Revolt Against Chivalry

Revolt Against Chivalry

Jessie Daniel Ames and the Women's
Campaign Against Lynching

Jacquelyn Dowd Hall

New York   Columbia University Press

As a dissertation much of this book was awarded the Bancroft Dissertation Award by a committee of the faculty of the Graduate School of Arts and Sciences of Columbia University.

Columbia University Press
New York   Chichester, West Sussex
Copyright © 1993 Columbia University Press

Library of Congress Cataloging-inPublication Data
Hall, Jacquelyn Dowd.
    Revolt against chivalry, rev. ed.

    Bibliography: p.
    Includes index.
    1. Lynching.   2. Ames, Jessie Daniel,
1883–1972.   3. Social reformers—Biography.
I.   Title.
HV6457.H34   364.6′6′0924   93-11815
ISBN 978-0-231-08282-2 (cl)   CIP
ISBN 978-0-231-08283-9 (pb)

Printed in the United States of America
c 10 9 8 7 6 5 4 3 2 1
p 10 9 8 7 6

For My Family

Contents

Preface

Twenty years have passed since I began to piece together the story of Jessie Daniel Ames and the Association of Southern Women for the Prevention of Lynching. At the time I thought I was feeling my way in relative isolation. Only later did I realize that I was in fact being borne along by the collective energy of a dynamic new field. From the start women's history has been capacious, inventive, and self-critical. It seems poised now for yet another burst of creativity, as research on the South and West moves from the margins to the center, as the literary turn in historical scholarship raises new questions about language, representation, and cultural meaning, and, above all, as we abandon universalized notions of gender for more complex definitions qualified by class, race, ethnicity, and sexual orientation. Our initial mission—to make invisible women visible, to recover what has been hidden from history—has lost none of its saliency. But we now seem closer to what appeared at the outset to be an impossibly utopian goal: by searching out the work of gender everywhere we have begun not only to document women's experience but also to transform history, and with it society, as a whole.

This new edition grew in part out of a desire to reconsider my early work in light of subsequent scholarship. But I was drawn back to *Revolt Against Chivalry* less by scholarly developments than by a heart-wrenching political event: the hearings precipitated by Anita Hill's allegations of sexual harassment against Clarence Thomas, George Bush's 1991 nominee to the Supreme Court. I saw distilled in the Thomas hearings many of

the preoccupations of my book: the links between language and
power, the ways in which race shapes both black and white
lives, the necessity of unraveling the race, class, and gender
subtexts not only of past events but of every situation that
demands a political response. Those issues are as pressing as
they were twenty years ago. Indeed, the hearings and their
reverberations—as well as the evolution of women's history—
give them more urgency than ever before.

In preparing this new edition, I have altered little and added
much. Except for correcting minor errors and infelicities, I have
not revised the main body of the book. To do so would require
an act of appropriation: an interpolation into a book of the 1970s
of evidence and perspectives that belong to later years. Instead
I have framed the original text with two commentaries from a
more current perspective. The first is an introductory chapter
written in the aftermath of the Thomas hearings. It draws on
my observations at the time as well as on my 1985 article,
" 'The Mind That Burns in Each Body,' " where I explored the
parallels between lynching and rape. The second addition is an
epilogue based on an article first drafted for a conference on
women's biography and autobiography in 1983. In it I reeval-
uate my treatment of Jessie Daniel Ames from the vantage point
of my own movement through time and of women's history's
progression. In both prologue and epilogue I have written in a
spirit of reflexivity, using my early work as an object lesson in
the ways in which personal, political, and intellectual contexts
shape the stories we tell.[1]

This too reflects current preoccupations. The winds of postmodernism have encouraged a new self-consciousness about
perspective, accompanied by a willingness to historicize and
contextualize not only the work of others but our own writing
and activism–a much harder task. To some this development
seems to raise the frightening prospect of a slide into relativism,
an endless struggle between opposing points of view, with no
hope of certainty or resolution. To me it offers endless opportunities. To reassess our memories and interpretations can be a
humbling experience. But it can be liberating as well. History

matters, not because it is written in stone but because it is a source of meaning for our lives. As we move creatively and responsibly into the future, inevitably we rewrite the past. But we don't rewrite it just as we please. We rewrite it in dialogue with others, past and present. The tensions produced by that dialogue—the conflict between respect for the self-understandings of others and our own interpretive ambitions, the tug between listening to our critics and forging our own vision—are what keep us honest and keep us alive.

In the case of a book published almost fifteen years ago, that dialogue is extensive indeed. My earliest scholarly debts are to John M. Hemphill, whose passion for history drew me to the field as a student at Rhodes College in the 1960s, and to Kenneth T. Jackson and William E. Leuchtenburg, who guided my research into its original form as a Columbia University dissertation. Kenneth Jackson, in particular, encouraged my turn to southern history and never blinked an eye when I metamorphosed into an historian of women. When I left Columbia and moved to Atlanta in 1970, I had the good fortune to find a job at the Southern Regional Council, where I worked for Paul M. Gaston, who was on a temporary sojourn as the council's research director. It was there that I came upon Jessie Daniel Ames's letters and began to formulate this study. At the University of North Carolina at Chapel Hill, where I began teaching and directing the Southern Oral History Program in 1973, I found a circle of friends who made it possible to turn a dissertation into a book. William H. Chafe, Sara M. Evans, Peter G. Filene, Anne Firor Scott, Joan W. Scott, and George B. Tindall gave me the benefit of searching criticism and warm support. Peter Filene, in particular, made suggestions that significantly improved the manuscript. Peter H. Wood's meticulous scrutiny of successive drafts went far beyond the call of friendship and of our mutual commitment to understanding the southern past. My sister, Jeanne Clark, and my then husband, Bob Hall, read every word of the manuscript. Jeanne came to my rescue at a crucial moment. The commitments Bob and I recognized and fostered in one another guide me still. Without the patience and dedication of my coworkers in the Southern Oral History Program—especially Brent G. Glass and Della Coulter—I could not have found time to complete the book. Darlene Roth, Virginia A. Shadron, and Mary Frederickson shared their parallel work with me. Lewis L. Gould, Norman D. Brown, Clara Scarbrough, and Louise Jackson supplied much-needed help with the Texas sections. I am indebted to Lee Alexander, archivist of Atlanta University's Trevor Arnett Library, for her steadfast and enthusiastic aid, to the staff of the Southern Historical Collection at the University of North Carolina, to the custodians of public libraries and local historical societies throughout the region for helping me to identify the Antilynching Association's members, to Page McCullough for research assistance, and to Secily Jones, Rosalie Radcliffe, and Lee Mullis for typing. I owe special appreciation to Rosalie, who has continued to support my efforts with wit and skill, and to Lee, whose leadership of the gay and lesbian movement in Chapel Hill was cut short by his tragic death. Bernard Gronert and Karen Mitchell of Columbia University Press saw the book through to publication with discerning care.

With this new edition I have acquired yet another set of intellectual debts. I experienced the first shock of the Thomas hearings in the company of Robin D. G. Kelley, and our conversations encouraged me to consider this project. Indeed, it was Robin who first suggested the timeliness of a new edition. Kate Wittenberg of Columbia University Press gave me the courage to carry the project through. Both read and reread the new material, as did Judith Bennett, Jeanne Clark, Richard Wightman Fox, Glenda Elizabeth Gilmore, Tera W. Hunter, Robert Korstad, Karen Trahan Leathem, Suzanne Lebsock, Della Pollock, and Joel Williamson. I could not have asked for wiser guidance or for more generous and inspiring friends. I also thank Emily Bingham, Joe Mosnier, and Anne Goodwyn Jones for giving me the opportunity to share my reactions to the Thomas hearings at the University of North Carolina at Chapel Hill in the fall of 1991 and at the University of Florida in the spring of 1992. Elsa Barkley Brown and Laura Edwards commented astutely on those talks, and Kathryn Wall and Karen Leathem provided careful and good-spirited research assistance.

Introduction

On October 11, 1991, the Senate Judiciary Committee, ready to approve Clarence Thomas's nomination to the Supreme Court, called Anita Hill to the witness stand. Hill, an African-American law professor at the University of Oklahoma, had worked for Thomas at the Department of Education and the Equal Employment Opportunities Commission in the early 1980s. Questioned by the committee's staff, she admitted that Thomas had badgered her with requests for dates, references to pornography, and boasts about his sexual prowess. The committee ignored Hill's allegations until the press made them public, setting off a rapid-fire mobilization of women's networks across the country.[1] The committee reopened the hearings, and both Hill and Thomas agreed to testify.

I watched the proceedings in a series of airports and hotels, on my way to conferences devoted to the scholarly dissection of the very issues of sex, class, race, and power that were suddenly exploding on our television screens. I listened to people in lobbies, on buses, and on street corners argue and commiserate as they looked for hope in what seemed to be a "tragedy and a travesty" and chose among a range of competing plots. In the months that followed, this torrent of conversation continued, and it shows no sign of abating.[2]

When Hill began to testify before the all-white, all-male Senate Judiciary Committee, however, we could not foresee the long-run consequences. What we saw at the time was the ineffectuality of the Democratic committee members and the well-practiced ferociousness of the Republican spin masters. "Anita

Hill will be sucked right into the maw," Republican Senator Alan K. Simpson predicted. "She will be injured and destroyed and belittled and hounded and harassed—real harassment, different from the sexual kind." [3]

Leaving to his supporters the task of besmirching Hill's character, Clarence Thomas overwhelmed the image of Hill's dignity and vulnerability with his righteous indignation. During the first round of hearings Thomas himself had insisted on substituting his personal character for a discussion of his constitutional vision. Now he challenged the legitimacy of just such an inquiry. By investigating Hill's charges, he claimed, the committee had subjected him to a "high-tech lynching." He was, he told a hushed Congress and a mesmerized national television audience, being "lynched, destroyed, caricatured by a committee of the U.S. Senate." [4] It was a brilliant rhetorical move, and with it Thomas succeeded in shifting attention away from the issue at hand—his treatment of Anita Hill (and what it revealed about his character)—and fixing it instead on what he considered "real harassment": the threat to his aspirations posed by the committee's decision to bring her accusations to light.

Thomas said in essence that his critics were using false charges of sexual misconduct the way white southerners had used false charges of rape to keep "uppity blacks" out of public life. The image was riveting, for there was Thomas before our eyes, a black man with southern rural roots confronting a jury/mob/committee made up entirely of white men. Cowed by the charge of racism, no Democratic Senator dared challenge the aptness of the metaphor. Indeed, from that moment on the Senate Judiciary Committee allowed Thomas to set the terms of the inquiry by declaring off-limits what he defined as his "private" life, just as in the first round of hearings he had refused to discuss his political and legal ideas. [5]

It was this moment in the hearings that first moved me to reread *Revolt Against Chivalry*. I was stunned by Thomas's appropriation of one of southern history's darkest themes. This was, after all, the same man who had chided African-Americans for blaming racism for their troubles. To call the hearings a

lynching trivialized the past. People who are lynched are dead—
not elevated to the high court or sent back to a comfortable
career.[6] If there *was* an attack on black people in progress, it
consisted in the appointment to the Supreme Court of a man so
ready to jettison the hard-won victories of the past thirty years.
For all these reasons I could easily dismiss Thomas's counterattack as a cynical ploy or, in psychological terms, as a classic case
of "reversal-fantasy" in which the perpetrator becomes the victim and the powerful unblinkingly proclaim their powerlessness.[7] Yet I could not help being moved by his testimony. I had
spent too many years immersed in the horrific details of mob
violence. I had written a book on women's activism in which
the victimization of black men was a central theme. Most important, I knew that the stereotypes and fears that fueled lynch
mobs are not a thing of the past. They are part of living memory. They surround us now.[8]

Thomas's use of the lynching metaphor resonated with my
own preoccupations in another way as well. First in *Revolt
Against Chivalry* and then more explicitly in " 'The Mind That
Burns in Each Body,' " I explored the links between the sexual
exploitation of black women and the lynching of black men. The
black women leaders I wrote about dedicated themselves to the
fight against mob violence, but for them the sexual abuse of
women was always a related and central concern. The efforts of
white southern women to confront that legacy of sexual suffering were, to my mind, among the most intriguing moments in
the Antilynching Association's history.

What made Thomas's evocation of lynching especially mere-
tricious—and especially effective—was the way in which it purged
the violation of women from the racial story. People knew what
Clarence Thomas was talking about when he cited the lynching
of black men. But in this battle over public memory, in which
symbols and images from the past were used to impose codes of
meaning on the present, they had no similar, accessible frame
of reference for understanding Anita Hill.[9] "The lynching story,"
as Nancy Fraser has put it, "requires a white woman as 'victim'
and pretext."[10] Thomas's testimony thus "whitened" Anita Hill

by displacing the televised image of a black woman harassed by a black man with the subliminal image of an hysterical white woman crying rape. Hill became an incomprehensible figure, and her indeterminacy allowed Thomas's supporters to discredit her in countless contradictory and mutually exclusive ways.

Into this confusion stepped commentators from across the political spectrum, scurrying to disaggregate what historians of women in recent years have spent so much energy trying to link: race, class, sex, and gender. At the outset, women's groups conceived the conflict as a gender story. White feminists saw Hill not as a woman of color but as Everywoman. African-American feminists never shared that illusion. They were all too painfully aware that this was also a racial drama: white inquisitors; white viewers/jurors filtering the action through racial stereotypes; a powerful black man, in Rosemary Bray's words, "burning the bridges that brought him over"; a black woman, bravely but dangerously putting "her private business in the street." [11] Yet for many African-Americans, Hill's character and motives remained inexplicable, while Thomas, monopolizing "race talk," appealed to a widespread and not unreasonable belief that white conspirators were trying to bring a black man down. Just as the struggle for manhood became the central metaphor of the civil rights movement in the 1960s, and women were enjoined to support their men, so this appeal to a collective memory of racial violence marginalized Anita Hill and cast Clarence Thomas as representative of the race.

At the same time Thomas's backers simultaneously obscured and played upon Hill's work identity. Focusing in mock horror and prurient detail on Hill's account of Thomas's sexual remarks, they deflected attention from the ways in which sexual harassment bolsters employers' power. No workers' representatives were called to explain how the structure of work interacts with racism and sexism to make women, and especially women of color, vulnerable to abuse. As Martha Mahoney has persuasively argued, a founding myth of capitalism, unchallenged by the voice of labor, undermined Anita Hill's credibility. Workers and employers, that myth holds, enjoy a mutual freedom of contract: workers are protected from exploitation by their right to leave. The question became, then, not what Thomas did but why Hill didn't leave. Seemingly too strong to be a passive victim yet failing to exercise free agency, Hill fit uneasily into a framework in which resistance and victimization are seen as mutually exclusive. In fact, abused workers, like battered wives, both stay and go. Committed to her work, Anita Hill resisted not by leaving but by working harder, not by cutting her ties with Thomas entirely but by staying put and refusing to give in.[12]

Thomas's supporters did more than suppress this class story; they effectively displaced it with another. By portraying sexual harassment as the hobbyhorse of "elite" white feminists and Hill as a cold-blooded careerist (ignoring her rise from rural poverty, which mirrored Thomas's own), they appealed to a potent mix of sexism and class resentment. This strategy, which concealed the fact that a disproportionate number of the complainants in sexual harassment cases have been African-American and working-class women, gained credence from real class cleavages.[13] Many working-class women, excluded from and unsympathetic toward a professional work culture based on the sponsorship of subordinates by powerful men, saw Hill as spineless and aloof. Orlando Patterson, an eminent sociologist, gave the "whitening" and "bourgeoisification" of Anita Hill a final twist. The outcry against Thomas, he argued, was the work of legalistic, puritanical white feminists who were shocked by African-American street talk, a style of obscene verbal sparring supposedly common to the culture that Hill and Thomas shared.

Feminist activists who saw Anita Hill only as another example of women's eternal sexual victimization were ill-equipped to intervene effectively in this confusing and segmented debate. Nor was a weakened labor movement, scrambling to adjust its strategies to a work force increasingly made up of women, in any position to fight such a discursive war. Needless to say, no one asked historians of women for their opinions. Given the reluctance of the media to seek out the views of African-American feminists, even the virtually overnight formation of a nation-

wide network called African American Women in Defense of
Ourselves could not shift mainstream discourse to an analysis of
the congruence between racism and sexual exploitation.[14] Instead, bureaucrats and handlers peddled pop psychology plati-
tudes about Anita Hill's repressed desires, assured us that pornography is utterly unknown in Washington except among
perverted psychopaths, and reduced the whole episode to a
case of "he said, she said."

When I set out to write *Revolt Against Chivalry*, I wanted to
subvert this habit of separating race, class, and gender and
pitting one brand of oppression against another. Women's history at the time largely ignored race, while southern history
ignored women and made race its central, and often exclusive,
theme. Working at the interface of these two fields, I tried to
understand how racial violence, and the struggle against it,
emerged out of the "alchemy" of race, class, and gender, though
I would not have put it that way at the time.[15]

I began by asking: Why a *women's* antilynching association?
Why did Jessie Daniel Ames, who cut her political teeth on
woman suffrage, go on in the 1920s to join a women's interracial
movement and then, in the thirties, to recast lynching as a
women's issue? Pursuing those questions, I arrived at an interpretation of the women's antilynching campaign as an instance
of feminist antiracism. I also proposed an analysis of the gendered subtext of lynching. And I tried to write a narrative of
violence against black men in which neither black nor white
women were displaced.

Revolt Against Chivalry argues that the racism that caused
white men to lynch black men cannot be understood apart from
the sexism that informed their policing of white women and
their exploitation of black women. Rape and rumors of rape
became the folk pornography of the Bible Belt. As stories spread,
the violation of the white woman was described in progressively
embellished detail, a public fantasy that implied a group participation in the rape that was as toxic as the subsequent lynching.
The lynch victim, literally, and the alleged rape victim, figura-
tively, became objects of voyeuristic fantasy. Violence against

women was "naturalized"—assumed to be a fixed reality, inherent in the natural order of things: black men pursued white women not only because they were black but because they were men, only less bound by civilization's restraints. The black man in this story was literally murdered; the white woman, ostensibly protected, was in fantasy pursued, looked at, and erased.[16]

I do not mean to downplay white women's complicity: they sometimes betrayed their lovers with false charges of rape; they helped to stir up rape scares; their faces can be found in the chilling photographs of crowds gathered to watch African-American men suffer and die. I do, however, argue that racism intensified sexual hierarchy and rape scares functioned as a means of both sexual and racial control. The fear of rape regulated white women's behavior and restricted their interaction with the world. The ideology of chivalry helped construct white womanhood; it shaped white women's identities and options even as it guarded caste lines.

Jessie Daniel Ames was engaged in a discursive struggle: a war of words. She sought to demystify and defuse the language through which white southerners expressed their racial fears and asserted their racial dominion. The black rapist, the chaste but vulnerable white lady, and her alter ego the wanton black woman—these were not just irrational fantasies. These were words invested with power, capable of shaping social reality. The Antilynching Association set out to turn this language on its head. In place of the black rapist as symbol of disorder, the association placed a white man—a lyncher of innocent black men, a fornicator, an exploiter of powerless black women.

Above all the Association rejected what Ames called "the crown of chivalry which had been pressed like a crown of thorns on our heads."[17] In this potent counterimage, the same emotional logic that burned black men at the stake crucified white women. The "false chivalry" of lynching cast women as Christ-like symbols of racial purity and regional identity and translated every sign of black self-assertion into a metaphor for rape—black over white, a world turned upside down. Dependent on white men for protection and circumscribed by an image of the self as a symbol, women could not assert—sometimes could not even discern—their own individuality, their human needs. By mobilizing traditional female networks to assert civic influence outside of official, male-dominated channels, the Antilynching Association displaced the image of the white lady as potential sexual victim with that of the woman citizen, requiring not the "crown of chivalry" but the equal protection of the law.[18]

My analysis of Ames and the organization she led was, like all narratives, shaped by choices regarding time frame, characters, and plot. *Revolt Against Chivalry* traces the history of lynching from its roots on the eighteenth-century frontier to its late-twentieth-century manifestations, but it focuses primarily on the nadir, the era after Reconstruction and Populism had been defeated and white southerners had closed ranks around a policy of disfranchisement and segregation. Its main characters are black and white middle-class women. It looks at the ways in which class, as well as race and gender, shaped these reformers' identities and actions, and it argues, as they did, against the convenient habit of blaming lynching on the irrational racism of poor whites. Its emphasis, however, is on the reciprocity between racism and sexism; class remains a relatively muted theme.

The exclusions entailed in these choices have become clearer to me in the course of my own and other scholars' subsequent work. Since *Revolt Against Chivalry* appeared, I have become more attentive to the class differences among white women, in part because of my own turn to working-class history and in part because of the discoveries of a new generation of women's historians. By shifting their focus from the nadir to the antebellum and post-Civil War eras and examining the treatment of rape in southern courts, these scholars have drawn a more nuanced picture of class-based attitudes and of change over time. Martha Hodes, for instance, has argued that under slavery white southerners displayed a degree of toleration for sexual liaisons between poor white women and black men, often blaming those relationships on the depravity of the women rather than on the dangerous sexuality of the men. Both before and immediately after the Civil War, African-American men accused of raping such women received relatively fair trials—at least by contrast to their treatment in later years. Moreover, as Victoria Bynum and Laura Edwards have shown, poor white women, like slaves and free black women, were fair game for upper-class white men.[19]

In the years of flux after the Civil War, poor women of both races fought for control over their own bodies by taking rape cases to court. Judges and juries, however, continued to view rape not as an act of violence against a woman but as an assault on her husband's or father's honor. The law, moreover, expressed profound distrust of women, demanding evidence of utmost resistance, corroboration by other witnesses in addition to the victim's word, and proof of the victim's chastity—all contrary to the rules of evidence in other forms of violent crime. Perforce, rape cases turned as much on the race, class, and reputation of the victim as on the evidence against the accused. The rape of a poor white woman, even by a black man, did not necessarily inspire public outrage or draconian legal response.[20]

The observation of legal niceties and, to a lesser extent, traditional distinctions among white women were buried by the pitched battles of Reconstruction and the rape scares that fueled turn-of-the-century disfranchisement campaigns. Democratic politicians equated black men's reach for political power with sexual aggression in order to justify vigilantism and undermine cross-race alliances. By extending the mantle of protection to poor white women, in rhetoric if not in reality, elites rallied their menfolk to the cause.[21] In 1931 the presiding judge in the infamous Scottsboro trial, in which nine black youths were accused of raping two hoboing white women, gave explicit voice to the assumptions that underlay this new mythology:

Where the woman charged to have been raped, as in this case is a white woman there is a very strong presumption under the law that she would not and did not yield voluntarily to intercourse with the defendant, a Negro; and this is true, whatever the station in life the

prosecutrix may occupy, whether she be the most despised, ignorant and abandoned woman of the community, or the spotless virgin
and daughter of a prominent home of luxury and learning.[22]

My own work in recent years has been focused less on the
uses of sexual discourse in social control and more on the history
of emotion and desire. Turning to the study of white working-
class culture and sexuality, I have tried to uncover dimensions
of southern women's lives hidden by *Revolt Against Chivalry's*
concentration on racial violence and middle-class reform. *Revolt
Against Chivalry* portrayed the sexual culture of the pre–World
War I South as relatively static and monolithic, in part because
of the book's preoccupation with the southern "rape complex."[23] Lately I have written about moments when white
working-class women deployed sexual symbolism for progressive political ends, and I have argued that the South—and
especially the urban, working-class South—experienced its own
prewar sexual revolution.[24]

Rereading *Revolt Against Chivalry* in the context of these
developments in my own work and in southern women's history, I was not surprised to find that working-class women,
whether black or white, appear mainly as objects of middle-
class aversion or concern. What did surprise me—indeed, what
leaped out at me in the Thomas hearings' harsh light—was how
little space I had actually devoted to the sexual exploitation of
black women. Four years later, in " 'The Mind That Burns in
Each Body,' " that theme assumed a much more prominent
role. Indeed, the purpose of that essay was to draw a parallel
between rape and lynching and to reiterate the importance of
opposing all forms of repressive violence. But in *Revolt Against
Chivalry's* analysis, black men and white women hold center
stage. And this is so despite my conscious efforts to make black
women integral to the story—by tracing the Antilynching Association's debts to their prewar institution-building efforts and
emphasizing their ongoing leadership of the larger antilynching
movement.[25]

This slighting of African-American women's experience offers a chastening example of why the scholarship of women's history, for all its achievements, did not prepare us for Anita Hill. In fact, as a graduate student in the early 1970s I considered writing a history of black women in America. Daunted by my own limitations as a fledgling scholar and as a white woman, as well as by the paucity of a secondary literature on which such a study might draw, I shifted to interracial reform and stumbled on Jessie Daniel Ames, the interracial Woman's Committee of the Commission on Interracial Cooperation, and the all-white Association of Southern Women for the Prevention of Lynching. With Ames as the leading character and her reconstruction of white womanhood as the action on which the plot turns, black women inevitably assumed supporting roles. This narrative difficulty suggests a deeper political problem: real differences between women mean that strategies that benefit some can easily ignore or marginalize others. In life as in art, no single, universalistic approach will do.[26]

Still, I did argue, too briefly in *Revolt Against Chivalry* but more forcefully in the later article, that sexual and racial violence are reciprocally entwined. In the antebellum South the sexual access of white men to black women, whether seized through force or granted within the coercive context of the master-slave relation, was a cornerstone of patriarchal power. It was used as a punishment or demanded in exchange for leniency. Like other forms of deference and conspicuous consumption, it buttressed planter hegemony. And it served the practical economic purpose of replenishing the slave labor supply.[27]

After the Civil War the customary sexual exploitation of slaves shaded into the use of rape as a political weapon. The records of the Freedmen's Bureau and the oral histories collected by the Federal Writers' Project testify to the sexual atrocities endured by African-American women as whites sought to reassert their command over the newly freed slaves. African-American women were sometimes executed by lynch mobs, but more routinely they served as targets of sexual assault, and their special vulnerability helped shape the former slaves' struggle for the prerequisites of freedom. The sharecropping system, for example, grew in part from black women's desire to avoid gang labor in the fields, thereby escaping white men's supervision and one venue of sexual assault.[28]

Just as Clarence Thomas ignored this legacy of sexual exploitation, most studies of racial violence pay little attention to women. Even rape appears less as an aspect of women's oppression than as a transaction between white and black men. Claude Lévi-Strauss's insight that men use women as verbs with which to communicate with one another (rape being a means of communicating defeat to the men of a conquered tribe) helps explain the extreme viciousness of sexual violence in the postemancipation era. Rape *was* in part an attempt by white men to stifle the freedman's efforts to assume the role of patriarch, able to provide for and protect his family. Nonetheless, rape was first and foremost a crime against women, a violent expression of both racism and misogyny.

Over the course of the nineteenth century, a belief in female passionlessness displaced ancient notions of women's dangerous sexual power. Yet even at the height of the "cult of true womanhood" views of women's sexuality remained ambivalent and double-edged. The association between women and nature, the dread of women's treacherous carnality, persisted, rooted perhaps in the earliest experiences of infancy. This lingering fear of and fascination with female sexuality was projected not only onto lower-class women but especially onto black women; the civilized, passionless lady arose in symbiosis with the primitive, sexual slave.

Ideas about black men's sexuality gained force from stereotypes about black women. Indeed Sander Gilman has argued that in Western Europe myths about black women's concupiscence predate those about black men's rapaciousness. In art, medicine, and literature, she served as an "icon for deviant sexuality in general."[29] In the United States hysteria about black men's sexuality merged with this timeworn theme. In the eyes of white observers black men were monsters because they were not restrained by wives and mothers who were "angels in the house." White men weren't rapists; they were civilized patriarchs seduced by Jezebel. Jessie Daniel Ames put it this way: "White men have said over and over—and we have believed it because it was repeated so often, that not only was there no such thing as a chaste Negro woman—but that a Negro woman could not be assaulted, that it was never against her will." [30]

Even today the myth of the willing black woman retains its power. Presumptions about African-American women's sexual availability make them susceptible to abuse and deny them the equal protection of the law. Black women are much more likely to be raped than white women, while black men convicted of assaulting black women receive milder sentences than assailants in any other racial mix. [31]

In the 1980s African-American women began to break the "code of silence" about an issue they had long discussed behind closed doors: the devastating impact of sexual violence on social relations in the black community. [32] In a society that defines manhood by power and possessions, black men lack the resources to fulfill their expected roles. All too often they turn to domination of women, one of the few means of manhood within their control. Just as racism undermines working-class unity and lynching sometimes pitted poor whites against blacks, sexual aggression divides African-Americans against themselves. The current economic devastation of black neighborhoods has exacerbated these sexual tensions. But black-on-black rape cannot be blamed on racism alone; it is not a "natural" reaction to social "emasculation." It is an act of violence that establishes gendered power relations.

Behind the Thomas hearings lay a dual system of formal and vigilante justice in which whites have looked the other way when it came to black-on-black crime. White men denied African-American men the authority to protect their women but *gave* them permission to inflict their own brand of abuse. [33] When Thomas spoke to the senators man-to-man he was in effect saying: You have canceled the historical bargain that put whatever went on between me and Anita Hill outside the white man's law.[34]

Like that of lynching, this legacy of sexual violence lives in memory, shaping the consciousness of women and men alike. Darlene Clark Hine has made this point eloquently. We know so little about the inner lives of African-American women, she argues, in part because they deliberately hid those lives from view. Victimized by black men as well as whites, they sought to shield themselves from negative stereotypes by creating a "culture of dissemblance" that masked their sexual practices and contributed to their historical invisibility. Some found themselves caught up in a politics of respectability, an effort to distinguish themselves from the mass of black women and to impose their own standards of morality on women whose behavior was different from their own.[35]

Viewed from the perspective of this history, Orlando Patterson's conversion of Thomas's verbal abuse into harmless word-play and his assumption that Anita Hill should have responded by cracking her own lewd jokes seems especially perverse. Ignored completely were the power relations of the work place, Hill's conservative Baptist upbringing, and the culture of dissemblance from which she came. White men seem to have found Patterson's comments particularly commonsensical. Once more we heard men talking to men, sharing their fear of feminist alliances, their ignorance of women's perspectives, and their anxiety about challenges to male prerogatives and power. What was new—and important—was a countervailing discourse. African-American feminists were quick to point out how Patterson's characterization of black culture duplicated the sexual slander that generations of women have struggled to combat. They offered an analysis of the meaning of Hill's hard-won probity and the pressures that ensure black women's silence about abuse by black men.[36]

In so doing, these writers and intellectuals could draw on a rich literature in African-American women's history. Ironically, in light of Thomas's assumption that men alone appear at the center of the racial story, that literature has revolved mainly around three central themes: African-American women's refusal to separate their interests as women from their devotion to the black community as a whole; their dual opposition to racial violence and sexual exploitation; and their leadership of the institution-building and welfare activities that offset the devastating impact of segregation and discrimination.[37]

These activists played a central role in *Revolt Against Chivalry*. Seeking to trace the steps that brought women such as Lugenia Burns Hope and Charlotte Hawkins Brown to the 1920 meeting that launched a southern women's interracial movement, I discovered a network of middle-class reformers linked together by their positions as founders of schools, women's clubs, and settlement houses. Their experiences during World War I, and especially their struggle for equality within the YWCA, served as the immediate catalyst for their postwar interracial efforts. This attempt to forge a women's alliance across the color line continued after the founding of the Association of Southern Women for the Prevention of Lynching in 1930. African-American women pursued their own separate strategies, joining with their counterparts in other regions to fight for federal antilynching legislation, creating local welfare services, and pursuing what they saw as the twin goals of defending their own sexual reputations and teaching lower-class women to lead moral lives. But they never quit trying to use their contacts with white women for the advancement of the race.

When I began looking for information about this women's network, I had to rely heavily on the writings of participants themselves.[38] By the time *Revolt Against Chivalry* came out, scholars such as Sharon Harley, Rosalyn Terborg-Penn, and Gerda Lerner were beginning to lay the groundwork for a renaissance of black women's history similar to the flowering of black women's literature in the 1920s.[39] Since then an intricate world of African-American women's activism has emerged from the deep shadows of historical neglect.

Elsa Barkley Brown has used Maggie Lena Walker's amazing career to illuminate the links between economic self-help and

Joint Meeting of the Central Council of the Association of Southern Women for the Prevention of Lynching and Special Committee of Negro Women of the Commission on Interracial Cooperation at Tuskegee Institute in 1938. The meeting was called to consider the advisability of maintaining the ASWPL as an all-white organization, structurally separate from the interracial CIC Woman's Committee. The women made elaborate arrangements to meet together in the Piedmont Hotel in Atlanta, traveled to Tuskegee by private car, then roomed together in Day Hall. They are posed in front of the famous bronze sculpture of Booker T. Washington lifting the veil of ignorance from his people.

Front Row: Mrs. John Hanna (Sallie L.), Dallas; Mrs. C. H. Thorpe (Ruth), Little Rock; Mrs. Charlotte Hawkins Brown, Sedalia, N.C.; Mrs. B. F. Zimmerman, Columbia, S.C.; Mrs. C. L. Read (Florence Matilda), Zebulon, N.C.; Mrs. W. A. Newell (Bertha Payne), Salisbury, N.C.; Mrs. R. B. Moton (Jennie B.), Tuskegee Institute; Mrs. Jessie Daniel Ames, Atlanta; Mrs. Mary McLeod Bethune, Daytona Beach, Fla.

Second Row: Mrs. O. O. McCollum (Bertha), Jacksonville, Fla.; Mrs. Walter S. Jones (Nell Rose), Jacksonville, Fla.; Arlene Rogers Park, Lithonia, Ga.; Fannie C. Williams, N.C.; Mrs. H. L. McCrory (Mary Jackson), Charlotte, N.C.; Mrs. George E. Davis (Kate T.), Orangeburg, S.C.; Mrs. J. W. Mills (Kate V.), Beaumont, Tex.; Miss Nannie Hite Winston, Louisville; Mrs. George Sexton, Shreveport, La.; Mrs. J. D. Lawhorn (Ethel Mae), Hugo, Okla.; Mrs. L. E. Brown (Onilee), Waxhaw, N.C.; Mrs. C. M. Mullino (Mary Addie), Montezuma, Miss.; Mrs. L. W. Alford (Bessie C.), McComb, Miss.; Mrs. J. A. Richardson (Alma Lipscomb), Richmond, Va.; Mrs. G. W. Hummel (Pearl C.), Louisville; Mrs. H. A. Hunt (Florence), Ft. Valley, Ga.; Mrs. Robert O'Neal (Bessie), Clarksville, Tenn.

Courtesy of the Jessie Daniel Ames Papers, Southern Historical Collection, University of North Carolina at Chapel Hill.

feminism. Jacqueline Rouse has written the first full-scale biography of Lugenia Burns Hope. Glenda Gilmore's ingenious excavation of untapped local sources has revealed new dimensions of turn-of-the-century political culture. By delineating the class and gender tensions inherent in African-American feminism, Deborah Gray White's study of black women's clubs has clarified the shortcomings of a history based on monolithic notions of "black womanhood." Elizabeth Lasch has documented the failure of northern settlement workers either to redirect their own efforts from European immigrants to African-American migrants after World War I or to recognize the efforts of black and white southern women to extend settlement work to the black community. Evelyn Brooks Higginbotham has provided an original and sweeping interpretation of the women's movement in the black Baptist church.[40] And this is to name only a few contributions to a surge of innovative research.

Much of the work emphasizes black women's separate institution-building efforts rather than on the flash points of interracial coalition that were *Revolt Against Chivalry's* major theme. These and other studies, however, have also helped to situate the interracial and antilynching movements of the 1920s and 1930s in a broad landscape of contacts across the color line. Gilmore has shown how women's interracial turn-of-the-century public health and temperance campaigns fed first into cooperation between segregated women's clubs and then into integrated war work councils and farm home demonstration projects during World War I. Higginbotham has revealed how the response of white women in northern missionary societies to the freedwomen's hunger for education helped to produce a cadre of educated African-American women leaders in the South. Mary Frederickson has surveyed the extensive and persistent interactions among southern Methodist church women.[41]

In a sense *Revolt Against Chivalry* might be seen as a bridge between the feminist scholarship of the late 1970s, which emphasized the "bonds of womanhood"—the values and disadvantages that defined women as a group—and this new wave of research, which focuses more on differences of race and class. Concerned as it is with interracial alliances among southern women, *Revolt Against Chivalry* examines the commonalities of class, religion, and rhetoric that brought its protagonists together, chief among which was a rejection of the double standard that allowed white men to have sex with black women but punished black men for any hint of crossing the color line. But the book's emphasis lies not on commonality but on difference: on what participants themselves called the "gulf of distance, of mistrust and suspicion" that made coming together so rare, painful, and hard.[42]

The deepening of the scholarship on African-American women and on women's interracial coalitions has been complemented by a broadening of the canvas that places southern women's history in the context of global developments. If I were writing *Revolt Against Chivalry* today, I would draw especially on the insights of scholars who have begun to construct a gendered history of imperialism, for their work—which has benefited in turn from studies of the American South—casts new light on how sanctions against interracial sex secured racial boundaries and on women's leadership of the antilynching campaign. Among the many benefits of that wider perspective is its challenge to the entrenched habit of making the South a proxy for race and reducing racism to a regional issue—a ploy that *Revolt Against Chivalry*, by its very subject matter, reinforced rather than revised.

This global perspective informs Gail Bederman's study of the British tours of Ida B. Wells, the African-American journalist who launched the antilynching movement in 1892. I underscored the symbolic centrality of white women to racial ideology; Bederman—reflecting a more recent concern with masculinity and with the ways in which gender structures men's lives—shows how "white man" became a synecdoche for "civilization." Wells's message to the British attacked the equation between whiteness, manliness, and civilization. As lynching became a cause célèbre among British reformers, white Americans found themselves cast in the uncomfortable role of un-

manly savages in the eyes of the "civilized" world. As Hazel
Carby has made clear, Wells and other turn-of-the-century black
feminists thus linked imperialism abroad to racism at home at a
time when most white feminists supported colonial expansion
as a means of spreading western gender conventions around the
world.[43]

In other ways as well developments in the South paralleled
larger currents of popular imperialism and the turn-of-the-century rationalization of colonial rule. Disfranchisement and segregation coincided .with the hardening of racial boundaries in
the European colonies and with the emergence of the United
States as an imperial power. White women in colonial societies,
like white women in the American South, were positioned both
as objects of protection and as keepers of the rituals of racial
dominance. Colonial authorities, like southern politicians, used
rape scares to justify repression and segregation.[44]

In the United States a dynamic women's movement helped
propel both white and black women into the public sphere and
encouraged some white women to question their assigned roles.
The "revolt against chivalry" that resulted had no counterpart
in the colonies, where organized white women had less room
for autonomous thought and action.[45] Viewed from the vantage
point of imperialism what is striking about the southern anti-
lynching campaign is not its limitations but that it occurred at
all.

Indeed, the more I have learned about the social construction
of race in Western societies generally and about the murderous
racism of the period in which the Antilynching Association
flourished, the more I have come to appreciate the courage and
prescience of the plain, small-town reformers who, lacking the
luxury of denouncing from a distance, struggled to change
themselves and their culture from within. In *Revolt Against
Chivalry* I assumed a sympathetically critical stance toward
Jessie Daniel Ames and the women she led. What I didn't
anticipate was the degree to which other historians would re-
peat my criticisms but not my admiration. Most subsequent
historians, if they mentioned the Antilynching Association at all,

did not laud it for its feminist analysis of racial violence or its fragile moments of interracial coalition. They faulted it for its conservatism or, conversely, dismissed it as unrepresentative of its conservative times.[46] And they continued to interpret racial violence in ways that fit neatly with Clarence Thomas's formulation: ignoring lynching's gendered subtext, they saw it exclusively as a means of keeping black men down.

One notable study, Joel Williamson's *The Crucible of Race,* departed markedly from that limited view. Where southern historians in general evinced little interest in women's history— and historians of women repaid the compliment by ignoring the South—Williamson was particularly sensitive to the interplay between race and gender. The agricultural depression of the 1890s, he argued, pushed white farmers off the land, depriving them of the economic autonomy on which their sense of manhood depended. Unable to play the role of breadwinner, they conjured up a fear of what Williamson calls "the black beast rapist" so that they could play another aspect of the masculine role—that of protector—to the hilt. At the same time white men suffered from sexual frustration. Emancipation deprived them of sexual access to black women, while they subscribed to an ideology of white female passionlessness that made them feel guilty about having sex with women of their own race. Only black men, as Williamson puts it, seemed to have "no fault sex"—by having intercourse with black women and raping white women. Lynching, then, became a means by which white men compensated for their own failures and punished black men for their imagined virility, for doing what white men secretly wanted to do.[47]

There were obvious similarities in Williamson's interpretation and mine. But there were instructive differences as well. Williamson seemed to posit a universal male sex drive, and he left the impression that the rhetoric about white female passionlessness reflected reality, that is, that white women were bad lovers and white southerners had bad sex. I saw rape not as sex but as violence. As a consequence, I read white men's identification with the so-called black rapist as an expression of misogyny rather than as a projection of desire.

Since *The Crucible of Race* appeared in 1984, a dialogue between women's history and southern history, as well as a cross-fertilization with African-American and labor history, has begun to challenge the earlier preoccupation with white middle-class women in the urban North. A lively, multicultural literature on women in the West has simultaneously emerged. These changes in women's history both reflect and shape broader debates. Advocates of "multiculturalism" and "diversity"—in the curriculum, the arts, and other areas—are grappling with an urgent and complex dilemma. They seek to recognize and celebrate the differences that situate individuals in particular cultures. Yet increasingly they do so while arguing against the notion that race, class, gender, and sexual preference are immutable givens of social identity. "Identity politics"—the assertion of knowledge claims and group solidarity based on such givens—have always propelled movements for racial and sexual equality. Yet the limits of such strategies have become ever more apparent. To be sure, we cannot remake ourselves each morning; we cannot opt out of the matrix of privilege or oppression into which we are born. At the same time, we are always coming into being; we become who we are in dialogue, in interaction with the world. The challenge and the anxiety of this intellectual moment lie precisely in the tension between these two realities. In practice we are learning to adopt what some have called "strategic identities"—identities that "allow opposition to one form of domination without being complicit in another." In our scholarship we are learning not to treat race and gender, racism and sexism, as ahistorical identities and ideologies. For those identities and ideologies are always in process, always being culturally constructed, and they have to be understood historically—or historicized—all the way down.

All of these issues—the differences among women, the urgency of coalition building, the necessity and perils of identity politics, and the political uses of our newly honed conceptual tools—were reflected in the Thomas hearings. Thomas's Republican advisers were determined to prevent the hearings "from turning into a referendum on 2000 years of male dominance and sexual harassment." [48] If the process of opinion making had stopped on October 16, 1991—when the Senate confirmed Clarence Thomas's nomination to the Supreme Court—they would have achieved their goal. But it did not. Instead the hearings set off political shock waves. They propelled women across the country into campaigns for political office, injected gender issues into 1992 presidential politics on an unprecedented scale, gave new visibility to a sturdy black feminist movement, opened a painful but overdue dialogue between women and men, and created new, if fragile, opportunities for cross-race and cross-class feminist coalitions.

The hearings also thrust into public consciousness issues that have been simmering since the contemporary women's movement began. [49] The demand for control over one's own body and the struggle against sexual objectification have been central to feminism because they are essential to a sense of being a person with needs and rights, able to make moral choices and to participate as an equal in social life. This struggle has involved litigation, institution-building, and political campaigns. Its driving force has been a decentralized, grass-roots "coming to voice," a process that has, over and over again, propelled issues out of the private sphere and into public discourse and public policy. [50]

In consciousness-raising groups and "speakouts" in the early seventies, women broke what in retrospect seems a remarkable silence about the body. Out of that process flowed an analysis that held rape to be a political act by which men affirm their power over women and a critique of the ways in which a "rape culture" victimizes *all* women by enforcing a muting of the body, a self-censorship, that limits their capacity to "walk freely in the world." After 1976 the movement broadened to include wife-battering, pornography, and sexual harassment. In landmark Supreme Court cases, first in 1977 and more decisively in 1986 and 1991, feminist legal theorists succeeded in convincing the courts that sexual harassment was not just a regrettable aspect of everyday life but a form of sex discrimination, a means by which women were disadvantaged as a group.[51]

These legal breakthroughs came in advance of any widespread public understanding of the issue. By forcing sexual harassment into public consciousness, the Thomas hearings triggered the publicity that could close that gap. Whatever their perspectives on the Hill-Thomas episode, women across the country responded to the hearings by revealing (or naming and thus reconceiving) experiences so patterned and pervasive as to counter any notion that sexual harassment is—as Hill's inquisitors would have us believe—the aberrant behavior of psychopaths. Claiming narrative agency, some women went on to claim political agency as well. Feminist writers and scholars, in the meantime, rushed to craft an analysis in which Anita Hill and Clarence Thomas made sense.

As they do so, I would argue, white feminists in particular must resist the urge to ignore the resonance of Thomas's testimony among African-American men and women alike. To do so would reinforce the racism that has distorted and confused the struggle against sexual exploitation. The antirape movement, for all its attempts to separate itself from the racist image of rape as the violation of white women by black men, has failed to dislodge the equation between whiteness and sexual vulnerability. This failure has enfeebled the movement itself, for it leaves intact a narrative of rape as a surprise attack by a (black) stranger— rather than as the outcome of pernicious but routine interactions between men and women generally known to each other and of the same race—and encourages strategies that depend on the punishment meted out by a racist and sexist legal system.[52] Similarly, the struggle against sexual harassment could find itself mired in legalisms and identified with a narrow range of women's interests if it neglects to take seriously the historical memories and contemporary realities that brought so many African-Americans to Clarence Thomas's side.[53]

The insights of feminist legal theory are a case in point. Catherine MacKinnon has made the important argument that sexual encounters cannot be "read objectively, from a 'point-ofviewless' perspective." The law of rape, for instance, views sexual violence from a male point of view. As MacKinnon puts it: "The law distinguishes rape from intercourse by the woman's lack of consent coupled with the man's (usually) knowing disregard of it. A feminist distinction between rape and intercourse," she continues, "lies instead in the *meaning* of the act from the women's point of view." The question then becomes, would a "reasonable woman" have experienced intercourse as rape, not would a "reasonable man" have believed he had the woman's consent.[54] Yet the reasonable woman, like the reasonable man, is a legal fiction. For real white women, historically, the meaning of rape might well have included a black man's whistle, a black man's inadvertent touch.

If Jessie Daniel Ames and the women of the Antilynching Association deserve a place in American history, it is for their willingness to grapple with that legacy. I hope this study of their efforts will stand both as a product of its moment, at the beginning of an endeavor that has blossomed beyond our wildest imaginings, and as a contribution to present debates. In Anita Hill, as Lauren Berlant has argued, we saw a black woman step forward as a messenger to the nation. Like Harriet Jacobs, whose autobiography exposed the sexual exploitation bred by slavery, Hill witnessed not just against the misuse of authority by a particular man but against a culture that permits and encourages such behavior.[55] Similarly Ames and her colleagues joined a long line of feminist opponents of racism, who, by linking rape and lynching, have witnessed against all uses of violence in oppression. Their example may remind white feminists of the dangers of excluding others by marginalizing issues that seem, on the surface, to relate not to gender or sexuality but to race or class. The next wave of women's history depends on such inclusiveness, as do the fragile feminist alliances that offer one of our best hopes for changing the world.

Revolt Against Chivalry

Chapter 1
Beginnings

Eleven miles from the Trinity River in the East Texas black belt lies a railroad junction called Palestine. Here, on November 2, 1883, Jessie Harriet Daniel was born, the third of four children. Only a decade before, the Ku Klux Klan had dominated the town, bringing an end to Reconstruction and paving the way for the reestablishment of white hegemony. In 1872, the coming of the International and Great Northern Railroad (I. & G.N.) had jolted Palestine into the industrial New South. A massive late-Victorian depot soon overshadowed the old courthouse square. "New Palestine," according to a disgruntled older citizen, overflowed with "active and hustling people . . . all running madly after the almighty dollar."[1] Among the influx of settlers drawn by the railroad and the boom-town atmosphere was Jessie's father, James Malcom Daniel.

Born in 1858 in Buffalo, New York, James Daniel was the son of a Scotch-Irish coal and wood merchant. Both his parents died when he was still a child, and by an early age James had become self-supporting. In 1876 he migrated to Camden, Indiana, where he worked as a railroad station agent. There he met and married Laura Maria Leonard, the daughter of a farmer and flour mill owner. Laura had attended Battle Ground Methodist Institute and had taught for one year in the county school. The Daniels' first child, Lulu, was born less than a year after their wedding, and Charley Leonard arrived in 1881. Ten days after the birth of their son, James Daniel,

"young, eager, and headstrong," left for the Texas plains.
Laura, despite her parents' strenuous objections and her own
reluctance to abandon the familiarity of the Indiana countryside
for the hardships of the frontier, followed her husband first to
Round Rock and then to Palestine, where he was employed by
the I. & G.N.

Laura Daniel saw her new home as a threatening place,
swarming with unkempt railroad workers and filled with black
faces. "Rain, rain," she recalled of her arrival, "and everything
awful." The family lived first in a hotel, then in one end of a
warehouse in the train depot amid noisy engines and flying cin-
ders. The birth of their third child, Jessie, in the fall of 1883,
put an impossible strain on domestic life; before winter arrived
the family had moved again, this time to settle in Overton, a
tiny railroad crossing northeast of Palestine. There, the Daniels' fourth child, James Malcom, Jr., was born.[2]

The town where Jessie spent the first ten years of her life
was barren and poor, dominated by the iron tracks that
stretched away to north and south. Her father served as train
dispatcher for the community, and its physical contours were
deeply etched in her mind. Years later, she recalled:

> One long, treeless road of white sand running parallel with the
> railroad track was the main street. Along one side of it was the
> business section of about ten unpainted, one story, barnlike build-
> ings occupied by three general merchandise firms, one drug store,
> three saloons, and a Saturday meat market. . . . Across the
> railroad . . . were the railroad eating houses and the Baptist
> church. Quite a bit south of these and separated from them by the
> old abandoned brick kiln was "nigger" town.[3]

To the east of main street lay the residence section: a scattering
of weather-stained frame houses. Monotonous sand hills
stretched off into the distance beyond the town, "ceaselessly in
motion with the rhythmical rise and fall of bluebonnets
whipped by the wind."[4]

Jessie's recollections of her small-town turn-of-the-century
childhood differed markedly from the popular myth of rural

simplicity and youthful innocence. In a time when epidemics of diphtheria, smallpox, and typhoid fever swept through communities with devastating regularity, an awareness of mortality and a fear of eternal damnation were part of the rhythm of daily life. Jessie's mother worked beside the town's only doctor, nursing the victims of each summer's epidemic. Often Laura Daniel left home for two or three days at a time, returning "dark around the eyes, and pale and silent," when another friend had died. One neighbor lost a baby every year: nine small graves in the family plot. When Lulu's best friend died one hot summer, they dressed her for burial in Lulu's own clothes, covered her with flowers so that only her "strange-looking pinched face" showed, and laid her out in a room "heavy and sickening with odor." After that, Jessie's sister recalled, "we children walked closer to death than we had ever done before."[5]

In this context, the protracted August revivals held between the planting and the harvesting of the cotton crop became the major unifying and cathartic rituals of community life. James Daniel, virtually alone in the community, emerged as an articulate and aggressive nonbeliever. He taught his children that a God who willed such pain was "inhumanly cruel" and manifestly unlovable. Torn between her father's skepticism and her own fear of damnation, Jessie developed the symptoms of a "sinner under conviction." Finally, during one disease-filled summer, at a revival conducted by a circuit rider who "believed profoundly in everlasting hell fire and sudden death for all sinners," all three Daniel children braved their father's scorn and joined the church.[6]

Physical violence, as well as death and disease, cast a shadow on the psychic life of Overton. One of the ten buildings in the business district stood vacant, supposedly because a terrible crime had been committed there. Men carried guns and used them. Collective violence against blacks was commonplace, and lynching reached a record high during the period of Jessie's childhood.[7] Although a conspiracy of silence usually kept such things from being discussed in the presence of children,

she remembered whispered stories of an especially sadistic
lynching in which the victim's eyes were burned out with hot
irons.[8] Almost forty years later, Jessie drew a vivid analogy between the epidemics that raged through the landscape of her
childhood and the contagion of mob violence. "With the coming of summer in East Texas in the late eighties and early nine-
ties," she recalled, "typhoid fever swept through the sun-baked
Redlands like a scourge. . . . Mob rule is the typhoid fever of
the emotional life of the South, as devastating and as shocking
in its implications as ever attended any of the physical scourges
which . . . undermined our social and economic life."[9]

Quarrels, emotional crises, and reconciliations disrupted the
Daniel family itself. James seemed to his children a complicated, even a tragic figure. Insensitive and domineering, he
sought to play the role of the Victorian patriarch, and he passionately attached his hopes for the future to the success and
upward mobility of his children. Laura Daniel served as the
guardian of family morality, shielding the children from their
father's harshness and upholding the values of evangelical religion. But she also possessed a fiery temper, a strong will, and
a decided mind of her own.[10]

Although Laura involved herself in the life of the community
as she cared for the sick and taught in the church, the Daniels
remained outsiders. They were, Jessie remembered, Yankees
in a locality where the resentments of Civil War and Reconstruction still smoldered. James Daniel was a Gold Democrat
and a railroad man in a stronghold of Populist insurgency. The
family was set apart from their neighbors by James Daniel's intellectual pretensions. Largely self-educated, he made his imposing, leather-bound books the center of the Daniel household. Lulu, the oldest child, recalled:

> Our books were kept in the darkened parlor. . . . No one ever
> touched [them] without permission except my mother and father.
> My father used to come home of evenings and after the work was
> done around the place and we were through supper, he would take
> down one of his precious books and read for a long time in the cool
> open hall. . . . My mother read them too, with her brows puck-

ered and a lead pencil in her hand making notes on paper. My father read them, I thought because he loved them; my mother
because she needed them for something.[11]

Both Jessie and Lulu emulated their father's intellectual interests and absorbed his religious skepticism.

James Daniel, however, seemed to Jessie to reserve his approval exclusively for his firstborn daughter. Lulu was "small,
dainty, with long brown curls and blue eyes. She was a little
lady." To their father, not only was Lulu lovely, she was also
"the only brilliant one in the family." Jessie, on the other hand,
he "never seemed to see . . . except as a . . . splendid foil for
the . . . beauty" of his favorite child.[12] While Lulu shared her
younger sister's impressions of death, disease, and family crisis,
the impact of those experiences was softened by her privileged
position in the family. And she recalled more positive events as
well: new dresses, the visits of a loving grandmother, battles of
will with teachers and other grown-ups from which she sal-
vaged, if not victory, at least a growing sense of self-determination. Rebelling in small ways, she ultimately made the transition to conventional womanhood.

Jessie, on the other hand, remembered only her own loneliness and feelings of rejection. Yet her very isolation brought
her into contact with aspects of southern life that were hidden
from her more successful sister.[13] She befriended the daughter
of an orthodox Jewish woman who ran a boarding house for
transients and, despite her parents' disapproval, regularly
crossed the railroad track to join the poor children of the community, both black and white, in their games. Here, she recalled, "we were judged and rewarded according to our abilities solely and without regard to sex." Forced to "make good
on my own merits," she learned to play roughly without crying, to take the least popular role without complaining, and to
survive. "From these socially outcast," she "learned the meaning of the word, equality." Then her friend moved away, and
Jessie absorbed lessons of a different sort. While her older sister played with dolls, Jessie sought access to her brother's pas-

times. "The boys made the laws which controlled my conduct," she remembered, "and which I found to my disgust did not apply to them. When I rebelled at the unfairness, I was dropped until I was amenable. . . ." Finally, she understood that she must "win modestly and deprecatingly. In time I became letter perfect in the proper conduct of little girls who would play with boys and for three years I was permitted to 'fetch and carry' for the gang." As Jessie's ninth birthday approached, she began to "withdraw from the boys," finding refuge in the solitary pleasures of her father's library. [14]

The summer of 1893 marked a turning point in Jessie's early life. First Lulu graduated from high school, and in celebration James Daniel took her to the Chicago World's Fair. For Lulu the greatest pleasure of the trip was arriving back home again, but for Jessie the episode remained an enduring symbol of her father's favoritism. [15] Returning from Chicago, James announced his intention to leave Overton behind. Lulu had reached sixteen, and her father insisted that she go away to school lest she "fall in love with one of the nice boys of the town and settle down in Overton for the rest of [her] life." Because—in Jessie's view—he could not bear to be separated from his daughter, he moved his whole family to Georgetown in Williamson County, site of Southwestern University, a small coeducational school established by the Methodist Church twenty years before. [16]

This move from the eastern blacklands to the hill country of central Texas transformed the context of Jessie's childhood and adolescence. The convergence of westward-moving white Southerners, German immigrants, blacks, and Hispanics gave the area an ethnic heterogeneity unique in the state. Austin, the capital and home of the University of Texas, lay less than thirty miles to the south. Although Georgetown's population numbered under 3,000, its social life was dominated by the local college and the Texas Chautauqua Assembly, and to the Daniels their new home seemed a haven of education, culture, and wealth. Lulu and then Charley entered Southwestern, and Jessie was placed in the college's private primary school. James and Laura attended lectures and participated in the activities of the elite Methodist Church. Daily routine underwent a radical change.[17] Jessie recalled:

> Instead of a deep well from which we drew our water, we merely stepped out of the kitchen door and turned on the hydrant; it was quite countrified to have milk from cows, so now we kept it in tin cans in the ice chest; we were no longer reduced to fried chicken or no meat, for we could step around to the market . . . and buy all the round steak we could eat for a dime. . . . There were more two story houses than a child could count and all the stores and the college buildings were of white stone. There were no saloons anywhere. Church bells sounded not only all day Sunday but almost every day in the week.[18]

The quiet surface of Georgetown, however, obscured a history of conflict. Saloons may have been banished to the outskirts of town and church bells may have rung every day, but no region in the country surpassed central Texas in acute, long-term violence. The Great Fear, which swept the South in 1860, culminated two years later in what may have been the largest mass lynching in American history: the illegal execution of 171 persons in four counties of central Texas. The brutal Indian wars along the Comanche-Kiowa frontier and the turbulent rise of the cattle industry reinforced a self-perpetuating mystique of individual self-defense and retaliatory violence. Only a decade before the Daniels' arrival, the cattlemen and town dwellers of Williamson County had waged a sustained vigilante offensive against a band of outlaws known as the Yegua Notch Cutters—who counted their victims by the notches on their guns. The hero of white folklore was John Wesley Hardin, whose career as a killer was inspired by partisan southern sympathies and rabid anti-Negro prejudice. Joining the other side of this ethnic warfare was his legendary female counterpart Cynthia Ann Parker: captured by the Comanches and acculturated to tribal life, she became the mother of Quanah Parker, the last of the great Comanche chiefs.[19]

Although the Daniels would eventually become respected

citizens of the town and Jessie would emerge as a leading opponent of the vigilantism endemic to the region, James's abrupt
attempt to improve his family's situation brought added anxieties as well as new opportunities. In Overton, the train dispatcher had been counted among the more affluent citizens. Now,
high rent and the cost of tuition strained the family budget.
The income that had seemed ample in Overton dwindled to insignificance before the needs of Georgetown. Moreover, the
children in Jessie's school came from the families of college
professors and professional men. "I tried humbly and painfully
to be like them," she recalled. "But I never learned to feel at
home." In this setting, Jessie's feelings of "unworthiness" intensified.[20]

Lulu at first fulfilled James's expectations. She was aware
that he was "vicariously . . . starting to college" with her; she
made good grades and achieved a requisite popularity. But in
the end neither she nor her younger brother Charley could live
up to James's imperious demands. Willful and sensitive, Charley refused to submit to his father's frequent thrashings; at the
age of fifteen, midway through his first year in college, he ran
away to California. Lulu retreated into sickness; though she
was graduated from college, she did not receive the high
honors James Daniel expected. When she married a few years
later and seemed to be drifting away from the family, her father was disconsolate.[21]

Jessie seized the chance to take Lulu's place in her father's
affections. In 1897 at the age of thirteen, she enrolled in the
local college. But James Daniel, embittered by the disappoint-
ing performance of his older children, held out little hope for
Jessie's success:

> The morning that I was to enter college, he called me into the sit-
> ting room and delivered to me a short and forceful speech. He was
> both sad and cynical as he looked me coldly in the eye and said,
> "Young lady, I am sending you to college because there is nothing
> else to do with you. But I want you to understand right now that
> . . . the first time that you fail in your classes . . . you come out of
> school and go to the kitchen. . . . I do not expect you to graduate.

If your sister could not stand the strain . . . there is no reason to believe that you will do as well."

Her father's attitude only stiffened Jessie's resolve. "My goal was to beat my sister," she recalled. She struggled on despite her youth and lack of preparation for the work, refusing to acknowledge her academic difficulties or to admit defeat.[22]

Women at Southwestern were segregated in a "Ladies Annex" and hedged about with special restrictions. Her father's refusal to allow her to attend college social functions further limited Jessie's student life. Dressed in her sister's discarded clothes, she was "cut off from all the intimacies of girlhood and thrown back upon books for companionship." When her father lifted his restrictions in her senior year, it was too late. "I longed despairingly to be like other girls," she recalled.

In sheer fright and embarressment [sic] I refused all engagements. As a result I achieved the reputation of hating boys. I did not hate them. I liked and admired them profoundly. . . . But I hid behind this as a means of saving my pride. I even boasted of a scornful contempt for them and I acted so well that I convinced everyone of the genuiness of my feeling.[23]

In 1902, with no suitors in sight and no encouragement to seek a career, Jessie graduated into the purgatory of spinsterhood. The only female relative who might have provided a model for a dignified and valued alternative to marriage was her father's half-sister, Annie Sturges Daniel; she had been graduated in 1897 from the medical school for women founded by Elizabeth Blackwell, was an early suffragist, a member of the Working Women's Society, and a participant in movements for tenement and prison reform. Jessie's father, however, viewed his sister as "degraded and unsexed," and Jessie met her aunt, whom she greatly admired, only in 1924, after she had launched her own career. Feminists of her aunt's generation had sacrificed marriage for professional careers, but Jessie saw before her neither the role of "new woman" nor the alternative of traditional family life. "In the South," she recalled, "an unmarried woman is an unwanted woman [and] marriage even to a 'gatepost' . . . is the only estate to which a woman should aspire. . . . Missing it, all is lost." At the age of nineteen, Jessie Daniel was (or believed she was) an "old maid," forced to live dependently in the house of her father.[24]

Two years later, however, James Daniel made another decision that changed the course of Jessie's life. Miserably unhappy in the same town with his married daughter and distraught "at the sight of her love for another man," he applied to the I. & G.N. for a transfer to Laredo, on the Mexican border. Laredo's large Latin population, together with the army officers from nearby Fort McIntosh with their "white uniforms and brass buttons," gave the town an ambience far removed from that of "quiet, conservative, religious" Georgetown. Like Kate Chopin's fictional heroine Edna Pontellier, on holiday among the Creoles of south Louisiana, Jessie was transfigured:

> At night the sweet perfume of blossoming oleanders, the velvet black shadows of the palm trees, the distant music in Mexico filled me with a spirit of exultation which I could not understand. . . . The throngs of dark skinned girls in bright colored . . . dresses, weaving in and out among the palms . . . flirting languorously with the sensuous-eyed men . . . appealed to my senses in a most un-Methodist manner.

For a season, she was filled with a gay abandon. "I was waiting," she recalled, "for the big event to enter my life." As if by magic, Jessie found herself being courted by a friend of her father's, an exotic man of the world from New Orleans, an army surgeon thirteen years her senior.[25]

Calamity ended this brief, idyllic interlude. In a fight with the opposing team at the end of a ball game, the youngest Daniel child, Jamie, was killed by a blow from a baseball bat. The Laredo *Daily News* described the event beneath the front-page headline, "CLOUD OF MOURNING PREVAILS OVER THE CITY." A "dead hush" followed Jamie's beating. "The poor boy staggered a few feet . . . exclaiming, 'Someone help me,' then fell to the ground face downward and . . . died instantly." One of Jamie's attackers was arraigned on a charge of murder but, to James Daniel's bitter disappointment, he escaped prosecution,

allegedly because of his father's connection with a notorious
South Texas political machine.[26]

Until the death of his youngest son, James Daniel had
seemed a paragon of masculine strength. Like other men of his
generation, he had tried to maintain a self-image and social role
being eroded by forces beyond his control. Bureaucratization,
the decline of rugged individualism—such invisible trends
posed an inchoate threat to the traditional ideal of manliness on
which James Daniel had based his life.[27] Transferred from
town to town, he had failed to rise above the post of station
master in a railroad empire dominated by the towering Jay
Gould. As the ambitions of his youth proved increasingly elu-
sive, James Daniel also had to bear the disappointment of his
waning authority over his wife and children. Lulu had deserted
him. Charlie was a reprobate. The death of his youngest and favorite son proved the final blow. "Out of his mind" with grief,
he paced the floor, refused to move anything in Jamie's room,
and suffered from incapacitating headaches. Their father, his
eldest daughter observed, was "always so persistently, so in-
domitably strong, and so bent on making his children likewise
strong, because . . . he was not inherently strong at all. He
had made himself strong in just the same way he made us
strong: through punishment, through lashing himself to an
ideal." Little by little Laura Daniel took over responsiblity for
the ongoing life of the family. Leaving the railroad, James invested in a local telephone company in Georgetown. In his last
years, he gave up his long rebellion against religious orthodoxy. He died in 1911, clinging to his wife and "consenting
. . . in the end to join her church and be baptized with her
baptism."[28]

1

In June 1905, a year after her brother's death, Jessie married
the handsome army surgeon, Roger Post Ames. She saw her

wedding as a "triumph," belated proof of her desirability as a woman. But far from supplying the security and affirmation she sought, Jessie's marriage at once foundered on sexual incompatibility and kinship pressures. When they arrived in Pascagoula, Mississippi, for a honeymoon at the Ames's summer home, the couple confronted the implacable disapproval of Roger's family. They viewed Jessie as a socially inferior interloper. Above all, they feared that Roger's marriage would deprive them of their chief means of financial support.

Born in 1870, Roger was the youngest of four children in a stormy Irish family. His maternal grandfather, captain of a Yankee clipper, had docked in Pascagoula and stayed on to marry a wealthy widow and manage a resort hotel. His paternal grandfather had left Ireland in 1828, settled in New Orleans, and became a dealer in coal, a cotton factor, and a slave owner. Frederick W. Ames, Roger's father, prepared for the Jesuit priesthood, but instead became a steamboat captain. By 1890, when their youngest son graduated from Tulane Medical School, the Ames's fortunes had declined. Roger's father had been injured in the Civil War; his two sisters were unmarried and dependent and his brother was an invalid. In order to support his family, he first went to work for a dredging company, then left for British Honduras where he was appointed post doctor at Belize. He enlisted in the army medical corps during the Spanish-American War, served in the Philippines, and worked with Walter Reed in Cuba on the famous experiments proving that mosquitoes transmitted malaria. His army salary continued to be the mainstay of the family economy.[29]

The hostility the couple met in Pascagoula forced Roger and Jessie to cut short their honeymoon and leave immediately for New Orleans, where Roger had been assigned to conduct antimalaria campaigns based on Reed's findings. But they fared little better on their own. After only a week, a yellow fever epidemic broke out, and Roger was ordered to Jackson Barracks. Rather than leave his wife in New Orleans, he sent her home to Texas. Jessie felt that she had been "sent away," that Roger regretted their marriage, that she had "failed him" in Pascagoula. This proved to be only the first of a debilitating series of long separations and brief reunions. Their sexual relationship was shrouded in fear, embarrassment, and jealousy. During their courtship, in what Jessie later viewed as an effort to persuade her to break their engagement, Roger had warned her first that he was syphilitic and then that he was impotent. After their marriage, he seems to have been unfaithful, while Jessie saw herself as frigid. "I was not a fully developed woman," she recalled. "I had not been allowed to grow up."[30] Sexual desire, she believed, was stronger in a man than in a woman. "A woman may be and in my day usually was a passive agent in this matter of conceiving a child. No man can beget a child except at a time when he is wide awake and in the throes of very strong passion. A woman can conceive in her sleep."[31] Fearful of intimacy, Jessie found herself incapable of sexual self-abandon.

Despite the birth of a son in 1907, the marriage, beginning badly, grew worse. Roger's family consumed most of his income. Jessie believed that they encouraged him to divorce her and sought "to blacken my reputation . . . in letters to him [and] in loose talk to everyone." She hid her "deep hurt and humiliation" in pride. In private she lashed out at him in words "that were intended as a release for my own pent up misery but which must have appeared to him as deliberately intended to destroy his self-respect. Our sexual relations were similar," she recalled. "This is the picture of our married life. I would leave him somewhere, New Orleans, Puerto Cortez, Puerto Barrios, at the end of my rope. . . . I could not live away from him. I could not live with him. I always returned in hope and joy; I was always sent away in despair."[32]

In 1910, Roger's sister precipitated a final crisis when she delivered an ultimatum in Jessie's presence "to the effect that unless he abandoned his wife and three-year old son, he could never return to Pascagoula to see his family." Roger responded by withdrawing from the family conflicts altogether; he left his wife with her relatives and spent the rest of his life in Puerto Barrios, Guatemala, where he became physician to the American Consul and the United Fruit Company. Even when his mother died two years later and his brother gained control of the family estate, he refused to return to fight for his inheritance. In nine and a half years of marriage, Jessie claimed, she spent less than ten months with her husband.[33]

Deserted and dependent, Jessie lived with her older sister, who had a devoted husband, an expensive home, "a life I would have given my eyes for." She fought back with the few resources at her disposal. Unable to win her husband away from the "complete domination" of his family, she journeyed for brief visits to Latin America and sought approval and security in pregnancy and motherhood.[34] Her first child, Frederick, she recalled, was conceived "much against Roger's desire and wish. He knew he could not support a family. . . . Ashamed of the situation, I forced the issue. . . . I was desperate." With Frederick's birth it seemed that even her father "came to tolerate" her. She became pregnant again in 1912. Once a daughter, Mary, arrived, Jessie at last induced Roger to support her.

In August 1914, Jessie journeyed to Puerto Barrios, a visit that in retrospect she believed was the only "happy and contented" time in her married life. Roger had "come to the place where he was able and willing to provide a home of my own for me and the family. . . . When the devil drives, needs must."[35] She returned to Texas pregnant with her third child, found a house, and made plans for a reconciliation. On November 15, however, Roger died of blackwater fever in Guatemala. Reluctant to face his family, Jessie refused to attend the funeral in New Orleans. She received only one thousand dollars from her husband's estate, but she was not in the "physical, emotional nor mental condition" to sue for more.[36]

A widow at thirty-one, with three young children to support, Ames began the transition from daughter, sister, wife, and mother to a new life devoted not to domestic duties but to what she proudly termed "serious social problems."[37] Changing historical circumstances would provide the settings in which her strengths could be realized; her identity would evolve through later stages of her life as she responded to the opportunities offered first by the women's movement and then by interracial reform. Yet no degree of public achievement and acclaim could permanently allay a private anguish rooted in the experiences of her youth. From the crucible of a particular family, time, and place came the qualities that would make her both a flawed and a brilliant leader of organized southern women.

Her political and cultural heritage was a complex mixture of frontier self-sufficiency and middle-class aspiration. Growing up in the small-town Southwest at the turn of the century, she acquired an abiding sense of place that shaped her self-definition and her point of view. This regional pride expressed itself as an identification with the South as well as a distance from it.[38] Because she had neither the southern antecedents nor the firm social standing of many white reformers in the region, she consciously struggled to maintain a life-style that would enable her to work with what she termed the "perfect ladies" of the interracial movement on a plane of equality. She sometimes claimed to come from an "old Southern family" or an "erudite Texas family," but she always saw herself as an outsider who assumed the role of southern lady for the sake of her work and her constituency.[39]

The image of her father and the misfortune of her marriage cast a permanent shadow over her interior life. She longed for the love of a man who encouraged neither achievement nor a conviction of feminine attractiveness. Her wedding had represented affirmation of her womanhood, but her relationship with her husband reinforced her feelings of unworthiness. She was ill-prepared for the intimacy of adult sexuality and found herself trapped in a permanent, and painful, emotional isolation. Her marital experience and her social situation made it unlikely that she would risk commitment to another man, nor were her affective needs fully met in relationships with

women. Terrified of rejection, she sought refuge in self-protective impersonality. The major theme of her emotional life became the need for control—over herself, her children, her sur-
roundings. She was by no means devoid of sensuality, but she
strove for a radical separation of mind and body, intellect and
emotion.[40] Above all, her strategy for survival rested on the
necessities of pride, of hiding one's feelings lest one's real self
be "found out." "Since the day of my husband's death," she
wrote, "I have put on a bold front to prevent anyone's feeling
sorry for me." Recalled her daughter: "she never let anyone
get close to her. And when they seemed to be getting close
. . . that was when she broke it off or she put the veneer on
thicker, the shell."[41]

Yet both her conflicts with her father and her marriage to
Roger helped pave the way for her accomplishments. Rescued
from the onus of spinsterhood, she had traveled into a world
beyond the bounds of her small-town, Protestant upbringing.
Her husband's early death clarified her status; as a young
widow, she would be granted a degree of social acceptability
she had enjoyed neither as an unmarried girl nor as a deserted
wife. On a deeper level, the abdication of men whom she both
desired and resented shielded her from the full brunt of female
socialization in a patriarchal society. Jessie Daniel Ames
scarcely had the option of remaining psychologically bound
within the family. The protective resources she developed
would, for the most part, serve her well in the political arena.
Although at a cost, her flight from a feminine role she equated
with powerlessness and inferiority would become a source of
enormous energy in a productive and useful life.[42]

The dynamics of Jessie's interaction with the women in her
family were more ambivalent, but no less formative. Her father's love for Lulu, she believed, had been obsessive and in-
cestuous; she and her sister, played off against each other for
the favor and approval of men, were locked in a relationship
compounded of dependence, admiration, and envy. Lulu presented a negative model of femininity: "a clinging vine, a para-
site," sustained by the love and patronage of men. Jessie's

identity would be bound up with self-sufficiency and independence. Yet Jessie's hostility toward her sister also prefigured competitive relationships with other women that would mar her leadership style and a denigration of femininity that would limit her identification with women as a group. Indeed, only in middle age could she fully admit her dislike of Lulu and pursue what she termed her "disenslavement" from a compelling and ongoing sibling rivalry. [43]

In contrast to her autobiographical comments about other family members, Jessie left little record of her mother's place in the mental landscape of her childhood. She viewed her mother, like herself, as a victim of James's rejection and thus both as an ally and an object lesson in the perils of womanhood. At the same time, Laura proved the stronger figure in the Daniel family, and Jessie came to believe that it was her mother who "embued me with [the] spirit of pioneering, keeping my chin up, fighting thro." As widows, the two women maintained close ties of mutual support, a practical reciprocity that made it possible for Jessie to combine motherhood with political activism. Their relationship, however, was marked by emotional reserve, rather than by personal confidences or the open expression of affection. In Jessie's youth, as she remembered it, her mother had been "too occupied . . . with her life as my father's wife to take seriously the small problems and difficulties of a child." Many years later, when Laura learned that she was dying of cancer, she asked to "go home to Jessie" rather than remain in her older daughter's care. Jessie reacted to this choice with feelings of pride and vindication. Her mother's death left her "deeply lonely," searching through her memories of the past for other signs of Laura's love. [44]

Out of the tangled web of her options and experiences, Jessie Daniel Ames gained a saving will toward competence and self-fulfillment. The initial sense of grievance, the early injury to the spirit that added an undercurrent of psychic isolation to an exuberant public persona was also part of the motive force for her transcendence of social norms. Neither in the protection of men nor in the model of her mother's and sister's lives could she find a fully satisfying personal and sexual identity. Rather, she was forced to become in the most profound sense a "self-made woman."[45] A desire to escape from the prison of solitude, a drive toward mastery of the irrational both within and without, an identification with victims of circumstance, and a need to care for others at a safe remove—these were among the emotional wellsprings of her career. Inevitably her journey into an unknown and unmarked future exacted a steep emotional price. Fierce and willful striving propelled her into the public forums that gave historic significance to her life. But throughout a long and distinguished career she retained a consciousness formed in adversity: competitive, insecure, and, in her words, "fighting every step of the way."[46]

Chapter 2
Out of Obscurity

Shortly after her husband's death in 1914, Jessie Daniel Ames took her first steps from the anonymity of private life to the public role of social reformer. Entering the suffrage movement at a time when much of its radical potential had been dissipated, she rose to prominence in Texas as an advocate of the goals of southern progressivism. In the process she became a "new woman," no longer a dependent, humiliated wife but an aggressive and effective leader. She developed the pragmatic style and the feminist consciousness that characterized the remainder of her career. Unlike most suffragists she also began, in the early twenties, to sense the limitations of a women's movement for whites only. A proponent of justice for blacks as well as of equality for women, she served as a vital link between a tradition of social feminism and the twentieth-century struggle for black civil rights.

1

The Seneca Falls Convention of 1848 marked the beginning of organized struggle for female equality and autonomy. Participants in the nineteenth-century women's movement drew their moral fervor from the romantic and perfectionist impulses that had also inspired the antislavery campaign. Through their central role in abolitionism, they learned the tactics of collective action, and they made the analogy of slavery central to the rhetoric of feminism. But their challenge to the sexual status quo met a wall of opposition even among abolitionists them- selves. Everywhere in middle-class America, the "cult of true womanhood" reigned, with its view of the family as the corner- stone of civilization, its extreme double standard, and its rigid separation of sexual spheres. Antebellum feminism threatened this whole set of social values.[1]

In the South, the stakes were higher: a challenge to the absolute dominance of the patriarch endangered slavery itself. Guilt over miscegenation and undercurrents of female discon- tent reinforced a pervasive uneasiness about the loyalty of white women to the peculiar institution, a loyalty made all the more precious by the moral authority granted women in the Victorian era. The cultural forces that suppressed indige- nous antislavery sentiment also precluded public advocacy of women's rights. As long as slavery and the subordination of women were thus intertwined, no organized women's move- ment could emerge in the slave states.[2]

After the Civil War, the historic connection between racial and sexual equality faded. The failure of the Fifteenth Amend- ment to secure for women the political privileges it granted to freedmen disillusioned feminists who earlier had been staunch abolitionists. Moreover, the defeat of Reconstruction, the derailment of Populism, and the nativist response to immigra- tion from southern Europe each reflected and then intensified a monolithic racism in which the rising generation of women's rights advocates shared. New leaders schooled in the politics of progressivism transformed a radical assault on social norms into a broad-based campaign for suffrage. As organizers within an intellectual milieu that encouraged compromise, they made pragmatism and coalition-building keystones of their struggle. By adopting the principle of autonomy for state organizations and separating the issue of black enfranchisement from that of votes for women, the National American Woman Suffrage As- sociation (NAWSA) cleared a way for the entrance of white southern women into the movement.[3]

The response of southern suffragists to the issues of race and sex ranged across a complex ideological spectrum. Moderate border-state leaders like Laura Clay of Kentucky advocated an educational requirement for women's suffrage, which would eliminate the poor, both black and white, from the political process. A minority led by Kate M. Gordon of Louisiana advocated the complete elimination of black voters and sought to forge an independent southern women's movement devoted to white supremacy and a state-by-state suffrage campaign.[4] By 1915, when Jessie Daniel Ames joined the movement, most southern activists had rejected Gordon's states' rights strategy and remained safely within the NAWSA fold. Like their progressive allies, they assumed the political prerogatives of the white middle class; acquiescing in the disfranchisement of blacks, they sought to ignore "the negro question" for the sake of expediency.[5]

2

In Texas the suffrage battle mixed the advantages of the West, where the first victories were won, with the problems of the South, where the campaign met its greatest resistance. The state became the second in the Old Confederacy to grant women the vote in primary elections and the first to ratify the Nineteenth Amendment. The movement drew its success from a divergent regional culture, a favorable political context, and a leadership dedicated to grass-roots organizing and practical coalition-building. Yet, as in the rest of the South, the drive toward suffrage was long and hard, triumphing only on the eve of war.[6]

Texas in the generation before the First World War provided a peculiar context for women's lives. The state had long been divided by geography and climate into two distinct regions. The Balcones Fault marked the furthest edge of the American South; to the west stretched the beginning of the Great Plains.

A heritage of slavery marked the eastern blacklands and piney woods, and the southern immigrants of the 1870s and 1880s brought with them the habits of living of the rural South.[7] Yet as nineteenth-century settlers poured into the Southwest, they modified their expectations and behavior to meet the exigencies of the frontier. Women's roles, like other social forms, succumbed to necessity. As women took on men's tasks, they were forced to cast off the trappings of gentility and to adopt more appropriate styles of dress and decorum.[8] A memorial on women's suffrage presented to the Constitutional Convention of 1869 acknowledged this frontier phenomenon when it congratulated the state for its generosity regarding "avocations" for women, and among the Reconstruction legislatures only Texas gave women's suffrage serious consideration. As the movement got under way, reports to NAWSA emphasized the liberalizing influence of Spanish law and pointed with pride to Texas' claim to be "a woman's State."[9]

The image of the independent frontier woman, however, pales beside the evidence of women's deep alienation from the arid plains, their loneliness, the added hardships they endured.[10] As the first stages of frontier life passed, both men and women sought to replicate familiar patterns, and the earliest organized demand for women's suffrage came, in Texas as elsewhere in the South, from women embracing their Victorian function as civilizers of an unruly masculine world. In 1887, frustrated in its attempts at moral suasion, the Woman's Christian Temperance Union (WCTU) turned toward political action. Temperance reformers sought to protect women's interests as mothers and homemakers by enforcing a single, feminine standard of personal morality and social ethics. Thus they provided a bridge over which Texas women could move into the public arena with their domestic self-images intact.[11]

Six years after the WCTU raised the suffrage issue, the Texas women's movement began in earnest. In 1893, a convention of 48 women met in Dallas to form the Texas Equal Rights Association. The organization, which immediately affiliated with the NAWSA, pledged to "advance the industrial, educational and equal rights of women, and to secure suffrage to them by appropriate State and national legislation." Five months later 300 women attended a Woman's Congress in Dallas and seven local societies were organized. After 1903, Annette Finnigan, who had attended Wellesley and joined the movement as one of Carrie Chapman Catt's lieutenants in the New York Equal Suffrage League, led a second flurry of organizational activity. But when Finnigan and her sisters left the state, the movement declined, leaving only one local group active in Austin. Controversy over the relationship between the state organization and the NAWSA and dependence on strong individual leaders plagued this first phase of the campaign.[12]

In addition to these internal weaknesses, the wider political context militated against the rise of an effective organization. Although women played important roles in the Texas Farmers Alliance and the Populist Party endorsed women's suffrage, politically significant support for enfranchisement came less from insurgent farmers than from their opponents. Only with the defeat of Populism and the disfranchisement of blacks did factions arise that viewed white women as a potential constituency and championed women's suffrage as a means of achieving their political goals.[13]

After the turn of the century, with the Democratic Party securely back in control, a new era of intraparty factionalism emerged.[14] The conservatives, led by Senator Joseph Weldon Bailey, sought political power in the name of states' rights, weak government, and unreconstructed racism. They kept alive the nineteenth-century identification of women's rights with black liberation, thus setting the terms of twentieth-century debate on women's suffrage. On the other side, Wilsonian progressives, under the leadership of Senator Morris Sheppard and a banker and insurance man named Thomas B. Love, advocated such mechanisms as the referendum and recall and favored governmental regulation of social life and personal behavior through prohibition. This identification of Texas progressivism with the prohibition issue provided suffragists with their most important allies. Seen by Democratic progressives both as a logical mode for promoting the cultural hegemony of a new middle class and as an avenue for gaining allies in the prohibition fight, women's suffrage gradually became a legitimate political issue within the party.

In 1912, M. Eleanor Brackenridge of San Antonio, "a woman of means, social prominence and wide acquaintance," assumed leadership of the Texas suffrage association. Brackenridge and her mother had made their home a center for the first women's literary society in San Antonio, the "Head of the River Mutual Admiration Society." As this society evolved into the first woman's club in the state, Brackenridge guided its activities into industrial education, legal reform, and women's suffrage. During her tenure as president of the state suffrage association, the agitation for an autonomous southern movement devoted to state legislation brought the latent dissension over tactics within the Texas movement to the surface. After lengthy debate at the convention of 1913—the first to be held since 1904—moderation prevailed and Texas remained loyal to the national organization. [15]

The period 1915–1916 marked a major turning point for the Texas suffrage campaign. The task of putting Carrie Chapman Catt's "winning plan" into action on the state level fell to a new president, Minnie Fisher Cunningham. Born in Walker County in 1882, Cunningham grew up amid the tenant farms of men and women who had once been slaves on her father's small plantation. She graduated from the University of Texas with a degree in pharmacy in 1901, and worked for three years after her marriage to an insurance salesman. In 1910, she began writing and speaking on behalf of women's suffrage. Her eagerness "to taste the experience of life lived as an 'equal' to the lords of creation" soon catapulted her to leadership in the movement, first as president of the Galveston Equal Suffrage Association, then as head of the state organization. [16]

Under Cunningham's guidance, the renamed Texas Equal Suffrage Association (ESA) adopted innovative and aggressive tactics. [17] In 1915, an inexperienced but determined group of lobbyists succeeded in bringing a women's suffrage resolution to a vote in the Texas legislature. Most importantly, Cunningham and her co-workers switched from petitions and pronouncements to the precinct by precinct organizing strategy pioneered by the New York movement. Their appeal to the increasing numbers of middle-class women who had gained experience in public life through local women's clubs and church societies met an immediate response. In one year the number of suffrage associations in the state rose by 400 percent, and Cunningham was able to announce support for women's suffrage from the Federation of Women's Clubs, the Texas Farm Women, the Texas Press Women, and the WCTU.[18] It was this growing rank-and-file constituency that demonstrated the political clout of organized women and convinced Democratic progressives to support women's suffrage in their own self-interest.

Among the younger generation who led the movement through its final, victorious phase were a number of women schooled, like Cunningham, in business and professional life. While there is little evidence of a correlation between the emergence of women's rights agitation and women's participation in the labor force, white-collar opportunities for middle-class women did help create the economic base and motivation for leadership in the suffrage movement. In 1870, only 10.4 percent of Texas women over ten were gainfully employed, while 20 percent of the women in the remaining ten ex-Confederate states and 13.1 percent in the nation had joined the work force. By 1920, when suffrage was achieved, the gaps between all three had narrowed, with Texas still trailing both the national and southern norms. Throughout the period, however, a larger percentage of working women in Texas were employed in white-collar positions than in any other southern state. In 1920, only 12.1 percent of employed women in the South were in professional and clerical service; in contrast, in Texas white-collar workers made up 21.7 percent of the total, 7 percent below the country as a whole.[19]

The Finnigan sisters, Eleanor Brackenridge, and other early leaders of the Texas movement were single, upper-middle-class graduates of female academies outside the state. After 1915, leadership roles were assumed by women in their early thirties, educated in Texas colleges and experienced in business and professional work outside the home. Cunningham, the association's president, had sought a place in a male-dominated profession. Jane Y. McCallum, who, as director of publicity, became Cunningham's closest ally, was the first married woman to attend classes at the University of Texas and combined a career in journalism and politics with her role as the mother of four children. The third member of this winning team was the recently widowed Jessie Daniel Ames.

3

Although few contemporary sources reflect Ames's developing feminism, at least some of her motivations and the influences upon her can be reconstructed. She was ten years old when her family moved to Georgetown in 1893, the year of the founding of the Texas Equal Rights Association. In response to the beginnings of suffrage agitation and the appearance of the state's second local suffrage association in nearby Taylor, the county newspaper editor launched a series of antisuffrage articles and editorials. A change in women's status, the editor plaintively warned, would deprive men of their last oasis from the pressures of economic competition. "What the true man wants is companionship, sympathy and love." A girl should be taught home economics and physical fitness in order to become an accomplished wife in a "well-developed body."[20]

The tensions that underlay local concern with sex-role prescriptions reverberated within the Daniel family itself. When Jessie's sister Lulu turned sixteen in 1893, she resisted the trappings of ladyhood.

The complete change from the simple clothing of a little girl to the longer skirts, tight bodices, and endless accessories of a young lady was bewildering . . . my bodily freedom was greatly hampered by my first stays. . . . Handkerchiefs to be carried all the time instead of just when you had a cold! Veils drawn over the upper half of the face! Gloves so tight that your hands looked wooden! A pocketbook with nothing in it, but which had to be held onto just the same! And layers of tight belted skirts coming to my ankles in modest folds. . . . I was a lady morning, noon, and night!

Lulu's restlessness with her role also found expression at Southwestern where she created a women's literary magazine called *An-X*, "a publication of unknown *quality*, just as the women were supposed to be an unknown *quantity*."[21]

Like her sister, Jessie claimed to have harbored women's rights convictions long before her involvement in the suffrage movement. Her interest in politics began early, growing directly out of her admiration for her father. In 1892, at the age of nine, she was allowed to stay up all night in order to raise the flag in honor of Grover Cleveland's election.[22] Her fondest memories of college days were of carriage rides with her father, "over the prairies or along the river roads," holding long pessimistic discussions about the decline of Cleveland's political fortunes, the future of the country under a Republican administration, and "the lack of stability in the Democrats as shown by their running after strange gods" in the person of William Jennings Bryan.[23]

After her marriage, she chafed under the inequities of the legal position of married women. In 1905, immediately following her wedding, she confronted a startled bank teller with the issue of married women's property rights: "I wanted to open up an account and the cashier looked at me and asked if I had my husband's permission. I hit the ceiling! I said, 'No, it's my money.' Then I found out about laws governing married women. The husbands owned everything—the clothes on her back! She owned absolutely nothing. . . . Women were considered not second-class citizens—ye gods, we were third-class, we were no class at all after we were married."[24] Her subsequent experience of married life deepened this indignation. Nine years of economic dependence on her relatives and an absent spouse convinced her that the most humiliating aspect of a wife's position was the ability of her husband to use money "as a bludgeon to make you conform."[25]

Although he had encouraged her interest in politics, Jessie's father maintained an implacable opposition to women's suffrage and to his daughter's nascent feminism. During her troubled marriage, he counseled her to remain with her husband in Latin America despite her unhappiness there. "Stay with [your] man," he warned, and don't "let the doctor know for one minute but what you are having the best time you ever had."[26] Her father loved her, Ames believed, only after she presented him with two grandchildren and as long as she was far away. But when she returned to Georgetown to live in 1911, the conflicts between them reemerged, centering this time on arguments over women's rights.

Laura Daniel, on the other hand, offered support for her daughter's convictions. Through the University Methodist Church she became friends with a Southwestern professor, John C. Granbery, and his wife, Mary Anne Catt, both of whom were staunch progressives and suffragists. As president of the local Methodist Woman's Missionary Society, Laura provided a forum for Granbery's early speeches on suffrage and other social issues. In later years, she attended suffrage lectures with her daughter and wrote admiringly of such illustrious visitors as Carrie Chapman Catt and Anna Howard Shaw.[27]

After 1914, when both women had been widowed, a new phase opened in their relationship with each other and with the larger community. Laura Daniel inherited the local telephone company acquired by her husband several years before his death. Choosing to keep the management of the business in her own hands, she soon found herself in an altogether unprecedented role. For years she had served as a mainstay of the church, organizing women's missionary societies, teaching Bible school, and performing community services that would later become the province of the medical and social work professions. Like other nineteenth-century women, Laura's neighbors called on each other in the crises of disease and death. It was her special role in the community to watch the sick, to prepare the dead for burial, and even to take the place of the minister in praying with the family of the terminally ill. Upon her husband's death, however, she began to relinquish this nurturing role within the female subculture, becoming instead what the local newspaper termed "a pioneer business woman in a field of great corporations and cold-blooded men."[28]

Jessie joined her mother in this endeavor, first as bookkeeper and then as manager of most of the day-to-day business of the company. The two women combined their resources, moving from the house in which Jessie had grown up to a more spacious residence closer to the company. With the aid of a cook and a full-time housekeeper, they shared the upbringing of Jessie's children. Despite their practical interdependence, however, the relation between mother and daughter was marked by recurring tension and conflict. Laura continued her devoted interest in the church. Jessie refused to participate. Laura maintained official control of the business, symbolically retaining her own private office in the small stucco building, while Jessie worked in the large common room with the telephone operators. Jessie, however, increasingly assumed responsibility for supervising not only the young women operators but, with more difficulty, the repair and linemen who viewed their new female superiors with ambivalence. "Mother," Jessie bitterly recalled, never gave any "visible evidence [that she knew] I had been a help to her in the business and that I had taken from her much unpleasant words and conduct."[29] Despite these problems, the company flourished, and both Laura and Jessie emerged as competent and toughminded competitors in a male-dominated business community.

For Jessie Daniel Ames, this experience offered unforeseen opportunities for growth. Whether arguing for a raise in telephone rates before the city council, or enforcing a strict bill-collecting policy, or traveling to conventions of her business peers, she demonstrated a new-found talent for administration and organization. She exhibited the blend of ladylike manipulativeness and pugnacity that marked the remainder of her ca-

reer. When, for example, an irate business man stormed into
her office, complaining that she had cut off his phone because
of an overdue bill, she handled the situation with unnerving
aplomb. "If you were a man," he blustered, "I would like to
cuss you out." "Now don't let that stop you," she replied. "You
just come right in here and get if off your chest." She "cut him
down," her long-time secretary recalled, "using the nicest
words. He was the worst whipped man you ever saw. He just
paid his bill and walked out."[30] In such encounters, and in the
daily experience of supporting her children and managing a
complex business operation, Ames gained the sense of competence she had never achieved as a student, a daughter, or a
wife.

Moreover, in her new situation Ames acquired both the psychic and the economic autonomy that made possible her role as
a public advocate of women's rights. Most married women, she
believed, "didn't see any advantage of the vote because they
were taken care of." Single women who worked for a living
"had sense enough to keep their mouths shut if they wanted to
hold their jobs. So it was only in the larger cities, where there
were a good many women who were . . . not only unmarried
but . . . financially independent, that we had any strength."[31]
While her activities put her in the public limelight and made
her vulnerable to criticism ("Frankly," recalled her secretary,
"most of the men just thought it was terrible that she was trying to wear the pants"), her position also enabled her to ignore
community pressures.[32] As Ames plunged into political life,
the local paper stood firmly, as it had twenty years before,
against "unsexing humanity" and called on God to "pity the
woman who . . . sighs for an opportunity . . . to dabble her
white robes in the cesspool of party politics."[33] Closer to
home, Ames's Georgetown neighbors were "highly distressed"
that she was "out after the vote. Ladies didn't do that," Ames
recalled. "But you see, they couldn't do anything about it and
I'll tell you why. . . . My mother and I owned the telephone
company and three or four telephone plants out in the country
and that was a monopoly."[34]

Ames's new status created both the material preconditions and the immediate catalyst for dissent. As an independent businesswoman she resolved to achieve the political power necessary to protect her economic interests. "All I wanted was the vote," she recalled, "for I was . . . the owner of property which voters could tax without the consent of the owners. It was a condition of taxation without representation and I was a female Patrick Henry."[35] As the ego-battered survivor of an unhappy marriage, she was determined "to grow up. For the first time I was responsible for the lives, the welfare and the development of others. I believed that I was escaping from myself. I believed that working for my children was a way to justify myself, acquire approval, mine and the public's, and keep faith with Roger. . . . I had to make good."[36] She had, in her daughter's interpretation, "what we now call an identity crisis. . . . She had to be something." Through with "being a lady," Ames was "looking for a fight." The suffrage movement gave her a double opportunity. Not only could she begin to translate her economic interests and her "sense of justice and fair play" into action, but also she could forge the personal identity toward which she had struggled with such tenacity and so little success.[37]

Ames's first opportunity for putting her sentiments into action came in 1916, as the suffrage forces gathered strength throughout the nation. "It was the longest time before I could get a small suffrage group in my town," she reflected. "People won't follow the lead of a woman they've known since she was so high." But when the ESA announced its precinct organizing drive, Ames was among the first local women to respond. On her own initiative, she organized a county association. Then on April 6, thirty-five men and women met in her home, formed the Georgetown Equal Suffrage League, and elected Jessie Daniel Ames its first president.[38]

Georgetown, Ames believed, was "the most promising field of work" in Senatorial District 20.[39] Indeed, long before state or national leaders appeared on the scene local women had engaged in an astounding number of voluntary organizations

and in a lively discussion of social issues. In a given week, the
Williamson County *Sun* might report on a "women's mass
meeting" for wartime food conservation, a half dozen ladies' aid
and missionary societies, literary and musical groups, a
woman's club, a Chautauqua gathering, and a variety of special
church activities organized by women parishioners. Ames herself had served as the first president of the Georgetown
Woman's Club, her mother led the Methodist missionary society, and both participated in a range of other community functions. Out of such self-activity emerged the constituency that
would transform a small elite band of suffragists into a broad-
based social movement.

At first the Georgetown suffrage group relied wholly on its
own resources, but soon Ames was sending pleas to state association headquarters that she "absolutely" could not "go any
further" without outside help. When the long-awaited organizer arrived, she helped form a men's suffrage league headed
by John C. Granbery. Together the two leagues sponsored
Georgetown's first public meeting on women's suffrage, a gathering in the county courthouse on George Washington's Birthday, February 22, 1917, with state president Minnie Fisher
Cunningham as the featured speaker.[40]

In Minnie Fisher Cunningham, Ames found the unam-
biguous mentor she had lacked as a child. Cunningham was the
great orator as well as the organizer of the Texas movement,
and she remained a power in Democratic Party politics for
another quarter of a century. She ran for the U.S. Senate in
1928 and for the Democratic nomination for governor in 1945,
earning the title "Mrs. Texas Democrat." A broadside for her
1928 campaign proclaimed, "Texas Women are Proud of having
the only woman candidate for the U.S. Senate; Are Proud that
she is womanly; Are Proud that she is learned. . . . Acclaimed
by thousands as the brainiest speaker of them all."[41] At her appearance in Georgetown she managed on the one hand to make
a dramatic appeal to her female audiences and on the other to
win the grudging approval of the press. Mrs. Cunningham, the
Williamson County *Sun* reported,

is convincing in her arguments, and is exceptional among suffragist speakers in that she brings no "railing accusations" against her brother man. She realizes that the present condition is a natural, historical development, for which no one is to blame, and makes an earnest and logical appeal to him that, having obtained suffrage for himself, he now help his sister to obtain the same privilege. [42]

Eleanor Roosevelt, who heard Cunningham speak at the second national convention of the League of Women Voters in 1921, thought her an "emotional idealistic" speaker who made you feel "that you had no right to be a slacker as a citizen, you had no right not to take part in what was happening to your country as a whole." [43]

This dynamic state leader brought Jessie Daniel Ames "out of obscurity" and started her on the road to regional prominence. With Cunningham's encouragement, Ames undertook a series of weekly "Woman Suffrage Notes" for the county paper. At first these articles were mere compendiums of arguments from elsewhere together with announcements of suffrage meetings, but soon Ames began developing her own salty style. [44] She derided the notion of women's "all pervading influence" and demanded that good government advocates cease to call on women for support while denying them the vote.

Consistency! Men never hesitate to ask and get from the women of the country everything that they wish for in the name of good government. Women will march in parades, serve hot coffee on the grounds the day of the voting, go to but not into the polling places. . . . Then after devoting themselves body and soul to this most trying work for so just a cause, they are brushed aside at the final and actual decision helplessly looking on while the men go in and in this county undo the labor of all the days. [45]

In addition to this foray into print, Cunningham gave the young widow from Georgetown her first opportunity to practice the oratorical skills upon which much of her later success would rely. At the May 1917 ESA convention in Waco, Jessie Daniel Ames appeared as one of the featured speakers. The subject she chose reflected both her growing restiveness with small-town life and the gap between her mother's mode of community participation and her own. By the time she joined the ESA, Ames had ceased to attend local social gatherings and had grown increasingly impatient with the institutional channels for female public life in Georgetown. Her speech at the Waco convention, entitled "Stored Culture," argued that such women's groups dissipated their energies on vague and uncompleted projects. Instead they should devote themselves to women's suffrage, where their "voices and efforts would count for something."[46]

Even more significant than this first platform venture was Cunningham's decision to circulate a family portrait of her new protégée throughout the state as part of a publicity drive for the 1917 meeting. Like suffragists elsewhere, Texans sought to allay antisuffragist fears that political participation was antithetical to femininity and a threat to domestic life. For women like Ames and Cunningham, however, such arguments were tongue-in-cheek. They were attracted to the movement, in part, because it gave them an outlet for their personal ambitions and an opportunity for self-actualization. For both psychological and strategic reasons they held to the notion of women's superior moral nature and responsibility for domestic life, but they also maintained a distance from that self-image which enabled them to manipulate and transcend it. Jessie Daniel Ames's family portrait is a case in point. In it she appeared amid the artifacts of a Victorian drawing room reading aloud to the three children gathered at her knee. At the moment of fleeing a domestic role in which she had been neither happy nor successful, she used the symbolism of motherhood as a justification for her actions. Her picture was circulated, she explained, because antisuffragists were claiming that only "old maids, unhappy married women, and childless married women wanted the vote." She didn't recall, she added ironically, that the fact that she was a widow at thirty-one "was given any publicity."[47]

The Waco convention had been shaped by wartime nationalism. Suffragists pledged their "time, strength, life itself" to the cause of war, and in the months that followed they diverted those precious commodities into Liberty Loan campaigns, the Red Cross, and above all, the formation of a Woman's Anti-Vice Committee to protect soldiers stationed in Texas training camps from the twin vices of alcohol and prostitution. Moreover, in a decisive repudiation of the "long and tortuous path" of state suffrage, the convention telegraphed a resolution to President Woodrow Wilson urging his support of the Nineteenth Amendment.[48]

Delegates like Jessie Daniel Ames returned to their local communities to find a receptive audience for their plea that women should be given political ammunition for their fight to strengthen the moral fiber of the country. By 1918, Ames could draw a crowd of one hundred women to her suffrage talks, and she had the satisfaction of seeing her county newspaper endorse votes for women.[49] In May, at the annual meeting of the ESA in Austin, Ames moved out of her local role: on the basis of both her business experience and her suffrage activities, she was elected treasurer of the state association. In that position she found herself at the vortex of the final drive toward victory.

As Jessie Daniel Ames's initiation into state politics began, suffragists joined in a spectacular battle with Governor James E. Ferguson. "Farmer Jim" (who had made his fortune in banking and real estate) had long been a major enemy of prohibition and women's suffrage. He rose to power in 1914 on a wave of agrarian insurgency, trouncing his progressive-prohibitionist opponent and gaining the governor's chair with a "forks of the creek" platform style, support from the liquor industry, and a program of land reform. An enigmatic figure who dominated Texas politics for two decades, Ferguson combined a

genuine—though largely ineffectual—recognition of the plight
of Texas farmers with casual bigotry and an unscrupulous pursuit of his own financial interests. [50]

Suffragist opposition to the governor had crystalized in 1916
at the state Democratic Party convention in San Antonio.
While women displaying yellow badges and banners looked on
from the galleries, Ferguson and Senator Joseph Bailey backed
a platform declaring "unalterable opposition" to the Nineteenth
Amendment and to national prohibition. With unprecedented
aggressiveness, suffragists in the galleries "descended to the
floor of the hall to mingle with the assembled representatives
of a government founded on the principle of equal rights to all,
and attempted to gain some recognition for the over-looked
half." [51] Despite such efforts, the Bailey/Ferguson forces swept
the convention. Ferguson then went on to humiliate Texas
suffragists by defending the minority resolution against wom-
en's suffrage at the national convention at St. Louis. [52]

Temporarily demoralized, Ferguson's opponents soon found
an opportunity for revenge. First they learned that the governor had received a series of mysterious loans and had mis-
applied public funds. Then Ferguson's hostility toward what
he regarded as an elite clique that ran the University of Texas
hardened into a resolve to purge the university's president and
six faculty members. By June 1917, when he vetoed a university appropriation bill, the governor's actions had fused the
disparate elements of Texas progressivism into a cohesive
force. The WCTU and the Federation of Women's Clubs satu-
rated the state with anti-Ferguson literature. Austin suffragists
were aghast at the governor's "outrageous behavior" and used
their positions in capital society as leverage against this "ignorant common personage." [53] Impeachment proceedings began
in August, and the ESA abandoned all other work to campaign
against "the implacable foe of woman suffrage." [54]

Suffragists arrived in Austin to find the city in an uproar.
"Hot-headed" university students, lawyers, legislators, and
2,000 farmers assembled for a Farmers Institute crowded the
capital, a participant recalled. "Mingling with the crowds and

noting every movement" were Texas rangers, reportedly summoned from the border to protect the governor. The files and contacts of the statewide suffrage organization were put at the disposal of the committee to impeach Ferguson. In addition, suffragists undertook a dramatic new tactic: a sixteen-hour street demonstration designed to place their message before the farmers upon whose support the governor relied.[55] On the main thoroughfare in front of the capitol startled onlookers found the women on a large dray flanked by two eight-foot banners emblazoned with the words WOMEN OF TEXAS PROTEST. From dawn until midnight they staged a "continuous protest" by one "earnest, able and . . . impassioned" speaker after another. This break with traditional decorum was engineered by the younger suffragists who were now in the forefront of the movement. But they were careful to demonstrate the respectability of their cause by placing a group of "distinguished, grayhaired" Daughters of the Confederacy on the improvised rostrum. Two months after the House brought impeachment charges, the Senate ousted the governor and barred him from ever holding state office again.[56]

With Ferguson out of the way, suffragists immediately pressed his successor, Lieutenant Governor William P. Hobby, to submit a bill to the legislature admitting women to the primary. Such demands had become the main focus of Carrie Chapman Catt's strategy for the South, for primary suffrage in one-party states was tantamount to full enfranchisement and could be conferred by simple legislation rather than by constitutional amendment. Moreover, it presented no threat to white supremacy. The first breach in the Solid South had come in March 1917, when the Arkansas legislature gave women the primary vote. But in no other southern state had women overcome the powerful antisuffrage forces arrayed against them.

Texas suffragists had cause for optimism. They had played an important role in unseating the new governor's major opponent and were exhilarated by their success at "throwing the rascals out." According to one legislator, their "unselfish, tireless, efficient" work in remote sections of the state had converted

many a "confirmed skeptic on the question of women's participation in public life."[57] Moreover, through the Woman's Anti-
Vice Committee suffragists had assumed a key position in the
dry coalition, thus gaining powerful allies for their own cause.
Nevertheless, despite his promises, Hobby vacillated between
former conservative loyalties and the exigencies of an altered
political climate. Although he capitulated to progressive-
prohibitionist pressure to call a special session of the legislature, he made prohibition its chief item of business, not wom-
en's suffrage.[58]

As soon as the legislature assembled, suffragists marshalled
the skills perfected in the impeachment campaign. In an organizational effort that was a "marvel of efficiency," they sent out
speakers to keep "the cities and towns aroused," channeled a
steady stream of letters and petitions in from the provinces,
and lobbied vigorously in the capital.[59] Finally, in March 1918,
a bill giving women primary suffrage was signed into law. For
the first time since the Terrell Election Law of 1903 provided
the legal basis for disfranchising blacks and many poor whites,
a measure significantly democratizing the political process had
passed the Texas legislature.[60]

The new bill went into effect on June 26. Although women
had been temporarily excused from poll tax payments, suffragists still had only seventeen days in which to conduct a
massive registration campaign before the primaries. The entry
of Ferguson into the governor's race—on the grounds that he
had resigned before the Senate rendered judgment and thus
was not bound by its decision—heightened their sense of
urgency. Admitted to the ranks of the Democratic Party,
women could now demonstrate their ability to deliver votes for
prosuffrage candidates from the county to the national level.

One of the most effective leaders in this effort to disprove
the antisuffrage argument that "southern women do not want
the vote" was Jessie Daniel Ames. At the Waco meeting the
year before, suffragists had set out to raise a budget of $30,000
through small pledges from individuals and local groups—at a
time when the state association's treasury held only $66.38.

Handling this crucial task fell to the already overworked headquarters staff. It was with great relief that Minnie Fisher Cunningham turned over the books to her lieutenant in Georgetown. "Bless you," wrote the headquarters secretary, Edith
Hinkle League, at last we can "work down to a business
basis."[61] In addition to her responsibility for the financial
aspects of the campaign, Ames acted as organizer for her district. She conducted schools of instruction and mock elections,
arranged rest rooms for voting farm women, and darted about
the county acting as "shepherd" to warring factions and teaching women their "a-b-cs."[62] By July 3, registrants were arriving in carloads from the surrounding towns in far greater
numbers than anyone had anticipated. The dream Ames had
expressed at the Waco convention was coming true: women
were comparing "ideas on politics and candidates not clothes or
recipes," and Ames did not intend "to let [them] fall back until
they are trained to be able to think."[63] "No man," she had
written, "would work year after year ploughing, sowing and
cultivating his fields with the knowledge that as surely as the
harvest time should come, some power greater than himself
would hold him back from gathering his grain."[64] At last the
enormous energy poured into women's voluntary organizations
would reap political power.

In the July heat, 3,800 Williamson County women came to
Georgetown "by wagon, by hack, by foot." On election day the
entire women's ticket was swept into office. The county, Ames
reported, "has been cleaned up from the Legislators to the
Janitor in the Court House." The women had thrown out the
courthouse gang and turned county politics "upside down."
"There's never been anything like it again," Ames would later
reminisce. For her, as for the movement in general, it was a
"glorious" moment of vindication and revelation. Ames's horror
of dependency—on men for her self esteem, on marriage for
economic survival, on indirect influence for social change—
was assuaged by a triumph of collective efficacy. Isolation gave
way to solidarity. "Hurrah for the women," Ames exulted; they
had thought and acted "as one body."[65] In the summer of

1918, Jessie Daniel Ames and her compatriots reeled with a conviction of their own powers.

On the state level, election returns revealed a wide margin of victory for every candidate endorsed by organized women. Hobby won the governorship, and the suffragist candidate, Annie Webb Blanton, became state superintendent of public instruction. Ferguson may have exaggerated when he blamed his downfall on "those high-brow, silk-stocking women," but the female vote had clearly turned a close contest into a rout. [66]

Immediately after the election, Williamson County women began to take their place in the machinery of the Democratic Party. At the county convention in August, the chairman first welcomed "lady voters" to the "political game," then corrected himself with condescending irony. "Lest I offend some of the delegates," he added, "I will say the cause of civic righteousness." [67] Undaunted by the discomfort and confusion that inevitably accompanied the breakdown of sexual segregation, Ames assumed a position on the platform committee and helped ensure that Williamson County would be one of the 233 conventions that endorsed full women's suffrage.

At the Democratic convention in Waco in September, the dry coalition completed its takeover of the party. The anti-Fergusonians, whose championship of "the Puritan ethic" made them supporters of electoral reforms designed both to undercut the influence of special interests and to consolidate the power of the white middle-class, had increasingly come to see women as potential constituents. In the context of Texas politics, women's suffrage, prohibition, anti-Fergusonianism, and support for the war effort had become the touchstones of an indigenous form of Wilsonian progressivism. [68]

Fortified by victory, Texas suffragists moved into phase two of the NAWSA strategy: the struggle for ratification of the Nineteenth Amendment. As the new year opened, congressional passage seemed at last within reach, and national suffrage leaders asked all state organizations to divert their resources to the federal arena. Accordingly, the Texas ESA sent a

strongly worded resolution to the legislature urging postpone-
ment of a proposed referendum on state suffrage; Minnie
Fisher Cunningham departed for Washington to aid in the final
drive in Congress; and Jessie Daniel Ames joined Jane
McCallum in Austin for what both believed would be a relatively painless lobbying effort for ratification of the federal
amendment.

Upon arriving in the capital, however, Ames found that the
legislature had, in Cunningham's words, " 'cursed' us suffragists 'with a granted prayer.' " In direct contradiction to
suffragist strategy, progressive-prohibitionists in the legislature
determined to submit a state suffrage amendment to Texas voters, along with a prohibition measure and a proposal to disfranchise aliens who previously had been permitted to vote upon
obtaining their first citizenship papers. Shocked by the high-
handedness of their male allies, Ames and McCallum searched
frantically for an appropriate response. [69]

A referendum—in which women could not vote—would not
only condemn activists to a "nerve-racking" organizational effort, but would also trap them in a hopeless conundrum. Antisuffragists had only to hold the thirteen southern states to
prevent ratifaction of the federal amendment. Losing the state
suffrage referendum would demonstrate that the Texas movement lacked a broad popular base and might seriously impede
ratification of the federal amendment—"a set back which would
be felt all along the line." [70] Moreover, even a miraculous victory would dissipate suffrage energies and do little to further
the national cause.

Despite communiqués from Carrie Chapman Catt urging
state leaders to stand pat against the referendum, Ames and
McCallum bowed to the inevitable. [71] As publicly visible
leaders in the cause, it seemed, they could hardly afford to
place themselves in the position of opposing something they
had been "enthusiastically urging for several years." They
squelched their suspicions and hesitations and galvanized their
elaborate organizational structure once more. Under their di-

rection, 29 senatorial district chairmen (out of 31 districts) and county chairmen in 236 of Texas' 253 counties set out to canvass Texas voters. [72]

In the state referendum campaign, both suffragists and their opponents were joining in familiar combat. ESA leaders regarded themselves not as "starry eyed" innocents, but as seasoned, if weary, politicians. They used a complex variety of arguments in their bid for the vote, some of which reflected deeply held convictions, some of which were chosen on the basis of expediency or to counter the charges of their opponents. They were idealists still, outraged at injustice and devoted to the principle of equal rights for "one half the people." [73] But their rhetoric now had the air of formula: the ready slogans of the campaign trail.

Through the years, opponents like Senator Joseph Weldon Bailey had employed the most blatant of racist scare tactics in order to maintain the traditional antebellum association between women's rights, miscegenation, and "Negro domination." Suffragists ignored such attacks or countered them with the statistical argument that enfranchisement would increase the white voting majority. [74] With the encouragement of the national office, they refused to admit to their sisterhood those doubly oppressed by sex and race. When, for example, a black woman from El Paso applied for membership in 1918, the Texas association was thrown into confusion. Asked her advice, Carrie Chapman Catt reaffirmed the NAWSA policy decision of 1903 that capitulated to racism by leaving membership requirements to the individual states. But Catt's reply to Texas suffragists went even further, demonstrating that the racial assumptions of Texas suffragists were but reflections of a consensus that many northern as well as southern activists shared. It was true, Catt wrote, that some individual black women had joined northern associations. But these were "women with a good deal of white blood and are educated women, otherwise they would not be asking auxiliaryship." As for the Texas situation, she cautioned against linking suffrage with a controversial stand on racial issues. Write to the applicant, she suggested, "and tell her that you will be able to get the vote for women more easily if they do not embarrass you by asking membership and that you are getting it for colored women as well as for white women and appeal to her interest in the matter to subside."[75] Texas women, operating in a state that had the smallest black population in the South, had no need to make the maintenance of white supremacy the chief argument in their repertoire. The association belonged firmly in the moderate wing of the southern movement, and Texas produced no aggressive racists like Georgia's Rebecca Felton or Louisiana's Kate Gordon. Yet by linking women's suffrage with the disfranchisement of ethnic minorities, the referendum campaign of 1919 made explicit the muted ethnocentrism of the state movement. Convinced that blacks, Germans, and Mexican-Americans would form a solid bloc against them, suffragists chose to stake their hopes for victory on the nativist fears of Texas voters.

Beneath the rhetoric of the 1919 campaign lay assumptions whose lineage could be traced all the way back to the Seneca Falls declaration of 1848: one of man's worst sins against woman, the first feminists had protested, was that "He has withheld from her rights which are given to the most ignorant and degraded men—both natives and foreigners." What one historian has termed the "elitist radicalism" of the first generation merged in the twentieth century with the progressive determination to assert the cultural hegemony of a new middle class in an urban industrial world.[76] Wartime chauvinism gave the old argument new force. Not only was political powerlessness an insult, but enfranchisement would enable "white loyal educated Southern women" to "offset disloyal and disintegrating forces." In a letter to Democratic county chairmen, Cunningham summed up this appeal:

> Is it not possible that when you substitute the loyal American women of this state as voters in place of the ignorant "First Paper" Mexicans on the Border, who have notoriously been exploited by corrupt politicians to the confusion of justice and the shame of our state, you will be bringing to a close a very black day in our history

and helping the dawn of a better day which shall see Texas on
record as an "All American" state? [77]

Even in the heat of this last major struggle, Texas suffragists
did not abandon the argument from justice. But this theme was
almost drowned out in the nativist call to arms.

When the final vote was tabulated on May 24, 1919, prohibition passed, but women's suffrage, together with the alien citizenship clause, lost by a narrow margin. Suffragists sought to
minimize their defeat by blaming it on the overconfidence of
their friends and on "the votes of Negroes, Republican Germans and nondescript foreign-born Mexicans." While demanding that Democratic legislators ignore this "Afro-Teutonic
voice," they turned at once to the task of lobbying for ratification of the federal suffrage amendment. [78]

With 10 out of 17 Texas congressmen swelling southern support, the Nineteenth Amendment passed the House for the
second time. On June 4, the Senate also bowed to the success
of the "winning plan," and Congress submitted the amendment
to the states for ratification. The Texas legislature met in special session on June 23, with progressive-prohibitionists firmly
in control, and the House quickly ratified the measure by a
vote of 96 to 20. The amendment faced stronger opposition in
the Senate. It was met by "heckling, threats, fervid oratory on
woman's sphere," filibustering, and an effort to prevent a
quorum by hurrying senators out of town under cover of
night—an effort thwarted by suffragists who "shadowed" the
passengers on outbound trains. Finally, on June 28, 1919,
Texas ratified the Nineteenth Amendment. [79]

On October 10, 1919, three months before the amendment
became the law of the land, the Texas Equal Suffrage Association was redesignated the Texas League of Women Voters
(LWV). Jessie Daniel Ames became the league's first president
and in that position set out to bring the tactics learned in the
suffrage battle to bear on the legendary complexity of Texas
politics. The movement she had led depended for its success
on its pragmatic role within a progressive-prohibitionist coali-

tion. Neither she nor her compatriots transcended the racial and class assumptions of their time. Yet in the pre–World War I South, the demand for participation in politics had implications of deep cultural significance: it altered the nineteenth-century doctrine of separate spheres and set women like Jessie Daniel Ames on the road to autonomy.[80] For Ames the suffrage movement was only the beginning of a long career devoted to challenging social norms. She had served her apprenticeship in Williamson County and in the halls of the state legislature; now, as president of the League of Woman Voters, she abandoned her position as Minnie Fisher Cunningham's protégée to become a leader of organized women in her own right.

Following the plan of action formulated by Carrie Chapman Catt at NAWSA's last gathering, Jessie Daniel Ames began organizing League of Women Voters' "citizenship schools" to prepare Texas women for their new rights and obligations. Like Catt, Ames believed that women should steer a middle course, neither segregating themselves as a separate interest group nor losing their collective identity in the maelstrom of party politics. She had faith that women, once trained in the art of politics, would expand their own opportunities while simultaneously ushering in an era of progressive reform.[81]

In addition to citizenship schools, Ames devoted the first months of her tenure as LWV president to a campaign for poll tax payments by women, modeled on her earlier successful voter registration drive in Williamson County. Although the tax had been suspended for new women voters in the 1918 primary, a special session of the legislature had enacted a bill making payments mandatory for all "as a protection to the state against possible influx of all kinds of voters in the event of ratification of the Nineteenth Amendment." Many years later, Jessie Daniel Ames claimed that even in this early period she had opposed the poll tax as a tool of black disfranchisement. But neither Ames nor the LWV officially fought the imposition of the tax on women. Rather, they took the opportunity to press for a bill giving women equal representation on all Democratic Party committees. When the poll tax passed, they made it their first order of business to register white women voters who could pay the fee, thus assuring that the female vote would be a middle-class, white, American-born vote as well. [82]

Black women in the South enjoyed little access to the newly won franchise. At first, they sought to register; in some places they evidently "took the registrars by surprise" and succeeded. In South Carolina, a group of women barred from the polls brought suit under the Nineteenth Amendment. But soon all the methods used to exclude black men were employed against women as well—"every means of trickery and brutality from vague statutes to shot guns." [83] On the eve of suffrage, W.E.B. Du Bois had written with eloquence and sensitivity of the goals of the women's movement. But the astute black activist and scholar had also foreseen that "The southern white women who form one of the most repressed and enslaved groups of modern, civilized women will undoubtedly, at first, help willingly and zealously to disfranchise Negroes." William Pickens, NAACP field secretary, posed the rhetorical question: "Will the women of the United States who know something at least of disfranchisement tolerate such methods to prevent intelligent colored women from voting?" [84] The answer, as Du Bois had prophesied, was yes. The Texas LWV offered no challenge to the prevailing patterns of racial exclusion.

Moreover, Texas women continued to pursue the progressive goal of "Americanizing" non-English-speaking immigrants. In keeping with the nativism of the times, the LWV succeeded in its advocacy of the compulsory use of English in all public schools and of citizenship as a qualification for voting. Adopted by the Texas legislature in 1923 (the same legislature that wrote the "white primary" into state law), these measures were meant to suppress the use of Spanish in Mexican-American border schools and to systematize the disfranchisement of the foreign born. [85]

The major challenge to the racial assumptions of Texas suffragists came not from advocates of equality but from extremists on the right. The final drive for women's suffrage coincided
with a nationwide wave of labor unrest, black militancy, and
white backlash. In June 1919 Governor William P. Hobby responded to a dock walkout in Galveston by placing the city
under martial law. Then in July, one of the first of the race
riots of the "red summer" erupted in Longview, a small town
less than twenty miles from Jessie Daniel Ames's childhood
home. It was precipitated by the formation of a Negro Business
Men's League and by the circulation of an article in the Chicago *Defender* claiming that a recent lynching of an alleged
rapist had in fact arisen out of an interracial love affair. When
blacks opened fire on their attackers, local officials had to call
in the state militia to restore order. [86] These signs of black protest and self-defense brought Senator Joseph Bailey back into
state politics in a gubernatorial campaign founded on vicious attacks on blacks, labor, and women's suffrage. However firmly
women might try to separate their cause from that of other
oppressed groups, they could not altogether escape the ancient
analogy of race and sex. [87]

Jessie Daniel Ames and Minnie Fisher Cunningham once
more joined battle with their old enemy. On March 6, 1920, a
mass meeting of Democrats opposed to Bailey elected the two
suffrage leaders to a resolutions committee, derided by Bailey
as a conclave of "six sissies and two sisters." [88] Ames sought to
separate her own participation in Democratic Party politics
from the nonpartisan program of the LWV and opposed direct
involvement of the league in the anti-Bailey drive. But when
she had to be hospitalized for an operation, Cunningham set up
a temporary league headquarters in Dallas and, in Ames's re-
trospective opinion, channeled the machinery laboriously built
up in the poll tax and citizenship school campaigns into a political struggle in which "the real purposes and objects of the
League were either forgotton or abandoned with intention."
Ames felt that her authority had been usurped and her program undercut; more fundamentally, this rift with her mentor
foreshadowed the fragmentation of the women's movement, as

new issues came to the fore and individuals began to ally themselves with party factions in pursuit of political influence and
position. [89]

Despite this disagreement over tactics, Ames enthusiastically
joined the campaign, serving as a delegate to precinct, county,
and state conventions and as an election judge. Fearful that if
Bailey were elected, he would disfranchise women in the primaries "exactly as the negros are," she helped rally the suffrage
forces. [90] Bailey's campaign manager attempted to frighten
women away from the state convention with images of masculine rowdiness. He warned them to be prepared for "stretchers
where the occasion will demand them." [91] Nevertheless, reported the press, the women "conducted themselves like veterans." Bailey's resounding defeat in the primary, and the election of Governor Pat Neff in August, spelled the final
denoument of prewar-style Democratic conservatism. Ames,
Cunningham, and two other women were elected delegates-
at-large to the Democratic National Convention in San
Francisco. [92] Attributing his demise to "the women and
preachers," Bailey at last disappeared as a force in state politics. [93]

Ames and Cunningham returned home in high spirits from
their first venture into national politics. But it soon became ev-
ident that the energy released by the suffrage issue could not
be automatically carried over into the age of normalcy. At its
height, the Texas Equal Suffrage Association had been able to
distribute 3 million pieces of literature through a network of
400 district, city, and county chairmen and to send 1,500
speakers into the field. By the first annual convention in El
Paso in 1920, the league could count only 280 members; only
10 women from outside El Paso—5 of them officers—bothered
to attend the convention. Moreover, the league's financial condition deteriorated so badly that over the next two years Ames
twice had to borrow money on her own signature to carry out
league activities. [94]

Ames and her co-workers, however, refused to accept the
facile observation of contemporary observers that women's suf-

frage had failed. Texas politicans feared the potentially disruptive surge of a mass of new voters into the political process, and at first the LWV was able to command respect out of proportion to its numerical strength. As one of her co-workers in the league recalled, Jessie Daniel Ames "would charge into the legislature, head high with fire in her eyes and left and meant to leave the impression on the helpless legislators that she was flanked by 10,000 irate and determined women."[95] And after the original downswing of support, the league under Ames's guidance gained back lost ground. The women saw the annual convention of 1921 in Fort Worth as a great success. An organizers' workshop in which 45 counties were represented brought the five-day meeting to a close. The convention engendered enough interest to liquidate at least part of the organization's debt and put it on a more secure financial footing.[96]

Most importantly, in 1922 the major women's voluntary organizations in the state determined to pool their resources in a Joint Legislative Council—"the quickest, most effective method of transforming their recently acquired voting privilege into legislative power."[97] Over the next year, the League of Women Voters, the Federation of Women's Clubs, the Congress of Mothers and Parent-Teacher Associations, the Woman's Christian Temperance Union, and the Texas Federation of Business and Professional Women's Clubs (joined later by the Texas Graduate Nurses Association) negotiated a platform, secured endorsements from their membership, and agreed upon a legislative strategy. The Dallas *Morning News* commented: "So quietly have these groups, representing thousands of women from all portions of Texas united their forces, and so harmoniously is the council working out a legislative program that speculation is rife as to the strength of this new political force henceforth to be reckoned with."[98] When the legislative session opened in January 1923, lawmakers found on their desks a six-point program calling for matching state appropriations for the Sheppard-Towner Maternity and Infancy Protection Act, a survey of the public school system made by out-of-state educators, stronger enforcement of prohibition laws, an emergency school appropriation, a survey of the prison system "with teeth in it," and a birth registration program.[99]

Dubbed the "petticoat lobby" by condescending legislators, the Joint Legislative Council proved remarkably effective. Careful planning, moderate demands, and "lady like . . . elusively intelligent" tactics disarmed opponents and eventually carried all six proposals to victory. The Sheppard-Towner bill, however, was pushed through only after a "vicious floor fight" in the Senate. The Senate Committee on Public Health refused to approve the bill on the grounds that it constituted "unjustified and unwarranted interference in the affairs of the state" by the federal government. Opponents attributed to it the power to foster "Communism, Anarchism, birth control . . . and free love." In response, women in each senatorial district forwarded letters and petitions to the legislature scoffing at states-rights arguments and pointing out the contradiction of accepting federal aid for agriculture and highways while refusing to appropriate funds for "the health of mothers and babies."[100] Eventually passed and signed into law, the Sheppard-Towner Act stood, on the state as on the national level, as the foremost legislative victory of enfranchised women.[101]

Jessie Daniel Ames's major contributions to the Joint Legislative Council program lay in the area of prison reform. Appointed to the Texas Committee on Prisons and Prison Labor, she gained first-hand exposure to the scandalous pork-barrel administration of the prison system and to the atrocious treatment of men and women on the state's vast penal farms. In 1925 the survey conducted by the committee resulted in the adoption of a constitutional amendment reorganizing prison administration. The plight of young black women prisoners engaged Ames's special concern. And in the 1925 legislative session, she led a lobbying effort on behalf of appropriations for a training school for delinquent Negro girls.[102]

With less success, Ames used her position as head of the LWV to lobby for protective labor legislation and legal rights for women. The Texas legislature did establish an Industrial Welfare Commission charged with the regulation of working conditions for women and children and added a women's division to the state Labor Statistics Department. A child labor act prohibited the employment of children under fifteen in factories and businesses, but made no provision for farm labor. Since almost seven out of eight Texas children employed in 1920 were engaged in agricultural pursuits, the law's impact was minimal. The Industrial Welfare Commission limited hours of work for women to 9 hours a day and 54 a week, but a study conducted in 1931 ranked Texas among the southern states in which such standards were most poorly enforced. A minimum-wage law for women passed in 1919 was repealed two years later.[103] Such "protective legislation" undermined the ability of working women to compete for jobs and did little to improve their standard of living. Indeed, in 1932, a survey conducted by the Women's Bureau of the Department of Labor at the request of the Texas Federation of Women's Clubs found that 20.9 per cent of women employed in industrial occupations earned less than $5.00 a week. Mexican-American women earned markedly less than native-born whites, even working side by side in the same establishments, and Negro women were altogether excluded from most industries.[104]

Even more frustrating were Ames's attempts to expand women's legal rights. To no avail she advocated equal guardianship of children, and protested that a mother's pension law passed by the legislature applied only to widowed mothers. With the Dallas lawyer and later state supreme court justice, Sarah T. Hughes, she formulated a married women's property rights bill and tried in vain to push it through the Texas legislature. Almost fifty years later, she vividly recalled an incident that illuminates both the relish with which suffragists fought these early battles and the entrenched resistence they met. Speaking before a legislative subcommittee, she challenged a committee chairman who employed all the insidious and effective arts of southern chivalry against her. The chairman, she recalled,

> was so considerate of me. He told me how the law protected women, how she was safe from everything. . . . Of course he assumed I didn't know anything about the law. . . . I knew we

weren't going to get the bill anyway so I might as well get something out of my system. . . . So I got up and asked a question (I don't know how I looked—I ought to have looked like a fighting peacock because that was the way I felt!). I said, "Since an unmarried woman or a widow could own her own property, while the wages of a working woman were 'community property,' then as long as a woman is married . . . she's *feeble-minded*, but just let the husband die and she gets her sense back, doesn't she!" [105]

Like her concern for working conditions and legal rights, Ames's interest in educational opportunities for women grew out of her own experience. As a college student she had confronted both the internal barriers of her own feelings of inadequacy and the external ones of her father's skepticism and her school's insensitivity to the aspirations of its women students. In adulthood, she viewed education as the means to both personal advancement and social progress, and she demanded intellectual achievement of her daughters as well as her son. In 1926, she helped found the Texas branch of the American Association of University Women (AAUW) and became its first president. Under her leadership, the AAUW urged state colleges to "offer women equal opportunities with those offered men in the best colleges . . . with special emphasis on the status of women members of the faculty as to pay, advancement and encouragement of advanced study." Women, she believed, should receive professional training that differed in no way from that available to men. [106]

As president and then legislative chairman of the League of Women Voters, executive committee member of the Joint Legislative Council and of the Texas Committee on Prisons and Prison Labor, political science chairman of the Texas State Federation of Women's Clubs, and founder and president of the Texas branch of the American Association of University Women, Jessie Daniel Ames participated in virtually every effort of Texas suffragists to effect legislative change in the nineteen twenties. First attracted to the women's movement by economic self-interest and a search for personal identity, she became a "social feminist," pressing forward the goals of the social-justice wing of southern progressivism. [107] Unlike most of her progressive allies, however, Ames soon perceived the limitations of the movement in which she found her start. The female bloc vote she had expected did not materialize. "We were idealists," she recalled. "We thought that when we got the vote the whole pattern of politics would be greatly improved and would be dominated by women."[108] Instead Texas women made little headway in gaining access to the sources of political power—what Carrie Chapman Catt called "the real thing in the center with the door locked tight."[109] Most importantly, experience in the political arena brought her face to face with the contradiction of a "women's movement" devoted to humanitarian reform that excluded black women from its ranks and racial oppression from its concerns.

Little precise evidence survives of the psychological bridge over which Ames moved from social feminism to the interracial movement. Her sensitivity to racial issues, however, seems to have grown out of a number of interrelated experiences. First, she discovered the efficacy of racism in undercutting the progressive goal of widening the regulatory functions of the state. The Joint Legislative Council got some social legislation passed,

> but such a small amount that it occurred to me a little research was in order. . . . Too frequently the whole . . . Committee . . . would be completely stampeded, when it was suggested that "nigger wenches" would be getting the same wages as "pure white girls" . . . ; or when it was suggested that the appropriation for maternal infancy would pass if there were a guarantee that Negro mothers and babies would be excluded from the benefits.
>
> Gradually it came over me that someone with enough background to do it was going to have to get out and tell white Texans—the women especially—that until we were ready to stand up and say in public that we would include Negroes in social benefits we might as well quit.[110]

Second, as her understanding of racism as an obstacle to social reform deepened, she also came into contact with the plight of blacks in her own county. For example, in 1921, one of Ames's co-workers in the local suffrage association, Mary Shipp Sanders, an instructor in English at Georgetown University, was "bold enough" to run for county school superintendent, an office never before held by a woman. Once elected, Sanders set out, with Ames's help, to investigate conditions in the black county schools. They found the high school a shack so dilapidated that "in any wind that blew, the building would have blown down." In a number of districts individual teachers taught as many as 90 pupils in a class, in part because state funds appropriated for blacks were actually being used by white schools. The two women set to work immediately to secure a grant from the Rosenwald Fund to match money raised by the black community. They succeeded in building a new high school, and in the process Jessie Daniel Ames became acutely aware of inequities that had always surrounded her.[111] Startled by this sudden visibility of injustice, she was even more affected by the experience of working with black parents struggling to educate their children. "I was being called by the Lord then and didn't even know it—I had to get busy. What those Negroes wanted was exactly what we wanted for our children."[112]

A third, and perhaps most important, factor in Ames's changing consciousness was the meteoric rise of the Ku Klux Klan.[113] In 1915, shortly after the film *Birth of a Nation* opened to national acclaim, William Joseph Simmons's fiery cross on Stone Mountain in Atlanta, Georgia, launched the twentieth-century version of the hooded order. The organization flourished amid the tensions of wartime migration to the cities, the rise of the "New Negro," and the arrival of immigrants from southern Europe. By July 1922, the Texas Klan was able to send Earle B. Mayfield, Railroad Commissioner and Klan candidate for the U.S. Senate, into a runoff primary against former governor James E. Ferguson, the hated "wet," antisuffragist whom Ames had worked to impeach in 1917.

The advent of Ferguson as the strongest foe of the Klan in Texas politics threw progressive women into confusion. Outraged by the Klan's lawless vigilantism, the LWV nevertheless remained neutral in the runoff contest, thereby helping to give the Klan one of its greatest political victories. The election of

Mayfield thrust the Klan into control of a majority of the state's counties and of the machinery of the state Democratic Party.[114] The almost overnight arrival of the Klan as the most powerful force in the political life of the state and the reassertion of racial politics discredited the prohibition cause and blunted the reform momentum of organized women.

Jessie Daniel Ames had received her political education in a movement that raised no fundamental questions about class and race. Indeed, disfranchisement and segregation could themselves be seen as seminal "progressive" reforms, for most white southern progressives welcomed this racial settlement as a means of burying the conflicts of Reconstruction and Populism in order to pursue the goals of public service and social order.[115] In Texas, progressive Democrats presided over the transition from an agrarian society to a corporate, capitalistic one, addressing neither the plight of displaced farmers nor the needs of blacks and Mexican-Americans who subsisted at the bottom of the new order. The postwar decades saw the rise of a society dominated by an oil-utility-banking axis closely identified with the party in power.[116] Within the state's reform coalition, organized women must be credited with keeping alive the claims of humanitarianism. But they shared the class interests and racial assumptions of their allies. Women with the vote offered no challenge to the institutions of economic inequality and racial exclusion.

In the years after World War I, however, Ames joined a small band of men and women across the South striving tentatively to reopen the closed issue of race. The failure of the promise of women's suffrage, the use of racism to prevent social-welfare reforms, the discovery of the inequity of black education and of the treatment of black prisoners, a revulsion against the bigotry of the KKK—all these developments combined to push her beyond progressivism "for whites only" and into the interracial movement. She came to view such groups as the League of Women Voters as "awfully good at organization for conservative people who always look many times before they leap. Then when they make up their minds to leap they find out that the rushing water has receded and they can walk across dry land, or else the floods have grown so great they have washed out the adjoining banks."[117] Impatient with the limitations of such an approach and convinced that the problem of race relations must be confronted in the coming era, she gradually shifted from women's organizations to the Commission on Interracial Cooperation. Through this institutional vehicle she set out to use the independence, self-confidence, and political skills forged in the suffrage movement in the twentieth-century struggle for racial justice.

6

With the eclipse of the women's rights movement in the thirties and forties, Jessie Daniel Ames's feminist concerns found less overt expression. She pursued the remainder of her career in a period when economic issues and black civil rights set the agenda for reform. Because her role in the suffrage campaign had been that of a local and state organizer rather than a national leader, her contributions were largely forgotten. Ames's claim to historical attention would rest not on her place in the women's movement but on her later identity as a white liberal in the racist South.

Nevertheless, Ames's experience as a woman and her commitment to sexual equality remained the touchstones of her emotional life and public activity. She felt an immediate affinity for women who had entered politics in the tough, turbulent days of the women's movement. Her "past activities in suffrage," she would write of a new recruit to the anti-lynching crusade, "make me feel that we could start off as tho we had been working together for a long time." Despite her disappointment in the results of women's suffrage, she continued to think of the vote as an essential "social tool." In the Texas movement she had drawn analogies between the disabilities of blacks and those of women. In the thirties, as she presented to women's groups her analysis of the causes of lynching, she suggested parallels between the position of blacks and the frustration of women before suffrage, and she pointed out the fallacy of the notion that the dominant group "will take care of your interest better than you could if you had a voice in government."[118]

Though persistent and deeply felt, Jessie Daniel Ames's sense of group identity and solidarity was far from unequivocal. "Women have always been a problem to masculine society," she reflected. As a result, "they have been a problem to themselves." The women who led the Texas ESA to victory were, in the words of one participant, "very immediately post-Victorian."[119] A member of a transitional generation, Ames was caught between a nineteenth-century world view and the attitudes of modernity. She had grown up in a society that segregated women and placed severe restrictions on heterosexual intimacy; but in such a culture feminists had been able to draw emotional support from intense, and sometimes sensual, relationships with other women. As sex roles became less rigid, women of Ames's generation enjoyed increasing options, but they may also have been deprived of the sustenance of the private, empathetic female networks of an earlier time. Ames herself, in flight from what Jane Addams called "the family claim," neither admired nor exemplified the traditional feminine virtues, and she sometimes viewed with contempt the concerns of the female subculture.[120] The expansion of women's rights, she believed, demanded a change in their self-concepts, a change she associated with education, discipline, and logical thought. "A well trained mind" was the first prerequisite for emancipation. "When I work with someone," she commented, "they are neither men nor women. Just competent or incompetent."[121] Because she equated femininity with frivolousness she saw men rather than women as her intellectual equals, and she could not but share in society's devaluation of her sex. Because she sought escape from what Caroll Smith-Rosenberg calls "the female world of love and ritual" in a culture that denied women full access to the male arena of politics and power, she suffered from loneliness and the pull of despair.[122]

The essence of Ames's feminism lay in her rejection of the ideologies of domesticity and paternalism. She was not, in her own view, "maternal by nature," and she knew from experience that women possessed no natural aptitude for nurturance. When she defined her home as "the whole wide world," she did so not in the belief that women should become the "mothers of civilization" but in her desire for entrance into the public arena on a basis of equality. Her own life had taught her to fear dependency. For herself, and for those women who could measure up to her standards of achievement, she asked not the deference of chivalry but the compliment of respect. Public acclaim, financial independence, the opportunity to affect the course of public events—these were the goals of her personal struggle and, for her, the measure of female emancipation.[123]

Jessie Daniel Ames's dilemma was both personal and historical. A consciousness formed in the last phase of the suffrage campaign found little cultural support in the South of the 1930s and 1940s. However temperamentally suited for public activity, she bore the lifelong responsibility of a demanding family life. Unable to enjoy the comfort of sexual love, neither did she have access to socially sanctioned intimacy with other women. Yet Ames's culture did offer a different kind of feminine support system. Not in the world of love and ritual but in women's organizations she discovered the setting in which she could gain the self-affirmation and solidarity that personal relationships did not provide. The twentieth-century women's movement, with its emphasis on pragmatism and politics, opened an alternative to the roles of wife and mother.[124] Transcending her private misfortunes and the decline of feminism, she found in the Interracial Commission a second forum in which her needs and capacities could be used in personally satisfying and socially constructive ways.

Chapter 3
A Bond of
Common Womanhood

On March 22, 1922, Carrie Parks Johnson, Director of Woman's Work for the Atlanta-based Commission on Interracial Cooperation (CIC), invited a small group of Texas women known to be concerned with social reform to a meeting in Dallas. Among the women in attendance was Jessie Daniel Ames. Her opposition to the Ku Klux Klan and her advocacy of educational opportunities for blacks in Williamson County made her a logical choice for chairman of the organization Johnson proposed to create: a woman's committee of the newly formed Texas Interracial Commission. Many of the women who came to this founding meeting "simply faded out of the picture . . . going home where it was safer to be."[1] But Ames took up her new responsibilities with the same aggressive energy she had demonstrated in the struggle for women's rights.

When Jessie Daniel Ames threw in her lot with the women of the Interracial Commission, she entered a movement long in the making. The founding of the CIC linked the drive of organized white women for efficacy in the public sphere with the rising militancy of black women. But the roots of this precarious alliance lay deep in the prewar history of black and white female self-organization. By the time Jessie Daniel Ames rose to prominence, becoming Director of Woman's Work for the regional commission in 1929 and founder of the Association of Southern Women for the Prevention of Lynching a year later, the parameters of women's role in the interracial movement were clear. From the women's missionary societies of the Methodist Episcopal Church, South, and the black and white branches of the Young Women's Christian Association, Ames drew the language and constituency upon which she built her own campaign for racial justice.

1

In 1919, the United States emerged from a war to make the world safe for democracy into a period of race riots, terror, and lynching. The Longview, Texas riot served as advance warning of a "red summer," climaxing in late September when at least 25 members of an incipient sharecroppers' union in Phillips County, Arkansas, were killed and hundreds more were arrested and charged with insurrection. Although the police power of the state was arrayed on the side of white vigilantes, blacks managed to inflict considerable damage on their attackers. Observers, both black and white, saw this defensive violence as a watershed in the black freedom struggle.[2]

Far-reaching demographic changes underlay this new militancy. In the era after Reconstruction, black farmers, the children of slaves, had worked the soil on shares, bound to the land and its white owners by the perpetual debts of the crop lien system. Every year some of these sharecroppers, pushed off the land and pulled by desire for a better life, had joined "the flight from feudal America." During World War I, however, the ravages of the boll weevil, the elimination of European immigration, and the expansion of industry turned this steady trickle to the city into a massive folk movement.[3] The Great Migration not only threatened the plantation system with the loss of its cheap labor force; it also gave blacks a political power base in the North from which to exert influence on both political parties and to launch an attack on racial proscription. The founding of the NAACP in 1910 signaled the revival of immediatism and agitation. In its first decade the association developed into a mass membership organization and won its initial Supreme Court victories over the grandfather clause and residential segregation.

These signs that Booker T. Washington's era of accommodation was coming to an end shocked the white South. Planters used force and intimidation to keep their tenants from leaving the land. State governments acted to repress local NAACP chapters. In Texas, for example, in the wake of the Longview riot, the state attorney general subpoenaed the records of the Austin NAACP, and a national NAACP secretary was assaulted in the heart of the state capital by a mob that included a constable and a county judge. Progressive Governor William P. Hobby condoned the beating and suggested to the association that it could "contribute more to the advancement of both races by keeping your representatives and their propaganda out of this state than in any other way."[4]

Rumors that "radical Negro organizations . . . are organizing in secret meetings and arming themselves" swept the region. John Hope, first black president of Morehouse College and later president of Atlanta University, arrived in his native state of Georgia from service overseas to see "colored soldiers and their families . . . being driven from their homes because of the hysterical fears of their white neighbors."[5] Political demagogues translated the assertiveness of the New Negro into a sexual threat. Only constant vigilance, they warned, could prevent returning soldiers from polluting white women with "the damned touch of the black."[6] In the first postwar year, more than 70 blacks were lynched, many of them after torture and mutilation.

Most white southerners, alarmed by this breakdown of law and order, demanded a reassertion of the prewar status quo in which racial hierarchy had been thoroughly established in law, politics, economics, and folkways. "We venture to say that fully ninety percent of all the race troubles in the South are the result of the Negro forgetting his place," proclaimed the Shreveport *Times*.

> If the black man will stay where he belongs, act like a Negro should act, work like a Negro should work, talk like a Negro should talk,
> . . . there will be very few riots, fights or clashes. Instead of the "societies" and "unions" floating propaganda to . . . lift them up to the plane of the white man, they should foster education that will

instill in the Negro the desire, and impress upon him the NECES-
SITY of keeping his place.[7]

A small group of white moderates responded, however, not
by calling for a return to old norms, but by seeking to accom-
modate black grievances. These men and women had spearheaded such organizations as the Southern Sociological Congress, the University Commission on Southern Race
Questions, and the Southern Publicity Committee. Drawn
together by anxiety over the postwar reaction, they met in
Atlanta in January 1919 to inaugurate an "After the War Program" and chose as their leader Will W. Alexander, a young
Methodist minister whose concern for social problems had led
him quietly—and permanently—out of the church and into the
YMCA War Work Council. They sought to "substitute reason
for force" by bringing moderate leaders of both races together
to negotiate the reduction of riot-producing racial tensions. Financed by the YMCA, black and white field workers set up
local interracial committees throughout the South. After a year
of effort, Will Alexander could proclaim, "We didn't have any
riots in any of the places where we worked."[8]

By the beginning of 1920, Alexander and his co-workers had
transformed the "After the War Program" into a permanent institution, the Commission on Interracial Cooperation. They
had also gained the support of the major foundations and
philanthropists concerned with black welfare: the Phelps
Stokes Fund, the Julius Rosenwald Foundation, the Laura
Spellman Memorial Fund, and the Carnegie Foundation.
Close personal and institutional ties with northern philanthropists made CIC leaders a major conduit for the flow of financial resources into black uplift and protest efforts, despite
their marginal position of influence within southern white society.[9] By the mid-twenties the CIC had grown into the major
interracial reform organization in the South.[10]

This interracial movement neither challenged segregation
nor advocated racial equality. Rather, it signified a recognition
on the part of middle-class whites of the emergence of a black

bourgeoisie with whom they could ally in attempts to ameliorate the "race problem" upon which progress in the South seemed perennially to founder. It also represented an acknowledgment that white violence could have extremely disruptive social consequences if blacks fought back, turned to the federal government for protection, or chose migration as an alternative to victimization. The Interracial Commission adopted a frankly paternalistic stance. The spiritual heirs of earlier southern moderates like Atticus G. Haygood, Edgar Gardner Murphy, and Walter Hines Page, its founders intended to resurrect a tradition of *noblesse oblige*. [11] In local interracial committees, reported Thomas Jesse Jones of the Phelps Stokes Fund, "the negroes draw up a prospectus of what they think they should have in the way of aid and recognition from the whites. The white committee then meets, considers the complaints . . . of the negroes, and devises means for bettering their condition." [12]

The CIC's founders believed themselves to be in the forefront of a significant departure in southern race relations. They had come of age in a society in which segregation was so thoroughly established in custom and in law as to seem an immutable fact of life. Their frame of reference was an era dominated by racist demagoguery, business progressivism, and scientific racism. In this context a region-wide interracial organization advocating improved housing, equal educational opportunities, justice in the courts, and an end to mob violence could be seen as the first thaw in a long winter of repression, an admission that one segment of the South's "ruling community" had faltered in the will to maintain white supremacy through absolute separation and overwhelming force. [13]

Black protest leaders, in contrast, took a skeptical view of the new organization. Post-emancipation proponents of black rights had searched diligently for white allies in the region. "There must be good people of the white South," one wrote in 1900, but "they are never heard from. . . . If they only would give some sign, protest in some form, it would have telling effect." [14]

Repeated disillusionment with the forces of southern moderation helped launch the NAACP. "The New South of Henry Grady," commented W. E. B. Du Bois, "had nothing new for the Negro. And since that time thoughtful Negroes have received professions of friendship on the part of the white South with much salt."[15] Du Bois saw the CIC as "one of the great results of the NAACP," a sign that "its persistent fight in the last ten years has aroused and even compelled the South to attempt its own internal reform." He took the opportunity to advise "our Inter-racial friends" to bring into their counsels "real black men who dare to look you in the eye and speak the truth and who refuse to fawn and lie." The success of a southern interracial movement, he believed, would depend on the vigilance of blacks who refused to be "lulled by false hope and vague promises," and on the ability of white liberals to deliver concrete results. "Do not merely talk," he admonished, "DO!"[16]

Within the South, the CIC met similar suspicions. Robert R. Moton, Booker T. Washington's successor at Tuskegee Institute, had played a key role in the initial planning stage, but after organization it was over a year before the "interracial" commission gained black members. Even Moton—whom Du Bois viewed as the epitome of "the sort of Colored men that we call 'WHITE FOLKS' NIGGERS"—expressed some reservations about cooperating. Others voiced "misgiving, unusual hesitation and apprehension," fearful that the real purpose of the CIC was to prevent the exodus of black workers.[17] John Hope in particular, who was seen by other black leaders in Atlanta as the "one colored man who will tell the truth to white folks plainly without insulting," placed little hope in professions of white good will.[18]

Finally, on March 23, 1920, the CIC admitted its first blacks: Robert Moton joined the group, along with Bishop R. E. Jones of New Orleans. Soon John Hope followed suit. By the June 24, 1924 meeting, 22 black men were present. Even the NAACP national leadership was mollified: in 1926, Du Bois confirmed that the work of the Interracial Commission indicated "the definite breaking up of the effort of the South to present morally and socially a solid front to the world." Mary White Ovington found Will Alexander, the organization's chief executive, to be "a humane, fair-minded man, without cant and without prejudice," trusted by radical and conservative Negroes alike.[19] A southern interracial movement had begun.

The process of incorporating women into the organization proved more difficult than the admission of black men. On a list of white southerners "known to be sympathetic and intelligent regarding the race situation" compiled at the outset of the movement, no female names appeared, and the first appeal for admitting women met spirited resistance.[20] Bringing "white women and colored men into interrelationships that symbolize equality" would open a Pandora's box of sexual fears and taboos. The CIC would be accused of fostering "social intermingling," miscegenation, and intermarriage. Delicacy would forbid an open discussion of lynching, related as it was supposed to be to sexual attacks on white women.[21] Moreover, the attitudes of white women were unpredictable. The Atlanta Baptist minister Dr. M. Ashby Jones declared that women were "the Hindenburg line" in race relations; more conservative and timid than men, they would remain the last holdouts for the status quo. Others maintained that women were emotional and sentimental and would become "wild-eyed fanatics" in behalf of reform. This debate reflected the wide gulf that divided men and women into separate cultures. What women thought and did in their own sphere mystified men as much as the endlessly puzzling matter of "What the Negro Thinks" and "What the Negro Wants."[22]

In fact, southern women had already provided abundant evidence of their approach to social problems, as Jessie Daniel Ames's own formative years in Texas politics make clear. The predominant channels for these concerns, however, were not

the secular organizations through which Ames entered public
life but the Protestant, and especially the Methodist, missionary societies that appeared throughout the South in the
1870s and the Young Women's Christian Associations that
spread slowly into the region after the turn of the century.
Most studies of the interracial movement have ignored its roots
in such women's activities, viewing the Woman's Committee of
the CIC as an afterthought of Will Alexander's and the Association of Southern Women for the Prevention of Lynching as an
organization that sprang full-blown from the mind of Jessie
Daniel Ames. A different angle of vision reveals that neither
development is explicable apart from the laity rights and social
Christianity movements within the Southern Methodist
Church and the struggle for racial equality within the YWCA.
For most middle-class southern women, it was the institutional
structure of the church that provided a basis for female solidarity, and evangelical religion that created a rationale for seeking
a female alliance across racial lines.

The women's missionary movement drew its inspiration from
an evangelical experience that had potentially liberating implications for female coverts.[23] A profoundly emotional conversion, a new birth, ushered them into a life of religious devotion
and missionary zeal. The direct infusion of the Holy Spirit
alienated them from the world and gave them membership in
an intimate community of believers. The rise of family religion
and the decline of clerical power invested women with responsibility for Christian nurture, and evangelical expansion
brought them into public assemblies and justified the creation
of their own prayer groups and aid societies. The ideal "evangelical woman" of the middle class was set apart from the lady
of the idle rich by her domesticity, piety, seriousness, and
commitment to benevolent action. For exceptional individuals
like Sarah and Angelina Grimké this world view could fuel radical abolitionism. For other southern women, it made service
to the slaves the measure of Christian commitment. In Donald
G. Mathews' words, women, like Afro-Americans, used evangelicalism "to fend off oppression, secure their personal and

group identity, and assert themselves in new and sometimes surprising ways."[24]

The social forces that undermined traditional sex roles in the late nineteenth century heightened the contradictions in the ideal of the evangelical woman and set in motion a struggle to alter women's place in the institutional church.[25] What one historian has called the "feminization" of American religion made women the mainstay of church life, yet they continued to be proscribed from formal avenues of power. The opportunity and necessity of work outside the home transformed the ideal of domesticity into a boundary to be maintained rather than an elevation of women's separate culture. The cumulative effects of educational opportunities strained the definition of evangelical seriousness, while middle-class women with increasing leisure demanded a wider expression for benevolence and piety.[26]

In 1878, spontaneous local efforts culminated in the first region-wide women's organization in the South, the Methodist Woman's Foreign Mission Society. In the name of evangelical expansion, Methodist women administered funds, made policy decisions, and managed complex overseas operations. Under their auspices, single women—whom "the then existing mission boards refused to send . . . to foreign fields on grounds of impropriety"—were able to assume independent professional responsibilities unavailable in their native land; at home, support groups emulated missionary heroines and identified with tales of conversion and institutional growth.[27]

Fortified by the self-confidence gained in this unprecedented work, Mission Society leaders petitioned the General Conference to enlist the aid of women in the westward expansion of Methodism. At first limited to collecting funds for parsonages, they insisted on the right to establish city missions and homes for "fallen women" as well. In order to mobilize "the broadest connectional spirit and effort" behind this local "woman's work for woman," they pressed for full control over their own organization. By 1898, they had parlayed the opening wedge of parsonage-building into an autonomous Woman's

Home Mission Society.[28] Under the presidency of Belle Harris Bennett, together with a remarkable group of Methodist leaders whose names would crop up again and again through decades of social welfare reform, the Home Mission Society grafted onto the evangelical idiom the language of the social gospel and used both to expand women's role in the church and the social order.

Belle Bennett's career epitimomizes the themes of the Methodist women's movement. By 1852, when she was born, the evangelical impulse had been institutionalized: the Bennetts were refined and respectable Methodist slaveowners, not religious insurgents. For the daughter of such a family, however, evangelical rhetoric could still give meaning to discontent and inspire a rebellion against the bondage of worldly prescriptions and expectations. Bennett was initiated into the cause of women's rights by her neighbor, the Kentucky suffragist Laura Clay. But like many other southern women she chose the church, not the state, as her arena of struggle. Interpreting evangelical seriousness as intellectual independence, she became a student of bibilical criticism and of the literature of the social gospel. Through the time-honored medium of a conversion experience, she found her calling: "I have spent my life in frivolity and idleness," she vowed. "Now I mean to give it wholly to the Lord."[29]

Bennett's first goal was the establishment of an institution of higher education run by and for women. She believed that women in the mission field should have access to training comparable to that "given to doctors and lawyers and professional men of all kinds." In 1892, Scarritt Bible and Training College opened its doors, financed and administered by the Woman's Foreign Mission Society. When the city mission movement was inaugurated a year later, Bennett insisted on the need for professionally trained home missionaries as well, and the Home Mission Society endowed a Chair of Christian Sociology at Scarritt, filled by a succession of inspiring and unusually progressive teachers.[30] By the thirties, according to the Fisk University sociologist Charles S. Johnson, Scarritt had become one of the two most significant white educational institutions in the South in fostering a "positive and dynamic response" to social issues.[31]

The next step in this effort to professionalize the traditionally voluntary work of church women was the creation of the office of deaconess. Already the leaders of the Home Mission Society had begun laying the groundwork for such an innovation. For example, the short stories and morality tales regularly published in the society's regional journal, *Our Homes,* contained the embryo of a new cultural image, a revision of the ascribed characteristics of southern womanhood. These stories upheld as a model not the selfless wife and mother but the single woman, distinguished by intelligence, civic-mindedness, and devotion to responsible action in the public sphere. The ideal church woman, though still expected to forego financial gain and worldly ambition, abandoned submission and suffering for knowledge, power, and authority.[32] Belle Bennett, while denying that she was motivated by an "egotistical desire for feminine assertiveness," clearly hoped to mobilize a formidable army. "We must have women filled with the Holy Ghost and with power," she wrote, "power to study and to think; power to wield the sword of the Spirit to the saving of life, as the skilful surgeon uses his knife; power to work under authority and to exercise authority, to project work and develop work." Opponents of the creation of deaconesses argued that women needed no special training or position, for their preeminent role in religious life rested on a natural aptitude for affection and intuition. Moreover, such official recognition might lead women to aspire to the ministry. But Bennett's rebuttal of such arguments was brisk and to the point. "We must have women who have power with God and man," she asserted; "we need no other kind."[33]

Through missionary education, deaconess activities, and city missions, Methodist women developed, for the first time, a visible and articulate leadership, able to speak to and for women as a group. In turn, Bennett and her co-workers used their position as acknowledged lay leaders in the general church to

forward the interests of a female constituency. Bennett told
the women of the Home Mission Society that they were

> the *leaders* of the great body of women who make up the auxiliaries
> in the individual Churches. These women expect you to act for
> them in every forward movement. To you is left not only the ex-
> pression of their openly avowed sentiments and convictions, but to
> you is left the interpretation of that larger and deeper inner life,
> which they have not yet formulated in words or proclaimed in ac-
> tion. This is what leadership means. [34]

Organizational autonomy, together with cultural assumptions
that channeled aggression and achievement into benevolent
reform, enabled such leaders to take a stance on social issues at
odds with that of the general church. When Home Mission Society leaders began to transform city missions into the South's
first settlement houses, opponents ridiculed their experiments
as "playhouses for women" or condemned them as centers of
secular radicalism. [35] Nevertheless, by 1920, the women had
created a network of more than 25 social settlements in mill
towns, coalfields, and industrial centers. They advocated equal
pay for women workers, protective legislation, and the elimination of child labor. Although, like many other progressives,
they deplored class conflict and hoped for amelioration of working conditions from the top down, they raised a wavering voice
in behalf of labor's right to organize. [36]

The position of Methodist women on racial issues, on the
other hand, testifies to the distance of late nineteenth-century
evangelicalism from its antislavery beginnings. The post–Civil
War retreat to segregated churches tore southern evangelicalism apart, and the mission to the slaves found no echo in the
treatment of the freedmen. [37] In 1899, when Belle Bennett
challenged the Home Mission Society to view the New South
as a "threshold of special privilege and opportunity," she went
on to assure her listeners that service to the poor had again
become possible because the South now had a *white* industrial
working class. [38]

As they took on ever-widening responsibilities, however,

Home Mission Society leaders inevitably confronted the question of race. Booker T. Washington's Atlanta Compromise and the spread of the industrial education idea encouraged Belle Bennett, after years of silence, to lay before the Home Mission Board a request for funds to build a women's annex at the Colored Methodist Episcopal Church's Paine College in Augusta, Georgia. The rationales presented for this "new and, as some felt, objectional work" reveal not only the master-servant model that characterized the Methodist women's approach to racial issues, but also a hint of identification with black women across racial lines. Their mothers and grandmothers, they argued, had exercised peculiar responsibility for the spiritual welfare of the slaves in general and of black women in particular.[39] Under their tutelage, blacks had taken the first steps toward civilization, but racial progress had been thwarted by premature emancipation and the "mistaken zeal of Northern philanthropists." The old, mutually satisfying relationship between white women and their black servants had been replaced by alienation. Black women—like their white counterparts—served as agents of Christian nurture; their degradation had stymied the development of the race.[40] The time had come, Belle Bennett admonished, for Methodist women to redefine "our relation to our colored sisters who live among us." Through setting individual examples for their servants and providing industrial training for girls, white women could lead the way toward the resolution of racial conflict and the gradual elevation of "a child race." At Paine College black girls could fulfill the contradictory goal of becoming competent servants to white women and moral guardians of their own families, under the tutelage not of egalitarian Northerners but of sympathetic southern whites.[41]

Within a decade after these maternalistic beginnings, Methodist women's work in the black community entered a new phase. In 1911, the first southern white woman—Mary De Bardeleben—presented herself for mission service to the Negro and opened the way to the first experiments in interracial cooperation among middle-class southern women. The daughter of a Methodist minister in Alabama, De Bardeleben dedicated her life to the mission field in the wake of a "deep religious experience." Courses at Columbia Teachers College had shaken her faith, but at Scarritt College she found herself among those "who were trying to be Christian and yet relate our Christianity to the social movement, then stirring mightily, and to the liberal interpretation of the Bible." Her parents, her bishop, "all the powers that be," urged her to reinterpret her calling and do her missionary service in the respectable, far-away field of Japan. Years of spiritual battle ensued. Everywhere the eyes of blacks she knew seemed to accuse her: " 'So my *Christian* friend,' they seemed to say, 'you are going to Japan. What about America, what about the South? What about us?' " Only her teachers at Scarritt understood. With their encouragement, De Bardeleben stood her ground and opened Bethlehem House in Augusta, Georgia. [42]

De Bardeleben had been motivated by a "decided feeling of superiority" and a desire to save the souls of her parents' former slaves. But, step by step, she realized that "the problem was deeper and vaster, more intricate than in my youth I had . . . dreamed." First at Bethlehem House, then as a teacher at Paine College, she came into contact with "the better class of Negroes." By World War I, she felt called to a different mission, the interpretation of "the new Negro to the new white youth," and she offered immediate support to the recently founded Interracial Commission. [43]

Following De Bardeleben's example, in 1912 Southern Methodist women assumed financial responsibility for a settlement initiated by the women of the Colored Methodist Church in Nashville, Tennessee. Two years later, they entered into a pioneering joint program with the Urban League and Fisk University to provide professional training for black social workers. Fisk students combined courses in economics and sociology with fieldwork at Bethlehem House. "The special aim of this training," the Urban League explained, "is to link the growing enthusiasm and knowledge of educated Negro youth with the pressing needs of the toiling thousands of the Negro people." [44]

The biracial staffs, governing boards, and welfare leagues associated with these Methodist settlements set a precedent for the postwar idea of interracial cooperation. Indeed, Will Alexander, then a young Vanderbilt University divinity student, gained his first interracial experience as a member of the board of the Nashville Bethlehem House. "On that board I grew accustomed to accepting the Negroes as human beings," he recalled. "The women had that attitude, and I learned something from them." His initial introduction to the racial justice efforts of southern white women led Alexander to become the major proponent of admitting women to the Interracial Commission five years later. Those who had grown up in this "sort of anteroom of the church," he observed, had the "freedom and liberty to think and act. . . . The most vital and imaginative and flexible part of the church's program was the one carried on by these women. I have felt for several years," he concluded, that the Woman's Home Mission Society "was the most progressive and constructive religious group in the South."[45]

Out of the experience of working with black women in the settlement movement grew a more sophisticated understanding of the social origins of the problems of the black community. In 1914, for example, Lily Hardy Hammond, first director of the Methodist Women's Bureau of Social Service, published an analysis of race relations of particular importance in shaping the consciousness of Jessie Daniel Ames's generation of interracial workers. The daughter of slaveholders who "thought slavery wrong," she learned about settlement work in the tenements of Chicago. After marrying the white president of Paine College, she returned to the South. She founded the Southern Publicity Committee to disseminate information about black achievements and, with Belle Bennett, served as one of the few women involved in such secular expressions of prewar racial liberalism as the Southern Sociological Congress.

Her book, *In Black and White*, employed a thoroughgoing environmentalism to dispel the notion of innate biological inferiority. Hammond justified segregation by distinguishing between "race prejudice," which should be discarded, and "race consciousness," a necessary and universal "instinct against amalgamation." Having touched these reassuring bases, she launched into the heart of her study: a catalogue of the injustices suffered by blacks in southern society. Most poignant among them were the indignities forced upon women of "education and refinement." White women, she urged, must revise the paternalism of their parents' generation. The "basis of racial adjustment" would be cooperation with the newly aspiring black middle class. [46]

Despite this steady expansion of women's roles and consciousness, Methodist leaders were well aware that "the places assigned to them in the councils of the church are regarded as privileges conferred rather than responsibilities that belong to able and loyal members." They had chafed under the condescension of "the reluctant brethren," but their goal had remained control of their own institutions rather than representation in the governance of the church. [47] In 1906, however, a show of force awakened them to the limits of persuasion and the consequences of political impotence. The General Conference, motivated in part by reaction against the entry of southern women into the national suffrage movement and in part by a desire to appropriate women's enormously effective fund-raising abilities, moved to curb the authority and autonomy of the women's societies. Without consulting women leaders, the General Conference ordered the unification of the Home Mission Society with the more conservative Foreign Mission Society and the subordination of both to the general Board of Missions. Although they successfully demanded representation on the board, women leaders proved unwilling to adopt the tactics of confrontation, and in the end they capitulated to unification. [48]

Like the refusal of the World Anti-Slavery Convention of 1840 to seat women delegates, this retraction of women's privileges gave birth to a demand for women's rights. It united the women of both mission societies in southern Protestantism's first struggle for women's voting rights within the church. A laity rights memorial, defeated twice by vote of the General

Conference, gained overwhelming endorsement in 1918 and was ratified by a three-fourths majority of the church's district conferences. While the structure of southern political life threw up formidable barriers against the secular suffrage movement, women whose public activities historically had been confined to the church were able to use the language of evangelicalism as a vehicle for the expression of dissent. [49]

Nevertheless, like suffrage itself, the winning of laity rights proved an ambiguous victory. Ten years later, the renamed Woman's Missionary Council commissioned a study of women's status in the church in order to ascertain whether women were in fact filling the elective and appointive offices open to them. It found that while women comprised a majority of church members, they constituted only 24 out of 230 lay delegates to the upcoming General Conference of 1930. From local congregations to general church boards, women held a tiny minority of salaried church positions. Excluded from professional careers in the church "*because* of sex," women remained in their time-honored roles of volunteers and bureaucratic functionaries. "The tradition of a man-dominated church," the study concluded, "is accepted by most men and many women as the unquestioned order. . . . Securing laity rights in the church and political enfranchisement in the state by no means end the struggle for equal opportunities. . . ." [50]

After documenting the limits of integration, the council turned to the question of autonomy. As long as man remained the measure of humanity, it maintained, women's special interests and abilities would be regarded as "erratic or inferior . . . variations" from a male standard. "An inherent belief in male supremacy" together with female deference meant that only in their own separate organizations could women develop leadership ability and "methods peculiar to their experience." In fifty years of women's work:

The obscure woman has been developed. There has been training for service and for leadership in an unhampered atmosphere where all people were equally inexperienced. Initiative has been cultivated. Self confidence, creative ability, purposive activity, tested power of accomplishment, sacrificial giving, mental independence, financial expertness, courage of conviction, administrative success, spiritual insight, appreciation of woman power, and a spirit of sisterhood which reaches around the world; these are some of the elements which have come to maturity.[51]

According to the council, this historical independence had enabled Methodist women's organizations to take a more forthright position on social issues than that of the church as a whole. "Women are more fearless in their attempts at civil and political reform," the council explained, "because they are freer from entangling political alliances or obligations, and because they are less hampered by business interests and economic interrelationships." Autonomy remained the prerequisite for benevolent action; involvement in social problems in turn had wrought a major change in women's consciousness:

Between the women of 1878 and 1928 there lies a whole hemisphere of experience and discovery. It amounts to nothing less than this: into the inner life of women there has crashed the whole of the world outside before closed off to them. They have entered into contact with all the forces social, economic, political, that made the world as men knew it, different from the world as women knew it. The artificial barriers have been washed away.

Only when this process of cultural change was complete, "when men and women have attained equality, both theoretical and actual, in church, state and society" will "the day of the separate organization of women anywhere . . . be over."[52]

On the eve of the creation of the Commission on Interracial Cooperation, then, Methodist women stood at a critical juncture. Fresh from victory in the laity rights campaign, they were confident, optimistic, at a peak of self-aware group identity. Yet the distance they had traveled could be seen in terms of declension as well as of progress.[53] The autonomy of the Woman's Missionary Council had been eroded, and the following decades would see a further loss of institutional vigor. The evangelical promise had enabled the pioneers to liberate themselves from worldly prescriptions through membership in a community of believers; the failure of the church to fulfill the egalitarian implications of the Gospel meant that for women, as for blacks before them, the community of believers had become "the man's church."[54] By 1920, Methodist women leaders implicitly saw themselves as a sisterhood within an alien institution. Following generations would carry on a tradition of social responsibility, but as the tenets of liberal theology diluted the idiom of evangelism, they would cease so confidently to ground their life's work on the emotional experience of a new birth; their critique of the social order would derive as much from secular theories of education and reform as from the righteous enthusiasm of the biblical prophets. A paradoxical mixture of triumph and defeat, optimism and disillusion, estrangement and bondedness had prepared them to join with other women to pursue their social goals outside the structures of the Methodist Church.

A second historical strand leading to the creation of the Interracial Woman's Committee emerged from the struggle of black women for equality and autonomy within the predominantly white YWCA. The women who led this campaign would provide the Woman's Committee with most of its black leadership in the 1920s.[55] After the creation of the Anti-Lynching Association, these same individuals would play an important behind-the-scenes role in educating and influencing Jessie Daniel Ames and her white constituency. Together the missionary societies and the YWCA formed the institutional foundation of southern women's involvement in race relations reform.

The women who spearheaded the YWCA effort were the children or grandchildren of slaves, the first generations of southern blacks born in freedom. Such women occupied immensely complicated positions both within their own culture and in relation to the larger society. Their familial roles were powerful, economically significant, and culturally valued. Because daughters were often sent to school while their brothers pursued farming and skilled trades, women played a major part in the struggle for education. As domestic servants they were caught up in the intimate dynamics of white family life and acted as mediators across caste lines. Yet they shared with black men all the burdens of subordination; in addition, they were denied the deference granted women as compensation for powerlessness and suffered as objects of sexual predation.[56] In the words of the black CIC leader Nannie H. Burroughs:

> The Negro woman "totes" more water; grows more corn; picks more cotton; washes more clothes; cooks more meals; nurses more babies; mammies more Nordics; supports more churches; does more race uplifting; serves as mud-sills for more climbers; takes more punishment; does more forgiving; gets less protection and appreciation, than do the women in any other civilized group in the world. She has been the economic and social slave of mankind.[57]

This historic role—which has yet to receive any but the most cursory attention—created the social base for the contributions made by women to the building of black institutions and of a resourceful, and ultimately insurgent, black community.

In the 1890s, these southern black women joined in a nationwide move toward self-organization. From the outset, the stimulus for voluntary activities was political: a search for a means of meeting urgent social welfare needs, protesting lynching, asserting ethnic pride, and counteracting the stereotyped image of black women in the white mind. The southern pioneer in this effort was a teacher and journalist, Ida B. Wells.[58] In 1892, Wells's journal, the Memphis *Free Speech*, published an editorial that charged white merchants with lynching three black grocery store owners in order to eliminate economic competition. "There is nothing we can do about the lynching now, as we are outnumbered and without arms," Wells proclaimed. "There is therefore only one thing left that we can do; save our money and leave a town which will neither protect our lives and property, nor give us a fair trial in the courts, but takes us out and murders us in cold blood when accused by white persons." Spurred on by Wells's daring leadership, Memphis blacks responded to the lynching with "earnest, united action . . . which upset economic and business conditions." Hundreds sold their property and moved west. Those who were left behind boycotted the streetcar system and stayed away from their jobs. Fearing retaliation, Wells bought a pistol: "I felt that one had better die fighting against injustice than to die like a dog or a rat in a trap. I had already determined to sell my life as dearly as possible if attacked."

In the beginning, even Wells, a veteran of resistance to discrimination, believed "that although lynching was irregular and contrary to law and order, unreasoning anger over the terrible crime of rape led to the lynching." But the Memphis incident convinced her that the rape charge was in fact an excuse to get rid of blacks who were acquiring wealth and property and thus "keep the nigger down." After a three-month investigation, she began asserting her belief that behind many lynchings lay not a case of forcible rape but an interracial love affair. "Nobody in this section of the country," she announced, "believes the old thread-bare lie that Negro men rape white women."

The Memphis *Press Scimitar* responded by calling on the white men of the city to avenge this insult to the honor of their women. It is their duty, the editors urged, "to tie the wretch who utters these calumnies to a stake at the intersection of Main and Madison Sts., brand him [*sic*] in the forehead with a hot iron and perform upon him a surgical operation with a pair of tailor's shears." On the evening that this incendiary editorial appeared, a committee of prominent men destroyed the office of the *Free Speech* and warned Wells, in New York at the time, not to return at the cost of her life. Taking a position on the New York *Age* (and later as chairman of the Anti-Lynching Bureau of the National Afro-American Council), she waged a campaign of muckraking journalism, lectures, and organizing that set a direct precedent for the twentieth-century NAACP anti-lynching drive. In addition, she inspired the formation of the first black women's clubs and helped initiate a national federation movement.

By 1920, a personal and political network of educated black women, tied together by membership in the National Association of Colored Women (NACW), had appeared in the South. In Atlanta, this network was represented by Lugenia Burns Hope, wife of John Hope, the president of Morehouse College. Her parents, "free issue" Negroes in Mississippi before the Civil War, married and moved north to Chicago after emancipation. When her father died, Lugenia gave up her education and worked for eight years as a dressmaker and bookkeeper. In 1897, she married John Hope and, despite her mother's hatred for the South, moved with him to Atlanta. From their new apartment, Lugenia Hope looked out not upon the green serenity of a college campus but upon an urban slum of the New South. Unpaved roads in Atlanta's West Side black community made travel difficult; the city refused to supply water mains or street lights; garbage was dumped and burned on the road. As Hope came "face to face with one aspect of injustice and oppression after another," she "rolled up her delicate muslin sleeves" and began to organize her neighbors into a core of volunteer social workers.[59]

By 1906, she had created the Neighborhood Union, a settlement house and community organizing project financed, administered, and controlled by black women. Unique in its scope and continuity, the Neighborhood Union furnished a wide range of social services to the black community.[60] The local white press saw the organization as a harmless attempt to elevate black moral standards.[61] Indeed, the group's activities did reflect the class interests of its members, as they sought to stabilize and improve the neighborhood surrounding the university by driving out the forces of crime, gambling, and prostitution.[62] But these educated, middle-class women also addressed themselves to issues of vital importance to the poor; and their efforts brought them into conflict with local merchants, the Sanitation Department, the Board of Education, and, in the thirties, the discriminatory administrators of New Deal relief agencies. [63]

In other parts of the South, black women undertook similar projects of education and self-help. Lucy Craft Laney, born in 1854, was the daughter of a carpenter and lay minister who had paid for his own and his wife's manumission from slavery. Taught to read by her mother's former owner, Lucy Laney graduated from the first class of Atlanta University. In 1886, she opened Haines Normal and Industrial Institute in Augusta, Georgia. At a time when custom limited black education to vocational training and when Georgia provided no public high schools for blacks, Haines Institute maintained a liberal arts curriculum that prepared students for college and careers in teaching. [64]

The most famous of the many black women who received their training at Lucy Laney's school was Mary McLeod Bethune. One of seventeen children born to slave parents in Mayesville, South Carolina (her mother, she remembered proudly, was "of royal African blood"), Bethune established Bethune-Cookman School in Daytona Beach, Florida, in 1904. Founder and president of the National Council of Negro Women and of the Southeastern Federation of Colored Women's Clubs, Bethune went on to become director of the National Youth Administration's Division of Negro Affairs, the only woman member of Franklin Delano Roosevelt's "Black Cabinet." [65]

Janie Porter Barrett and Charlotte Hawkins Brown, also protégées of Lucy Laney, kept black education alive in a period when white society regarded all but the most rudimentary public education for blacks as a useless and even harmful luxury. In 1890, Barrett organized the Locust Street Social Settlement, the first settlement house in Virginia and among the first for blacks in the country. Fourteen years later, she created the Virginia Industrial School for Colored Girls in Peaks Turnout, supported by the fund-raising efforts of the Virginia State Federation of Colored Women's Clubs. Charlotte Hawkins Brown opened Palmer Memorial Institute in Sedalia, North Carolina, in 1902, and maintained it by a mighty effort of will until her death in 1961.[66]

Many of the institutions founded by such clubwomen, educators, and social workers grew out of a concern for the special plight of black girls; and in the years before World War I, these women began to look toward the YWCA, a national organization especially devoted to the spiritual and physical welfare of young working women, as a means of coordinating and broadening their efforts. Under the leadership of Lugenia Hope, they pressed for the inclusion of black women in the YWCA on a basis of equality. When these efforts failed, they became a moving force in the creation of the women's interracial movement.

The YWCA, like the women's missionary societies, was rooted in Protestant evangelicalism. It spread to college campuses and urban centers in response to the entry of women into higher education and wage labor. Ministering primarily to middle-class girls, it offered opportunities for self-organization and leadership unavailable in the churches and "the influence and protection of a Christian home" for rural women in the city for work. In the decade before World War I, the "Y" developed vigorous industrial and student departments and moved from its early emphasis on moral protection to a concern for the working conditions confronted by its constituency. In 1920, industrial members convinced the national organization to adopt as its platform the "Social Creed of the Churches," calling for economic justice, collective bargaining, and the workers' right to organize.[67]

For southern college students in particular, participants recalled, the YWCA offered a window on "the great wide world" and an entry into an inspiring and sustaining female network. While the YWCA did not directly challenge cultural definitions of women's place, it did provide its members with the basis for solidarity and group identity. Like Scarritt College, the YWCA's National Training School prepared women for new professional roles in the service sector. Industrial secretaries like Lois MacDonald, author of a classic study of southern mill villages, and Louise Leonard McLaren, founder of the Southern Summer School for Women Workers in western North Carolina, served as models for women too young to have been directly touched by the suffrage movement. From across the South, these field workers recruited potential women leaders on college campuses and introduced them to experiences and values outside the norms of their regional upbringings. [68]

Like the Methodist Woman's Missionary Council, the YWCA found it easier to promote professional opportunities for middle-class women and to address the conditions of the white industrial working class than to offer a critique of racial proscription either within its own ranks or in the larger society. [69] The first black branch was established in 1893, and segregated locals appeared here and there in northern and western cities. When the National YWCA was organized in 1906, it accepted de facto segregation as official policy and began chartering black YWCAs as subordinate branches of the central white association in each city. In 1915, an interracial conference was held in Louisville, Kentucky, to lay the groundwork for expansion into the South. [70] But in that same year only one black representative attended the national convention, and her experience there left her with the "feeling that the 'Y' was a spiritual farce, rather than a spiritual force." [71]

After the outbreak of World War I, the YWCA, like other volunteer organizations, channeled its resources into the war effort. Through its War Work Council, the YWCA supplied recreational facilities to soldiers and aid to young women entering war industries. In belated recognition of the needs of black soldiers and the fact that black as well as white women were entering war industries, the "Y" appropriated $200,000 for a "Colored Department" of the War Work Council one year before the armistice.

The YWCA placed Eva Bowles, its first black field secretary, in charge of this work and furnished her with a small staff. Plunging into public service with the same sense of "joyful release" felt by many white women during the war, Bowles and her staff established recreational and industrial centers in 45 communities by the end of 1919. Paid black local workers rose from 9 in 1915 to 86, and 12,000 young women enrolled in YWCA branches.[72] In Atlanta, Hope's Neighborhood Union formed the core of an Atlanta Colored Women's War Council, which led public protests against the mistreatment of black soldiers on streetcars and the harassment of black civilians and soldiers by police officers. On the basis of her outstanding work in Atlanta, Lugenia Hope was appointed a Special War Work Secretary and placed in charge of training hostess house workers at Camp Upton, New Jersey.[73]

When the war ended, a sense of impending doom replaced the euphoria of home-front solidarity. Black women were forced to abandon their precarious foothold in industry, and race riots shattered the hopes raised by wartime rhetoric. "The war," wrote Eva Bowles at the end of 1919, "has given opportunity to the colored woman to prove her ability for leadership. She had her chance and she made good."[74] But instead of building on these accomplishments, the National Board moved to dismantle Bowles's wartime staff.

Returning from five months at Camp Upton, Lugenia Hope collided with the realities of the postwar South as she attempted to form a black YWCA group in Atlanta. The president of the Atlanta central "Y," Susan L. Davis (who would later become a founder and chairman of the CIC Woman's Committee), encouraged Hope's plan. But Adelle Ruffin, field supervisor of colored work in the South, objected to the site chosen for the Phillis Wheatley branch and accused Hope of using the organization not to aid aspiring middle-class women but to "save" immoral "Alley Girls."[75] Other southern black women joined Hope in raising objections to Ruffin's leadership.[76] Ruffin, however, had gained the support of the white field staff headquartered in Richmond; they were determined to use their authority to bolster her position, and to prevent the black secretaries of the National Board, with their aggressive northern ways, from setting foot "on Southern soil." In

1920, they launched a campaign to replace the black national student secretary, Catherine D. Lealtad, with a southern white woman "who was really sincere and just in her attitude toward colored people."[77]

In response to these encroachments, Hope and her co-workers raised the first public demand for integrating black women into the "Y" on a basis of full equality. On April 6, 1920, Hope called southern black women to a meeting at her home in Atlanta to clarify the principles on which work in the black community should be based. "Northern women," Hope explained, "thought they knew more about it than Southern women—Colored women believed they knew more than both and that's why they wanted to represent themselves."[78] Black women, the caucus asserted, never agreed to the principle that work in the field should advance only as fast as "the Southern whites will permit," nor that young women who needed the "Y" most (Adelle Ruffin's "Alley Girls") should be excluded, nor that black national secretaries could be prohibited from working in the South. They drew up a petition asking that Adelle Ruffin be removed on the grounds that she "does not know her own people," that "in all work affecting our people, full recognition of leadership be given Negro women," and that blacks be allowed to form independent organizations.[79]

Expressing high hopes and unity of purpose, Hope, Lucy Laney, and Mary Jackson McCrorey presented this petition to the YWCA national convention in Cleveland, Ohio.[80] But the convention avoided taking action by deferring to the authority of the southern field staff to handle all problems in its jurisdiction. Disappointed by the evasiveness of the National Board, Mary McCrorey concluded that "the whole policy is to keep us strictly subordinated" and urged the caucus to "keep wide awake and remain fearless."[81] A follow-up meeting in the Richmond, Virginia, headquarters of the southern field staff proved equally fruitless. Not only were the demands of the black committee rejected, but in the official account of the meeting sent to the National Board, they were ignored altogether. The report made it appear, protested McCrorey, "that there were no complaints, no issues—*nothing* but an outing to Richmond to see the South Atlantic Field Office and its 'dignitaries.' "[82]

Frustrated by the failure of their efforts to work from within established channels, the black caucus brought public pressure to bear on the "Y."[83] As a consequence, a Louisville, Kentucky, "Conference on Colored Work" adopted several general resolutions and appointed Charlotte Hawkins Brown to a figurehead post as member-at-large of the southern field staff. But even this victory proved illusory, for the southern field staff appropriated no travel funds to bring the "non-resident" member to Richmond, nor did they inform Brown of scheduled meetings or encourage her to attend.[84]

Firing off one final protest, Hope expressed her moral indignation and disappointment: "I have no regrets for the stand that I took . . . even if I had to be misrepresented and rather cruelly treated because of it." She had grown increasingly disillusioned with the emphasis of YWCA officials on "technique" and compromise. But she had not given up her belief that black women "could stand side by side with women of the white race and work for full emancipation of all women."[85]

The black women's caucus that met in Lugenia Hope's home in April 1920 had discussed not only "some vital interracial work of the YWCA," but also the possibility that "the time was ripe [to] go beyond the YWCA and any other organization and reach a few outstanding white and Negro women, Christian and with well-balanced judgment and not afraid."[86] By cutting across the boundaries of existing organizations, they hoped to bring the strongest black women leaders together with the most progressive whites in an organization specifically devoted to improving race relations.

This desire meshed fortuitously with events taking place at

the same time within the Methodist Woman's Missionary Council. At the annual meeting of April 1920 in Kansas City, Missouri, Belle Bennett delivered a presidential address calling upon newly enfranchised southern women to join in the movement for interracial cooperation. Her plea was emphasized by a special guest speaker, Will Alexander. Over the previous decade, a few dedicated Methodist women leaders had followed the call to social service into the black community. They had conceived of their work in settlement houses and schools as their duty to a "weaker race," and had made little attempt to involve rank-and-file church women in a larger educational program on race relations. Now Bennett and Alexander urged upon the council a new departure. Missions to the poor should be replaced by cooperative ventures with black women on the local and regional level. In response, the council created a commission empowered to "study the whole question of race relationships, the needs of Negro women and children, and methods of cooperation by which better conditions can be brought about."[87] The motion to create the commission was put forward by Sara Estelle Haskin, who had served as supervisor of the Nashville Bethlehem House, editor of the *Laity Rights Advocate,* and a leader of YWCA interracial work in the South. Her proposal was seconded by Mary De Bardeleben. Carrie Parks Johnson, who had demonstrated her unusual "powers of initiative" by securing petitions from throughout the church in behalf of the laity rights memorial, assumed the chairmanship of the group.[88]

Lugenia Hope, informed by Will Alexander of the creation of the Methodist commission, seized this opportunity to carry forward "the spirit and purpose" of the YWCA effort. She invited Johnson and Haskin to attend the biennial conference of the National Association of Colored Women at Tuskegee Institute in July. Afterward she arranged a meeting in Mrs. Booker T. Washington's home between the two white women and her southern co-workers.[89]

Tuskegee Institute, founded by Booker T. Washington in 1881 and presided over in 1920 by Robert R. Moton, provided an appropriate location for such a unique and unconventional venture: an encounter of white and black women on a black college campus. The white women did not expect to find any surprises at Tuskegee; its beautifully landscaped grounds, its industrial courses for inculcating morality and preparing southern blacks for manual labor, and its genteel, Victorian atmosphere made it an ideal showcase for visiting northern philanthropists interested in black education.[90] When they arrived, Johnson and Haskin were offered segregated housing and dining facilities in Dorothy Hall. But when they appeared at the first session of the NACW conference, they were startled to find themselves treated simply as members of the group rather than as honored white guests. In contrast with white interracial leaders, whose influence for the most part was limited to local communities or channeled through the southern church, many of the southern club women present had gained national recognition as members of a rising black middle class. Amazed at the intelligence and seriousness of the delegates, Johnson sat quietly in the audience: "I had a new world opened to me, a world I had never conceived before."[91]

Black women, for their part, viewed the Tuskegee meeting with mixed emotions. As they sat down together around a teakwood table in Booker T. Washington's library, the black and white southern women faced each other across "a gulf of distance, of mistrust and suspicion." The black women suspected, as well they might, that the concern of their white visitors for "Negro betterment" was related to their desire for more efficient and presentable domestic servants. "I am glad you have not any Negro servants," Charlotte Hawkins Brown privately reflected, "and I am not going to help you get any." The hostility of black women toward whites, the inability of white women to comprehend the meaning of that hostility, and the confusion of etiquette and expectations threw participants into paralyzing discomfort.[92]

Typically, shared religious conventions provided a formal structure in which the women could regain their bearings and overcome their uneasiness. "Only after an hour spent in the

reading of God's word and in prayer, face to face on the platform of Christ Jesus," reported Johnson, "did these white
women and black women come to a liberty and frankness that
made possible a discussion."[93] Lugenia Hope broke the ice:
"We have just emerged from a world war that cost the lives of
thousands of our boys fighting to make the world safe for democracy— For whom? . . . Women, we can achieve nothing
today unless you . . . who have met us are willing to help us
find a place in American life where we can be unashamed and
unafraid." Black participants saw Hope's words as exceedingly
frank and courageous; they waited tensely to see how Johnson
and Haskin would respond and then followed Hope's lead with
statements of their own grievances and concerns. Looking back
thirteen years later, Mary McCrorey felt that "the spirit of that
meeting will last me the remainder of my life."[94] I saw in "the
hearts of those Negro women . . . all the aspirations for their
homes and their children that I have for mine," Johnson remembered. "My heart broke and I have been trying to pass the
story on to the women of my race."

Johnson and Haskin returned to Will Alexander's office in
Atlanta convinced that "the men might as well hang their harps
on a willow tree, as to try to settle the race problem in the
South without the aid of the Southern white woman."[95] They
had discovered a network of educated black women engaged in
self-help and institution-building quite apart from the sporadic
activities of their white sisters. "While we have thought we
were doing the best we could, a race has grown up in our very
midst that we do not know," Johnson explained. "We know the
cook in the kitchen, we know the maid in the house, we know
the man in the yard[,] we know the criminal in the daily papers, we know the worst there is to know—but the masses of
the best people of my race do not know the best of the Negro
race."[96] If only the Tuskegee experience could be duplicated
for larger numbers of women, Johnson and Haskin argued, the
indifference of white middle-class women and the assumption
of black inferiority could be effectively challenged. "We had
some pretty belligerent women in the Methodist Church," Jes-

sie Daniel Ames recalled, "and they had some pressure and they brought it on Dr. Alexander . . . and pushed and pushed and pushed until eventually he decided to set up a woman's committee separate from the men." [97]

Overcoming the skepticism of his co-workers, Will Alexander persuaded the CIC to sponsor a South-wide women's conference in Memphis, Tennessee, on October 6–7, 1920. Ninety-one women representing the major Protestant denominations, the women's clubs, and the YWCA accepted a vaguely worded invitation to a gathering for the consideration of "important problems." Four black women agreed to address the meeting. Determined to avoid publicity of any sort because "the whole situation was too strange and delicate," Alexander arranged for the conference to be held in a small dingy room in a Memphis YMCA, where it would be possible to "control the press." [98]

Johnson and Haskin opened the meeting with an account of their sojourn at Tuskegee and "informed the rest of the group that they had been invited to hear the stories these Negro women had to tell." Anyone who objected could withdraw before the afternoon session when the black women would appear. Fearful that the black speakers would be "embarrassed or insulted" or that the audience would be scandalized, Alexander and three other CIC men "sought a seat in a corner as nearly out of sight as [they] could get" and watched the proceedings with some trepidation. [99]

The afternoon session opened with a speech by Margaret Murray Washington. Born in Macon, Mississippi, in 1865, she grew up after her father's death in a household of Quaker teachers, was graduated from Fisk University in 1889, and assumed the position of Dean of the Woman's Department of Tuskegee Institute. There she became the third wife of Booker T. Washington and, as Director of Girls' Industries, collaborated with him in the building of Tuskegee. As the organizer of an exceptionally effective local women's group and the first president of the National Federation of Afro-American

Women, she played an important role in her own right in the
founding and expansion of the black women's club movement.
Like her more famous husband, Margaret Washington was a
proponent of accommodation, combining an assertion of black
cultural achievements and racial pride with a conciliatory
stance toward whites. Seen by the other speakers as "the most
conservative type of our Negro women," she operated as a me-
diator between them and the white leadership and as a brake
on their self-assertion and militancy.[100] "I belong to the South
and I love it," Washington assured her audience. Referring
delicately to "the system" that had, through no fault of the ladies present, destroyed the black home, she recounted her
own efforts at Tuskegee to impress upon black field workers
the necessity of "legally solemnized marriage, and legal children." She described the inequities of black education and portrayed the difficulties faced by black mothers working long
hours in a white woman's home. "Give us a chance," she
ended, "and you won't find a more law-abiding people in the
world."[101]

Elizabeth Ross Haynes spoke on the second day of the conference. Born in Lowndes County, Alabama, the daughter of
former slaves, she had graduated from Fisk University, taught
school, and, in 1908, had become the first black YWCA national secretary. During World War I she served with the
Women's Bureau of the Department of Labor and, in later
years, authored a number of articles on black women.[102] She
acknowledged (but did not endorse) an earlier statement by a
white participant who "believed in segregation" and then described some of the daily humiliations of life under Jim Crow.
She ended her low-key address with the dramatic tale of So-
journer Truth who, after forty years in slavery, became not
only a spell-binding abolitionist, but a staunch feminist. At an
Akron, Ohio, women's rights convention in 1851, Truth had sat
quietly on the edge of the crowd through two days of antifeminist testimony. Finally, she rose and, amid murmurs of
disapproval, moved to the platform. "The tumult subsided at

once, and every eye was fixed on this almost Amazon form,
which stood nearly six feet high, head erect, and eyes piercing
the upper air like a dream."

That man over there says that women need to be helped into carriages, and lifted over ditches, and to have the best place everywhere. Nobody ever helps me into carriages, or over mud-puddles,
or gives me any best place! And ain't I a woman? Look at my arm! I
have ploughed, and planted, and gathered into barns, and no man
could head me! And ain't I a woman? I could work as much and eat
as much as a man—when I could get it—and bear the lash as well!
And ain't I a woman? I have borne thirteen children, and seen
most of 'em sold off to slavery, and when I cried out with my
mother's grief, none but Jesus heard me! And ain't I a woman?[103]

The final speaker was Charlotte Hawkins Brown. She was
born in Henderson, North Carolina, in 1882; when she was six
years old, her father deserted the family and her mother led
her clan of twenty children north to Cambridge, Massachusetts. Through the patronage of Alice Freeman Palmer,
president of Wellesley, Brown secured an education. In 1901,
she returned to North Carolina to work "among her own folk."
A year later, she opened Palmer Memorial Institute, a prepara-
tory school, supported for the most part by New England
philanthropists, whose aims were "to teach the dignity of labor,
and to emphasize politeness."[104] Brown described herself as "a
radical," but her militancy consisted primarily of a demand for
white recognition of the black bourgeoisie. Proud of her white
ancestry, indebted to a white benefactress, and dependent on
whites for the survival of her school, Brown was charged by
W.E.B. Du Bois with, in fact, "representing the White South."
Yet sharing as she did the class values of her audience, Brown's
presence functioned as a dramatic contradiction of their expectations of black humility and cultural inferiority. In the context
of the 1920s, her uncompromising demand for "the respect of
others" was, if hardly radical, certainly much more than white
society was prepared to grant.[105]

Marshaling all her rhetorical skills, Brown brought the Memphis meeting to a surprising and emotional close. She opened

her speech with the story of her trip from North Carolina to Tennessee. A menacing crowd of white men had forced her out of a Pullman berth into a Jim Crow day coach. "And the shame of the whole affair was that southern white women passing for Christians were on that very car" bound for the Memphis meeting. She arrived at her destination, shaken with anger, and Johnson and Haskin gingerly kept her off the first day's program. By the last morning of the conference she had translated her rage into an electrifying piece of oratory, perfectly tailored to her audience. "I came to Memphis crushed and humiliated," she told the gathered women. But with a great effort of will she had at last attained a transcendent and forgiving state of grace. Like an Old Testament prophet she could now deliver "the message which God had given me." [106] Her message was first of all a challenge to southern white women to confront the evil of lynching:

> The Negro women of the South lay everything that happens to the members of her race at the door of the Southern white woman. . . . We all feel that you can control your men . . . that so far as lynching is concerned . . . if the white women would take hold of the situation that lynching would be stopped. [As for the excuse that lynching is necessary to protect] the chastity of our white women . . . I want to say to you, when you read in the paper where a colored man has insulted a white woman, just multiply that by one thousand and you have some idea of the number of colored women insulted by white men. [107]

Brown then pursued a theme that she and other black women on the Interracial Commission would bring up again and again: the oppressiveness of the myth of the promiscuous black woman. One symbol of that myth was the refusal of whites to address a married black woman as Mrs.—"whether she be cook, criminal or principal of a school." Brown pointed out that a terrible assumption lurked beneath this seemingly trivial discourtesy: the belief that all black women were immoral and therefore not entitled to protection from sexual exploitation. [108] Finally she brought her address to a close with the familiar language of sin, damnation, and salvation-through-works. In a statement that was both an appeal and a warning, she concluded, "I know that if you are Christian women, that in the final analysis you are going to have to reach out for the same hand that I am reaching out for but I know that the dear Lord will not receive it if you are crushing me beneath your feet."[109]

Far from recoiling in anger, the white delegates rose to their feet in the ritual response of the evangelical church: heads bowed, spontaneously singing a familiar hymn of Christian fellowship and solidarity. Years later participants still recalled the sacred, ecstatic quality of the Memphis conference. Confronted by proud and articulate black women, exhorted passionately, yet in acceptable generalities and in the language of a shared religious tradition, to accept responsibility for the plight of women whose aspirations were so much like their own, the white women present responded with an outpouring of emotion that would become the paradigm for—and often the only accomplishment of—interracial meetings for a decade.[110] Charlotte Hawkins Brown described the Memphis meeting as "the greatest step forward . . . taken since emancipation."[111]

Adopting a platform based on a statement of grievances drawn up by the black women at the Tuskegee Conference, the delegates asked the Interracial Commission to create a Committee on Woman's Work funded jointly by the CIC and the Woman's Missionary Council.[112] Carrie Parks Johnson, who had chaired the Council's Commission on Race Relationships and served as an initiator of the Tuskegee and Memphis meetings, was chosen to lead the new organization. A native of Athens, Georgia, Johnson was the daughter of an itinerant Methodist preacher who had served as a missionary to the slaves before the Civil War. She had married the pastor of the First Methodist Church in Decatur, Georgia; after her children were grown, she had started a second career in the work of the Woman's Missionary Council. A leader in the struggle for laity rights for women, she had been elected a delegate to the first General Conference that admitted women. Johnson brought to her position in the Interracial Commission a number of invaluable qualities: a combination of the aristocratic benevolence of her slave-owning grandparents and the religious fervor of her missionary father, the ability to translate social issues into the language of the southern Methodist pulpit, and a strong identification with the problems of women as a group. She had been influenced by the social-justice wing of the progressive movement and had read "scientific" studies of the race question. But for her, solutions to the problem of racial justice lay neither in science nor in social engineering but in Christian perfectionism and feminine compassion. Not as intellectually able, as ambitious, or as capable an administrator as her successor, Jessie Daniel Ames, Carrie Johnson was nevertheless a fitting choice to direct a movement that derived its constituency from a network of woman's missionary societies and its ideology from the "call to Christian service."[113]

The women's interracial movement had begun in the mood of heightened expectation common to the evangelical revival experience. But the vision of a bond of common womanhood that made the Tuskegee and Memphis conferences so memorable faded as the new Interracial Woman's Committee attempted to develop an analysis of concrete social problems and a program for change. When conference participants set about the task of building an organization, spontaneity gave way to a reassertion of traditional hierarchies and assumptions, and black participants found themselves in a struggle for "self-determination and self-expression" not unlike the YWCA battle from which they had just emerged.[114]

The black women's caucus had hastily drafted a position paper meant to serve as the basis for CIC women's work. It dealt with a wide range of issues: the working conditions of domestic servants, child welfare, transportation, education, lynching, the treatment of blacks in the white press, and the right to vote. Without consulting the authors, however, Johnson read a version of the statement to the Memphis conference that added to Lugenia Hope's straightforward condemnation of lynching a preface deploring "any act on the part of Negro men which excites the mob spirit." She omitted the resolution on suffrage altogether. Most significantly, she left out the preamble demanding for black women "all the privileges and rights granted to American womanhood."[115]

Angered by these changes, the black delegates at first accepted Margaret Washington's counsel of silence and moderation. "Let us stand shoulder to shoulder with the two white women and their followers," she admonished. "This Mrs. Johnson, in my mind, is a sincere southern white woman and certainly will need our cooperation and sympathy. . . . We are expected to mark time." But when Johnson decided to publish the black women's statement in this altered form, Hope led a protest against the plan. "Mrs. Johnson's crowd," she wrote to her ally, Charlotte Hawkins Brown, "refuses to . . . believe that we are ready for suffrage and . . . are trained in all activities of American life."[116] Convincing Johnson to delay the printing of the pamphlet, Hope called a meeting of the original Tuskegee participants to reaffirm their commitment to the original platform.[117]

In a series of letters written in the following weeks, Hope summed up her own position and pointed out some of the fundamental weaknesses of the interracial movement. "It is difficult for me to understand why my white sisters so strenuously object to this expression of colored women as put forth in the discarded preamble," she wrote on March 1. "After all . . . when we yield to public opinion and make ourselves say only what we think the public can stand, is there not a danger that we may find ourselves with our larger view conceding what those with the narrow view demand?" The white women, she continued, "may be too cautious, with too little faith in [their] own people."[118] In the same letter, Hope went on to attack the assumption of racial inferiority underlying objections to the preamble and the limitations of the white women's avowed desire for "a frank and open" statement of the black women's point of view:

> Ignorance is ignorance wherever found, yet the most ignorant White woman may enjoye [sic] every privilege that America offers.. Now I think that the ignorant Negro woman should also enjoy them to the best of her ability. We learn by doing and what is good for one race is good for the other. I therefore canot [sic] understand why this clause should be cut out, since this is the Negro woman's viewpoint, and that is what you asked us for, our point of view not the White women's point of view.[119]

After months of negotiation, the two groups drew up a compromise statement. But before it could be submitted for approval to the black woman's committee, Johnson decided to drop the matter and notified the black women that there would be no printed pamphlet at all.[120] In a frank letter to Johnson on June 24, Hope expressed the frustration of being forced to spend an inordinate amount of time and energy in efforts to influence white moderates who were, in any case, largely outside the mainstream of political and economic power. While racist demagogues plied their trade and the Ku Klux Klan surged to power, Interracial Commission leaders quibbled over the nuances of wording and used their position as mediators between the black community and the white power structure to impose their own interpretations of what was strategic and timely on even the most cooperative of black leaders. "In the meantime," Hope continued, "the forces of darkness manage to agree about what is 'best for Negroes.' "[121]

Four days after this letter was written, the Southeastern Federation of Colored Women's Clubs, meeting in Atlanta, adopted the black women's statement as the platform of the federation. Published in pamphlet form under the title *Southern Negro Women and Race Co-operation*, the statement omitted the controversial preamble, retained the suffrage plank, and adopted a conciliatory tone in its discussion of lynching. The publication of this pamphlet represented a strategic retreat, a willingness on the part of Hope and her supporters to compromise rather than "retard progress."[122]

Progress was slow indeed. Woman's Committee leaders assumed that white women would take the initiative in organizing state women's groups, then locate black women to form a "parallel committee"—a procedure not unlike that followed by the YWCA.[123] Lugenia Hope's experience in Georgia indicates some of the problems faced by black members in such an organization. Responses to her invitation to "outstanding, forward thinking, level-headed women" from the smaller towns of southwest Georgia expressed fear of local whites as well as suspicion of the motives of white women. Nevertheless, Hope organized local black committees in a number of localities, but no white groups appeared with which to "cooperate." In Atlanta, on the other hand, the Neighborhood Union and other black institutions provided a base for the development of self-confident and experienced black women leaders, and an active and successful local women's committee flourished.[124]

Even a relatively strong committee faced the problem of developing an acceptable description of its purpose and focus for its work. Just as black scholars in the period were confined to racial topics and black members of civic organizations were expected to deal with "interracial" matters, so women, guided both by their self-images and by cultural expectations, tended to see their public activities as an extension of their nurturing function in the home. Within the Interracial Commission, black members as well as white assumed that the "point of contact" across the color line lay in women's mutual experience of motherhood; "women's work" would naturally take as its central concern the integrity and well-being of "the Negro home." "A white mother," Carrie Parks Johnson hopefully explained, "cannot labor with a colored mother on a given piece of work for the common good, without having her heart beat in unison with the desires of the colored mother for her own young and her own home." Johnson confidently believed that "from such contacts, and such only, can genuine understanding take place. The plans and methods of your Woman's committee have been projected upon this psychological basis."[125]

In the view of the Woman's Committee, the chief threat to the black family lay in the sexual double standard and the exploitation of black women by white men. In a speech to the male members of the Interracial Commission, Carrie Parks Johnson graphically described her position on this issue:

> If any black man publicly advocated the amalgamation of the white and colored races by marriage, he would be, if not burned at the stake, hung in effigy. The race problem can never be solved as long as the white man goes unpunished, and loses no social standing, while the Negro is burned at the stake. I shall say no more, for I am sure you need not have anything more said. When the white men of the South have come to that position, a single standard for both men and women, then you will accomplish something in this great problem.[126]

Similarly, the work of each state organization began with a public pronouncement calling for the abolition of lynching and a single standard of morality. An Arkansas group asserted

> that the degradation of women is the doom of any race and that among the number of underlying causes of the present racial situation in America is the lack of respect and protection for Negro womanhood. Recognizing with sympathetic appreciation the high standards of virtue set by the best element of Negro women, we pledge ourselves to an effort to emphasize the single standard of morals for both men and women to the end that righteousness may prevail, and that racial integrity may be assured, not to one race, but to both.[127]

While black participants shared these concerns, they could scarcely have assented to all the implications of the white women's words. The protests of white CIC women reflected sympathy for female vulnerability and placed the blame for sexual irregularity on men rather than on black women; at the same time, however, they expressed a revulsion against "amalgamation" as such, a desire to suppress not only rape and seduction but interracial sex in all its forms. Black women viewed the situation from a different perspective. Opposition to lynching and a desire to defend black womanhood against aspersions of immorality had stimulated the formation of black women's organization since the 1890s. But the notion of "racial integrity," which white women asserted as a fundamental goal, functioned for blacks as a code word for segregation. Indeed, a number of the original black members of the Interracial Woman's Committee were themselves products of interracial unions, and they were motivated more by outrage at sexual abuse and sexual mythology than by opposition to legitimate human relationships.[128]

At the same time, their attitude toward sexual morality demonstrated the class values they shared with their white compatriots. Charlotte Hawkins Brown, for example, protested against the refusal of whites to differentiate between "that class of women who were prostituted years ago to save the women of the white race" and those who, like herself, "through fifty years of training and service" had achieved a level of middle-class respectability. In fact several of the black participants at the Memphis conference had gone so far as to argue that since they themselves had little contact with "the masses of black women," white women bore a special responsibility for social uplift in their capacity as mistresses of domestic servants.[129] In the confusing junctures of race, class, and sex, efforts of women at mutual understanding were inevitably fraught with irony and contradiction.

In essence, the activities of the women's interracial movement were not designed to fulfill specific social welfare needs or to challenge the caste system. Rather, CIC women sought to register disapproval of sexual relations across the color line, and, most importantly, to provide in ritualistic meetings between "the best type of white women and the best type of colored women," a recognition of the development of a black middle class. In Gunnar Myrdal's term, the color line was "tilted up"; black and white women could recognize some of the common concerns arising from their class and sexual positions, while at the same time maintaining between the groups a proper social distance.[130]

Even this symbolic purpose was by no means easy to accomplish. Little open conflict between black and white members erupted after the issue of the black women's statement had been settled, but a number of incidents illustrate the subtle and not-so-subtle racist stereotypes under which black participants labored. For example, Mrs. T. W. Bickett, chairman of the Interracial Woman's Committee and wife of the governor of North Carolina, introduced Charlotte Hawkins Brown to the CIC meeting of 1921 with the following backhanded compliment:

> The memory of slavery is very dear to me because in the women of that day, the colored women, there was the same loyalty of purpose, integrity . . . that I find among the women who are leading their race today. [It was] my old Negro mammy [who] endeared [me] to the people of her race, however little I might find in them individually to appeal to me today. . . . I cannot say anymore, Mrs. Brown, for your race today than . . . that you are as fine as was my Negro mammy.[131]

Black CIC women, often cast in the role of representatives to white women's groups, were acutely conscious of such social slights. "When we colored people come to your assemblies and churches and you send us to the galleries or put us in a corner," admonished Janie Porter Barrett, "it is as humiliating as if you hung a banner over us with flaming words 'UNCLEAN' written across it."[132] Mrs. H. A. Hunt was introduced as "the wife of Mr. Hunt" to a regional meeting of church women unwilling to accord her the title of "Mrs." "It was very difficult to talk to those women," she remembered. "Everybody looked as if they were scared to death . . . their faces looked so funny."[133] Another black participant described an incident in which a group of Baptist women invited her to address them "about the work of the 'niggers' " and instructed her to enter the meeting by the back door.[134]

In contrast, here and there black and white women formed

lasting alliances based on mutual respect. In South Carolina, for example, Alice Spearman Wright, the daughter of a wealthy planting and banking family, returned home from a year at the YWCA's National Training School and a YWCA-sponsored trip around the world to become a mainstay of the state branch of the Interracial Commission. The most militant black member of the group was Modjeska Simkins, a young teacher and social worker from Columbia. Over the years, they found themselves on the same side in confrontations with their paternalistic colleagues in the movement. When the post–World War II drive for black civil rights began, Wright was appointed the first director of the South Carolina Council on Human Relations and waged a lonely battle to mobilize white liberal support for integration. Simkins helped organize the NAACP legal offensive in the state and, as head of the Richland County Citizens Committee, supported the shift out of the courts and into direct action. An outspoken critic of "exponents of the power structure," both black and white, Simkins saw Alice Spearman Wright as "a vigilant and almost a radical spirit," whose work had a very positive "leavening influence" in the state. [135]

Unevenly and with varying degrees of difficulty, CIC women's committees materialized across the South. By 1924, eleven statewide groups had appeared. Although a concerted effort was made to cross denominational boundaries and to engage the cooperation of civic as well as religious groups, Methodist leaders dominated the organization and Methodist missionary societies continued to afford the major channels for local interracial activities. Each local women's auxiliary in the Methodist Church, for example, received instructions to set up a committee charged with conducting a detailed survey of housing, sanitation, and recreational facilities in black neighborhoods and with leading a study group within the church on black achievements and progress. Armed with this knowledge, they were to work cooperatively with black women on community improvement projects. The number of such Methodist committees grew from 110 in 1922 to 606 by 1927. Their activities consisted mainly of securing access for blacks to public services and upgrading segregated facilities. They helped establish dental and health clinics in public schools, secured library and hospital privileges, and set up municipal playgrounds. Monthly bulletins kept local auxiliaries informed of the Interracial Commission's work, and local officers were invited to attend regional commission meetings and to send representatives to state commission branches. [136]

The most important institutional avenues for black women's participation in the interracial movement, however, were the Southeastern Federation of Colored Women's Clubs and the YWCA. State federations took as their central concerns the eradication of lynching and the establishment of state training schools for delinquent girls. Within the YWCA, the World War I campaign of southern black women bore fruit, as that organization became a major conduit for bringing a younger generation of southern women into the movement.

In 1923, for example, a Southern Division of the National Student Council was organized, which included black and white co-chairmen and a department on interracial education. The CIC supplied the group with literature, speakers, and campus advisors. Katharine Du Pre Lumpkin (author, in later years, of *The Making of a Southerner* and other studies in regional sociology) served as student secretary for the South. Traveling through the region with black staff members Juliette Derricotte (later Dean of Women at Fisk University), Grace Towns Hamilton (whose mother had been a founder of the Neighborhood Union and who herself became the first black woman elected to the Georgia legislature), Frances Williams, and Juanita Sadler, she urged upon students in the small women's colleges of the South "more emphasis on the ills and injustices of America." Those early years of interracial work in the YWCA, Lumpkin recalled, were "something very special." A sense of solidarity, a group identity as southern women "working on these things" formed lasting bonds of friendship among black and white student leaders. [137] By 1928, the National Student Council had begun to move beyond the tactic of "interracial contacts" between individuals as a means of affecting racial attitudes. In 1933, it adopted a policy statement demanding "basic changes in our economic and educational institutions, our legal systems, our religious organizations, and in our social customs." A year later a joint YMCA-YWCA interracial committee called for "the ultimate elimination of all segregation and discrimination." As the thirties progressed, this cadre of YWCA-YMCA student leaders assumed prominent roles in the development of regional sociology, the workers' education aspect of the labor movement, and the southern wing of the New Deal coalition. [138]

The Woman's Committee, like the Interracial Commission in general, thus encouraged and coordinated the first stirrings of racial liberalism in the region. Here and there it helped ameliorate the worst injustices of segregation and break down the most blatant of racial stereotypes. It signified the beginnings of regional self-criticism and rendered interracial work respectable in the conservative South. [139]

While individual perspectives were broadened and friendships developed, however, tangible signs of organizational effectiveness were few. Early in 1924, Johnson admitted that "not one State Committee has adequately organized." A few months later, she felt that "the achievements in this section of the work have scarcely been commensurate with the opportunity." She noted that while nearly every woman's state committee had adopted a definite plan of work at the outset, "some of these have brought concrete and worthwhile results—some have not. Some content themselves with a declaration of principles, some with public speaking and some with real achievement provided no publicity is attached." Of all those chairing state committees, only Jessie Daniel Ames in Texas seemed able to "submit reports on results in any coherent form." [140]

The weakness of these groups reflected the limitations of a reform movement dependent on the tactics of conciliation and moral persuasion. In addition, women faced the problem of defining a distinct role for themselves within a male-dominated organization. Local and state women's committees were subordinate to local and state men's committees. Male chairmen hesitated to convene women's groups or to take them seriously once they had been organized. In many places male chairmen chose women representatives, and, as Jessie Daniel Ames believed, they often chose women "not because they represent something but because they have met them somewhere and they are pleasant and easy to look at." The Woman's Committee acquired neither autonomy nor adequate funding; its policy decisions and programs were submitted as recommendations to the Interracial Commission as a whole.[141]

Progress was also hampered, Woman's Committee leaders believed, by deeply ingrained hierarchical attitudes. Their assumption of superiority made it difficult for white women to distinguish between interracial cooperation and charity. Cut off from the exercise of political and economic power, women tended to substitute sentiment and emotion for practical activity. Carrie Parks Johnson had begun her work confident in the belief that women's special religious sensibilities and maternal roles would guide them to right action. Understanding would take place spontaneously: at the outset of the movement, she supposed, "the silent anguish and the cry of the mother heart of the Negro race leaped the chasm and found response in the mother heart of the white race." But by the middle of the decade she was complaining that too often women assumed that once their emotions had been stirred their duty had been accomplished. They were willing to study "the history of the Negro" or "the Negro woman"; they might even issue a statement of principles calling for law and order and "racial integrity." But to take action to which "publicity is attached" in the atmosphere of the early twenties required more courage and perception than any but the boldest few could muster.[142]

Almost a century before the founding of the CIC Woman's Committee, Sarah Grimké had begun closing her correspondence with the phrase, "Thine in the bonds of womanhood." Implicit in her choice of words were the premises of the early feminist movement: women's oppression combined with their common experience of domesticity to create a bond of sisterhood that transcended class and racial lines. From the outset, such assertions of collective identity had obscured profound structural differences in women's lives. Black women in particular had been ignored and excluded and, for the most part, they had seen their interests in racial rather than in sexual terms. As the earliest attempt to build a women's organization in the South explicitly devoted to overcoming the barriers of race, the Woman's Committee testified to the tenacity and motivating power of the ideal of female solidarity. At the same time, it was shaped by the hierarchical social order from which it emerged, and the goal of meeting as equals on what Johnson called "the platform of Christ Jesus" and the "psychological basis" of motherhood had proven easier to assert than to accomplish in day-to-day institutional life. [143]

By the end of the 1920s, interracial gatherings had begun to lose their symbolic impact. The novelty of meeting educated black women had worn off; white leaders as well as blacks began searching for a more effective mode of operation, for more realizable goals. Increasingly, the director of the Woman's Committee turned to the work of Jessie Daniel Ames in the Southwest as a model for plans and precedures. Ames brought to the movement an instrumentalist approach to social issues that set her apart from her more religiously oriented coworkers. Spurred by a rise in racial violence at the onset of the Depression, this "person of practical mind" would channel the Woman's Committee away from interracialism and into an elaborately organized single-issue campaign against lynching. [144] In doing so, she would link the language and assumptions of the evangelical women's movement with the pragmatic, issue-oriented style of the secular struggle for women's participation in public life.

Chapter 4
The Double Role

While the CIC Woman's Committee struggled for self-definition and concrete results, the state chairman from Texas pursued a vigorous program of interracial cooperation and social
welfare reform. Jessie Daniel Ames's efficiency and assurance
attracted the attention of the leadership of the regional Interracial Commission, and she rose to a position of prominence
within the organization. But beneath the surface of her successful career lay a continuing source of tension: the effort to balance "women's two roles"—public work and private, family
life.[1] In the Texas interracial movement, Ames developed the
social analysis she brought to the anti-lynching campaign of the
thirties; in the experience of family tragedy, her characteristic
patterns of feeling and behavior were both supplemented and
intensified. The political activism of the suffrage generation
subsided, but Jessie Daniel Ames remained in the public
arena, exchanging her identity as a Texas progressive for a
place in the ranks of an indigenous southern racial liberalism.

1

In the first years after suffrage, Ames perceived no conflict
between her dawning interest in the situation of blacks and her
commitment to women's rights and progressive reform. She
did not use her position as head of the League of Women

Voters to speak out on racial issues, but she did employ her influence and contacts behind the scenes in behalf of her new cause. In order to train herself both academically and practically in the field of race relations, she enrolled in extension courses offered by Robert E. Park's pioneering sociology department at the University of Chicago. As she studied the "Principles of Collective Behavior" and "The Negro in America," she acquired a library of books on race relations that ultimately included over two thousand volumes; soon she was adding to her repertoire lectures on racial problems "both learned and interesting."[2]

The argument Ames presented on the Texas lecture circuit was a standard synthesis of the themes of the early interracial movement. In the context of the times, however, she and her co-workers considered their message "a difficult . . . and a dangerous one." On the one hand, they confronted moderate whites loath to admit the existence of racial problems; on the other, their plea for change was almost drowned out by the voice of the Ku Klux Klan. Ames's carefully worded addresses thus stressed the interdependence of the races and the necessity of a better-educated and more efficient black labor force. She assured her audiences that the Interracial Commission—unlike such earlier biracial groups as the NAACP and the Urban League—was southern born and southern led. The Negro must be given "fair living conditions," she pled, "a square deal in the courts," protection from mob violence, and "a chance to grow up as a worthy product of the South, wherein his destiny was unalterably cast."[3]

By 1929, with her broadening responsibilities in the regional CIC, she had begun to deliver stronger fare. She distinguished her own brand of paternalism from that of bourbon traditionalists. The comforting image of the "old darkies" must go. Technological progress left no room in the economy for "12,000,000 . . . servants." In their place stood the articulate and demanding "New Negro." The South perched on the edge of industrialization, and the task of the coming decade was the assimilation of "the New Negro into the New Southland."[4]

The major problem Ames faced was how to turn study into concrete action. She had fled the world of female evangelicalism; yet, she recalled, "I knew the language." And when secular women's organizations proved unresponsive to her new concerns, she looked to missionary societies as a means of reaching women in the rural and small-town south.[5] A card file on each Southern Methodist social service chairman in the state provided a mailing list for CIC literature; once these local leaders had been "cultivated" from Ames's office in Georgetown, she visited each of them personally, "clinching sentiment" for interracial cooperation in areas "that had never been touched with the germ of citizenship" and involving church women's groups in investigations of black living conditions in their own communities.[6]

Jessie Daniel Ames's efficient methods brought such "relief and satisfaction" to Carrie Parks Johnson that in January 1924 she offered Ames a salaried staff position as field worker for Texas. "I didn't come cheap," Ames recalled, and she accepted the position at a salary greater in proportion to her part-time services than Johnson received for her full-time regional work. No longer a high-powered volunteer, Ames had taken a decisive step toward defining her professional career. In the space provided by a shifting caste system, individuals like Jessie Daniel Ames began to function as race-relations experts speaking to and for the white middle class on behalf of racial moderation.[7]

Within a few months, Ames expanded her activities beyond the borders of Texas, answering speaking requests throughout the South and taking over more and more of Johnson's responsibilities. Soon she was presiding over regional CIC Woman's Committee meetings, as Johnson became increasingly incapacitated by ill health and overwork. By the end of 1924, Ames had been named the first woman executive director of a state interracial committee as well as salaried field representative for the whole Southwest.[8]

Appropriately, Ames won her first triumph in her new professional role in a setting dominated by her older sister. In 1912, Lulu's husband, James Chappell Hardy, had assumed the presidency of the Gulf Coast Military Academy in Long Beach, Mississippi. As head of the Mississippi Federation of Women's Clubs, Lulu, in Ames's opinion, had become the "most influential woman in the state." Mississippi women were present at the Memphis meeting of 1920, but women's interracial work had made virtually no headway there. In April 1924, Ames took on the task of bringing the message of interracial cooperation to this formidable and socially elite group.[9] "After worrying myself sick over the kind of an impression that I should make for the cause," she recalled, "I discarded my three speeches, rose up when I was introduced and spoke for thirty-five minutes. . . . I was quite amazed when I finished at the length of applause I received." In addition to Ames, the president of the Mississippi Federation of Colored Women's Clubs appealed to the convention for cooperation in improving the treatment of domestic servants. In response, the federation—a number of whose members were "kluxers"—set up a Committee on the Condition of the Colored People. The way was open for Johnson to organize a CIC woman's committee in Mississippi. "I had," Ames concluded, "the experience of my life."[10]

A few months later, Ames reported another successful undertaking to central CIC headquarters. In response to the tensions of neighborhood transition and black migration in the early twenties, a Community Protective League had been organized in Dallas. Its purpose was ostensibly to "conserve civic righteousness and promote friendly relations between races." In practice, it sought to remove blacks from the zone of emergence between the inner city and the white residential fringe and to isolate them in an area of Dallas that it "pictured as the Ilysian Fields in the land of Utopia." Mass meetings were held and violence threatened. Ames's successor as director of the Texas Woman's Committee had done nothing about the situation, "feeling that it was a man's job." But the new field worker swept into town, met with black CIC women, called on newspaper editors and influential friends, and convinced the state CIC to proceed expeditiously with a survey of housing conditions in the black community. The plan for a survey was presented both to the City Commission and to the Protective League, in the hope that each would defer action— "the white people because they do want a frictionless solution and the [City] Commission because they are not sure yet whether the Klan or the Anti-Klan element will predominate in the spring election." [11] .

The Interracial Commission's research revealed that over half the black homes in Dallas were unfit for human habitation. The solution advocated by the group typified the stance of white racial liberals in the period. Tensions arising from what the Dallas press called the "age old problem of the 'border line' " could be reduced by enforcing residential separation of lower-class whites and blacks. At the same time, the inequities bred by segregation must be ameliorated. Only improvement in the housing conditions of blacks—particularly those "educated . . . toward thrift and refinement by the white man"—could prevent encroachments on white neighborhoods. [12]

In addition to speaking engagements, cultivation of local women's groups, and crisis management, Ames also undertook special projects. She continued the effort, begun by the Texas Joint Legislative Council in 1923, to establish a training school for delinquent Negro girls. Although the state legislature had approved construction of the school, no appropriation had been forthcoming. Consequently, the Texas Federation of Colored Women's Clubs took matters into its own hands, purchasing the land for the school and enlisting Jessie Daniel Ames's aid in convincing the state to take over the project. On a six month tour in 1926, Ames presented the need for such a facility to women's organizations, conferences of social agencies, and members of the legislature. She solicited letters and petitions from organized women to key legislators. In 1927, the state finally provided funds to sustain the project. [13]

Ames's most extensive endeavor as CIC field representative was an educational and legislative campaign against lynching. During her youth in East Texas and her activities in William-

son County, Ames had encountered at first hand the sexual
fears and racial stereotypes that nurtured mob violence. In
1915, the Williamson County *Sun* reported a narrowly averted
lynching: If the "brute" who had committed the "dastardly
deed" of attempted rape of a farmer's wife had not been spirited away, the paper claimed, three fourths of the citizens of
Georgetown would have joined in executing him. A few weeks
later the *Sun* carried the story of the lynching of Will Stanley,
"Black Fiend, Rapist and Murderer of Three Innocent Little
Children," in nearby Temple, Texas. An "orderly crowd" of
5,000 people burned Stanley at the stake. "The will of the people had prevailed," concluded the paper. In the 1920s, the
paper deplored mob violence in general and applauded officials
who upheld the law, but it continued to maintain that lynching
was an inevitable reaction to rape. "Abstractly we are against
mob violence," concluded one editorial, "but negro rapists,
North or South, must die; by the law if possible; without the
law if need be." [14]

The local approbation Ames had enjoyed in her rise to leadership in the League of Women Voters and Democratic Party
politics did not extend to her new role. She found herself
speaking against mob violence to audiences who assumed "that
no Southern woman of fine sensibilities would speak the word
'lynching' in private, to say nothing of talking from a platform
about it by name." "Nigger lover" was whispered behind the
back of Georgetown's most outspoken citizen, and anonymous
letters denounced her betrayal of caste solidarity. Warned one
writer, "God will burn . . . the Big African Brute in Hot Hell
for molesting our God-like pure snowwhite angelic American
Women." [15]

Undeterred by public opinion, Ames moved quickly from
pronouncements to action. "We could talk . . . in little circles
if we wanted to but we had to get enough people behind us
and that was what we set out to do," she recalled. She began
by conducting on-the-scene investigations of lynching incidents. Discovering a wide disparity between the facts as she
knew them and the way lynchings were reported in the press,

she confronted newspaper editors with the effects of their biased and inflammatory coverage and succeeded in winning the support of the influential owner of the Dallas *Morning News*. In addition, she sought the cooperation of county sheriffs and lobbied for an anti-lynching law in the state legislature.[16]

The tactics used in this early crusade against lynching reflected Ames's conception of the task of the reformer: she considered personal investigations, public speaking, pressure on newspaper editors and local law-enforcement officials, and state anti-lynching legislation not as ends in themselves but as methods of changing public opinion. A lobbying campaign for anti-lynching legislation, for example, was predicated on the notion of legal reform as a vehicle of public education rather than on faith in the power of the state to restrain lynch mobs. "A legislative program," Ames explained,

> is valuable in proportion to the amount of educational work accomplished. We are no longer susceptible to propaganda pure, so that in order to reach the thinking person, some action must be involved. The legislative method of education cannot be too highly recommended in all social work. The more that social projects are in conflict with the accepted prejudices, traditions and habits of society, the more valuable is a legislative program as a method of procedure in educating people.[17]

Ames's attempt at "educating people" about the consequences of extralegal violence brought her into confrontation with neighbors and friends who joined the growing ranks of the Klan. By 1922, Williamson County Klavern no. 178 was able to attract a large crowd to an open-air initiation of one hundred new members. In the following months, Klansmen consolidated their support by appearing at local churches in full regalia and placing ads in the county newspaper.[18] In April 1923, Georgetown witnessed one of the more notorious of the period's incidents of Klan brutality when local members savagely beat a salesman named Robert W. Burleson, accused of an illicit sexual relationship with a widow in nearby Taylor.

Brought to trial in September, two of the Klansmen, one of whom was a Georgetown Baptist minister, were convicted and given prison sentences. This case helped end the violent phase of Klan activity in Texas, and it provided a springboard for the political ambitions of the young Williamson County prosecuting attorney, Dan Moody. Ames, who sat through the entire Burleson trial and thought the young attorney "acquitted himself nobly," helped throw the weight of the interracial committee and of organized women behind Moody's career and against the Klan.[19]

In 1924, the Klan, led from Atlanta by ambitious, Texas-born Hiram Wesley Evans, moved into presidential politics. The organization controlled a large majority of Texas's 254 county conventions and chose two-thirds of the delegates to the state nominating convention in Waco. But owing partly to the work of Jessie Daniel Ames, Williamson County sent anti-Klan representatives, including Ames herself, to the state convention. At the Democratic National Convention in Madison Square Garden, the Texas delegation had to be restrained from demonstrating its sentiments with a fiery cross, while Ames gained statewide attention by advocating a plank in the party platform condemning the Klan by name. With Ames voicing her dissent, the Texas delegation, bound by the unit rule, went down the line for William Gibbs McAdoo and the Ku Klux Klan.[20]

Returning home, Ames continued her fight against the hooded order by supporting Dan Moody in his successful campaign for state attorney general. When James E. Ferguson placed his wife's name in nomination against the Klan's gubernatorial candidate, Judge Felix D. Robertson, Ames foreswore old animosities and moved into the Ferguson ranks. Mrs. Miriam Amanda "Ma" Ferguson gained the backing of a broad, incongruous coalition that included "dry" middle-class progressives and "wet" urbanites, big businessmen who feared the chaos engendered by the Klan, traditionally pro-Ferguson tenant farmers, the major daily papers, and nervous politicians who saw a chance to end the Klan's unpredictable effect on state politics.[21] For many organized women, however, the preeminent issue remained—as Robertson insisted—not the Klan but prohibition; and Ames was hard-pressed to defend her support of Ma Ferguson to her allies in the LWV and the WCTU. Ames said later that supporting Ferguson "was a perfectly awful thing to do. But I supported her because the man running against her was a scoundrel. . . . a Ku Kluxer [who] had suddenly become a prohibitionist. . . . I made speeches all over the state, but I didn't speak about Ma Ferguson. I spoke about this man."[22] With Ames's help—but against the opposition of most women's groups—Ma Ferguson became the first female governor in Texas history.

Two years later, when Dan Moody entered the governor's race, organized women once more united behind a political candidate. Through the Texas Women's Citizen Committee for Dan Moody for Governor, Ames worked "to the limit of [her] endurance" for the election of the young man whom she regarded as her protégé. Secure in her position as a veteran of tough "wrestling matches" with Texas politicians, she demanded for the Women's Committee an equitable share of campaign funds, a well-paid chairman, and a full-time secretary. "Men always have plenty of money to spend on campaigns," she remarked; she was "past the day when she thought women should stint and economize."[23] On the campaign trail, Ames drew enthusiastic audiences and favorable press coverage. The county attorney of San Saba, Texas, for example, commented with poor spelling but great enthusiasm:

Mrs. Jesse Daniel Aimes of Georgetown, Texas, spoke here last night. . . . Mrs. Aimes is a wonderful woman, talented, capable, earnest, tactful and very beautiful in her language and manner. . . . She brings "first hand" information about Mr. Moody, having sat althru the now famous Klan trial at Georgetown and she told of Mr. Mood's having personally conducted the trial and successfully destroyed the first efforts of the hooded order to get controll of the politics and the courts of this State. . . . I only wish that every woman in Texas, all the men to, could hear this good woman deliver her address; if they could surely there would be but one result on the 24th, and that would be Mr. Moody's carrying the State by an overwhelming majority over both candidates, which he deserves to do.[24]

Dan Moody did carry the election on the twenty-fourth, and with his election, Jessie Daniel Ames believed she had an ally for the interracial cause in the governor's mansion. Contrary to her expectations, however, Moody's prosecution of the Burleson flogging case did not signify a commitment to ending racial violence. She was bitterly disappointed by his failure, once in office, to take strong measures to prevent lynchings and prosecute mob members. Her disapproval widened into an open rift during the presidential campaign of 1928, when she believed that Moody betrayed the principles of the progressive coalition by failing to push for a strong prohibition plank in the national Democratic Party platform.[25]

By the end of the decade, Ames's involvement in the interracial movement, together with her disputes with Dan Moody, had increasingly alienated her from her suffragist allies. Interpersonal conflicts rose to the surface as the unity and optimism of the women's rights crusade faded, new issues came to the fore, and party politicians extended token recognition to individual women leaders. Minnie Fisher Cunningham and Jane Y. McCallum, in contrast to Ames, maintained unwavering loyalty to Dan Moody and the Democratic Party. McCallum, in particular, held "that boy" in reverential esteem. As head of the Women's Citizen Committee for Moody in 1926, she had viewed Ames as a potential rival "brainy enough and attractive enough to be dangerous." When Moody won the governorship in 1928, he rewarded McCallum with the position of Secretary of State—an appointment that Ames considered a means of undermining the adversary stance of organized women.[26]

Even more serious than her political disagreements with Moody and McCallum was Ames's break with Cunningham. After years of campaigning for her male allies, Cunningham decided to make her own bid for political office. The results were devastating. In a 1928 primary race for the U.S. Senate, she came in a poor fifth in a field of six. "She organized bril-

liantly for others," observed a contemporary, "but she couldn't
do it for herself. Something withered within her after the campaign." Cunningham blamed her defeat on progressives who
assumed that a woman couldn't win and on Democratic women
who stayed out of the primary to vote for Herbert Hoover in
the general election.[27] Jessie Daniel Ames was among those
who withheld active support from Cunningham's bid for office,
and the two women never regained their former friendship.

Ames parted ways with McCallum and Cunningham over
questions of principle and political strategy. But her conflicts
with them had a personal dimension as well. McCallum, described as "the gently reared daughter" of a prominent family,
was a member of the Colonial Dames and the wife of the superintendent of the Austin public school system. Even during
the suffrage campaign, she seems to have taken offense at the
rough-edged manner of the "country woman" from Georgetown. Cunningham managed to keep peace between her two
lieutenants, urging McCallum to make allowances for Ames's
lack of "acquired poise" and to appreciate the contributions of a
co-worker who "does three women's work every day of this
world." For her part, Ames refrained from critical personal
comments; she seems, however, to have identified McCallum
with the pretentious *crème de la crème* of southern womanhood
and to have had serious reservations about her "political acu-
men."[28]

Ames and Cunningham, on the other hand, possessed markedly similar personalities. Contemporaries saw the two women
as "whirlwinds in themselves": charismatic, highly intelligent,
with a consuming interest in political life. Both were "prima
donnas." Perhaps inevitably, as Ames became a leader in her
own right, both women turned elsewhere for what Cunningham termed "friendship & loyalty & backing."[29] In the
late twenties, Ames developed a close relationship with an unconventional Williamson County woman named Frank King,
who ran a large ranch and dressed as a man. The two women
shared an ironic sense of humor and a cynicism about a "Democratic machine" that could so readily be "stolen or bought" by

"masked bandits." Most importantly, King adopted a warm, protective loyalty toward the woman she addressed as "my general." Ames and Cunningham, too competitive and strong-minded to supply each other's need for unquestioning admiration and loyalty, grew apart. Whatever the complex sources of their estrangement, it formed another link in a pattern that marred Jessie Daniel Ames's affective life. Only one oblique reference indicates her feelings about this lost friendship: Minnie Fisher Cunningham, like her father, her sister, and her husband, had "used [her] devotion," had betrayed her love. [30]

Despite these disappointments, Ames's years in the Texas interracial movement were among the most satisfying of her reform career. For all its caution and moderation, the movement represented a significant departure for white southerners like Jessie Daniel Ames. It offered participants an exhilarating conviction of unlimited and unknown potential. "Movements such as ours must gather momentum," Ames remarked. In the decade of the twenties, she had no doubt that she was in on the beginning of a campaign that would bring about substantial social change. It was a period when convincing a conference on social welfare to include the subject of race relations on a program could be considered "a truly progressive accomplishment"; and Ames felt that her record of such successes in the field was "dynamite." Her new job was hard work, she wrote, "but intensely interesting . . . calling for all the tact, the brains, the training and the mentality which I have been accumulating in these last seven years of handling all kinds of people in all conditions. . . . My years of working with wild-eyed women and suave politicians have stood me in good stead." Ames was a "fighter by nature," and the drama of the race issue during the era of the Ku Klux Klan suited her temperament perfectly. With equal relish, she acted as a gadfly to bastions of conservatism like a Methodist Bishops Conference, filled a speaking engagement in "a Klan hotbed," and acted as a troubleshooter in areas where other women feared to tread. [31] Under Ames's leadership, the Texas CIC became one of the few state councils to achieve financial independence and one of the more successful and sustained CIC efforts.[32]

2

By the end of the decade, Jessie Daniel Ames was rapidly divorcing herself from a "local outlook" and moving into a position of regional standing. Gone was the diffidence of her years as a "private in the ranks" of the suffrage movement.[33] Within the sphere of influence carved out by organized women, she took second place to no one, and her letters of the period reflect the self-confidence and optimism of a woman at the height of her powers.

Yet Ames's public success was accompanied by unremitting private struggle. Unlike many of her associates in Texas politics and the interracial movement, she was not motivated by the need to fill the leisure time created by middle-class affluence and technological progress. On the contrary, she pursued her reform activities against a backdrop of economic necessity as she worked to support herself and her three children. Her official positions in the women's movement brought no remuneration, and the opportunity for gainful employment contributed to the eagerness with which she offered her services to the Interracial Commission. Even this modest salary, however, was never adequate to her family's needs. Corporate consolidation made survival increasingly difficult for small telephone companies like that of the Ames women; and in 1927, they sold their business to Southwestern States Telephone Company. After 1933, when her mother lost her investments in the Depression, Ames's financial situation worsened. "I stayed in the ring for another ten and a half years," she recalled, "but only by grim will power." Her two oldest children, Frederick and Mary, entered medical school, adding to her economic difficulties: "furniture mortgaged, car mortgaged . . . bank notes up to the hilt." [34] Throughout her career, Ames was forced to reconcile her duties as a provider with her will toward achievement and public work; and she did so in a society that offered neither cultural sanctions nor institutional support for women who made such a choice. "When I undertake a piece of public work," she said,

> I give out from my home every piece of work that I can employ done without harm to my family, but which would relieve me of a drain both on my own time and strength. I find that a woman can be borne down . . . with the making of gingham dresses and darning stockings in her leisure hours instead of keeping fit in order to be able to go before people in a none-too-popular cause and convert them to her belief. [35]

Her Georgetown neighbors found much to criticize in the unorthodox Ames household. Her children, comparing their situation to that of their peers, sometimes felt "orphaned and neglected"; at the same time they labored under the demand to live up to their mother's model of personal strength, professional success, and intellectual ability. [36] For her part, Ames strove to demonstrate her competence as a mother no less than her ability as a reformer. In the end, her financial sacrifices and her children's resentment became a source of grinding family conflict. "I had to play the double role" of mother and father, she wrote, "and the strain produced a sort of frustration which will go with me to my death." [37]

Most importantly, after 1920, Ames carried more than the ordinary burdens of family life. In November of that year, she was summoned home from the annual meeting of the Texas Federation of Women's Clubs in the middle of the night. She arrived to find her five-year-old daughter Lulu near death. With the aid of her husband's medical books, Ames correctly diagnosed the illness as one of the most dreaded childhood diseases of the time: infantile paralysis. Although Lulu lived through the night, the effects of polio were permanent and crippling. [38]

The years that followed, Ames wrote, were "the hardest of

any of my entire life."[39] Two months after Lulu's paralysis, Ames placed her in a Dallas sanatorium. Over the next six weeks she traveled back and forth from Georgetown, each parting more difficult than the last. "I was on the fourth or fifth floor," Lulu recalled. "And when she left me the first time, she could hear me screaming for her all the way down." This separation from her mother left the child in "an hysteria of terror," and Ames became increasingly convinced that the treatment her daughter received could not justify its emotional costs. Ignoring her doctor's advice and trusting her own intuition, she removed Lulu from the hospital and began to care for her at home.[40]

Over the next six years, Ames focused her will, her intelligence, her tremendous energy on her youngest child. She consulted friends, physicians, and parents of other stricken children. She ordered medical texts and, through trial and error, devised a regimen of "psychology, physical training, massage, hydrotherapy, splints [and] crutches." Against her own judgment, she bowed to community pressure to explore the promises of faith healers and chiropractors.[41] Feeling her way through a maze of contradictory advice and medical ignorance, she lived in dread that she was "making mistakes which will later warp [Lulu's] whole life." She vacillated between despair and the hope that her daughter was "bound to recover completely, given time and patience and perseverance."[42]

By the summer of 1923, it had become apparent that physical therapy could not prevent the onset of deformity, and Ames submitted her daughter to a series of excruciating operations. The worst of these took place in a charity hospital in Dallas during the first six months of 1924. The ordeal began as Ames fought to have Lulu admitted to an institution open only to the absolutely destitute. When a physician warned her that her prominence in the state might hinder her daughter's entrance to the hospital, she reacted with pent-up bitterness.

> I have always known . . . [that the Shrine Hospital] was being built not so much from a desire to serve crippled children as to serve the vanity of prosperous middle aged men under the guise

[of] philanthropy. . . . I am not poor from the standpoint of some tho heaven knows I would be considered poverty stricken from the standpoint of others. I have credit and always can borrow on it to secure whatever I need for Lulu and shall do so to the last penny. I am a self supporting widow who seems to have gained enough prominence to withold [sic] from her the most necessary thing of my life.[43]

By the time Lulu gained admittance to the hospital, Ames was "skirting the edge of a nervous collapse." To spare Lulu the jolt of frequent partings and herself the humiliation of losing her self-control, she remained at home in Georgetown while doctors labored to straighten her nine-year-old daughter's crippled body.[44]

The relationship between mother and daughter that grew out of these experiences was one of painful ambiguity. "Wholly dependent, therefore wholly defenseless," Lulu took refuge behind a self-protective barrier of silence and a "reputation for courage." To her aunt and most trusted advisor, Dr. Annie Sturges Daniel, Ames described this dynamic:

> when Lulu has to face a thing, like a hospital or an operation, she has steeled herself to do so without outward protest. She always smiles and never complains. She is obsessed with a fear of other people except members of her immediate family. When she had her last operation she suffered for days and could not speak for pain. In the first hospital the nurses told me that she would wake at two in the morning and sing softly to herself. They thought it was lovely. I thought it was tragic.[45]

Lulu perceived herself as a lifelong burden to her mother. Craving acceptance, she suffered under the conviction of having failed to live up to her mother's expectations of recovery. She believed that her mother, after an unhappy marriage, had been energized and liberated by the suffrage movement. "The children were coming up all right . . . and she could live a life, she could be something." Then tragedy struck. "I always knew what it did to mother," she recalled. "That was one thing she couldn't whip."[46] As she reached adolescence, Lulu became bitterly hostile toward the woman on whom she depended so

completely. Many years later, she came to believe that only
her mother's death freed her to accept the reality of her physical condition.[47]

Like her contemporary, Eleanor Roosevelt, whose refusal to
accept her husband's invalidism in 1924 enabled him to return
to politics, Jessie Daniel Ames ensured her daughter an active
and useful life. When Lulu eventually finished college and followed her mother into business and politics, Ames viewed her
daughter's self-sufficiency as her own "greatest achievement."
But unlike Eleanor Roosevelt, Ames nurtured not a strong and
self-defined man but a small and uncomprehending child. As
her determination seemed at times clinical and oppressive to
her daughter, so it may have seemed, at times, even to Jessie
herself. Undoubtedly this experience helped transform Jessie
Daniel Ames into a woman of unusual maturity and force of
character. Yet it reinforced other traits as well. "I think
[mother's] emotions burned out on me," Lulu recalled. "And
thereafter it was strictly mind, intellect, and no emotions."
Steeling her heart against her child's suffering, Ames became a
more controlled and less accessible person.[48]

In 1928, Maud Henderson, who had replaced Carrie Parks
Johnson as Director of Woman's Work, resigned from the Interracial Commission. When the Woman's Committee recommended that Jessie Daniel Ames be named to the post, she accepted the opportunity without hesitation. By moving to
Atlanta, she would abandon sustaining community ties, but she
would also escape the entangling watchfulness of small-town
life and increasingly unsatisfying political relationships. Although periodically she would long to "shake the red clay of
Georgia off my feet" and return home, Texas no longer offered
the means of meeting her financial needs or the avenues for advancement, public acclaim, and social service she desired.[49]

Jessie Daniel Ames moved to Atlanta in May 1929 to become

Director of Woman's Work for the Commission on Interracial Cooperation. She had not, however, left personal conflicts and internal organizational controversies behind. On the contrary, her move had been delayed because of friction with CIC Director Will Alexander, who viewed the assumption of responsibility and authority by the "younger professional woman" from Texas with mixed feelings.[50] When Ames had tried to discuss with him the possibility of becoming permanent field worker for the Southwest, the results had been unsatisfying. "I am never sure," she commented, "that he has spoken freely when he talks to me. I am left with a general idea that he didn't go as far as he might have if I were a man. And I am so used to fighting every step of the way that this lovely consideration of me as a woman is absolutely new."[51] Now that she was being offered the position of Director of Woman's Work, Alexander resisted her appointment "like the dickens." According to Ames, he "expressed this great admiration for the work I had done in Texas" but pointed out that the Southwest was "so different from the Deep South. . . . He told me that I had such a definite way of walking and talking that I would be marked as not a southern woman. . . . He went on," she concluded, "until he made me mad and I decided to terminate the interview and I said, 'Now listen, I'm coming here and I'm coming here for a year. . . . And if I find out that I can't get any acceptance . . . I'll go back home.'"[52]

The impression Ames made on her co-workers at CIC headquarters did little to allay Alexander's fears. Robert E. Eleazer, Educational Director, believed that a woman's role was to be a "gracious hostess," and the new Director of Woman's Work could scarcely have been further from his ideal. Another staff member recalled, "she had a touch of the suffragette about her, in revolt against a male-dominated world." At issue seems to have been the degree to which Ames conformed to the normative demands of ladyhood. Her admirers perceived her as brilliant and compelling. She had a "built in self-charging dynamo," reflected a friend. Jessie "held her head high." Her critics saw her as abrasive and domineering. Whether in admiration

or dislike, her contemporaries agreed that she bent expectations of gentleness and gentility. She was assertive, outspoken,
unsentimental, and accustomed to being in charge. She made
people "want to listen to her by virtue of her animation and
dynamism," summed up one astute observer. "I would say she
was a kind of a fervent person, but she did not have any
warmth in the sense of southern femininity; she did not have
that."

In any case, Ames made no effort to cover up what she
termed "my disposition and my origins." And by the end of her
trial year she had won the support of the Woman's Committee
and the grudging respect of the CIC staff. Latent friction remained, but not until the end of the decade did it erupt into
serious questions of policy and authority.[53]

Partly because of this inauspicious beginning, Ames's first
move was designed to strengthen her official position within
the CIC. She had been proud of her ability to work with men
on a basis of equality in Democratic Party politics and in the
Texas Interracial Commission, and she was determined not to
remain for long the head of a subordinate women's auxiliary.
"At the annual meeting of the Commission," Ames recalled dis-
dainfully,

> the Woman's Committee would meet the day before the men and
> then we would come in and sit with the men and *listen* to what was
> being done! . . . Well, I was Director of Woman's Work but my
> first determination was to do away with the Woman's Committee
> and get us right into the main stream. I don't believe in segrega-
> tion. . . . I didn't make the approach to Dr. Alexander—I was still
> a politician. . . . I sold it to the women and they took it up with
> [him]. I didn't know whether he had any idea that I was back of it,
> but if he didn't he was more feeble-minded than I think he was.[54]

The Woman's Committee, in its meeting on September 21,
1929, resolved to develop state committees along "lines which
would eliminate a division on the basis of sex," and Mary
McLeod Bethune, the black commission member whose support was to prove most valuable to Ames on other occasions,
moved that the title of Director of Woman's Work be changed

to Assistant Director of the General Commission. Nevertheless, despite Ames's careful plans, men's and women's work remained officially separated.[55]

Soon after this setback, Ames also faced the disaffection of an important element of her constituency—Southern Presbyterian Church women. Mrs. W. C. Winsborough, the founder and superintendent of the Presbyterian Women's Auxiliary, had become increasingly impatient with the slow progress of the Interracial Woman's Committee and unhappy with the predominance of Methodist women in the organization. Will Alexander feared the effects of bureaucratization and was firmly committed to creating a "movement" rather than an organization.[56] But Winsborough believed that "Dr. Alexander has always been misunderstood about this—We can surely not hope to carry a program without *well* organized and functioning groups behind it." The New York–based Commission on Race Relations of the Federal Council of Churches, she argued, had exactly such an organizational base. She threatened to pull Southern Presbyterian women out of the CIC and join "the northern group, with their [will] to accomplish things [rather than] go forward with tentative plans and no force behind them."[57] Alarmed at this threat to her organization, Ames sought and received the backing of her executive committee. Mary McLeod Bethune reassured her that only the decade of work done by the CIC had enabled the Federal Council of Churches "to get glimpses" of the interracial work they were now attempting. "Our strength is our weakness," wrote another executive committee member. "All great beneficent movements are slow."[58]

Encouraged by this support, Ames arranged a meeting with Winsborough at which they hammered out a new organizational plan for CIC women's work, calling for grass-roots interdenominational cooperation. In a pilot project in Tuscaloosa, Alabama, under Winsborough's direction, Methodist and Presbyterian Christian Social Relations chairmen were to work together on a survey of "conditions of Negro life" in their localities. Resources in the form of study guides, books, and speakers would be supplied by the CIC. The plan, reported the Methodist Woman's Missionary Council, was "a long-needed device for making our 'paper' interracial Committees truly active in the communities and in welding all denominations in the common cause." The "quality and quantity" of interracial activities among local church groups seemed to increase, and observers attributed the improvement to "the generalship, the insight, and practial ability of Mrs. Ames."[59]

Thus during Ames's first year in Atlanta, she continued, with some success, to conduct CIC women's work along the lines developed in the early twenties by Carrie Parks Johnson and the Methodist women. Outside the churches, however,. interracial groups remained discouraged and uncertain of their purpose and direction.[60] They could not satisfy Jessie Daniel Ames's desire for concrete results and a visible impact on public life. When 1930 brought an upsurge in racial violence, she seized the opportunity to launch a women's campaign against lynching: single-issue in focus, elaborately organized, and part of a larger movement that ultimately brought an end to the long reign of lynch law in the South.

With the founding of the Association of Southern Women for the Prevention of Lynching, Jessie Daniel Ames dedicated herself to this one cause with extraordinary single-mindedness. Lynching, she believed, was preeminently a women's issue, generated by cultural assumptions as degrading to white women as they were oppressive to blacks. A women's campaign against mob violence would allow her to fuse her feminism with her perception of racial inequity and to pit her skills as an organizer and publicist against a phenomenon she associated both with arbitrary power and with the dark underside of the "emotional life of the South."[61] As a CIC leader in the Southwest in the 1920s, Ames had asserted that the excuses of lynch mobs frequently had little to do with their true motives. Now she undertook to discover the roots of a practice deeply obscured by the mythology of white racism. To understand the import of this attempt at social analysis and political strategy we must turn, in the chapter that follows, to lynching itself: to its history and function in southern political culture and, most importantly, to the relationship between lynching and inter-racial sex.

Chapter 5
A Strange and Bitter Fruit

On May 9, 1930, a Sherman, Texas, mob lynched a black farm laborer named George Hughes. Hughes was accused of raping his employer's wife in revenge against "the white folks [who] hated him and his race." But the story told in the black community, and whispered in the white, was both chilling and prosaic: an altercation over wages had ended in mob violence.[1]

The community where the lynching took place lay in a sparsely populated farming region in East Texas, where, for a decade, white farmers had been forcing blacks off the land. "Nigger, don't let the sun go down on you here," was a common phrase in the region, and by 1930 most remaining blacks lived in or near the larger towns. In Sherman, a relatively prosperous black middle class had grown up, while poorer blacks found employment in service and domestic jobs. The success of black merchants was a smoldering affront to the caste system, and the onset of the Depression exacerbated tensions between black and white wage earners. Hughes himself was a newcomer to the town. Illiterate and allegedly "feeble-minded," he and his wife were said by local Negroes to be "denizens of the underworld."

Once Hughes had been arrested and indicted, lurid rumors had begun to circulate through the county: the defendant had raped the woman three times in succession, mutilated her, and infected her with venereal disease. Hughes, reported the local county attorney, was a "beast who knew what he wanted and meant to have it, hell and hanging notwithstanding." By the

time the trial began, white farmers from the surrounding countryside were converging on the town. Although Governor Dan
Moody sent four Texas Rangers in a halfhearted attempt to
forestall violence, the crowd, emboldened by word that Moody
had instructed the rangers not to shoot and enraged at the
sight of the woman carried into the courtroom on a stretcher,
set fire to the building. Left in a second-floor vault, Hughes
died in the flames. The police directed traffic, while men
dragged the corpse to a cottonwood tree in the Negro business
section. There it was burned; afterward the crowd looted and
destroyed most of the black-owned property in town. In the
months that followed employers were warned to dismiss their
black laborers, and many black families left the area altogether.

In addition to George Hughes, nineteen black men and one
foreign-born white died at the hands of lynch mobs in 1930.
This sudden upsurge of mob violence, after a decade of steady
decline, became the impetus for the creation of the Association
of Southern Women for the Prevention of Lynching. The size
of the Sherman crowd, the burning of the courthouse, and the
complicity of a moderate governor gave the Hughes lynching a
special notoriety. But in its origins, development, and aftermath, it typified the deeply rooted tradition of extralegal racial
violence these women reformers set out to combat.

1

The American tradition of vigilante justice first emerged on
the eighteenth-century frontier. The terms "lynch law" and
"lynching" gained currency during the Revolutionary War
when Charles Lynch of Bedford County, Virginia, formed a
vigilante association to rid the area of plundering Tories. After
the war, the Virginia legislature exonerated Lynch for his actions on the grounds that circumstances may arise under which
"measures taken . . . may not be strictly warranted by law, although justifiable from the imminence of the danger."[2]

Throughout the nineteenth century, frontier elites routinely banded together to impose social order in areas where population was sparse, officials few, and legal machinery rudimentary. Such "establishment violence" became a half-accepted aspect of American political life.[3]

In the antebellum South, lynch law helped suppress both white dissidence and slave rebellion. The planter's self-interest and the ideology of pateralism gave a measure of protection to the slaves, and before the Civil War many victims of vigilante violence were white.[4] Nevertheless, the cycle of slave-insurrection panics, in which vigilance committees conducted mock trials, extracted confessions by torture, and staged public executions, set a bloody precedent for racial lynchings.[5]

When the war began, lynching took on new significance as a systematic weapon of terror against blacks. As early as 1866, while white southerners still maintained political control, the head of the Freedmen's Bureau in Georgia reported that bands of vigilantes were committing the "most fiendish and diabolical outrages on the freedmen." During the decade of Radical Reconstruction, the lynching of black men and the rape of black women became the most spectacular emblems of a counter-revolution that convulsed almost every former Confederate state. By the time federal troops withdrew in 1877, signaling the North's abandonment of the ex-slaves, private, collective violence in support of white supremacy was embedded in southern political culture.[6]

Lynching, however, reached its height not during the pitched battles of Reconstruction but during the transition between 1877 and the establishment of a new caste system. Through the 1870s and '80s, southern farmers suffered a sustained decline in agricultural prices, capped by the severe recession of 1893. Bourbon regimes, anxious for a share of Gilded Age profits, sought to lure northern and British capital into the region with promises of cheap labor and natural resources. As the rigid adherence of a private banking system to the gold standard and a contracted currency, mediated through the furnishing merchant and the crop lien system, forced small farmers off the land, they fought back through the Farmers Alliances and the Populist Party. When white Populists pragmatically allied with blacks, their opponents responded with an extralegal campaign of physical and psychological intimidation that reawakened the passions of Reconstruction.[7]

Lynching became a major issue in the movement, for blacks turned to the third party in part for protection against the whims of southern justice.[8] Populist politicians, however, were tragically unable to shield their potential constituents from terrorism. In 1892, 255 persons were killed by lynch mobs, "the most staggering proportion ever reached in the history of that crime."[9] In some cases lynching was a specific mode of political repression. In others, it represented a diffuse reassertion of white solidarity. For example, a study of racial violence in 59 Louisiana parishes found a marked increase in lynching during election years at the height of Populist voting strength. Although the victims tended to be alleged criminals rather than Populist activists, mob violence undoubtedly served as a general warning to blacks of the dangers of political assertiveness. More signifcantly, lynching functioned as a means of uniting whites across class lines in the face of a common enemy, thus rekindling one of the major stumbling blocks to Populist success: the fear of "Negro domination" and the powerful pull of the notion of the Solid South.[10]

Defeat in the election of 1896 spelled the end of the Populist challenge to the emerging capitalist order. Formal disfranchisement eliminated the third party's constituency in the black community and restricted white political participation as well. By 1906, blacks had been excluded by law from primary elections in every southern state. Landowners replaced white tenants with more easily exploited blacks, and white farmers, who had once sought an interracial alliance, now, in Lawrence Goodwyn's ironic phrase, competed with blacks "for the rights to peonage." The textile industry, harbinger of southern industrialization, became a whites-only enclave for an emerging southern proletariat, and mill owners systematically used racial fears to undercut the organizing efforts of their workers.[11]

As the remnants of planter paternalism gave way to competition, a reinforcing system of debt peonage, disfranchisement, physical segregation, and terrorism replaced the "distant intimacy" and condescending tolerance of an earlier era.[12] Industrialization increased class differences and sent landless workers like George Hughes wandering across a once fixed agrarian landscape. A new generation of blacks, born in freedom and less willing to act out the etiquette of obsequiousness, seemed to many whites to betoken a society whirling away into the unknown.[13] The ideology of racism reached a virulent crescendo, as the dominant image of blacks in the white mind shifted from inferior child to aggressive and dangerous animal. Lynching, the ultimate weapon of social order in a society wracked by economic and racial tensions, seems to have become increasingly sadistic: emasculation, torture, and burning alive replaced the hangman's noose.[14]

With the new caste system in place, lynching gradually declined from an average of 188 a year during the decade 1880–1899 to 93 a year during the first decade of the twentieth century. But from 1905 until World War I, little further change occurred. Throughout the period, the average number of lynchings never fell below two or three a week. After a resurgence during the "red summer" of 1919, mob violence dropped steadily, only to rise temporarily with the beginning of the Great Depression. Although twice as many threatened lynchings were prevented as were carried out during the decade of the twenties, the thwarted lynch mob frequently demanded that public officials impose the death sentence in a hasty mockery of a trial. If these "legal lynchings" were included in the statistics, the death toll would be much higher. Moreover, the proportion of lynchings taking place in the South increased from 82 percent of the total in the 1890s to 95 percent in the 1920s; over the same period the proportion of lynch victims who were white decreased from 32 percent to 9 percent. Lynching had become virtually a southern phenomenon and a racial one (tables 1 and 2).[15]

While these statistical changes lessened the chance that any one individual might lose his life to a lynch mob, they did little

Table 1

Number of Persons Lynched, by Region and by Race for Five-Year Periods, 1889–1928

Years	South	Non-South	Black	White	Totals
1889–1893	705	134	579	260	839
1894–1898	680	94	544	230	774
1899–1903	492	51	455	88	543
1904–1908	362	19	354	27	381
1909–1913	347	15	326	36	362
1914–1918	311	14	264	61	325
1919–1923	287	14	273	28	301
1924–1928	95	5	91	9	100

Source: Compiled from data in NAACP, *Thirty Years of Lynching* (New York: NAACP, 1919) and *Supplements* (1919–1928). Southern states are Alabama, Arkansas, Florida, Georgia, Kentucky, Louisiana, Mississippi, Missouri, North Carolina, Oklahoma, South Carolina, Tennessee, Texas, Virginia, West Virginia—the fifteen states in which the ASWPL was active.

Table 2

Number of Persons Lynched, by States, 1882–1930

State	Whites	Blacks	Total
Alabama	46	296	342
Arizona	35	1	36
Arkansas	64	230	294
California	42	4	46
Colorado	70	6	76
Connecticut	0	0	0
Delaware	0	1	1
Florida	25	241	266
Georgia	34	474	508
Idaho	16	6	22
Illinois	15	16	31

State	Whites	Blacks	Total
Indiana	33	19	52
Iowa	19	1	20
Kansas	34	18	52
Kentucky	62	151	213
Louisiana	60	328	388
Maine	0	0	0
Maryland	3	27	30
Massachusetts	0	0	0
Michigan	4	4	8
Minnesota	6	3	9
Mississippi	45	500	545
Missouri	53	63	116
Montana	91	2	93
Nebraska	55	5	60
Nevada	12	0	12
New Hampshire	0	0	0
New Jersey	0	1	1
New Mexico	39	4	43
New York	1	1	2
North Carolina	14	85	99
North Dakota	12	2	14
Ohio	9	13	22
Oklahoma	116	44	160
Oregon	22	3	25
Pennsylvania	1	5	6
Rhode Island	0	0	0
South Carolina	5	154	159
South Dakota	34	0	34
Tennessee	44	196	240
Texas	143	349	492
Utah	6	3	9
Vermont	0	0	0
Virginia	16	88	104
Washington	30	0	30
West Virginia	15	35	50
Wisconsin	6	0	6
Wyoming	38	7	45
Total	1,375	3,386	4,761

Source: Monroe Work, ed., *The Negro Year Book: An Annual Encyclopedia of the Negro, 1931–1932* (Tuskegee: Negro Year Book Publishing Co., 1931), p. 293.

to undermine the psychological impact of mob violence. In the decades before World War I, the expansion of communications, the development of photography, and the popularity of yellow journalism gave reporting a vividness it had never had before. The rhetorical evocation of intimate human suffering implicated white readers in each act of aggression and drove home to blacks the consequences of powerlessness.[16]

The most relevant measure of the importance of lynching was never the percentage of blacks directly involved, for, like whipping under slavery, lynching was an instrument of social discipline intended to impress not only the immediate victim but all who saw or heard about the event. And the mass media, together with the late-Victorian relish in the details of death, spread the imagery of rope and faggot far beyond the community in which each lynching took place. Writing of his youth in the South of the 1920s, Richard Wright recalled:

> The things that influenced my conduct as a Negro did not have to happen to me directly; I needed but to hear of them to feel their full effects in the deepest layers of my consciousness. Indeed, the white brutality that I had not seen was a more effective control of my behavior than that which I knew. The actual experience would have let me see the realistic outlines of what was really happening, but as long as it remained something terrible and yet remote, something whose horror and blood might descend upon me at any moment, I was compelled to give my entire imagination over to it, an act which blocked the springs of thought and feeling in me, creating a sense of distance between me and the world in which I lived.[17]

As long as lynching survived in any form, Jessie Daniel Ames argued, it remained the most vivid symbol of black oppression, shaping the consciousness of southerners both black and white. Under her leadership, the Association of Southern Women for the Prevention of Lynching would pursue its campaign until socially sanctioned mob violence disappeared from southern society.

2

Despite the central place that lynching occupies in the southern imagination and in the idea of the South in the rest of the country, historians have paid remarkably little attention to the phenomenon. The imagery of the lynch mob pervades black autobiography and fiction and provides a chief dramatic device for the southern novel of gothic terror. But no modern historical analysis has appeared, and the classic account remains *The Tragedy of Lynching*, written by the sociologist Arthur Raper for the Interracial Commission in 1932.[18]

This neglect stems in part from a more general failure of historians to look systematically at the role of violence in American political life. Until recently, historians have tended to see American development as the unfolding of a pluralistic democracy based on a broad consensus of values, and this notion has militated against attention to the function of coercion in maintaining political and economic arrangements. The practice of lynching represents a notorious contradiction to such norms. Precisely because of its fanatical quality, however, it has been viewed as a pathological aberration, easy to deplore but difficult to assimilate into an understanding of the nature of the American past.[19]

Sociologists, unlike historians, have developed a considerable body of literature on the subject. Studies have related the incidence of lynching to seasonal rhythms, the structure and autonomy of southern county governments, economic fluctuations, the isolation of southern rural life, inadequate legal institutions, frontier conditions of rapid in-migration, revivalism, and the proportion of blacks in the population.[20] Social psychologists have suggested that lynch mobs were made up of frustrated poor whites using blacks as scapegoats for displaced aggression and have delineated an "authoritarian personality" typical of mob leaders.[21]

Arthur Raper found that most of the lynchings of 1930 occurred in counties with a high rate of tenancy and below-average per capita tax evaluations, bank deposits, and educational facilities. Within these counties, lynchings took place in the open countryside or in towns of less than 2,500 population and then spread contagiously from one community to another. In a larger survey of the period 1900–1930, he discovered that blacks were most vulnerable to mob violence in newer, more sparsely settled areas where they constituted less than one fourth of the population. Here, he hypothesized, institutions were less stable, role and status less sharply defined, and blacks were sometimes able to secure a foothold in the economy and to assert a measure of autonomy (see figure on number of lynchings).[22]

Only when historians have integrated the often contradictory hypotheses of such words into analyses of empirical evidence and change over time will we have an understanding of lynching's ebb and flow, its impact on the lives of black and white southerners, and its eventual decline. The social function of

Figure 1[*]
Number of Lynchings per 10,000 Population
in Southern Counties, 1900-1930

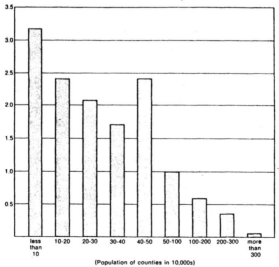

(Population of counties in 10,000s)

Source: *Data from Arthur F. Raper, *The Tragedy of Lynching* (1933, rpt.; New York: Dover, 1970.)

mob violence in the context of the twentieth-century South, however, seems relatively clear. By definition, lynching consisted of "an illegal and summary execution at the hands of a mob, or a number of persons, who have in some degree the public opinion of the community behind them."[23] It thus could be seen as a form of what the sociologist Emile Durkheim termed "repressive justice," designed not to punish or to rehabilitate the individual but to enforce social conformity.[24] Despite the pull of the forces of modernization, whites in the small-town and rural South resisted the delegation of law enforcement to the orderly administration of the police and courts. Instead they responded to the threat of black aggression with a communal ritual that demonstrated and reinforced white unity, intimidated blacks as a group, and ensured allegiance to caste roles on the part of both whites and blacks.

Twentieth-century southern liberals increasingly blamed lynching on ignorant, irrational poor whites. In fact, lynching drew its repressive power from the extraordinary caste solidarity it expressed.[25] Seldom was any attempt made to disguise the identity of participants; in the files of anti-lynching organizations appear one front-page newspaper photograph after another in which members of a lynching party look solemnly and confidently into the camera. Only in rare instances did state political leaders take effective action against lynching, and southern congressmen consistently opposed federal anti-lynching legislation. As Arthur Raper discovered in a survey of 100 lynchings, at least half were carried out with police officers participating, and in nine-tenths of the others the officers condoned the mob action. Nor did Protestant ministers often break caste solidarity by speaking out against racial violence. As one local woman wrote about the Sherman lynching and its aftermath, "I heard that the preachers in their pulpits today deplored the horrible tragedy, but if they had lifted their voices against mob law when sheeted figures were sowing the seed that ghastly fruit would never have hung from the court yard tree."[26]

Lynch mobs, like frontier vigilante movements before them,

counted among their leaders members of the "county seat elites" who controlled local political life. Apologists sometimes sought a casuistic distinction among the participants in a mob. The "leaders" were said to be "from outside the county." The best people were "in but not of" the crowd. In fact, a lynching typically involved large segments of the population, and it was the presence of "men of property" that tipped the balance against sheriffs who sought to uphold the law. "I went into that cell block with every intention of fulfilling my oath and protecting that man," one officer reported, "but when the mob opened the door, the first half-a-dozen men standing there were leading citizens—businessmen, leaders of their churches and the community—I just couldn't do it."[27]

In rural areas, planters sometimes used lynching as a quasi-official instrument of coercion for enforcing labor contracts and crop lien laws.[28] The incidence of lynching rose in the summer months when the hard work of planting was done and only the lucrative harvest remained. "Now is the season," explained a Georgia editor quoted in one ASWPL publication, "when the tenant with the best crop gets run off the place." The implicit purpose and end result, Jessie Daniel Ames believed, was "intimidated inarticulate and cheap labor for the farms and domestic service."[29]

Indeed, lynchings often took the form not of frenzied killings but of deliberate, purposeful extensions of the administration of justice. Blacks were eliminated from juries, and courts meted out disproportionately harsh sentences to black defendants. In a system of what one scholar has termed "underlaw," police officials exploited areas of discretion in the legal process to translate local white custom into effective social control, regardless of the letter of the statute books. The broad discretionary power in the hands of local and county officials routinely verged on vigilantism. Whites acting as special deputies or posse members eagerly assisted in manhunts. If the lawful authorities failed to measure up to community demands, the initiative for law enforcement could easily pass into the hands of private citizens. The lynchings that followed were modeled after the public hangings that, until the second decade of the twentieth century, were carried out by local and county government officials.[30]

In addition to its ritualistic affirmation of white unity, lynching functioned as a mode of repression because it was arbitrary and exemplary, aimed not at one individual but at blacks as a group. White supremacy was maintained by psychological repression as well as by economic and political control, and lynching worked effectively to create a general milieu of fear that discouraged individual or organized black assertiveness. Many whites believed that lynching struck terror into the black community in a way that court proceedings, nominally bound by constitutional guarantees of due process, could never do. With care and constant vigilance, an individual might avoid situations that landed him in the hands of the law. But a lynch mob could strike anywhere, at any time. Once the brush fire of rumor began, a manhunt was organized, and the local paper put out special editions announcing a lynching in progress, there could be few effective protestations of innocence. If the individual accused of a crime could not be found or if his identity were unknown, then a guiltless bystander could serve as well. Those threatened with lynching sometimes fought back; the black community acted to conceal them or spirit them out of town. But resistance could bring retaliation against the victim's family. A lynching could serve as prelude to widespread destruction of property or pogroms against the whole black community.[31]

In day to day life, psychological intimidation resisted on an elaborate code of racial etiquette. Southerners, noted an observer during Reconstruction, "perceive insolence in a tone, a glance, a gesture, a failure to yield enough by two or three inches in meeting on the sidewalk." Talking back to a white man, seeking employment "out of place," refusing to obey an order—the transgression of a whole range of nebulous taboos could lead to a verbal rebuke, a beating, or a lynching.[32] Indeed, in 26 percent of the 4,715 known lynchings committed between 1882 and 1946, the victim was accused only of some minor infraction or of no crime at all. Men lynch most readily, Ames observed, when the victim has "offended that intangible something called 'racial superiority.'"[33] A black child thus had to learn from birth "the ethics of living Jim Crow." "To wander from the paths of behavior laid down for the group," wrote the black novelist Ralph Ellison, "is to become the agent of communal disaster." The threat of lynching penetrated black family and community life, demanding the repression of a child's individuality in order to protect him against the forces within himself that might urge him to reach out for the symbols of dignity and equality in a white world.[34]

Aimed ostensibly at blacks, this process also operated as a means of indoctrination and social control over whites. It served the essential educational function of establishing "in the public emotions the conception of the Negro race as inherently and everlastingly inferior." "Sometimes even Southern white people forget their caste in a biracial society," Jessie Daniel Ames pointed out. "When they do, though they are admonished, the outcome may be death to a Negro." If some white people "were not prone to be familiar with Negroes and socialize with them, allowing them reasons to suppose their presence among white people is acceptable," warned a North Carolina editor, "there would still live in the heart and soul of the Negro the fear and dread of swift and sure punishment in case of wrong doing."[35]

Even in the worst of times, it is crucial to remember, the southern black experience was never bound by fear alone. We know little about the effects of coercion on the inner lives of black people, for the world whose psychic horizons were dominated by Judge Lynch has remained for the most part invisible to historians. The evidence of music, folklore, and oral testimony, however, indicates that southern blacks fashioned a vital and sustaining culture out of conditions that can only be described in the language of the tragic and the absurd. The quality of black life in the region found expression not only in the statistics of violence and the witness of "silent sorrow," but also in the life-affirming idiom of the blues.[36]

Individuals in this culture adopted strategies for survival ranging across a continuum from internalized victimization to open rebellion. Richard Wright, for example, suggested some of the ways in which blacks of his generation confronted their destiny:

> They could accept the role created for them by the whites and perpetually resolve the resulting conflicts through the hope and emotional catharsis of Negro religion; they could repress their dislike of Jim Crow social relations while striving for a middle way of respectability, becoming—consciously or unconsciously—the accomplices of the whites in oppressing their brothers; or they could reject the situation, adopt a criminal attitude, and carry on an unceasing psychological scrimmage with the whites, which often flared forth into physical violence.[37]

It was this final choice, the adoption of a "criminal attitude," which dominated the fears and fantasies of the white South. The "desperate" Negro, like George Hughes, seemed to many whites to reveal the true nature behind the black mask. To blacks he represented both catharsis and warning. Like the pre-political "avengers" described by the British historian Eric Hobsbawn, the black desperado proved "that even the poor and weak can be terrible." But his explosions of fury also taught that the wages of violent resistance were death.[38]

All God's Dangers, the autobiography of Nate Shaw, an Alabama sharecropper born in 1885, bears eloquent witness to another alternative to victimization: the strategy of a strong rural black man, wedded to the soil, who took insults, accommodated, had "to fall back," but never admitted defeat. Shaw went to work in the fields at the age of nine. Because of his industry, ambition, and intelligence, he prospered; by the early thirties he was on his way to owning an eight-acre farm. When individual effort failed, Shaw joined the Alabama Sharecroppers Union. For thus standing up against "this southern way of life," he went to prison for twelve years. An obsolete "mule farmer in a tractor world," Shaw greeted the civil rights movement of the 1960s as a continuation of his own struggle to "bring light out of darkness . . . to make a clearer life to live."[39]

Nate Shaw's story on the one hand and Richard Wright's furious rebellion on the other provide evidence of the limits of coercion. And the violence endemic to southern society can be seen in part not as the badge of oppression but as the result of an ongoing, if unequal, battle. An observer in 1910 characterized black/white relations in the United States as a perpetual "state of war." James Weldon Johnson spoke of "the tremendous struggle which is going on between the races in the South."[40] "You let the Negroes think they are somebody," summarized an anonymous critic of the ASWPL, "and you will have a job on your hands."[41]

The use of "repressive justice" never stilled the desire for self-determination. Blacks never finally "knew their place," and the black community found means of survival, cohesion, and resistance. As a result, whites felt themselves continually under seige. Lynching persisted as much to reaffirm solidarity and demonstrate power *to whites themselves* as to punish and intimidate blacks.

World War I marked a turning point in the history of lynching, as in the larger struggle for racial equality. The war itself called into question the long-standing American acquiescence in private violence, for national conscription and the creation of a mass army signaled the emergence of a nation state that possessed the means successfully to monopolize the use of physical force within its territory.[42] During the decade of the twenties, the logic of economic and political change demanded, and to some extent engendered, the substitution of "modern" forms of law enforcement for the repressive justice that lynching represented. But modernization, as recent scholars have shown, is not a unilateral process; cultural forms often lag behind economic changes, and values carried over from earlier times affect the way men and women respond to new material conditions. In a deeply racist society, determined to maintain the subordination of a large black population, racial beliefs and practices persisted independently of and sometimes in conflict with social and economic exigencies.[43] Even as lynching was increasingly discredited in the eyes of the world and disavowed by southern leaders, it survived in the small towns and rural areas of the South as a communal ritual that articulated and thus helped to maintain a set of entrenched cultural preoccupations.

In their effort to devise a theory and practice for antilynching reform, Jessie Daniel Ames and the women she led were forced to confront the historical roots and social functions of racial violence. It was the sexual tensions in southern society, however, that provided the emotional link between their self-perceptions and their public activities. The dimension of the problem that most concerned them, the basis for their campaign and its chief motive force, was the association between lynching, sex roles, and sexual attitudes.[44]

Of all aspects of racial etiquette, those governing sexual relations aroused the strongest emotions and carried with them the severest sanctions. Nowhere were the ethics of living Jim Crow more subtle and treacherous than when they touched on the proper conduct of black men toward white women. Any act of a black man, however innocent, that offended or frightened a white woman might cost him his life. Any transgression of the caste system was a step toward "social equality"; and social equality, with its connotations of personal intimacy, could end only in interracial sex. The white man, explained a participant in the Montgomery race conference of 1900, "regards the rape of white women by Negroes not as ordinary criminality, [but as] an attack on the integrity of the race."[45]

The main rationalization for lynching followed from this deeply felt taboo: only the threat of immediate and terrible retribution stood between the white women of the "lonely, isolated farmsteads of the South" and the overpowering desire of

black men. Rape of a white woman was "THE MOST TERRIBLE
CRIME ON THE FACE OF THIS EARTH" for which legal punishment was inadequate and too uncertain. Moreover, a woman
who had already suffered, as the editor of the Conyers,
Georgia, *Times* put it, a fate "many times more brutal than
death itself," could not be "put on the stand in full view of a
packed courtroom and then required to again look into the face
of and publicly proclaim her assassin." As the anti-lynching reformer Ida B. Wells pointed out, "there could be framed no
possible excuse more harmful to the Negro. . . . Humanity
abhors the assailant of womanhood, and this charge upon the
Negro at once placed him beyond the pale of human sympathy."[46]

Southern moderates as well as racial extremists justified
lynching for the one crime of sexual assault. The notion of black
retrogression, which continued to influence both popular and
academic thought into the 1930s, was closely bound up with
the question of black sexual behavior. Freed from the restraints
of slavery, the "new issue" Negro had supposedly reverted to
African primitivism. The chief evidence was sexual immorality:
family feeling, the cornerstone of social order, was unknown in
the black community; black women were lapsing into prostitution and illegitimacy; above all, black men were acting upon
the innate lasciviousness of the savage beast.[47]

Central to this national mythology was the image of the black
rapist. Propagandists of white backlash nurtured the imagery of
white women ravished by "lustful black brutes." Senator James
K. Vardaman, "Pitchfork" Ben Tillman, and Coleman L. Blease
built political careers around "The Crime of Rape." The southern historian Phillip Alexander Bruce offered a rationale for
lynching that drew no protest from his white peers. Black men,
he wrote, find "something strangely alluring and seductive
. . . in the appearance of the white woman; they are aroused
and stimulated by its foreignness to their experience of sexual
pleasures, and it moves them to gratify their lust at any cost
and in spite of every obstacle." Having encouraged the Atlanta
riot of 1906 with extra editions headlining a nonexistent wave

of assaults on white women, the respected journalist John Temple Graves went on to warn black Atlantans that "No law of God or man can hold back the vengeance of our white men upon such a criminal. . . . We will hang two, three, or four of the Negroes nearest to the crime until the crime is no longer done or feared in all this Southern land we inhabit and love."[48]

Even as the new social sciences began to undermine retrogressionist theory and southern spokesmen began to condemn lynching as a disruption of social order, specific lynchings (particularly those close at hand) were still defended as inevitable results of the passions aroused by the beastly nature of the crime of rape. In a debate published in a national magazine in 1928 on the subject, "Is Lynching Ever Defensible?," both pro and con contributors cited as extenuating circumstances the feelings aroused by rape atrocity stories. In 1926, Warren A. Candler, senior bishop of the Southern Methodist Church and brother of Coca-Cola founder Asa Candler, warned that "possible danger to women is inherent in every offense against the white man." Nine years later, he still claimed that lynching was not caused by the "base passion" of greed (like gangland slayings in the North), but by righteous indignation over "the most repulsive forms of crime." The Jackson *Daily News* published what it felt was the *coup de grâce* to antilynching critics: "What would you do if your wife, daughter, or one of your loved ones was ravished? You'd probably be right there with the mob." Nor was violence condoned only by the racist press and a few outspoken conservatives. In a survey made by the anthropologist Hortense Powdermaker in 1939, 64 percent of her white respondents still believed that lynching was justified in cases of sexual assault.[49]

This southern obsession with rape touched a responsive chord in the nation at large. It was rooted in the deepest of American communal preoccupations: the conflict between "civilization" and "savagery," historically acted out in the destruction of the Indians and the subjugation of African slaves.[50] In a culture that insisted upon work, instinctual repression, and acquisitive behavior, men struggled to separate themselves from nature; what James Madison called "the black race within our bosom [and] the red on our borders" became the repositories for those parts of the self which, in the process, had to be conquered and repressed.[51] For nineteenth-century Americans, the association between "savagery" and sexual passion was central to the problem of social order. By setting white women apart as asexual guardians of morality, men could pursue acquisition and expansion secure in the knowledge that they were not abandoning the values of civilization. By projecting onto blacks the "animal within," the buried parts of themselves could be objectified and controlled. But this separation from spontaneous emotional life and heterosexual love generated longings, fantasies, and fears that could never be kept altogether at bay. The result was a society prey to "visions of violent, immoral possession." The image of black over white, of a world turned upside down, symbolized the ever present danger of the return of the repressed, of a regression to a primitive natural world of sexuality and violence.[52]

The myth of the black rapist reached pathological proportions at the turn of the century, in part because of its congruence with the exaggerated sexual tensions of a dying Victorianism. Sexual strivings—rejected, feared, and projected onto others—beat like a "distracting savage drum" beneath the genteel discourse of white middle-class life. The erotic revolution, ushered in by theorists Sigmund Freud and Havelock Ellis, together with the threatening specter of the "new woman," engendered an hysterical counterattack from the spokesmen of sexual orthodoxy. The purity movement, capped by the white slavery campaign of 1906, represented in part the rearguard action of Victorian prudery at bay, an attempt to reassert social boundaries against sexual defiance.[53] No image so dramatically symbolized the most lurid of Victorian fantasies and fears as that of violent sexual congress between a black man and a white woman.

In 1915, D. W. Griffith, the talented son of a Confederate cavalry officer, captured the popular imagination with his screen version of Thomas R. Dixon's *The Clansman*. The attempted rape of the virginal "little Flora" and the lynching of her monstrous attacker represented a critical moment in the transformation of white America. As Victorian sexual attitudes seemed to crumble, the primal image remained: *The Birth of a Nation* harnessed the enormous myth-making potential of the modern film to a pernicious set of racist stereotypes and sexual obsessions.[54]

Despite its tenacity, this southern "rape complex," was never founded on objective reality. Of the known victims of lynch mobs in the period 1882–1946, only 23 percent were accused of rape or of attempted rape.[55] Every study of the crime has underlined the fact that despite the persistent mythology of black attacks on white women, rape has remained an overwhelmingly intra-racial event, and the victims have been predominantly black women.[56]

A major strategy of anti-lynching reformers, beginning with Ida B. Wells in the 1880s and carried on by the NAACP and the Association of Southern Women for the Prevention of Lynching, was to use facts and figures to undermine the rationalizations for mob violence. But the fear of rape, like the practice of lynching, was embedded far beyond the reach of factual refutation—in the heart not only of American racism, but of American attitudes toward women as well.

For blacks, lynching reinforced social boundaries that became, quite literally, a matter of life and death. For the white women involved, the practice can be seen more accurately as a dramatization of cultural themes, a "story" white southerners told themselves about the social arrangements and psychological strivings that lay beneath the surface of everyday life.[57] The archetypal lynching for rape thus served as a symbolic expression of sexual attitudes as well as a sanction against interracial sex.

The imagery of lynching—in literature, poetry, music, in the minds of men—was inescapably erotic. The mulatto Joe Christmas in Faulkner's *Light in August*, child of an interracial love affair, was himself doomed to castration and death by lynching. The white lyncher in James Baldwin's "Going to Meet the Man" tosses on his bed in sexual frustration before he rises to join the manhunt at dawn. Lynching is the culmination of an interracial love affair in Jean Toomer's "Blood-Burning Moon." Billie Holiday, the great jazz singer, made famous the indelible image of the "strange fruit" of race and sex in the American South:

> *Southern trees bear a strange fruit,*
> *Blood on the leaves and blood at the root;*
> *Black body swinging in the Southern breeze,*
> *Strange fruit hanging from the poplar trees.*
>
> *Pastoral scene of the gallant South,*
> *The bulging eyes and the twisted mouth;*
> *Scent of magnolia sweet and fresh,*
> *And the sudden smell of burning flesh.*
>
> *Here is a fruit for the crows to pluck,*
> *For the rain to gather, for the wind to suck,*
> *For the sun to rot, for the tree to drop,*
> *Here is a strange and bitter crop.* [58]

Rape and rumors of rape became a kind of acceptable folk pornography in the Bible Belt. As stories spread, the attacker became not just a black man but a ravenous brute, the victim a beautiful, frail, young virgin. The experience and condition of the woman (who could not be put on the witness stand to suffer the "glare and stare of public curiosity") were described in minute and progressively embellished detail: a public fantasy that implies a kind of group participation in the rape of the woman almost as cathartic as the subsequent lynching of the alleged attacker. [59] Letters berating Jessie Daniel Ames and other ASWPL women for their work typify the way in which a lynching could become the occasion for the expression of ag-

gressive fantasies ordinarily repressed. "The crowds from here
that went over to see [the victim] for themself," wrote an anonymous Floridian, "said he was so large he could not assault her
until he took his knife and cut her, and also had either cut or
bit one of her breast [sic] off."[60]

The small percentage of lynchings that revolved around
charges of sexual assault gripped the southern imagination far
out of proportion to statistical reality. In such scenes, described
in the popular press in strikingly conventionalized words and
phrases, the themes of masculinity, rage, and sexual envy were
woven into a ritual of death and desire. Participants might see
in "lynch law" their ideal selves: the protectors of women,
dispensers of justice, and guardians of communal values. But
they must also have seen themselves in the alleged rapist, the
lynch mob's prey. In this bloody drama were caught up "man
and beast, good and evil, ego and id, the creative power of an
aroused masculinity and the destructive power of loosened an-
imality."[61]

The story that such rituals told about the place of white
women in southern society was subtle, contradictory, and de-
meaning. The frail victim, leaning on the arms of her male relatives, might be brought to the scene of the crime, there to
identify her assailant and perhaps to witness his execution. Humiliation mingled with heightened worth as she played for a
moment the role of the Fair Maiden violated and avenged. For
this privilege—if the alleged assault had in fact taken place—
she might pay with physical and psychological suffering in the
extreme. In any case, she would pay with a lifetime of subjugation to the men gathered in her behalf.[62]

The lynch mob in pursuit of the black rapist thus represented the trade-off implicit in the code of chivalry, for the
right of the southern lady to protection presupposed her obligation to obey. The connotations of wealth and family background attached to the position of the lady in the antebellum
South faded in the twentieth century, but the power of "ladyhood" as a value construct remained. The term denoted chastity, frailty, graciousness. "A lady," noted one social-

psychologist, "is always in a state of becoming: one acts like a lady, one attempts to be a lady, but one never *is* a lady." Internalized by the individual, this ideal regulated behavior and restricted interaction with the world. If a woman passed the tests of ladyhood, she could tap into the reservoir of protectiveness and shelter known as southern chivalry. Women unable or unwilling to comply with such normative demands forfeited the claim to personal security. Together the practice of ladyhood and the etiquette of chivalry functioned as highly effective strategies of control over women's behavior as well as powerful safeguards of caste restrictions.[63]

The proslavery stance on the status of women exemplified this dialectic. The "essence of manhood," wrote the conservative theorist Thomas R. Dew, is "predation." The essence of womanhood is allure. Historically, women had served as the spoils of war: to the conquerer belonged the female bodies of the vanquished. The progress of civilization, the rise of the bourgeois family, immeasurably improved women's lot. Under the protection of a freely chosen marriage, Dew argued, she could find safety from the predatory instincts of other men. Stripped to its bare essentials, the difference between the sexes was the opposition between the potential rapist and the potential victim of sexual assault.

Dew's notion of female passivity, however, did not deny her passions of her own. On the contrary, because her social role was "not to seek, but to be sought . . . not to woo, but to be wooed," she was forced to suppress her "most violent feelings . . . her most ardent desires."[64] When, almost a century later, women began to assert their right to sexual expression and to challenge the double standard Dew's injunctions implied, the twentieth-century inheritors of the plantation legend responded with an extremity that revealed the sanctions at the center of the chivalric ideal. William Faulkner's *The Sanctuary*, published in 1931, embodies the most violent of these reactions to the fall of the lady. The unchaste woman, who had already lost her most precious possession, gave up the right to protection. The corncob rape of Temple Drake—a "New

Woman" of the twenties—was the ultimate revenge on the ab-
dicating white virgin. Her fate represented the "desecration of
a cult object," the implicit counterpoint to the idealization of
women in a patriarchal society.[65]

Thus the threat of rape cannot be seen, as reform rhetoric
claimed, simply as a rationalization used to obscure the real
function of lynching. Rather, the two phenomena were inti-
mately connected, for the fear of rape, like the threat of lynching,
served to keep a subordinate group in a state of anxiety and
fear. It may be no accident that the vision of the Negro as
threatening beast flourished during the first organizational
phase of the women's rights movement in the South. Certainly
the women of the ASWPL, born for the most part around the
turn of the century, inherited a legacy of terror. Women reformers of their mothers' generation, like Belle Kearney and
Rebecca Felton, had combined a discontent with women's circumscribed roles with a conviction that they were hedged
about on all sides by a "nameless horror." The South, wrote a
southern woman in 1898, had become "a smoldering volcano,
the dark of its quivering night . . . pierced through by the cry
of some outraged woman."[66] Thirty-two years later, Anti-
Lynching Association critics voiced the same sense of fear:
"Nowhere in the country are we safe. Even on the public
highways, the situation has become so serious that frequently
one or more male escorts fail to protect the fragile and helpless
woman, innocent of any wrong."[67] As the women of the
AWSPL sought to undermine the rationalizations for lynching,
they found themselves entangled in the reinforcing myths of
black sexuality and female vulnerability. The abject dependence on white men for protection against sexual aggression
that the fear of rape engendered could not be overcome without a significant psychological breakthrough.

Moreover, Anti-Lynching Association members learned that
the black rapist was not the only source of danger, for when the
southern white woman attempted to abandon her place on the
pedestal, she was subject to attack by her protector. For example, Ames reported that women who sought to convince

officers to guard their prisoners against mob violence "found themselves in receipt of anonymous letters conveying nauseating threats in slimy words—threats against Southern white women by Southern white men." [68] Indeed, even the eminent respectability and moderation of the women of the Anti-Lynching Association did not shield them from the charge that only the desire to sleep with a black man could account for their scandalous betrayal of caste solidarity. "You may have yourself a nigger if you want one, but do not force them on others," wrote one expatriated southerner. "If you want a Negro man, OK. Otherwise lay off white supremacy," read a telegram to an ASWPL leader in Mississippi. [69]

Such accusations further illuminate the importance of the sexually constrained woman to the preservation of the mores of white supremacy. Lynching was not just a punishment for forcible assault; it was also a severe sanction against voluntary sexual relations. "I have always been curious about the . . . white mentality," Jessie Daniel Ames commented, "which as far back as I remember assumes that only segregation and the law against intermarriage keep . . . white women from preferring the arms of Negro men." [70] White civilization, wrote Doris Lessing in her powerful first novel, "will never, never admit that a white person, and most particularly, a white woman, can have a human relationship, whether for good or for evil, with a black person. For once it admits that, it crashes, and nothing can save it." On the presumption—held not only in popular opinion but very often in law—that any white woman having intercourse with a black man had been "raped," untold black men were lynched or legally executed. [71]

The double standard that buttressed such attitudes was scarcely confined to the American South. The chastity of women in western European societies has been hedged about with an array of legal, social, and psychological restrictions. Unfaithfulness was more serious in a woman than a man, in part because the adultery of a married woman might produce children to make claims upon the father's estate. More fundamentally, this notion was "the reflection of the view that

men have property in women and that the value of this property is immeasurably diminished if the woman at any time has
sexual relations with anyone other than her husband." Rape
has been defined at law as a transgression not so much against
the woman as against the property rights of the man to whom
she belongs.[72]

In the South, the double standard took on special and explosive force. White women were viewed *collectively* as the repositories of white racial legitimacy. Theodore Bilbo, for example,
in a long treatise on "separation or mongrelization" advanced
the perverse logic that even though miscegenation practiced by
white men may have "poured a broad stream of white blood
into black veins," white racial purity had been in no way im-
paired. "Southern white women have preserved the integrity
of their race, and there is no one who can today point the
finger of suspicion in any manner whatsoever at the blood which
flows in the veins of the white sons and daughters of the South."
As absolutely inaccessible sexual property, white women became the most potent symbol of white male supremacy.[73]

Ironically, such symbolism may have created an objective
basis for the fear of black attacks on white women. "When men
sow the wind," warned Frederick Douglass in 1892, "they will
reap the whirlwind." In the rhetoric, if not the reality, of the
1960s and '70s, the fantasies of generations of white men at last
came true. Writers like Eldridge Cleaver, Calvin Hernton,
LeRoi Jones, and Frantz Fanon asserted that the assault of a
white woman, the taking of the forbidden fruit, could indeed
be seen as an act of political retribution.[74] Whether or not
George Hughes—victim of the Sherman, Texas, lynching of
1930—actually explained his motives for attacking his employer's wife in the words attributed to him, the white community's ready belief that he acted in protest against white racism
reveals a significant and deeply felt tension in southern society.[75]

The double standard had similarly pernicious effects on attitudes toward black women. The traditional American split
image of women as Virgin and Whore, Fair Maiden and Dark

Lady, was reified in the South. The association between darkness and eroticism cast white women *en masse* in the role of the "ice goddess"; upon black women were projected the fears and fascinations of female sexuality.[76] "White men," Jessie Daniel Ames pointed out, "hold that white women are their property [and] so are Negro women." Recoiling with "horror and madness" from the image of sexual relations between white women and black men, white men regarded their own sexual crossing of the color line as "welcome attention" to black women.[77] The inability of black men to protect their women from sexual assault and the threat of death by lynching against black men who had sexual relations with white women were complementary aspects of a system of repression.[78]

The white man's "sexual gain" may also, in the context of the Protestant South, have been fraught with a sense of sin and guilt. The illicit relationships between white men and black women could never be openly acknowledged. White women had to be compensated, "the revolting suspicion in the male that he might be slipping into beastiality got rid of, by glorifying her."[79] And the reality of the lust of white men had to be projected upon black men and exorcised by the ritual of rope and faggot. In C. Vann Woodward's words: "The ultimate horror might be the tragedy of Charles Bon in *Absalom, Absalom!* or that of Joe Christmas of *Light in August*. But the ultimate cost has never been reckoned. It is still unpaid, still mounting, and it could run much higher."[80]

The ritual of lynching, then, served as a dramatization of hierarchical power relationships based both on gender and on race. The women of the ASWPL came to maturity in a region still very much in thrall to sexual and racial attitudes rooted in the slavery past. Masculine guilt over miscegenation, the veiled hostility toward women in a patriarchal society, the myths of black sexuality—a dense web of sexual violation and desperate rationalization lay behind the practice they sought to stamp out. Jessie Daniel Ames and the women she led made it their special mission to challenge this complex phenome-

non. Around the realization that lynching had profound implications for white women as for black men, they would organize
the first extensive public protest on the part of the white
South against an evil perpetuated for decades in their name.

Chapter 6
A Movement of Southern White Women

Six months after the lynching of George Hughes in Sherman, Texas, a small group of white southern women met in Atlanta to found the Association of Southern Women for the Prevention of Lynching. The goals of the organization were ambitious indeed: it proposed to use the moral and social leverage of organized women to prevent lynchings in the rural and small-town South. More broadly, it hoped to create a new climate of opinion by challenging the association between racial violence and sexual attitudes. To implement these goals, Jessie Daniel Ames designed an organization that provided her with the utmost independence and flexibility. It enabled her to gather a small, stable, active membership explicitly devoted to combating mob violence, while at the same time facilitating the participation of larger numbers of women with widely varying degrees of commitment. This chapter will examine the structure Ames created and the women who filled the association's ranks—the vehicle and the leaders who would translate Jessie Daniel Ames's private convictions into a public movement.

1

On May 9, 1930, the day of the Sherman lynching, Will Alexander, director of the Interracial Commission, appeared as a featured speaker at the Quadrennial Convention of the

Southern Methodist Church, meeting in nearby Dallas. Since the year of the commission's founding, lynching had slowly declined. In 1930, however, the lynching rate doubled. Fearing that the onset of hard times signaled a permanent reversal of the downward trend, Alexander convinced the Methodist convention to adopt a strong anti-lynching resolution. In vain, he also urged the white ministers of Sherman to speak out from their pulpits and to lead their congregations in making restitution to the black community. [1]

When Alexander returned to the CIC's headquarters in Atlanta, he determined to reinvigorate the commission's anti-lynching drive. The means he chose reflected both larger intellectual currents and the exigencies of finance. From the end of the Populist challenge until World War I, white southern intellectuals had settled into a virtually monolithic defense of regional institutions. But the literary renaissance of the twenties and the growth of regional sociology sent cracks through this brittle protective shell. By 1930, a significant group of southern writers, centered primarily at educational centers like the University of North Carolina, had begun to produce a body of regional self-criticism. The failure of a fund-raising campaign in 1929–1930 and the findings of a program evaluation convinced Alexander that the CIC strategy of local interracial committees was foundering and that its major philanthropic supporters would prove more responsive to social science research. The upsurge in lynching in 1930 provided the opportunity for a change in emphasis. Abandoning to the NAACP the battle for civil rights in the courts and in Congress, the Interracial Commission turned increasingly to the factual documentation of the region's ills. [2]

In the fall of 1930, Alexander secured a grant from the Rosenwald Fund to establish a "Southern Commission on the Study of Lynching." For half a century the Chicago *Defender*, Tuskegee Institute, and the NAACP had been collecting and publicizing lynching statistics; and southern white newspapers printed yearly press releases detailing the fluctuation of mob violence. Alexander's commission sought to provide an added dimension to such research: a case by case analysis of the social origins of extralegal racial violence. For the task, it chose Arthur Raper, an activist scholar trained in the techniques of regional sociology at Howard Odum's Institute for Research in Social Science at Chapel Hill. In addition, Alexander formed a special Commission of Law School Deans to study the legal aspects of lynching. The findings of both groups appeared in two pamphlets entitled "Lynchings and What They Mean" and "The Mob Murder of S. S. Mincey" and in two full-length books that have remained the standard texts on the subject: Arthur Raper's *The Tragedy of Lynching* and James E. Chadbourn's *Lynching and the Law*.[3]

These study commissions were composed of white men of impeccable academic and professional credentials and a "colored advisory committee" consisting of the small circle of black leaders who worked on most CIC projects: Robert Moton and Monroe Work of Tuskegee, John Hope of Atlanta University, and Charles S. Johnson of Fisk. Neither group, however, included a woman among its membership.[4]

As in the creation of the Interracial Woman's Committee in 1920, the impetus for bringing women into the campaign came from two directions: the ranks of organized black women and the white leadership of the Southern Methodist Woman's Missionary Council. In October 1930 Mary McLeod Bethune informed Will Alexander of her intention to issue a statement to the press demanding that southern white women assume responsibility for halting the rise in racial violence. The following month, the Methodist executive Mrs. J. W. Downs protested vigorously against the exclusion of women from the commission. "I am not a stickler for the appointment of a woman in recognition of sex," Mrs. Downs explained. "But if I had been a member of the selection committee I'm sure I would have suggested the name of a woman who was as well trained as the men."[5]

Jessie Daniel Ames shrewdly grasped this chance to create an autonomous women's organization. Her search for a new institutional form for women's work reflected a maneuvering for position within the internal politics of the CIC; but it was also a logical outgrowth of her approach to reform. She never whole-heartedly supported the commission's turn toward social science research; instead she raised a consistent voice in behalf of decentralization and work in the field. Moreover, Ames's skills lay in the mobilization of a middle-class female constituency around specific pragmatic reforms; a women's campaign against lynching would provide a better vehicle for her abilities than the diffuse, and largely symbolic, efforts at interracial cooperation that had characterized the work of her more religiously and domestically oriented predecessors. Assuring Alexander that it would do no good to appoint a token woman to the existing commissions—"because what woman would have any influence on a commission made up of eight or ten prominent men?"—she persuaded him to underwrite the expense for a region-wide conference in which women could devise their own independent program. [6]

On November 1, 1930, twenty-six white women from six southeastern states answered Jessie Daniel Ames's call to a meeting in Atlanta. In the decade since the Memphis conference introduced women to the interracial movement, such gatherings had become fairly commonplace. Moreover, from the beginning, the black and white women of the CIC had taken as their special concern the twin evils of the sexual exploitation of black women and the lynching of black men, and Jessie Daniel Ames herself had adopted anti-lynching reform as the programmatic focus of the state organization she led. But in 1930, Ames meant to go beyond denunciations and moral pronouncements. She intended to translate the social analysis of southern intellectuals into a theory of racial violence that could be readily understood by her constituency; and she intended to build on that theory a politically effective anti-lynching campaign. "The men," she remarked, "were out making studies and . . . so the women had to get busy and do what they could to stop lynchings!"[7]

The women who responded to Ames's invitation had, for the most part, a long history of involvement in interracial activities.

A substantial majority represented church organizations, equally divided among Southern Presbyterians, Baptists, and Methodists. Women were also present from Jewish women's groups, the YWCA, and civic organizations like the Parent-Teachers Association and the Southeastern Federation of Women's Clubs. But of the core group of twelve who proved willing—in Ames's words—"to stand under fire" by becoming the founding members of a new organization, all were officials of Protestant church groups, and a majority had been active both in denominational race relations programs and in CIC women's work. From its inception, the anti-lynching campaign was rooted firmly in a tradition of evangelical reform.

Will Alexander and Jessie Daniel Ames opened the Atlanta conference with a review of the history of lynching and of the efforts of the CIC to combat it. Despite overwhelming evidence to the contrary, many southerners still denied that lynching was peculiar to the South or had anything to do with race. "Lynching," Alexander told the gathered women, "is distinctively a Southern white institution . . . as much a part of us as mint juleps or hot biscuits, or camp meetings or evangelists or hookworm, or eloquence." He then touched on two themes that would become staples of anti-lynching publicity: first, that lynching was an embarrassment to the United States abroad; second, that it grew out of the South's failure to provide for the educational and social welfare of both its black and poor white populations.

Jessie Daniel Ames presented more precise information: in the 204 lynchings of the previous eight years, she told the assembled women, only 29 percent of the victims were even accused of crimes against white women. This simple statistical fact would form the cornerstone of the anti-lynching campaign. As the program and methods of the new organization evolved over time, its leaders developed a variety of strategies to combat racial violence and to link it with other issues. But throughout the twelve-year history of the group, its main purpose would be to hammer home the argument that black men did not provoke lynching by raping white women.

"Convinced by the consideration of facts," Ames reported, the women resolved "no longer to remain silent in the face of this crime done in their name." Constituting themselves the Association of Southern Women for the Prevention of Lynching, they issued a statement to the press, putting themselves "definitely on record as opposed to this crime in every form and under all circumstances." In addition, they sent telegrams to each southern governor calling upon him to use his "power and influence" to prevent mob violence and pledging the political support of organized women to public officials who upheld the law. Six days later a similar group of southwestern women meeting in Dallas adopted an anti-lynching resolution and agreed to join in a region-wide women's movement against vigilante justice.[8]

Both the white and Afro-American press greeted the founding of the ASWPL with enthusiasm. "Southern women, whose chastity has been saved, according to a widespread belief, for the past hundred years by lynchings, have initiated a movement to eradicate this protection by rope and faggot," announced the *Nation*. "The daughters of the south are not content with hurling denunciatory phrases; they are militantly marching out to make war upon barbarism that has flourished in their name."[9] "The greatest gain of the anti-lynching [fight] is to be found in the support now being given by the white women of the South," editorialized the Atlanta *World*. "The South moves forward with women taking the lead as usual," commented the Philadelphia *Tribune*. The black educator and Baptist church leader Nannie Helen Burroughs summed up the opinion of many when she reported in her Pittsburgh *Courier* column that the ASWPL was the most important anti-lynching group in the country.[10]

Such a positive evaluation was by no means unjustified. Yet it must be stressed that Jessie Daniel Ames did not organize the first extensive female resistance to mob violence, nor did her campaign exist in the historical vacuum implied by many of the Anti-Lynching Association's contemporary supporters and critics. For decades, black women had filled the front ranks of the fight against lynching. They had developed an analysis of the relationship between racial violence and sexual exploitation that the white ASWPL adopted only haltingly and with mixed feelings. Together with black men, they had long sought the white southern support that the CIC and the ASWPL belatedly offered. Indeed, years of black struggle against lynching shaped the social and political climate that made the founding of the Anti-Lynching Association possible.

After 1910, the NAACP had expanded Ida B. Wells's one-woman anti-lynching crusade into a multifaceted offensive against mob violence. Access to funds and legal talent had enabled the organization to respond swiftly to lynching incidents—publicizing the facts, urging the incorporation of anti-lynching planks in national party platforms, and lobbying for the passage of state and federal anti-lynching legislation.[11] In 1922, the NAACP formed a women's group called the Anti-Lynching Crusaders to mobilize support for the Dyer Anti-Lynching Bill. Led by Mary B. Talbert, president of the National Association of Colored Women, the Crusaders sought to enlist one million women and raise one million dollars for the lobbying effort.[12] Within three months after its formation, the 16 original members had expanded to 900, and William Pickens, NAACP field secretary, characterized the movement as "the greatest effort of Negro womanhood in a generation."[13]

The structure of the organization closely resembled that of the ASWPL eight years later. Each state was to have a voluntary, nonsalaried director, each town or county its "key women." The campaign was to be devoted exclusively to the lynching issue and was to disband when its purpose was achieved without creating permanent sinecures or an ongoing bureaucracy. The organization's letterhead proclaimed its religious orientation. "To your knees," it read, "and don't stop praying." The Anti-Lynching Crusaders differed from the ASWPL, however, in several significant respects. It was organized and controlled by black women; it hoped to enlist the help of white women and to become an interracial movement; and its major strategy for stopping lynching was the passage of national anti-lynching legislation.

The Anti-Lynching Crusaders made a concerted, though largely futile, attempt to bring white southern women into its ranks. "This is the first time in the history of the colored women that they have turned to their sister white organizations and asked for moral and financial support," Mary Talbert declared, "and as we have never failed you in any cause that has come to us, we do not believe that you will fail us now." Talbert sent 1,850 letters to white women known to be sympathetic to social reform. She sought to make contact with the CIC state women's committees in Arkansas, Texas, and Alabama, and a pamphlet published by the Crusaders included the anti-lynching resolution of the CIC Committee on Woman's Work. Mrs. H. K. Harring, a white woman whose efforts had stopped a lynching in Manassas, Virginia, promised to cooperate, approximately 900 white members enrolled, and individual CIC women indicated their support. But the hoped-for response from southern white women never materialized.[14]

Although the Anti-Lynching Crusaders were unable to accomplish their fund-raising objectives, they did help publicize the anti-lynching movement. Articles were sent to the leading women's periodicals in the country; the wire services gave national distribution to their press releases. Commented James Weldon Johnson: "Had the Anti-Lynching Crusaders done nothing but show America and the world that women, colored and white, North and South abhor and disclaim any such excuse as the protection of womanhood for the lynching evil, its efforts would not have been in vain."[15]

By 1930, when the ASWPL was founded, years of black-led publicity and agitation had thus made inroads on the consciousness of the nation. No aspect of regional life contributed more to the galling image of the benighted South, and during the decade of the twenties, a number of white southern journalists began to condemn lynching in general, though most newspapers continued to justify specific instances close at hand.[16]

Partly to circumvent the threat of federal legislation, southern governors increasingly took steps to prevent lynchings, and southern legislatures passed anti-lynching laws that, while virtually never enforced, did indicate a pro forma disavowal of mob violence upon which the women of the Anti-Lynching Association could draw. [17]

To say that the way had been prepared for the Anti-Lynching Association, however, is not to deny the importance of its campaign. Even though most southern leaders had ceased to defend the practice with the assurance and virulence of earlier generations, lynching had by no means been extirpated from southern society, and a strong current of public opinion still condoned vigilante action for the crime of rape. Moreover, while Jessie Daniel Ames and her co-workers were not the first to attack the sexual justification of lynching, no one could drive home the point with the dramatic force of a group of white southern women. Repeatedly, the black women of the Interracial Commission had emphasized that lynching was carried on for the protection of white women and that "when Southern white women get ready to stop lynching, it will be stopped and not before." The formation of the Association of Southern Women for the Prevention of Lynching signified an acceptance of this responsibility. The construction of a region-wide women's group that could carry the anti-lynching message into the rural South and take concrete steps to prevent mob violence would be a feat requiring extraordinary organizational genius, courage, and commitment. At the same time, women's willingness to involve themselves in an issue with such profound psychosocial implications in itself constituted a sign of social change: a rebellion, as Jessie Daniel Ames eloquently put it, against the "crown of chivalry which has been pressed like a crown of thorns on our heads." [18]

The background for such revolt lay in the half-century of black and white female self-organization described in previous chapters. The secular suffrage campaign, the interracial movement, and the struggle for women's rights within the church had significantly revised traditional images and set individual white women on the road to questioning the racial as well as the sexual status quo. Yet until World War I, they acted within the confines of an essentially static society. The war, bringing rapid industrialization and shattering the isolation of the region, marked a turning point for southern women as well as for blacks. By 1930, the political force of the Ku Klux Klan was spent; the CIO drive for an industrial democracy and the rise of New Deal liberalism were about to begin. The South, noted one historian, "stood between two worlds, one dying and the other struggling to be born."[19] The forces of modern capitalism that had transformed the lives of women in other parts of the nation came to the South in the twenties and thirties, bringing with them a new context for feminine reform.[20]

In this period, the southern textile industry overtook and bypassed its New England competitors, while industrial diversification scattered new factories through the Piedmont. Even the Depression failed to halt this process, and southern industry continued to improve its relative position in the nation. Southern cities grew at a faster rate than those of any other region: in 1910, one out of every five Southerners lived in an urban area of over 2,500 persons; by 1930, one out of three did so.[21] Farmers, sharecroppers, and mountaineers, pushed off the land by hard times and New Deal agricultural policies, came to the towns and cities or commuted from farm to factory. Throughout the region, rural men and women were confronted with new concepts of work discipline, authority, and social order.[22]

The emergence of a highly visible white anti-lynching movement reflected these trends, for it drew its leadership from an urban middle class in conflict with the agrarian demagogues who had dominated southern politics since the turn of the century. In a trenchant review of Gunnar Myrdal's *An American Dilemma*, the culminating statement of interwar liberalism, Ralph Ellison described this phenomenon. The Depression and the problem of national recovery, he argued, challenged the assumption of northern industrialists that the social isolation of the South offered "the broadest possibility for business exploitation." Franklin Roosevelt's characterization of the South as the nation's number one economic problem bespoke a realization that "Northern capital could no longer turn its head while the Southern ruling group went its regressive way." Southern New Dealers and northern industrialists agreed: capitalist development required the orderly administration of the law; economic necessity demanded cultural change. Gunnar Myrdal's liberal environmentalism, Ellison concluded, *"is the blueprint for a more effective exploitation of the South's natural, industrial and human resources."* [23] In a speech delivered to the Kentucky branch of the Interracial Commission in 1939, Jessie Daniel Ames anticipated Ellison's insight. "We have managed to reduce lynchings," she said, "not because we've grown more law-abiding or respectable but because lynchings became such bad advertising. The South is going after big industry at the moment, and a lawless, lynch-mob population isn't going to attract very much outside capital. And this is the type of attitude which can be turned to advantage much more speedily than the abstract appeal to brotherly love." [24]

Southern middle-class women shared with their male counterparts this experience of economic and ideological change, but the forces of modernization presented them with quite different options and dilemmas. Women moved to the cities in even greater proportions than men; once there, they entered white-collar positions at a slightly faster rate than did women in the country as a whole. Nationally, the critical shift of women into professional and clerical occupations occurred before 1920; in the South, such opportunities became widely available only in the following decades. In 1910, for example, 16.4 percent of employed women in the nation were engaged in white-collar occupations, while only 7.4 percent of working women in the South Atlantic states were so employed. By 1940, these figures had changed to 41.5 percent and 30.5 percent respectively. More strikingly, in the region's cities, the proportion of em-

ployed women in professional and clerical occupations had
risen to 37.1 percent. At the same time, regional differences in
women's education decreased. In 1910, only one out of twenty-
eight female college students lived in the South Atlantic states;
by 1942, one in eight did so. Perhaps an even more important
index of the relative change in the situation of southern women
can be found in the rapid decline of the region's birthrate. In
1910, the South had the highest birthrate in the nation, in both
rural and urban areas. In the South Atlantic states there were
760 children under five for every 1,000 women between the
ages of 20 and 40, while in the nation as a whole there were
609. By 1940, regional differences had narrowed to 400 for the
nation and 464 for the South Atlantic region. In urban areas the
change was even more marked: by 1940, there were 305 children for every 1,000 women in the urban areas of the South
Atlantic states, in contrast to a national average of 311. This is
not to say that by the interwar period the position of southern
women coincided with the national norm. It is clear, however,
that by World War II, the distance between southern women
and their northern counterparts had begun to close and that,
especially in the towns and cities, a new female middle class
had arisen whose social situation more closely resembled that
of their northern urban counterparts than it did that of their
southern rural predecessors. [25]

While their husbands moved into a masculine sphere of business and politics increasingly linked to national institutions,
these women, like their northern sisters before them, found
themselves confined to a home with ever narrowing functions.
If they joined the work force, they did so under Depression
conditions that curtailed work opportunities for married
women; they moved in and out of jobs as their marital condition changed, restricted for the most part to lower-echelon,
sex-typed white-collar occupations. Even though education,
leisure time, and economic opportunities set them apart from
both the world of the tenant farmer and the ethos of the
planter class, they remained hedged about by cultural prescriptions rooted in the antebellum patriarchy. The women's cam-

paign against lynching allowed women caught in such contradictions to disassociate themselves from a racial ideology that linked white women with the region's most notorious ills; it gave them an opportunity for social action compatible with their traditional church and community roles; and it identified them with an ideal of social order that looked to the urban-industrial future rather than to the agrarian past.

4

Before the anti-lynching campaign could be set in motion, Ames had first to secure the indispensable basis for autonomy: adequate financing with no strings attached. Will Alexander had given her a "free hand to carry on an independent movement among southern white women." When she persuaded the CIC to throw out the itemized budget treasurer R. H. King had prepared and present her with a lump sum to be used as she saw fit, she had the means to carry out this mandate, although her program budget, averaging only $2,000 per year, was minuscule in comparison with the $100,000 annual expenditure of the commission as a whole.[26] The anti-lynching campaign remained a voluntary effort, with Ames herself as its only salaried official.[27]

Stringent funding seems to have posed few problems for the Anti-Lynching Association's director, however, for the strategy she pursued reflected her long involvement with middle-class voluntarism and her belief in the collective power of enfranchised women. As in the suffrage and prohibition movements, she sought to mobilize an existing network of women's church and civic groups with their own program budgets around an issue consistent with their preoccupations and concerns. From the ranks of these organizations, she hoped to attract leaders like herself, who had "fought for political freedom," or "younger women . . . educated in the increasing numbers of co-educational schools, [who] did not accept the dictum of the man-made society."[28] These women—strategic elites within the feminine subculture—would be predisposed against lynching and ideally placed to wage an educational campaign aimed first at southern white women in general and then at the larger society.

The institutional structure Ames designed was exceptionally suited to these goals. While she retained the nominal title of Director of CIC Woman's Work, she was able to channel virtually all her resources into the work of the ASWPL. She met annually in Atlanta with a Central Council of dedicated leaders to set policy, issue resolutions, and provide members with inspiration and encouragement. An executive committee, with Ames at the helm, carried on the program on a day-to-day basis. In addition, the founding members solicited endorsements of the movement's goals from every major women's organization in the region, at the same time asking these organizations to send to Central Council meetings delegates who would accept responsibility for disseminating the association's ideas to their broader membership. Once this central organization had been established, state councils were created to spread the anti-lynching message within their own borders. A state chairman, a central council of ten to twelve women, and an executive committee of five were expected to interpret the ASWPL program to the state's women's groups, investigate and respond to local lynchings, and bring political pressure to bear on local and state politicians. State chairmen recruited local supporters by presenting an anti-lynching program to women's clubs and missionary societies, outlining concrete steps women could take to prevent lynchings in their areas, and asking everyone present to sign pledges indicating their commitment to take those steps. Women who signed such pledges did not become ASWPL "members," nor did they pay dues or attend regional meetings (though they were sometimes recruited for community forums or state anti-lynching institutes); rather, ASWPL officials integrated their names into a file of local contacts and supplied their organizations with a steady stream of literature, arming them with facts and statistics that refuted popular justifications for lynching and explained "What One Woman Can Do" to oppose the practice.[29]

Immediately after the founding meeting in November, the twelve original ASWPL members began a round of speaking engagements in their home states and within the regional organizations they represented. By January 1931, local organization began, when a group of Georgia women constituted themselves the Georgia Council of the ASWPL. Two exceptionally dedicated Methodist missionary society leaders from Mississippi, however, created the model for the operation of these state councils. Bessie C. Alford of McComb and Ethel Featherstun Stevens of Jackson returned from the Atlanta meeting to recruit representatives from each women's organization in the state; these Mississippi State Council members then launched an energetic drive to collect anti-lynching pledges from county sheriffs as well as from women in every county seat. By November 1931, almost 700 Mississippi women had signed the pledge. Their names were filed in a card index that enabled Alford and Stevens to call on local women to move into action whenever a lynching threatened. In addition, supporters' names, along with information on all state lynchings, were sent to central headquarters in Atlanta. State leaders released statements to the press condemning every lynching that occurred in the state, offered political support to sheriffs who prevented lynchings, and filled numerous speaking engagements. By 1935, women from all but one of Mississippi's eighty-two counties had joined the movement.[30]

The immediate success of these efforts prompted the adoption of the "Mississippi Plan" at the first ASWPL annual meeting in 1931. Over the next two years, Jessie Daniel Ames traveled throughout the South setting up organizations on the state level that mirrored the Mississippi structure and strategy. Eventually, councils formed in all eleven ex-Confederate states plus Kentucky and Oklahoma. ASWPL councils were not, however, evenly distributed throughout the region. Ames reserved her greatest effort for what she termed the "lynching states." Special meetings were held for women from areas with the highest incidence of mob violence; and as a state enjoyed a period of racial peace, she ceased actively to solicit support within it. Mississippi (which consistently led the country in vigilante violence) had the most active state council. Georgia, Texas, and Florida—among the most notorious lynching states—also received extensive ASWPL attention. Virginia, with one of the lowest lynching records in the South, never had more than a "shadow organization." Areas that had no recent history of lynching—like western Texas, northern Kentucky, and the Appalachian highlands—were ignored by the ASWPL campaign.[31]

In addition, the quality of individual state chairmen significantly influenced the vitality of state councils. An aggressive leader, working through a network of other women's organizations, could sustain a fairly high level of ASWPL activity even without a strong council behind her. Kate T. Davis, chairman of the South Carolina ASWPL, for example, backed by a handful of women centered in Charleston, carried on a vigorous campaign.[32] The Tennessee ASWPL, on the other hand, while contributing a number of able members to the Central Council, never enjoyed such sustained state leadership. Despite the central role of the state chairman, however, the most effective councils were not those dominated by a single leader but those, like Mississippi and Georgia, that combined a dedicated chairman with active council members scattered in small towns throughout the state.

Along with the organization of these central and state councils explicitly devoted to the anti-lynching campaign, Jessie Daniel Ames expended much effort in securing endorsements from larger preexisting women's groups.[33] Such support was crucial to the association's strategy, but it also posed the difficulty of gearing policy to widely divergent constituencies, and some of the association's caution may be attributed to its efforts to avoid alienating the more conservative of these institutional affiliates. For example, a serious setback occurred in 1931 when the Baptist Women's Missionary Union of Virginia refused to endorse the ASWPL program and registered its disapproval "of the action taken which speaks for Southern Women on the subject of lynching." Fearing that without the cooperation of the Baptists—the largest religious group in the South— the ASWPL would prove unable to attract an interdenominational membership, Ames took immediate steps to prevent such disapproval from spreading to other states.[34] The emergence of opposition within the Southeastern Federation of Women's Clubs became even more serious. At the annual meeting of 1935, the president of the Georgia federation and Mrs. J. R. Cain, a disaffected member of the ASWPL executive committee, blocked a move to endorse the anti-lynching campaign by arguing that ASWPL women were "communistic" and supporters of federal anti-lynching legislation. In response, Jessie Daniel Ames turned for support to club women on the state and local level, and they successfully appealed to the national federation for endorsement.[35]

Despite these difficulties, the association enjoyed remarkable success in buttressing its claim to speak for organized southern women. By February 1937, eighty-one state, regional, and national endorsements had been secured. By the early forties, 109 women's associations whose membership totaled over four million had joined the ASWPL campaign. These included the women's auxiliaries of the major Protestant denominations, national and regional federations of Jewish women, the YWCA, and the Business and Professional Women's Clubs.[36] Such endorsements did not necessarily signify a commitment to make an anti-lynching campaign part of an ongoing organizational program. But the ASWPL's staunchest supporters—church women's groups—not only passed resolutions of support, thus lending their names to ASWPL publicity, but also actively incorporated the issue of racial violence into educational materials used by a network of women's missionary societies that reached into the most remote of rural counties.[37]

Predictably, the Methodist Woman's Missionary Council served as the Anti-Lynching Association's most important endorsing group. Bertha Payne Newell, superintendent of the Methodist women's Bureau of Christian Social Relations, became secretary of the ASWPL and one of Jessie Daniel Ames's closest friends and confidantes.[38] Louise Young, who in 1919 had been one of the first white southern women to teach at a black school, assumed the position of professor of sociology and social work at Scarritt College and succeeded Carrie Parks Johnson as chairman of the bureau's Committee on Interracial Cooperation. Both as a teacher and as a church official, she worked with Newell to recruit Methodist support for the anti-lynching campaign.[39] Sara Estelle Haskin, whose role in the laity rights struggle and the creation of the CIC Woman's Committee has been noted, played an equally active part in the ASWPL. As editor of literature for the Woman's Missionary Council, she served as publicist for the anti-lynching campaign.[40] At the outset of the ASWPL effort, these women notified conference officers to give all the assistance in their power to Jessie Daniel Ames's organizational work in the states; under their leadership, the lynching issue was routinely incorporated into the programs of local missionary societies throughout the region. By 1934, Newell could report that "thousands and thousands of women all over the South" had signed the ASWPL anti-lynching pledge presented to them in Methodist zone, district, and conference meetings. In addition, over half of the association's numerous pamphlets, posters, and flyers were distributed through this Methodist network.[41]

Women who occupied similar positions in other denominations also furnished the ASWPL with official members and solicited grass-roots support. Prominent among these was Hallie Paxton Winsborough, founder and first superintendent of the Women's Auxiliary of the Southern Presbyterian Church, and Una Roberts Lawrence, president of the Baptist Woman's Missionary Union. Neither woman, however, enjoyed the authority within the church won by their Methodist counterparts. Baptists and Presbyterians had participated in the post–Civil War expansion of women's missionary societies, but in each case both ideology and institution militated against autonomy and an aggressive pursuit of the goals of social Christianity. The atomistic congregational structure of the Baptist Church and the synodical form of Presbyterian church government blocked the avenues of joint decision-making that the connectional structure of Methodism made possible. Both Winsborough and Lawrence fought an uphill battle against church fathers who feared that a leader of a separate women's organization might become a dreaded "ecclesiastical suffragette." Only in 1927, after she had served full-time for fifteen years, did the Presbyterian General Assembly confer on Winsborough a title comparable to that of other church executives and grant her the privilege of reading her own report to the assembly. Neither the Presbyterian nor the Baptist women's organization controlled its own finances or initiated its own programs. Each functioned primarily as a fund-raising body for the general activities of the church; and on the state and local level Baptist women were responsible not to a regional women's organization but to a state convention dominated by men. As a result, despite their personal commitment to the anti-lynching campaign, neither Winsborough nor Lawrence was able to mobilize the extensive church-wide support encouraged by the Methodists' unique historical experience.[42]

The Episcopal Church, traditionally the denomination of the upper class, endorsed the ASWPL program and contributed a number of leaders to its ranks, but the Episcopal Woman's Auxiliary enjoyed little independence or self-conscious group identity and made minimal effort to incorporate the anti-lynching issue into the church's program. Jane Cornell, the Episcopal chairman of the Florida ASWPL, for example, could get little cooperation from her own denomination and had to rely on the Methodist organization, which, she commented, "sort of carries itself in spite of personalities."[43] In North Carolina, the Society of Friends endorsed the ASWPL, and a Quaker minister, Clara Cox, served as an effective and progressive state chairman. No Catholic women occupied prominent positions within the ASWPL. In contrast, Mrs. Joseph Friend, president of the National Council of Jewish Women, and Rebecca Mathis Gershon, president of the Southern Interstate Conference of that organization, led Jewish women in strongly backing both the ASWPL and the interracial movement as a whole.

Like the Methodist Woman's Missionary Council, the YWCA proved a major conduit for ASWPL programs and publicity. Mrs. John Hanna, national president of the YWCA and vice-president of the National Council of Federated Church Women, worked with Jessie Daniel Ames in the Texas interracial movement and served as chairman of the Texas ASWPL. The national YWCA endorsed both the ASWPL's educational campaign and the NAACP's legislative program. And YWCA public affairs chairmen in many southern cities took an active part in the anti-lynching effort. [44]

Leaders of secular organizations performed less conspicuous functions in the Anti-Lynching Association. Geline MacDonald Bowman, national president of the Business and Professional Women's Clubs (BPWC), joined the ASWPL executive committee and secured the endorsement of the Southeastern Regional Conference of her group. Bowman's participation was considered "a feather in the hat" of the ASWPL woman who recruited her; but few other BPWC leaders followed her example. [45] While a number of active ASWPL leaders, like Kate T. Davis of South Carolina, were state chairmen of federations of women's clubs, the Southeastern Federation refused to endorse the campign; nor did the League of Women Voters offer more than perfunctory aid in spreading the anti-lynching message.

In the early months of the campaign, Ames hoped to balance these members who had "official connections" with "Southern women who have national standing." She sought to enlist well-known writers and journalists like the North Carolina journalist Nell Battle Lewis and the novelists Ellen Glasgow and Julia Peterkin. [46] Lucy Randolph Mason, director of the National

Consumer's League, provided support in organizing the Virginia ASWPL. George Madden Martin, a widely read author of children's books, was chairman of the ASWPL Central Council throughout its twelve-year history and the association's major link with national political figures and publicists. Pulitzer Prize–winning journalist Julia Collier Harris and novelist Willie Snow Ethridge both served as at-large members of the Central Council.[47] But once the institutional structure had been set up and the actual process of education, prevention, and investigation was under way, Ames placed less emphasis on what she derided as "paper organization" and more on concrete programs and dedicated local women. Moreover, while she worked tirelessly to "find a solid ground in civic and lay organizations," she increasingly turned to the church, the South's traditional "sanctuary for women's undisturbed activities," for the campaign's rhetoric and constituency.[48]

Through organizational endorsements on the one hand and signature pledges on the other, the Anti-Lynching Association thus sought to uncover and mobilize anti-lynching sentiment among a broad cross-section of white southern women. At state and regional gatherings of endorsing organizations and local meetings of clubs and missionary societies, approximately 6,000 new women each year signed the ASWPL's anti-lynching pledge (see table 3). As of 1936, 29,269 women had indicated their support in this way; by 1942, the ASWPL could claim over 43,000 such personal endorsements.[49] By working through these local women and preexisting organizations, the ASWPL hoped to avoid the stigma of outside interference. "With a knowledge of the psychology of State's rights and to what extent it is used as an alibi," Jessie Daniel Ames explained, the ASWPL "has developed a method of procedure which makes it possible for us at headquarters to encourage State women to act when their particular State [or county unit] is involved."[50] Moreover, by garnering support in this way, the Anti-Lynching Association enlisted a strategic constituency: small-town church women, schooled for decades in running their own affairs within women's clubs and missionary socie-

Table 3

Signature Pledges Against Lynching
Annual Totals

	Counties	Towns	Women	Men	Officers
1932	587	1,324	7,910	139	
1933	918	2,252	17,051	647	
1934	1,018	2,655	26,631	829	283
1935	1,033	2,808	29,269	1,189	673
1936	1,059	2,912	35,468	1,799	887

Source: Compiled from summaries and reports in ASWPL files.

ties, familiar with the social gospel, and sensitized by the prohibition and suffrage movements to issues of law enforcement and social order.

While the organizational affiliations of the women who joined the Anti-Lynching Association are relatively easy to ascertain, their social backgrounds are more obscure. Their first and perhaps most important characteristic was their race. The decision to create an organization for white women only, which set the ASWPL apart from the interracial movement and shaped its rhetoric and style, flowed from a number of attitudes and perceptions. White southern women, Ames believed, occupied a position both circumscribed and exalted. On the one hand, the notion of the white woman as passive victim lay at the heart of the mythology of lynching. On the other hand, the southern lady enjoyed extraordinary moral authority, and mob violence spectacularly breached the social order and amity supposed to be her special responsibility. Ames hoped to draw on women's resentment at the anachronistic chivalric ideal and to assert middle-class feminine values against the violent ethos of a masculine world. Secure in the privileges granted family and social standing in the region, the association's white leaders could act with some immunity in situations where blacks would encounter hostility and even personal danger. They could use their own hard-won political rights and their husband's economic positions as leverage against county officials and local police. Most importantly, they were strategically placed to make maximum use of the cultural symbol of the southern lady. Apart from any specific programs she might devise, the very existence of the Anti-Lynching Association embodied Jessie Daniel Ames's major strategy: an organization of impeccably respectable white southern women expressing their abhorrence of masculine violence would, she believed, have an impact on white public opinion that a biracial or black protest movement could not achieve.

In addition, Ames's policy of exclusion followed from her view of the weaknesses of the CIC Woman's Committee and her desire to broaden its base of support. In the ASWPL, she could bypass the "obstacle of distrust" between black and white women that hindered women's interracial work. Moreover, Ames surmised that, despite the CIC's careful disavowal of any association between interracialism and integration, white fear of social equality had reduced the movement to a "little group of like-minded people talking only to themselves."[51] By separating her new organization from the CIC, she hoped to attract women who had not previously been linked with any race-related activities and to form a coalition that would include the entire range of southern white middle-class women's organizations.[52] Accordingly, she stressed again and again that this was "not an interracial movement, but a movement of Southern white women interested in law observance and law enforcement."[53]

Although black CIC women greeted the advent of the ASWPL with enthusiasm, they took strong exception to Ames's statement that she "frankly" could not see any "contribution the Negro race itself could make in the eradication of lynching." Such a belief, wrote Nannie Burroughs, denied "the power of God to work through the persecuted and thereby help change the heart of the persecutor."[54] The ASWPL received no public criticism from blacks, but on several occasions black members rose on the floor of CIC conventions to question the organization's policy of exclusion. While never officially included, black women continued to participate in ASWPL meetings as guests of the organization, and as we shall see, they worked behind the scenes to influence the white antilynching campaign.[55]

Clearly, the decision to create an organization for white women only reflected the limits of Ames's approach to race relations as well as her devotion to traditional modes of private power and public influence. Like most white southern liberals of the time, she believed implicitly that social reform would come about not through the efforts of blacks but through the mediation of white interracialists between the black community and the white power structure; appealing to Christian and democratic ideals, white leaders would control the process they themselves set in motion. Undoubtedly an effective tactic arising naturally out of the context of the times and Ames's prior experience, the ASWPL's membership policy eliminated the very participants who could have kept the organization accountable to changing black agendas for reform.

A second characteristic of the ASWPL's membership was its urban/rural distribution. Most of the women who attended the founding meetings in 1930 and returned to set state organizations in motion lived in large population centers. Moreover, they were urged by Ames to hold the first statewide organizational meetings in urban areas where, she assumed, the heads of other women's organizations usually resided.[56] In a survey of 122 women who were active members of the ASWPL's central or state councils, 49 percent came from metropolitan areas of over 100,000 persons; a total of 72 percent lived in cities of over 25,000.[57] Thus, despite some exceptions, the ASWPL, whose program was aimed at the rural South, drew most of its leaders from the cities.[58] It was headquartered in Atlanta, the region's major transportation and commercial center and the undisputed capital of the aggressive new middle-class spirit. Nashville, boasting of the largest proportion of college students of any city in the country and vying for the position of southern financial center, supplied the organization with its coterie of strong Methodist women leaders. [59]

It would be a mistake, however, to exaggerate the urbanity of ASWPL leaders. Almost all those whose ages are known were born before the turn of the century; their average age was forty-eight in 1930, and a small but significant group was born in the 1860s. Thus many of these residents of newly expanding cities probably shared with Jessie Daniel Ames origins in the countryside. Such women came of age as sexual tensions and racial violence wracked in the region; their political consciousness was shaped by the search for order in the progressive era. Their deepest premises were informed by moral conviction rather than by cosmopolitan rationalism, and their concern with the dynamics of chivalry and the consequences of interracial sex betrayed their roots in the Victorian past.

Moreover, a number of active members did live in rural counties. Of these 122 women, 13 were from towns of less than 2,500, and 21 from towns with a population of between 2,500 and 25,000. In Mississippi, the most rural of southern states, ASWPL leadership was drawn almost exclusively from small communities. Bessie Alford, chairman of the Mississippi council throughout the life of the organization, lived in McComb, population 10,000. Montie B. Greer, who, as Superintendent of Christian Social Relations for the Mississippi Conference of the Southern Methodist Church, played a major role in the anti-lynching movement in Mississippi, resided in the tiny town of Potts Camp. In other states, too, key women emerged in small towns. Kate T. Davis, influential chairman of the South Carolina ASWPL and later field representative for the CIC, was from Orangeburg, population 10,521. Isa-Beall Neel of Forsyth, Georgia, and Bertha McCollum of Atlantic Beach, Florida, were other active state chairmen from similar communities. "There is nothing that gives me so much hope as the simple steady work that the women are doing in these small towns all over the South," Ames wrote. A report of the work of such Mississippi women, she continued, "moved me to tears."[60]

Moreover, the ASWPL's broader constituency—the 44,000 individuals who signed the anti-lynching pledge—consisted, in the main, of women in small towns, recruited through the missionary societies of the large Protestant denominations. "We set our goal for the first year as one thousand signatures from each of the thirteen Southern states," Ames noted.

> At the end of the first year we found that through the missionary societies in the cities alone it was easy to secure even more than the minimum of one thousand, but we realized the cities rarely lynched and our program, though it might show up a great deal more forceful, was not really doing the work we wanted to do. The next year we changed our goal by setting a minimum of one thousand names from each state in towns of less than five thousand. At the end of the third year we found we could go a little farther and set our goal as a minimum of one thousand names from towns of twenty-five hundred or less.[61]

Thus, even though the ASWPL's founding leaders tended to be members of an urban bourgeoisie, they evinced an increasing commitment to organize where lynching actually took place rather than limit themselves to disavowals of mob violence from the safety of the cities.

The high incidence of city and town dwellers among the association's leaders is mirrored in educational and occupational backgrounds that set them apart from southern women in general. An unusually high percentage worked outside the home for at least some portion of their adult lives. Of the 122 women surveyed, one-half were gainfully employed and all were in clerical or professional positions. Of these 61 employed women, 13 were salaried church executives; others were social workers, journalists, college instructors, librarians, or businesswomen; one was a state legislator, two were lawyers, one a Quaker minister. A smaller proportion were clerks, bank tellers, or WPA employees. One Mississippi woman was a secretary who brought to her job the first typewriter seen in the county. Of the 53 women whose educational background is known, all had attended a college or female academy; of these, 19 had taken graduate courses or attained professional degrees. The ASWPL thus drew its major leaders from a group of women who had already, to some extent, stepped outside the domestic sphere. Like Jessie Daniel Ames, they had been among the first generation of women college graduates in the region, and had acquired the altered self-perceptions associated with economic autonomy.

Whether or not they held jobs, however, most ASWPL members were married women with children; few maintained long-term careers, and doubtless their primary identity lay not in their occupations but in their roles as wives, mothers, and leaders of women's voluntary organizations. Of the 79 women whose husbands' occupations are known, most were the wives of managerial or professional workers. Professional men and politicians made up 42 percent of this group, businessmen 32 percent, and ministers 18 percent. Although their positions ranged from postman, deputy sheriff, pharmacist, and railroad inspector to bishop, governor, and company owner, all were white-collar workers who could supply their wives with a degree of leisure, domestic help, and opportunity for travel. The wives of such men, of course, derived their status in the society at large from that of their husbands. Yet, unless their husbands were very prominent, ASWPL leaders acquired their importance within the association from their *own* positions within organized women's groups, or, to a lesser extent, from their personal accomplishments, not from their husbands' occupations or activities.[62]

The pattern of religious affiliation of ASWPL members flowed directly from the enthusiasm with which denominational women's groups promoted the anti-lynching campaign. Of the 103 leaders whose church membership is known, 55 percent were Methodists, whereas Southern Methodism, the second largest denomination in the region, accounted for only 29 percent of white Protestants. Presbyterians and Episcopalians, who composed 8 percent and 4 percent of white

Protestants, each claimed 16 percent of ASWPL leaders. The Southern Baptist Convention, 34 percent of white Protestants, contributed 11 percent of active ASWPL leaders.[63]

7

Whether housewives, professional workers, or leaders of voluntary organizations, ASWPL women took part in the antilynching campaign under the options and limitations they shared as women. Their secure positions in the middle class gave them certain privileges and immunities; as long as they did not step beyond permissible bounds, they could engage in unconventional activities without endangering either their husbands' jobs or their own social standing. Although some ASWPL leaders were married to men who were also involved in the interracial movement, it appears that in many cases these women took a more active interest in civic affairs than their husbands. Mississippi ASWPL organizer Ethel Stevens, for example, was a vivacious, outspoken participant in a range of voluntary activities, in sharp contrast to her quiet, reliable husband's single-minded devotion to his legal practice. She prided herself on taking a more liberal stance on social issues than her husband's, but at the same time it was he who—in their daughter's opinion—provided her with "the social status so that [she] could express [her] views without suffering."[64] Curious about the prominence of women in social reform in the South, Methodist church leader Louise Young asked an older co-worker why southern men allowed their wives to engage in such "outrageous" activities. "Let them, child," the woman replied. "Why they're so proud of them they don't know what to do. . . . They're so glad that . . . the women can do things their husbands couldn't get away with."[65]

As this anecdote implies, however, the choices of ASWPL women were circumscribed by the sufferance of the men in their lives. The degree of participation by married women depended markedly on the sympathy of their husbands toward the anti-lynching campaign. Bessie Alford, Mississippi chairman, contributed a great deal of time to the ASWL, in part because of her optometrist husband's "deep interest in all that had been accomplished." But Alford's equally dedicated sister-in-law was forbidden by her husband to take part in anti-lynching activities. "I appreciate very much the fact that you consider me enough of a leader for good to want me to be one of your ten key women in the state to fight lynching," she wrote, but

> I am married to a man who does not see things as I do and I have enough opposition to meet from him where my work with the negros is concerned that I do not feel like undertaking any thing else that he is not in sympathy with and like a great many other southern men, he thinks that we women should keep our mouths out of this and let the men take care of it as they think best. Now of course that isn't right but unfortunately for us there are too many men who feel exactly that way about it. However I do not and I deplore the fact that Mississippi leads in this horrible thing but under the circumstances I cannot afford to be militant about it and trust that you will understand my position.[66]

A number of ASWPL women faced with their husband's disapproval or protectiveness hid their activities from their families. Montie B. Greer of Potts Camp, Mississippi, was criticized by the Jackson *Daily News* and received a number of threatening letters; she concealed these threats from her husband and told him about her investigations of lynchings only after they were completed.[67] A Mississippi member searching for women to take leadership responsibilities summed up this fundamental problem: "Of the two ladies who were to have served with me, one has been ailing constantly since our meeting and the other asked to be relieved because of the opposition of her husband. And right there I believe I have discovered my Waterloo."[68]

Moreover, despite their relative affluence, married ASWPL supporters carried time-consuming burdens of housekeeping and child care. In many cases, the inexpensive labor of black domestic servants made their race relations activities possible (an irony that did not go unnoticed among some of the more reflective leaders). Yet members frequently failed to carry out their commitments to the anti-lynching campaign because of family crises and responsibilities. Only a woman who was "fairly free in her domestic responsibilities, having no small children and . . . of especially strong health," Jessie Daniel Ames believed, could carry on the simultaneous roles of home-maker and social activist. [69]

Like their neighbors, ASWPL women also suffered the economic hardships of the Depression. By the mid-thirties, a number of women who had given time to the organization as unpaid volunteers found themselves in financial straits and began searching for some way to carry on their social welfare work as paid professionals. Even a wealthy novelist like George Madden Martin claimed to be financially handicapped as never before and sought payment from the CIC for her services as chairman of the ASWPL. [70] Bessie Alford had to resign the Mississippi state chairmanship to take a job with a relief agency, and many women could not attend ASWPL meetings for lack of travel money. [71] Although in later years, Ames did manage to supply some state chairmen with small stipends to cover the expenses of their work, the CIC never funded additional ASWPL field staff. [72]

The prominent role played by employed women in the anti-lynching campaign indicates that work outside the home may have broadened women's interest in public life as well as provided them with the independence and self-confidence to contravene social norms. On the other hand, only church executives occupied positions of authority and autonomy; most ASWPL women were forced to guard their precarious professional niches from the dangers of controversy. For example, Ruth Atkinson, Director of Community Organization and Negro Welfare for the Florida State Board of Public Welfare, while an enthusiastic ASWPL supporter, felt she had to do her volunteer work behind the scenes in order not to jeopardize her effort to extend state welfare programs to blacks.[73] Jane Cornell, dedicated chairman of the Florida ASWPL, was almost forced to resign because of pressure from her employer.[74] Kate H. Trawick's superior in the Tennessee Public Health Department refused to allow her to take the chairmanship of the state ASWPL. And an Arkansas woman who invited Ames to speak to a conference of social workers cautioned her not to "let anyone know I suggested it."[75]

Writers and journalists enjoyed more freedom from daily scrutiny by their superiors, but the experience of Julia Collier Harris suggests that the frustration of striving for professional recognition while fulfilling the demands of the feminine role may have drained the energy of women sympathetic to the anti-lynching cause. Harris began her career only after raising five younger brothers and sisters for whom she became legal guardian after her parents' deaths. She had, in addition, two children of her own, both of whom died at an early age. As assistant editor of the Columbus *Enquirer-Sun*, she participated fully in her husband Julian's crusade against lynching and the Ku Klux Klan. Both Harrises began writing for the Atlanta *Constitution* after losing their paper in 1929, but Julia gave up her efforts because all the work she did was "contributed gratis and merely to help" her husband. When Julian became editor of the Chattanooga *Times* in 1935, she served as a regular staff columnist and in that position gave the ASWPL extensive press coverage. In the end, however, a "nervous breakdown" sent her to the Asheville, North Carolina, hospital where Zelda Fitzgerald had also been confined, and her illness made both writing and participation in the anti-lynching movement impossible.[76]

Whatever the difficulties of their lives as wives and working women, Ames and her co-workers clearly thought of themselves as southern ladies, and they proposed to work within the conventions of the role, using whatever leverage their position supplied while at the same time confronting the most indelicate of racial and sexual issues. Accordingly, ASWPL members placed a great deal of emphasis on their southern origins. For example, a potential chairman for the Tennessee ASWPL was rejected because she had lived in Nashville only ten years and was not "firmly entrenched" enough.[77] Ames exercised great caution about admitting women who had not been in the South long enough to acquire a "southern viewpoint." Moreover, she explained, "there isn't any use in trying to get the Northern women to lead out in this kind of thing. Either they are timid because they are from the North and easily abashed, or else they are aggressive and give offense."[78] Jane Cornell, chairman of the Florida ASWPL, had lived in the South for thirty years and had "many southern ancestors." Yet she wrote despairingly to Ames that her New Jersey origins had been "thrown in my face . . . and I believe it is one reason why my work as Chairman of the Association is not making the headway it might." Nine months later, she continued to feel that her northern heritage was "bad for the cause."[79]

Dwelling in towns or cities, linked to a national middle-class community through a network of women's groups, yet firmly rooted in a distinctive regional culture and identity, the women of the Anti-Lynching Association were prepared by habit and experience to act out their discontents and moral impulses not through solitary intellectual effort, career ambitions, explicitly feminist protest, or private rebelliousness, but through church-based female institutions. In a generalized profile, an association leader would be seen, above all, as a woman active in a broad range of voluntary organizations. She would owe her primary allegiance to the women's work of the Methodist Church and she would be likely to occupy an elected position on the conference level of the Woman's Missionary Council. At the same time, she would belong to a local women's club or YWCA. She would be in her late forties and would be married to a man who occupied a middle-level professional or managerial position. She would have attended at least one year of college, usually at a small southern women's school. She would not pursue a full-time career, but she would be more likely than southern women in general to have worked at least part of her life in a white-collar, sex-segregated occupation.

The social origins of the anti-lynching campaign's 43,000 local supporters, on the other hand, can only be surmised. Ames denied the charge of elitism occasionally leveled at the ASWPL. When, for example, a speaker pointed out that "poor white trash" were not represented at ASWPL meetings, she insisted that the organization's grass-roots, pledge-signing constituency cut across class lines.[80] All that can be said with certainty is that these local women lived in small towns and that they belonged to the main-line Protestant churches, especially to Southern Methodism. They were undoubtedly less highly educated than the Anti-Lynching Association's leaders and less likely to work outside the home. It seems probable that, despite Ames's claims, many of these local supporters were wives and mothers whose husbands, while certainly not as prosperous as those of the ASWPL's leaders, could be found among small-town and rural elites. What seems primarily to have distinguished these 43,000 women was a hunger for knowledge of an outside world to which they were increasingly linked and participation in a network of missionary societies that exposed them to changing social ideals couched in the language of evangelical reform.

Chapter 7
Deeply Buried Causes

Within a year after sending her band of eleven church leaders out to raise the lynching issue in women's forums across the South, Jessie Daniel Ames had placed herself at the head of a carefully structured new voluntary association. The group's first and most ambitious purpose was ideological: it hoped to persuade southern white women that lynching posed a threat to their own interests and to use such women as a medium for crystallizing public sentiment against the crime. The arguments devised by ASWPL members for their educational campaign reflected the conservative goals of middle-class reform; at the same time, however, their ideas and methods evolved under the impact of changing historical circumstances. Jessie Daniel Ames self-consciously assumed the task of guiding her constituency toward a complex view of the "deeply buried causes" of mob violence.[1] Under her leadership, the Anti-Lynching Association sought not only to bring the region into line with national norms of law observance and social order but also to modify the definition of womanhood in southern society. As a result, the group's internal discussions and public utterances provide a rare and instructive view of the self-images and assumptions of a cross-section of middle-class white women in the twentieth-century South.

1

As we have seen, the first and central argument in the
ASWPL's repertoire pivoted on the role of the southern lady.
Neither Jessie Daniel Ames nor her followers rejected the
norms of ladyhood outright; indeed the anti-lynching campaign
relied for its impact precisely on its members' exemplification
of this ideal.[2] Nevertheless, ASWPL members sought to strike
down the apologetics of lynching by disassociating the image of
the lady from its connotations of female vulnerability and retaliatory violence. With even fewer reservations, they attacked
the paternalism of chivalry. The claim that lynching was necessary as a protection of white women, they argued, masked the
racism out of which mob violence really sprang. The presump-
tive tie between lynching and rape cast white women in the
position of sexual objects—ever threatened by black lust, ever
in need of rescue by their white protectors. Asserting their
identity as autonomous citizens, secure in their own rectitude
and their confidence in the established agents of law enforcement, the women of the ASWPL refused to play the part assigned to them. "Public opinion has accepted too easily the
claim of lynchers and mobsters that they were acting *solely in
the defense of womanhood*," they declared. "Women dare no
longer to permit the claim to pass unchallenged nor allow
themselves to be the cloak behind which those bent upon personal revenge and savagery commit acts of violence and lawlessness."[3]

In language resonant with indignation, the women of the
ASWPL thus exposed hypocrisy and declared their independence from political manipulation. Nothing provoked a quicker
response from the organization than the invocation of "white
southern womanhood" by a politician using "the negro as a political bludgeon" to stir up race hatred and fear and increase
lynching totals.[4] In the summer of 1930, South Carolina
Senator Cole L. Blease based his campaign for renomination in
the Democratic primary on a sensational defense of lynching;

ASWPL state chairman Kate T. Davis reacted quickly with a widely circulated protest. "Whenever the Constitution comes between me and the virtue of the white women of the South," Blease fulminated, "I say to hell with the Constitution!" Replied Davis: "Hundreds of thousands of white women in the South feel that the law . . . is their honorable and reliable protection and avenger. The women of the South are not afraid to stand by the Constitution." When southern congressmen filibustering against federal anti-lynching legislation used the argument that lynching was necessary to prevent rape, ASWPL women deluged them with letters enjoining them to "quit dragging the good name of southern white women through the mud."[5]

Response to the ASWPL campaign indicated the effectiveness of this persistent reiteration of a simple, dramatic motif. To be sure, here and there the women's efforts were greeted with ridicule. A newspaper in a small town in Georgia, for example, published an editorial characterizing the delegates to the first annual meeting as "all fat and forty. . . . We cannot imagine an association of twenty prize fighters and wrestlers," it continued, "more independent or able to protect themselves than the group picture indicates these women to be. But they forget that all women are not endowed with such a formidable line and, if attacked, would be helpless."[6] Even such condescension, however, indicated that the ASWPL's message had hit home, and most southern papers that covered the campaign at all gave their readers a favorable interpretation of its meaning. The formation of the ASWPL, editorialized the Hattiesburg *American*, showed that white women would no longer allow the "perpetrators of such atrocities to hide behind their skirts." Women, noted the Macon *Evening News*, had "announced to their red-handed 'protectors' that they want no more of this rope-and-faggot courtesy."[7] Nor was the significance of this argument lost on later commentators. Looking back from the vantage point of 1949, Lillian Smith, the most eloquent of white critics of the racial and sexual status quo, located herself in a tradition begun by the ASWPL. By 1930, she wrote, white women had ceased to believe the lies of men who "went on with their race-economic exploitation, protecting themselves behind rusty shields of as phony a moral cause as the Anglo-Saxon world has ever witnessed. . . . The lady insurrectionists gathered together in one of our southern cities. . . . They said calmly that they were not afraid of being raped; as for their sacredness, they could take care of it themselves; they did not need the chivalry of lynching to protect them and did not want it." It was, Smith concluded, "a truly subversive affair."[8]

The ASWPL's second argument, like its first, reflected the special concerns of a female constituency. It suggested that lynching "brings contempt upon America as the only country where such crimes occur, discredits our civilization and discounts the Christian religion around the globe." To women schooled in the idiom of evangelicalism, no appeal could be more appropriate; in order to reach a larger audience, however, this argument blended into a more secular defense of U.S. interests abroad. One ASWPL pamphlet stated that lists of lynchings were published throughout the Orient and in Africa and "presented as a reason why [foreign peoples] should not be deceived by American missionaries and exploited by American business men."[9] By the mid-thirties the contention that lynching gave Christianity a bad name included a warning that the practice created "a fertile field for . . . communistic doctrines subversive of American democracy at home."[10] Like other southern liberals, ASWPL leaders undertook the risky course of arousing anticommunist fears as a means of extracting concessions for blacks, while at the same time nervously reassuring white southerners of black patriotism and loyalty. Interracialists warned that the failure to punish lynch mobs would give blacks "every right to feel that there is no help for them except in these most radical organizations [and] the outside world will have some basis for believing the accusations which the Communists are making and will pour hundreds of thousands of dollars into the Communists' treasury for the defense of Negroes in the South."[11] At the same time the CIC circu-

lated a statement by Tuskegee's Robert R. Moton claiming that
if only the practice of lynching were obliterated, American
blacks could be expected to be the staunchest of anticom-
munists. [12]

A third claim that appeared from the beginning in ASWPL
literature insisted that lynching discredited legal processes and
undermined respect for officers of the law. Instead of providing
protection against black aggression, it actually lessened the
ability of the established authorities to maintain social control.
According to the original ASWPL anti-lynching resolution,
lynching was "a menace to private and public safety, and a
deadly blow at our most sacred institutions. Instead of deter-
ring irresponsible and criminal classes from further crime, as it
is argued, lynching tends inevitably to destroy all respect for
law and order." [13]

This analysis, designed to appeal to the interest of women in
domestic peace and of the middle-class in social stability, could
be dangerously double-edged, for it reinforced the racial attitudes that Ames and other ASWPL leaders, in their more in-
sightful moments, saw as the deeper causes of lynching.
Usually implicitly, but sometimes openly, the demand for law
and order promised that blacks could be kept in their place
more efficiently, more permanently, and with less social disorganization by a legal system firmly under the control of whites
than by extralegal lynchings. As one black critic pointed out:
"Your argument that 'the courts will convict Negroes' and that
therefore Negroes need not be lynched, is a cold-blooded proposal to regularize lynching under legal forms." [14]

Almost immediately after the women's campaign began, the
infamous Scottsboro case pushed the issue of "legal lynching"
into the forefront of the struggle for black rights and challenged
the adequacy of the ASWPL's law-and-order argument. [15] In

March 1931, four months after the association's founding, nine young blacks hopped a boxcar at Stevenson, Alabama. A group of white youths, including two women, Ruby Bates and Victoria Price, were also aboard the train. A fight ensued, and when the train arrived in Paint Rock, the nine blacks found themselves charged with rape. Although Ruby Bates later repudiated her claim that the two women had been sexually assaulted, all of the accused were convicted in a hasty trial at Scottsboro, the county seat, and all but the youngest were sentenced to the electric chair. The fate of the Scottsboro boys was not an atypical miscarriage of justice. Represented by an ill-prepared defense counsel appointed by the local court and tried by an all-white jury in an atmosphere of threatened mob violence, they would ordinarily have joined the long ranks of anonymous victims of white justice. Even the NAACP at first held aloof from the case. But the intervention of the Communist-led International Labor Defense (ILD) precipitated a court battle that ended only with the release of the last prisoner in 1950 and made Scottsboro the period's most celebrated symbol of oppression.

The Scottsboro case posed a new dilemma for anti-lynching reformers, for it focused worldwide attention on the court system and demanded that white southern liberals take a stand on more fundamental questions than whether legal formalities had been observed.[16] "Just as we adjust our thinking and action to one line of cooperation and justice something new comes up," wrote one Alabama ASWPL member. As soon as she heard of the arrest of the Scottsboro boys, the Alabama ASWPL chairman, Mary McCoy, had urged a supporter to forestall a lynching by quieting "intemperate talk." But when the defendants had been convicted and the ILD entered an appeal in the case, McCoy was reluctant to attempt any further action that might "connect the Interracial Movement with Communism."[17] None of the Alabama women Ames contacted believed that the Scottsboro defendants deserved to die, but the only solution they could offer was a quiet appeal to the governor or an effort to have the sentences commuted to life imprisonment.[18] Nor were they willing to try even those measures, believing that "if any action was taken by them to protest the verdict it would cut the ground from under their feet in their campaign to prevent lynching."[19]

Meanwhile, northern liberals urged the ASWPL to make public its position on the case. The Southern Commission on the Study of Lynching agreed that the Scottsboro affair lay within the bounds of its research, and Will Alexander and the CIC conducted private investigations and worked to discredit the ILD, thus aiding the NAACP's attempt to gain control of the defense. Jessie Daniel Ames, however, answered an appeal for help from Theodore Dreiser and the National Committee for the Defense of Political Prisoners by reaffirming her commitment to a single-issue campaign against lynching.[20] Her organization would make no headway, she replied, if it took official action on the Scottsboro case. "The women are proving courageous and thoroughly undaunted under all circumstances, but their only argument to which they can get any hearing at all is that constituted law protects womanhood and society." Moreover, she believed that southern blacks themselves saw the eradication of lynching as the first priority for reform. She had talked to Negroes all over the region, she claimed. "They have said that above all things lynchings were the most horrible thing that could happen to them."[21]

Like Will Alexander and other southern interracialists, Ames came to believe that the Scottsboro case had assumed spectacular proportions primarily because of the intervention of the ILD. The overwhelming endorsement of the ILD's efforts by the black press did nothing to mitigate her conviction that the radical organization was exploiting the affair for the sake of propaganda and fund-raising.[22] What concerned her most, however, was that Scottsboro had given lynchers a new rationale for their crime. The ASWPL, she argued, was accomplishing one of its major goals: southern editors were becoming less willing to "lay themselves open to ridicule" by defending lynching on the grounds of gallantry.[23] But now they had a new justification: loopholes in the law and clever radical lawyers made legal procedures against blacks too slow and uncertain. "A great, liberal and influential daily paper," for example, blamed the Tuscaloosa, Alabama, lynchings of 1933 not on the "hot-heads who took the law into their own hands," but on the defenders of the Scottsboro boys. The paper concluded, "The maggoty beaks of the belled buzzards of the International Labor Defense League are stained with the blood of the three Negroes whose torn bodies this morning lie in newly turned graves." Lynching, a law enforcement club told Jessie Daniel Ames, "is a warning to the Courts from the public" that black defendants were no longer being punished quickly and harshly enough under the law. [24]

However much she might deplore the use of the Scottsboro case by the left on the one hand and by the defenders of lynching on the other, Jessie Daniel Ames perceived that the questions raised by this *cause célèbre* could not be avoided. Indeed, she herself took advantage of the opportunity it offered to "deepen the thinking" of the women of the ASWPL. "Picture the courthouse under guard by several thousand men down from the hills to join the mob to see that justice is done," she admonished.

> The jury sitting within the court room hearing the evidence but listening to the noise of the rioters, trying to render a "fair and impartial" verdict guaranteed by the Constitution to every American citizen regardless of race, yet sensing the restive stirring of the human mass gone mad, knowing that the shouts of gratified passion greeting each sentence of death will be turned into snarls of rage against them if they interpret the evidence contrary to the verdict of the mob.

Such "legal lynchings," she concluded, rocked the foundations of American democracy. [25]

Throughout the period, the ASWPL probed the implications of the court's treatment of blacks. "Which is Better—A Lynching or the Prostitution of the Courts and a Prevented Lynching?" became a recurring discussion topic at ASWPL meetings. Beneath the symptom of lynching, Jessie Daniel Ames argued, lay the disease of a legal system that punished blacks with disproportionate severity while letting mob members escape unscathed. Far from slipping through "legal loopholes," blacks uniformly received perfunctory trials and maximum sentences. The public's low estimate of the black man's worth, she pointed out in a report to ASWPL members, "the ready assumption of his guilt, his ignorance of court procedure, his lack of money and friends and political influence, all make his arrest and conviction easier than that of the white man." In contrast, perpetrators of mob violence broke the law with impunity. In a leaflet entitled *Whither Leads the Mob?* she cited case after case in which troops were called in to uphold legally constituted authority—but not a single instance in which mob leaders were prosecuted for their criminal acts. As in the Scottsboro case, the court cringed "before the mob's mad ravings." Complying with the demand for a verdict of guilty, the government itself carried out "legal lynchings . . . and the Constitution and the law become a hollow mockery."[26]

By the late thirties most participants in ASWPL meetings seem to have agreed that the legal system was weighted against blacks. But rather than act on this realization, ASWPL leaders continued to reassure whites that legal processes could be as "swift and sure" as lynch mobs and gave tacit support to critics of the Scottsboro defense by campaigning for legal reforms to ensure speedy trials. An executive committee meeting in 1936 condemned "legal lynchings" vigorously but finally concluded that such corruption of the courts posed less "danger to social institutions" than mob violence.[27]

Just as the Scottsboro case raised the question of legal justice in a manner that the ASWPL could not ignore, so it challenged the organization to confront the issues of rape and interracial sex. In the beginning, ASWPL discussions revealed a distress-

ing ambivalence about what participants could bring themselves to refer to only as "the unspeakable crime." Although
the women gathered for the founding meeting were united in
their opposition to extralegal violence, they did not necessarily
assume that white women's fears of sexual assault were without
foundation. Ames tried to close the subject with statistical
proof that only a small proportion of lynch victims were accused of rape. But however conscientiously she might steer the
discussion toward what she regarded as the main topic—
"lynching as a lawless act"—other participants kept returning
to the subject of rape itself. "The white women are afraid," asserted Mary McCoy of Alabama. Was anything being done in
the counties to speed up the trials of Negro rapists? asked
another participant.[28] These doubts and fears surfaced once
more at a joint meeting between the ASWPL and the black
women of the CIC held in 1933. "What program should be
carried on by Negro women to educate their people?" asked
Ames. Teach their sons "that rape is a worse crime than murder," answered a white ASWPL member. "Doing away with
rape would do away with lynching."[29] Such preoccupations
were aired only in private discussions, never in public pronouncements, and after the first few years they were less often
voiced at all. Nevertheless, the fact remained that many of the
women whom the ASWPL education campaign hoped to reach
felt constrained and intimidated by their own sexual vulnerability. And the image most powerfully embodying their fear
was that of the black rapist.

Although Jessie Daniel Ames herself never admitted to such
feelings, she could not discount altogether the effect on women
of the danger of sexual assault. In a letter to Ames in 1931,
Theodore Dreiser offered a not atypical hint of the attitude of
the left toward rape when he criticized the imposition of capital
punishment for a crime which was, after all, "natural human
conduct." Indeed, as a North Carolina ASWPL supporter indicated, rape might be seen as an extension of ordinary masculine attitudes toward women, but that fact in no way mitigated
its seriousness. Whatever his race, she wrote, a man who "se-

duced and ruined" a young girl should be "put out of the way
. . . like a mad dog."[30] The ASWPL responded to such views
not by discounting them but by trying to separate them from
their racial implications. In the end, Ames could only say that
"whether their own minds perceive danger where none exists,
or whether the fears have been put in their minds by men's
fears," the terror of sexual assault was deeply embedded in the
feminine psyche. "Someday someone is going to be bold
enough to write fully and completely about the Southern white
women through slavery up to the present," Ames concluded,
"but that day is far off."[31] Meanwhile she held to her task of
convincing women as well as men that the way to prevent the
crime of rape did not lie in extralegal violence.

The Scottsboro case, however, provided Ames with another
dilemma, for it posed the disturbing possibility that behind
many accusations of rape might lie clandestine interracial affairs. The character of Ruby Bates and of Victoria Price quickly
became a central issue in the Scottsboro controversy. Although
the defense attorney Samuel Leibowitz's effort to picture Victoria Price as a "cut-rate prostitute" infuriated Alabamians, by
1933 many metropolitan dailies in the South and many southern moderates believed the women had not in fact been raped
by the Scottsboro defendants.[32]

Convinced by the efforts of the defense and by the CIC's
own investigation that the Scottsboro women were indeed
"common prostitutes," Ames began delving beneath the surface of lynchings in which a white woman was involved. As she
did so she was "shocked" to find that white women did indeed
voluntarily "cohabit with Negro men."[33] In the late 1930s, the
accusation of some black anti-lynching reformers that white
women commonly covered up their own transgressions by sac-
rificing their black lovers to the lynch mob was given a psychoanalytic twist by writers like Helene Deutsch. False rape
charges, Deutsch suggested, reflected the masochistic fantasies
of white women. White men, sensing the psychic reality of
such declarations, "react emotionally to them as if they were
real. The social situation permits them then to discharge this

emotion upon the negroes."[34] Finding little evidence for such claims in her own investigations, Ames placed the blame on men who, in revealing contradiction to their espousal of the code of chivalry, falsely and knowingly portrayed their own wives and daughters as victims of sexual assault. At the same time, by the end of the decade most ASWPL leaders were thoroughly disabused of the notion that, as one Mississippi editor claimed, there had never been a southern white woman so totally depraved as to "bestow her favors on a black man."[35]

The organization's literature, however, usually shied away from a direct confrontation with this issue. For one thing, as the Scottsboro defense had learned, an attack on the virtue of white southern womanhood could be extremely unpopular. The jury did not even discuss, let alone consider, Ruby Bates's testimony denying her earlier story. Victoria Price "might be a fallen woman," commented a spectator, "but by God she is a white woman." The prosecution pleaded for conviction in order to ensure "that it doesn't happen to some other woman." And in his charge to the jury, Judge William W. Callahan remarked that when a white woman had intercourse with a black man, the presumption must be that she had been raped. At a district meeting of the Methodist Woman's Missionary Council in Scottsboro, reported an ASWPL supporter, "All were agreed that the punishment fitted the crime, since the assailants were *black*. No white woman would be safe if such crimes were not punishable by death. Regardless of the status of the girls justice must be meted out and quickly, since they were *white* girls."[36]

Certainly the ASWPL's admission that intercourse between white women and black men was not *prima facie* evidence of rape was, in the context of the times, an important step. But the reaction of some members to this insight also typified the more repressive impulses of white interracialism. Jessie Daniel Ames, for example, wrote to ASWPL members in Alabama that "we women must consider . . . some kind of action against loose white women who do cohabit with Negroes."[37] And in 1935, Kate Davis of South Carolina indicated just what such "action" might entail. A lynching, she reported, had been narrowly averted when a white woman in Orangeburg gave birth to a black man's child. The grand jury considering the case suggested that the city council adopt a segregation ordinance to prevent the "racial intermingling" that gave rise to such affairs, and Davis played a significant role in seeing that the law was finally enacted. [38] Five years later, she was still working to enforce and extend housing segregation in South Carolina. "I had a map drawn," she reported to the ASWPL executive committee, "with every home marked where it was black or white." Then she contacted property owners who were renting houses in "Negro sections" to whites. "The first thing we knew they were exchanging renters. . . . It was all done in a fine way." Of course, Davis concluded, "it is going to take another year or two to correct some of the problems. There are women in all towns who cater to Negro men." [39]

The ASWPL's urge to control sexual mores also led, more positively, to a process of internal education about the exploitation of black women. In 1920, CIC leaders had launched the women's interracial movement with protests against the sexual double standard. In the winter of 1931, Jessie Daniel Ames continued this tradition by organizing a meeting with black CIC women for what she hoped would be a "free and frank" discussion of their mutual grievances against masculine behavior. The women, she felt, should gather in closed session with no men present "because there are some vices of Southern life which contribute subtly to this crime that we want to face by ourselves, and we Southern white women still have a feeling that many things we know we should not know. Consequently, when there are . . . men present we feign ignorant [sic] because of our traditional training." The black leader Nannie Burroughs agreed: "All meetings with white and colored women on this question should be held behind closed doors and men should not be admitted." [40]

Ames opened the discussion with the question, "Have slavery and reconstruction in the South produced a *Double Standard of Ethical and Moral Conduct* based upon race? If so, does this *Double Standard* contribute to the phenomenon of lynching in the South?"[41] The conversation that followed touched on the ways in which legal, political, and economic discrimination against blacks created a climate of opinion conducive to violence. But the group's most impassioned exchanges focused on the status of women. White male attitudes, they concluded, originated in a slave system in which black women "did not belong to themselves but were in effect the property of white men." To rationalize sexual exploitation the myth arose that "Negro women invited and preferred promiscuous relationships with white men. . . . Negro women were looked upon as degraded creatures, quite without instincts of personal decency and self-respect. As a corollary to this conception of Negro women in terms of animal wantoness, white public opinion conceived all white women in terms of angelic purity." This double standard had resulted in a society that "considers an assault by a white man as a moral lapse upon his part, better ignored and forgotten, while an assault by a Negro against a white woman is a hideous crime punishable with death by law or lynching."[42]

Throughout the ASWPL campaign ran the core themes of female moral reform: the desire to control male sexuality, erase the double standard, and impose the ethics of domesticity on the larger society. Confronting the sexual abuse of black women, Ames felt, "is logically the next step in our whole program." She urged ASWPL members to encourage respect for black women by personal example and to build community institutions providing "moral and spiritual safeguards for adolescent girls."[43] "The relationship of the Negro woman to the white woman here in the South," she commented to Charlotte Hawkins Brown, "is so very close, and such immense power rests in the hands of the white women to establish the status of the Negro woman that I have taken every opportunity which has come my way to open the minds of the southern white women in regard to their . . . responsibility in this matter."[44] Nevertheless, the issue of rape, like the demand for courtroom justice, remained a latent preoccupation, never surfacing as a major argument in the association's repertoire.

4

The ASWPL's final argument attempted to grapple with the class nature of lynching and with the relation of racial violence to the operations of the plantation economy. Lynching occurred most often, a typical ASWPL analysis ran, in sparsely populated rural counties during the summer months; it was brought on by idleness, pent up emotions awakened by revivals and "competition between lower class whites and blacks." Blacks guilty of raping white women were "illiterate and feeble-minded" and thus themselves victims of society. Lynchers were often "mentally defective" unskilled laborers. Lynching was, then, a manifestation of social pathology, a "reversion to barbarism" by the deprived poor whites of the countryside. Ames sought to convince her constituency that "fairer treatment, better schools . . . certain human considerations will do more [to preserve racial peace] than a lynching." [45] By placing blame on the rural poor, this interpretation of racial violence could absolve middle-class whites of responsibility. But it also enabled the ASWPL to link the anti-lynching campaign with an issue increasingly in the spotlight of national attention: the plight of the southern tenant farmer. The Works Progress Administration, the Farm Security Administration, and other New Deal agencies, Ames emphasized, were making an important contribution to the fight against lynching by giving "debt-ridden, bankrupt, and poverty-depressed families of both races . . . a new lease on life." [46] Most importantly, as ASWPL women inquired more closely into the economic causes of racial violence, they began to stress not the racism of "poor whites" but the roots of lynching in white supremacy itself.

This focus on the structural implications of lynching increased through the decade of the thirties as mob murders gave way to new, less spectacular, forms of violence against blacks. [47] By 1933, ASWPL leaders were discussing the "changing character of lynching," and Ames began to suggest that lynchings were being carried out with greater frequency by small groups of upper-class men acting with quiet premeditation.[48] In fact, she claimed, "prominent people," especially in Deep South plantation areas, engineered over 50 percent of the lynchings. Such a condemnation of reactionary plantation owners came with relative ease to urban-based reformers like Jessie Daniel Ames. But she, and other ASWPL leaders, went one step further. Whether ruling elites actually participated or not, ASWPL literature pointed out, lynching survived only because of the tacit collaboration of the whole white community. "What group benefits most by the cheap and subservient labor guaranteed by a system of white supremacy and enforced in the final analysis by lynching?" Ames asked participants in an ASWPL annual meeting. "We ourselves profit most by cheap labor," she replied.[49]

At the annual meeting of 1934, the ASWPL adopted a resolution that Ames regarded as a landmark in the development of ASWPL thought:[50]

> We reaffirm our condemnation of lynching for any reason whatsoever. . . . We declare as our deliberate conclusion that the crime of lynching is a logical result in every community that pursues the policy of humiliation and degradation of a part of its citizenship because of accident of birth; that exploits and intimidates the weaker element . . . for economic gain; that refuses equal educational opportunity to one portion of its children; that segregates arbitrarily a whole race in unsanitary, ugly sections; that permits the lawless elements of both races to congregate in these segregated areas with little fear of molestation by the law; and finally that denies a voice in the control of government to any fit and proper citizen because of race.[51]

There had been "many public statements on the subject, emanating from social welfare groups," commented the black editor of the Norfolk *Journal and Guide*, "but we have never seen one that was as unequivocal" as the 1934 resolution of the ASWPL. "All honor and glory to the Association of Southern Women for the Prevention of Lynching!"[52] Clearly, ASWPL leaders had added to their concern for law enforcement and sexual morality a more penetrating analysis of the functional significance of racial violence.

Writing about the ASWPL six years after its dissolution, Lillian Smith commented that few of these anti-lynching reformers "had disciplined intellects or giant imaginations and probably no one of them grasped the full implications of this sex-race-religion-economics tangle."[53] Indeed, the leaders of the women's campaign against lynching were primarily moralists, not social theorists. None, including Jessie Daniel Ames, were original thinkers, and their attitudes toward social questions ranged across a broad political spectrum. The lowest common denominator of their crusade was an impulse toward social order, and many of the women whose names appear on ASWPL membership lists probably shared the white supremacist views of their contemporaries. Nevertheless, the ASWPL provided a forum in which women drawn from the entire range of middle-class women's organizations in the region confronted issues whose implications went far beyond the substitution of legal for extralegal forms of social control. In ASWPL discussions, black and white women explored together their position in southern society, and Ames took every opportunity to use the prism of lynching for exploring sexual as well as racial oppression.

Many of the arguments employed in the ASWPL educational campaign could also be found in the research of sociologists and of the NAACP. But the ASWPL conveyed this information to men and women who would be unlikely to read such scholarly works and who viewed the northern-based black protest group as a threat to their most keenly felt values. Association literature simplified and reiterated the claims of other anti-lynching reformers and translated social research into palatable and comprehensible forms. Most significantly, it shaped its rhetoric in accord with specifically feminine interests and assumptions. Through the decade of the thirties, the leaders of the women's campaign against lynching succeeded in disseminating their central message, if not their more complex ideas, to an ever widening audience in the white South.

Like ASWPL arguments, the means used by the organization to communicate its message evolved over time, reflecting a creative search for social efficacy. First among the media employed was the printed word; the ASWPL issued approximately 10,000 pieces of literature a year—a barrage of pamphlets, flyers, and articles, many of which were composed by Ames herself. In a period when social activists increasingly turned to the visual power of documentary photography and vivid first-person reportage, ASWPL material relied on a low-keyed mixture of facts, statistics, and declarations of principle.[54] Unlike the NAACP, which endeavored to shock white Americans into moral outrage, the ASWPL seemed deliberately to avoid making lynching too real to its readers. For example, in 1937 the NAACP emphasized the debasing effects of mob violence on the white children who witnessed it by circulating photographs of a crowd of men, women, and children staring at the mutilated body of a lynch victim. At the same time, the ASWPL decided that its own posters should avoid "over-sensational or emotional" illustrations in favor of simple statistical graphs.[55] Behind this caution lay Ames's belief that while few of the middle-class women who received ASWPL literature would be aggressive proponents of mob violence, many of them would view lynchings as unfortunate but inevitable affairs that should not be talked about in polite society. "These happenings," wrote one woman, "are purely local affairs and shouldn't be broadcast through the papers. There are skeletons in county and state closets, as well as in the family closet. Just keep the door closed."[56] For the most part, ASWPL literature attacked not the open racism of potential lynchers but the entrenched apathy of the comfortable middle class. The last thing a women's club or missionary society wanted, Ames felt, was the intrusion of unsavory tales of horror upon its weekly meeting.

Yet in its careful, factual way, ASWPL literature did hammer

away at the truth of murder and humiliation behind the fa-
cade of racial peace. Of the four Negroes lynched in South
Carolina in 1933, read one ASWPL leaflet, two were not even
charged with a crime. One, a farm tenant, was shot to death in
his home at midnight by a masked mob after he repeatedly
asked his white landlord for a crop settlement. Near Moultrie,
Georgia, an innocent Negro was lynched when the mob could
not find its intended victim. At Tuscaloosa, Alabama, a helpless
paralytic was lynched on the charge of attempted rape.[57] Moreover, as Jessie Daniel Ames and the more active ASWPL
leaders learned about the concrete terrors of lynching, they
tried in turn to convey their experience to other women. "I
don't know whether they will get perfectly furious with me or
not," Ames commented, as she fired off a graphic account of
the slow torture, castration, and death of Claude Neal to all the
women on her mailing list in Jackson County, Florida, where
the lynching took place.[58]

In general, however, Ames issued her most hard-hitting
rhetoric from the podium rather than the printed page. Though
the ASWPL did produce brief, simple flyers meant as "popular
literature," its publications served primarily as adjuncts to first-
person testimony. The ASWPL's audience, Ames believed,
could be divided into three groups: those who already shared
its outlook, those who were fanatically opposed, and a "large
middle group with open minds willing to be convinced." It was
to the last that she directed her efforts, and she perceived that
they could be most effectively reached through their own
trusted reference groups. Speaking as insiders to women's
clubs and church organizations, ASWPL leaders could vastly
amplify the meaningfulness and acceptability of their message.
The only way to "bridge that gap between a selected group
. . . and the masses," Ames argued, was through "personal
presentations and contacts—a word of mouth campaign."[59]
Like Frances Willard, who used prohibition to lead into the
political arena women who would never have entered otherwise, Ames hoped to make lynching a compelling "women's
issue." When asked to speak on any subject, "you will be sur-

prised how perfectly easy it is to close on lynching," she told her supporters.[60] With such encouragement, ASWPL women found ways to raise the lynching issue before hundreds of audiences throughout the region.

Ames herself was the most prolific of ASWPL lecturers, and until her pace began to slow in the late thirties, she kept up a steady itinerary of speaking engagements. In one eighteen-month period she spoke to thirty-six separate groups scattered throughout the South. These speeches served as Ames's chief means for propagating her political ideas, as well as for reinforcing her position of authority and leadership.[61] Carefully tailoring her words to her audience, she could be a master of circumspection. An audience of PTA women, a gathering of 150 northern women in Miami, a black women's club, a police officer's association—each required its subtle differences of language and approach, and she cultivated an ability to match her message to the "peculiar psychology" of each. At the annual ASWPL meeting of 1937, Ames instructed other ASWPL leaders in this method. When talking to a women's club or other civic organization, she explained, "I talk on World Peace—something I know they are working on. . . . You can tie lynching up with Peace, you can tie it up with such hard knots that they can hardly proceed on Peace." When talking to a women's missionary society, "there is only one approach and that is . . . on the Bible." By making careful use of biblical references, "you don't have to talk about social equality, you don't have to talk about lynching in regard to women, you don't have to talk about the alleged crimes for which lynchings are committed—you can talk about the crime of lynching and its relation to Christian brotherhood." In conclusion, Ames urged her co-workers to develop an ability extemporaneously to shape their rhetoric by a sensitive reading of audience response. "We can't talk to people except in . . . mental images of the kind that they understand."[62]

Once her audience was prepared for "mental images" of a more challenging kind, Ames could deliver an incisive critique of racial violence. The soul of judiciousness in printed literature, she achieved her greatest clarity and persuasivenes in her speeches. Like many reformers of the progressive era, she saw herself primarily as an educator of a middle-class public that, once informed and enlightened, could be counted on to rectify injustice. But she also subscribed to an understanding of racial attitudes rooted in William Graham Sumner's theory of "folkways" and applied to regional problems by the sociologist and Interracial Commission leader Howard W. Odum. Racial practices, Odum held, were embedded in a folk culture amenable only to a slow process of evolutionary transformation.[63] Such a notion resonated with Ames's own experience, both political and personal. She had seen the failure of women's suffrage to alter basic sexual attitudes; the interracial movement had scarcely shaken the ideology of white supremacy. Moreover, she recognized the dichotomy between her own emotional life and the controlled, rational demeanor she presented to the outside world. For these reasons, she evinced a sharp perception of the irrational depths of racism that liberal environmentalists of the period often sought to minimize or deny. "Back of all mob outbursts," she believed, lay "psychological factors which are not responsive to reason." And when she could confront her audience face to face, she sought not only to persuade the intellect but to touch the emotions as well. She called herself a born "rabble-rouser." "If I had been a man," she observed, "I would have been an awfully good revivalist."[64]

Before a gathering of Southern Presbyterian women, for example, she juxtaposed the complicity of the church in maintaining the notion of black inferiority with the function of the Gospel as a judgment on manmade traditions, developing the theme with eloquence and anger. She ended by calling on church women to transcend their own culture by identifying themselves with prophetic tradition.[65] In another talk delivered to several audiences that same year, she pointed to the way in which political and church leaders "pounded into the minds of the white South nearly a century ago [a monolithic ideology of racism] and all for the purpose of establishing and maintaining an economic kingdom built on cotton." After the

Civil War and the destruction of slavery, racial solidarity was ensured and "the Negro re-enslaved by condoning crimes against the persons of Negroes." The Negro race, she continued,

> was cast outside the law. . . . Added to this was—and is—the peculiarly construed chivalry, which of necessity—if the belief in racial superiority was to be maintained—must place all white women in a category characterized by physical frailty, goodness, purity, and chastity, and all Negro men in a category characterized by brutish build and sex perversion.
>
> To establish in the public emotions the conception of the Negro race as inherently and everlastingly inferior, disfranchisement was secured. . . . Segregation of the Negro . . . sets even more firmly in the public emotions the feeling that Negroes as a race of people are not only inferior but unfit and unclean. . . .
>
> Through the process of disfranchisement and segregation, the Negro has been reduced to a state of helplessness to the local white man's will against which he rebels at the peril of his life. He is to work when, where and for how much he is told to work. Failure to comply is punished according to the white man's state of mind or digestion. [66]

Ames's reputation for forthrightness preceded her, and often she was able to gain access to an audience only through the intervention of a few strong supporters. In South Carolina, Alice Spearman Wright and her friend Rebecca Reid, a former YWCA secretary from Sumter County, invited Ames to speak to the state interracial commission despite the opposition of other members of the group. Once there, Wright recalled, Ames was able to "muster the facts and make a most effective presentation." [67] Moreover, while Ames's appearances often received only the perfunctory press coverage routinely given to women's activities, they occasionally drew a storm of protest. In 1935, for example, Ames was speaking in Austin, Texas, when two black youths were lynched in Columbus for allegedly raping and murdering a nineteen-year-old girl. Ames assailed the local county attorney—who had announced that he considered the mob's action "an expression of the will of the people"—and called on the governor to investigate the incident. In response, the Columbus Chamber of Commerce adopted a resolution denouncing the ASWPL director, and a local attorney suggested that her organization should "enter upon a campaign of education for the purpose of teaching the colored brother to keep his black hands off our white women and girls."[68] Afterward, Ames had to confess that "it did take a lot of courage to live for the next week or ten days, when anonymous letters and threats were sure to come in."[69]

Gradually other women initiated their own speaking engagements. "In some states," Ames recalled, "there was expressed keen resentment against women assuming leadership in an open educational program to eradicate lynching. . . . The best way to take care of this, the women believed, was not to argue but to increase the number of women willing to undertake to speak against lynching." By 1936, several hundred ASWPL women were able and willing to deliver public addresses in the organization's behalf, and state speakers' bureaus had relieved Ames of the burden of representing the anti-lynching campaign throughout the region.[70]

One of the most successful of these state speakers was Mississippi ASWPL chairman, Bessie Alford. She dreaded her first appearance before the state federation of women's clubs. "The higher ups," she wrote, "have such a Superiority Complex"; moreover, the lynching issue lacked "the popularity they are ambitious for." Nevertheless, Alford overcame her trepidation and succeeded in winning the organization's support.[71] Almost as intimidating was a speaking engagement before the Mississippi Baptist Convention: "One dear old Sister," Alford reported, "took the floor [and] came out four square against the program." As a result, Alford was not able to secure a single signature on the anti-lynching pledge.[72] Even the women of her own Methodist church could be "very evasive." Some objection to the ASWPL program, she believed, was keeping the signatures from coming in. Methodist men were more recalcitrant; it took Alford five years to convince the Mississippi Conference of the Methodist Church to pass its first anti-lynching resolution. Finally, at the annual meeting of 1936, when the Conference Board refused to put her on the program, she presented an anti-lynching resolution from the floor and had a supporter planted in the audience ready to second her motion. The passage of the resolution, she reflected, was the high point of her life. In 1939, almost sixty-five years old and nearing retirement, Alford was still "using all methods" to get the anti-lynching program before the people of Mississippi and was trying to branch out into appearances before college groups. By the late thirties, when the organization was at the height of its power and self-confidence, Alford and her Mississippi women inaugurated state anti-lynching institutes that were announced in the press and open to the public, and thus designed as "mass meetings." [73]

Other ASWPL leaders reported similar difficulties and triumphs. Not until 1935, for example, was Jane Cornell of Florida able to appear before the state Episcopal Convention without confronting open hostility and "black looks" from the audience. Like Bessie Alford, Ethel Mae Lawhorn of Oklahoma reported that signature pledges gathered at a church women's meeting had been lost, and "the only explanation for the disappearance was that they had come to the hand of an unsympathetic listener." Similarly, Ruth Knox complained that an anti-lynching resolution adopted by her synod had been deliberately omitted from the published proceedings of the meeting. [74] "Some of us," Ames reflected, "have traveled half the night in a day coach to speak for three minutes to an audience which most reluctantly received us. The state leaders have sunk their personalities so completely in the purposes of the cause that they have forgotten the meaning of the word rebuff." ASWPL women had been shocked by the hatred and prejudice demonstrated by "educated people" from whom they had expected understanding and cooperation. On the other hand, they were "confounded and humbled by the generous spirit and big heart of others who in our ignorance and pride we assumed would oppose us." They had, Ames concluded,

"been up against real conditions and we are going to continue
to go up against them." [75]

6

One of Jessie Daniel Ames's more innovative tactics for confronting ASWPL participants with the "real conditions" that
surrounded them was to cast them in the role of investigative
reporters to their female constituency. At first, she "had no
thought of going . . . to the scenes of lynching after it occurred and talking with the citizens of the community—men
and women in all walks of life." But as ASWPL leaders fanned
out to speaking engagements across the South, they continued
to encounter audiences willing to denounce lynching in general
but convinced that an incident in their own communities was
either an unavoidable eruption of irrational violence or a case
of justifiable retribution for rape. In order to pierce this veil of
myth, rumor, and deliberately suppressed fact, they decided to
venture out into the field. At first Ames led each investigation,
accompanied by women from the state and, if possible, the
county in which the lynching occurred. For example, Ames
and Dorothy R. Tilly of Atlanta traveled hundreds of miles
through rural Georgia probing lynching incidents in counties
"solid for Eugene Talmadge" where there was "not a railroad
or an inch of paved highway." [76] But soon local women, especially in Mississippi, Georgia, and Florida, were initiating their
own inquiries. From 1933 to 1935, Ames investigated 20 lynchings, all of which involved an alleged attack on a white woman.
By 1941, ASWPL women had conducted 46 such case studies. [77] In many of these inquiries, ASWPL representatives relied on the testimony of local whites. But on a number of occasions, they overcame their own biases and the suspicion of a
recently terrorized black community and gained access to the
black version of lynching incidents. [78] The information they

gathered in this way enabled ASWPL leaders to convey to their constituency, through periodic bulletins and word of mouth, the genesis of specific acts of racial violence.

As the decade progressed, Ames began to explore new, more dramatic channels for broadcasting the anti-lynching message. Influenced by the documentary movement of the times and by the genre of folk drama made famous by the Carolina Playmakers at Chapel Hill, she sponsored a contest for original plays on the theme of lynching. The two winning entries were "Country Sunday," written by Walter Spearman of the University of North Carolina, and "Lawd, Does You Undahstan?" submitted by Ann Seymour and first produced by the School of Dramatics at Paine College in Augusta, Georgia. Performed before church and college audiences across the South, these folk dramas represented an attempt to make vivid to a middle-class audience the human suffering caused by mob violence. [79]

Precisely because they succeeded in graphically portraying the realities behind the statistics that were the staple of the ASWPL's printed literature, these dramatic productions drew strenuous opposition. The vice-president of the South Carolina Federation of Women's Clubs "blew up" when Ames tried to present the plays to the federation. [80] In the midst of a production at Peachtree Christian Church in Atlanta, Jessie Daniel Ames, sitting inconspicuously in the audience, was attacked by Mrs. J. E. Andrews, editor of the right-wing *Georgia Woman's World*, who accused her of fostering intermarriage "just as fast as possible." "In the meantime," Ames recalled, "all my would-be friends were getting out of the church as fast as they could because there was a lot of noise . . . and it did look as though we were going to have a fight. Mrs. Andrews said, 'Just for a nickel I'd slap you in the face.' And I said, 'Well, I have a nickel.' And she skirted herself around and flapped out of the place." [81]

In practice, most ASWPL literature, speeches, and plays reached an audience of organized women; [82] consequently, in her effort to reach the general public, Ames relied heavily on a fourth medium: a sympathetic press. Ames had energetically sought the support of influential newspaper editors while lobbying for women's rights and social welfare measures in Texas. In the anti-lynching campaign, she made it her particular task to cultivate close relations with the southern press. Editors like Grover Hall of the Montgomery *Advertiser*, Mark Ethridge of the Louisville *Courier-Journal*, Virginius Dabney of the Richmond *Times-Dispatch*, Josephus Daniels of the Raleigh *News and Observer*, and George Fort Milton of the Chattanooga *Times* were already speaking out against lynching. Many of them were supporters or members of the CIC, and they gave the ASWPL its most extensive publicity.[83] Although Ames was grateful "for editorial commendation of our courage and nobility in openly working against lynching," she was convinced that the real power to affect attitudes lay in news coverage. Accordingly, she set out to "reach the men who control this power."[84] From the outset of the campaign, she encouraged ASWPL women to register their disapproval of local editors who covered black crimes in lurid detail or announced impending lynchings days in advance.[85]

These efforts culminated in 1936 when Ames sent curt letters to newspaper editors through the South complaining about the discrepancies between their anti-lynching editorial policies and their inflammatory reporting of the news.[86] In return, she was invited to speak to the annual meeting of the Southern Newspaper Publishers' Association—an address that was one of the high points of her career. Few women had ever been asked to appear before this almost exclusively male conclave, and only three women were present in the audience when Ames made her presentation. It was the kind of gathering Ames most respected and seldom had access to: hard-bitten, politically sophisticated, influential men. Moreover, she would speak on a subject that she believed to be of vital importance. The rise of facsism and communism in Europe had intensified her interest in the use of propaganda and the influence of the mass media on public consciousness.[87] And she was convinced that a trans-

formation in the way lynching was depicted in the popular
press would go farther than any other single acomplishment in
changing public attitudes toward it.[88]

Citing examples garnered from the ASWPL's large collection
of news clippings, Ames pointed out to the assembled journalists the contradiction between editorial denunciations of lynching and the conventionalized rhetoric of news stories that
whipped up hatred and encouraged violence. Headlines reading "Girl Sobs Story," "Fugitive is Believed in River Bottoms,"
and "Feeling is Intense as Posse Scours Woods" echoed like a
Greek chorus, commenting on the developing tragedy and
creating the atmosphere in which it was certain to take place.
Alleged rape victims were invariably "young, lovely, innocent,
devout in her religious life, loving, affectionate; now broken and
ruined, a glorious future and proud womanhood destroyed and
blasted." Details that might cast doubt on the guilt of the accused or on the motives of his pursuers were suppressed. After
such stories, the dignified language of editorials was "like the
silent fall of dew after a terrific hail storm." This sometimes unconscious use of "propaganda," she concluded, had established
in the public mind the conviction that "all white women of the
South are categorically pure and noble and sacred," and all white
men of the South were their defenders against "spoilation by a
Negro."[89] Ames was immensely gratified by the reception of her
address, which was reprinted in pamphlet form by the Publishers' Association. By the end of 1937 she claimed to have observed a marked change in the handling of mob violence by
newspapermen across the South.[90]

The women of the Anti-Lynching Association had opened
their educational campaign with three primary arguments.
First, far from protecting white women from sexual assault,
lynching made them unwilling pawns in a deadly and disruptive masculine conflict. Second, mob violence crippled the missionary efforts of evangelical church women, undermined the
political and economic interests of the United States abroad,
and generated propaganda for radical movements in the black
community at home. Finally, lynching discredited legal au-

thorities and undermined social order. But as ASWPL women went into communities where mob violence had recently erupted and grew familiar with the literature of regional self-criticism and with the thinking of black scholars and activists, their ideas and arguments changed.[91] Lynching, they came to see, was rooted in poverty and the deprivation of the black and white rural poor, and, beyond that, in the presumptions and institutions of white supremacy. Middle- and upper-class southerners like themselves benefited from the economic exploitation it enforced and were directly or indirectly responsible for its persistence. While the infamous bloodthirsty mob itself might be restrained, the threat of violence and coercion would continue as long as the caste system survived.

For the women who participated in it, the campaign became what Ames called a journey "along a disillusioning road of hard reality": a political education in a patriarchal world. In the context of a period and a region profoundly inhospitable to feminist protest, ASWPL women articulated and acted upon a sense of group identity, registering a significant, if muted, dissent against the cultural shibboleths of their time. In all their endeavors, they held proudly to the image of the southern lady, while at the same time seeking to remake that image according to their own definition of responsible womanhood. The crusade against lynching, like earlier female reform efforts, was bounded by women's traditional religious and domestic concerns. But within those limits, and with the resources accessible to them, the women of the ASWPL led a revolt against chivalry that was part of a long process of both sexual and racial emancipation.[92]

Chapter 8
A Choice of Tactics

The Association of Southern Women for the Prevention of Lynching aspired, in the long run, to forward a slow process of cultural change, but it also sought to devise more immediate ways of inhibiting mob violence. In pursuit of this second goal, Ames and her co-workers made ingenious use of southern folkways and institutions together with the modes of influence available to them as middle-class women. This aspect of the ASWPL campaign, aimed explicitly at bringing pressure to bear on local officials and indirectly at restraining lynch mobs themselves, improvised on the familiar tactics of suffrage and evangelical reform; at the same time it drew on the persistent localism of the association's constituency—the attachment to and identification with place that has remained a distinctive feature of southern ethnicity.[1] The roots of lawlessness, Ames believed, were "buried in local communities. Its branches spread over the country only slightly stirred by the agitating winds of reform." Accordingly, she sought to overcome the historic isolation of southern liberalism by intervening in the community dynamics out of which lynching arose. To a limited degree, the ASWPL's tactics developed over time as its members confronted what Ames termed "real conditions."[2] Yet the commitment to localism that accounted in part for the organization's unique effectiveness also limited its ability to evolve in response to new issues and opportunities. Largely because of Ames's intransigence, the association's search for political and moral leverage stopped short of support for federal

anti-lynching legislation, the chief means by which black reformers and increasing numbers of white southern liberals
hoped to translate public disapprobation of lynching into law
enforcement at the local level.

1

"The women are of the opinion that conscientious sheriffs,
determined to guard their prisoners at all costs, can do more to
stop lynching than any other one factor," commented Willie
Snow Ethridge at the beginning of the ASWPL campaign.[3]
Subsequent investigations drove home this original impression.
In isolated incidents, sheriffs—and even sheriffs' wives—risked
their own lives to protect the men in their custody. But social
pressure and role expectations weighed heavily against such exceptional behavior. Locally elected officials shared the fears
and prejudices of their white constituency; they were, moreover, dependent for their livelihoods on the electoral support
of the mob that confronted them. Dereliction of duty seldom
brought negative sanctions; indeed, in the period before 1933
not a single case can be found in which a southern sheriff was
convicted and ousted from office for collusion with a lynch
mob. Consequently, as ASWPL women discovered, peace
officers regularly cooperated with or even led mobs bent on
lynching their prisoners. Frequently a sheriff's posse became a
lynch mob as soon as the bloodhounds located their victim.
Sheriffs who gave up their prisoners claimed to have been
"overpowered," but in most cases, Ames believed, political expediency rather than fear of bodily harm discouraged them
from defying their white constituency.[4] As long as blacks were
excluded from the polls, she argued, they could not expect protection from white elected officials.

At an anti-lynching institute in Georgia in 1938, Ames offered a graphic illustration of the way in which political powerlessness left blacks at the mercy of lynch mobs. On July 9,

1938, John Dukes, a black turpentine worker accused of drunkenness and murder, was lynched in Arabi, Georgia. The local sheriff had driven to the scene of the impending violence but had done nothing to prevent it.

> It was an hour before the mob decided what to do: they discussed shooting him, another suggested cutting his throat. Somebody thought that was too much pleasure for one person. After an hour they decided they would soak him with gasoline and burn him. Nothing was done and nothing is going to be done about it. [The sheriff] walked off and left the Negro to be burned [because] he looked the mob over and saw back of them voters, and he saw back of that dying Negro nothing. . . . Back of that mob was his bread and his butter and the shoes and clothes and schooling for his children, and back of that Negro nothing. [5]

Ames persistently raised the issue of black disfranchisement, as she presented her analysis of lynching to regional women's groups. The elimination of blacks from electoral politics allowed white officials to mistreat them with impunity; moreover, this "condition of helplessness contributed to a belief in inherent superiority on the part of white people." Beginning in 1924, when a Klan-dominated legislature extended the white primary throughout the state, Texas black activists had joined the NAACP Legal Committee in one court battle after another challenging the right of a political party to limit participation in primary elections on the basis of race. Jessie Daniel Ames had watched this litigation attentively, and under her leadership ASWPL members became increasingly convinced that only "recognition of the Negro as a citizen due the same privileges accorded the whites" could protect them from arbitrary violence.[6] In 1941, when the NAACP's Thurgood Marshall began arguing *Smith* v. *Allwright* in the lower courts, the Women's Division of the Methodist Church declared itself in favor of removing "all barriers to the use of the franchise such as . . . the white primary." Within a few months—two years before the Supreme Court ruled in the NAACP's favor—the Anti-Lynching Association issued its first pamphlet condemning the white primary as an "extra-legal institution."[7]

During the thirties, however, neither the CIC nor the ASWPL took an official stand on black voting rights. Rather, Ames's major strategy for bringing pressure to bear on law enforcement officials called for the use of political and social influence by white women. Though sheriffs might not see black power back of "a dying Negro," she hoped they might begin to see an array of disapproving white women armed with the ballot.[8] County officials in the South, Ames pointed out, enjoyed an extraordinary autonomy. The lucrative office of sheriff was subject to little interference from state or federal authorities. Only county seat elites and local voters could subject sheriffs to demands that they could not ignore.[9] It was at this point, she claimed, "that woman suffrage made its contribution to the decrease in lynching."[10]

The female vote had failed to bring concrete results, Ames believed, in part because women themselves misperceived the dynamics of political power. Especially in the South, significant political decisions took place at the state and local level, where officials jealously guarded their prerogatives from outside interference. Consequently, while women contented themselves with moral pronouncements and turned their attention to such "distant evils" as the enforcement of national prohibition, male politicians reasserted their control over the political process. "Years have passed," Ames concluded. "Local politicians no longer fear the woman vote. They control the social order at home." Through the ASWPL, Ames hoped to reverse this trend.[11]

Once its local, pledge-signing constituency had been convinced by the testimony of their peers that the very men entrusted with the maintenance of law and order were in fact the agents of lawlessness, the ASWPL encouraged them to call their elected representatives to account. It is important to remember that for women in communities where lynchings took place the southern sheriff assumed a vivid human reality. He might be a relative or friend, someone to greet by name, someone with whom one routinely exchanged civilities. On the other hand, he might be seen as the "half-drunk" representative of a courthouse gang whose ways were as alien to the world of the southern lady as the ethos of the lynch mob itself.[12] In either case, it took more than ordinary commitment for a local woman to carry the anti-lynching message out of her church society and into the sheriff's office. "Whatever else may be said about Southern women," Ames commented on this aspect of the ASWPL campaign, "it cannot be said that they lack the moral courage to act according to their convictions. . . . When from their own investigations of lynchings allegedly committed to protect Southern womanhood, they found that they were used as the shield behind which their own men committed cowardly acts of violence against a helpless people, they took the only action they could." They began to speak "as citizens who had the assurance born of the knowledge that they had the power to affect the political lives of local and county politicians."[13]

The tactics through which the ASWPL sought to exercise this power combined personal confrontation with behind-the-scenes manipulation. Supporters in county seats would present a petition to a local sheriff as evidence of the support he would receive for upholding the law—and the opposition he would face if he did not. In addition, they asked each sheriff to sign a statement declaring that lynchings were never justified, that he would spare no effort to prevent them, and that lynchers should be prosecuted.[14] As they gained confidence from these ventures into the county courthouses of the region, ASWPL women took on more intimidating tasks. For example, in 1934, Ruth Knox, a choir director and president of a Presbyterian women's auxillary, secured a place on the program of a meeting of the Louisiana Peace Officers Association. Fearful of venturing alone into such a male preserve, she asked her husband to drive her to the gathering. Once she arrived, her speech proved a resounding success; 109 officers signed the anti-lynching pledge, and the group invited Mrs. Knox to appear again the following year.[15] By 1941, 1,355 peace officers had signed the ASWPL pledges, and the organization could report that in 40 incidents in one year alone peace officers, many of whom were committed in writing to the ASWPL program, had protected their prisoners from threatening mobs. [16]

For those sheriffs who proved oblivious to persuasion, the ASWPL attempted to apply negative sanctions in the form of region-wide publicity. By the mid-thirties, ASWPL bulletins began naming names. *Where Were the Peace Officers?* asked a 1938 publication. It then went on to list the name of every sheriff that year who failed to uphold his oath of office, detailing his complicity in the death of a black prisoner. [17]

In addition to these local activities, ASWPL women also exerted political pressure on state officials. The campaign had opened with an appeal to southern governors to use their executive powers to prevent lynching and punish lynch mobs. In preparation for the first annual meeting in November 1931, Ames asked the ASWPL's most influential supporters in each state to contact their governors, urging them to call out the national guard, remove from office sheriffs who connived in mob violence, sponsor anti-lynching legislation, and encourage state district attorneys to prosecute lynchers. [18] ASWPL women sent questionnaires to candidates for public office asking for their position on lynching and conducted vigorous lobbying campaigns in state legislatures and at annual southern governors' conferences. [19] Once a governor offered any indication of support, however pro forma, Ames added his name to her file of contacts; when a lynching threatened, she called upon him to make good his commitment. [20]

A report from Jane Cornell, chairman of the Florida ASWPL, affords a vivid example of the ASWPL system at work. On May 17, 1933, a black man named Robert Hinds allegedly attacked a white woman in Apalachicola, Florida, a small Gulf Coast town thirty miles east of Panama City. Cornell immediately warned local citizens of impending violence. She contacted the governor of Florida, the sheriff of Apalachicola, and the circuit court judge, asking them to protect the prisoner and pledging public support for their efforts to do so. She maintained close communications with the head of the Associated Press, who promised "to notify her immediately if any trouble develops." When the case went to trial, Cornell commended the sheriff and the governor for protecting the prisoner and kept in touch with both the prosecuting attorney and the state-appointed counsel for the defense, applauding the latter's decision to seek a change of venue. [21]

In McComb, Mississippi, state chairman Bessie Alford operated with similar dispatch through the personal and kinship networks of small-town community life. In July 1939, she reported "an exciting afternoon" in which she had mobilized her friends and relatives to avert a lynching in Monticello, a neighboring county seat. At 2:00 P.M. a Monticello man came into her husband's jewelry store, where she worked as a salesperson, and asked to speak to her "very privately." Learning that vigilantes were gathering to punish a white man accused of assaulting his own daughter, Alford began to phone for help. First she called her brother-in-law, a highway patrolman, asking him to inform the Monticello sheriff of the threatened lynching and of her intention to contact the governor and the head of the Mississippi State Highway Patrol. Soon another Alford relative arrived at the jail; within thirty minutes he had called the ASWPL chairman to assure her that the highway patrol had removed the prisoner to the state capital for safe-keeping. [22]

Six months later, Alford was again sending daily bulletins to Jessie Daniel Ames about the trial of two black men in Prentiss, forty-five miles from her home. From the day the two men were arrested until the trial began, she maintained contact with the sheriff, the governor, and the highway patrol. When the governor called out the national guard, she warned their commander that the guardsmen were "imbued with much the same spirit as the mob itself." Alford kept up her "frantic efforts" on the scene while Jessie Daniel Ames relayed the information she had received to the head of the Associated Press in Atlanta, urging him to give the incident widespread publicity. "If the citizens of a small community come to realize that they are not going to be able to keep a lynching secret," she explained, "it will be another tool for preventing lynchings." Finally, Alford reported, the Prentiss town mayor "called the people together and the citizens agreed there would be no lynching."[23]

On occasion the flow of information between state chairmen and regional headquarters was reversed, as Jessie Daniel Ames took advantage of the pre-notification mobs often gave of their murder plans. "Mobs . . . frequently give public warning of their intention to lynch hours and even days before the capture of their victims permits them to act," Ames explained. Through the cooperation of the Associated Press, this forewarning gave the ASWPL time to mobilize its network of supporters. Indeed, in a number of cases, Ames's newspaper contacts advised her of an impending lynching even before local and state women knew it was about to occur.[24]

The first such incident took place in Mississippi: "When I got hold of the state chairman," Ames recalled, "she said there was nothing in the paper. I said, 'The morning paper's not out yet but it's going to be in there that the mob is forming.' And it was. She got in a car and she went to see the sheriff at 7:00 in the morning. He summoned the state patrol and they got that Negro out of McComb and up into Jackson before the mob was well organized." A similar case occurred in Tennessee. "The AP phoned me about a lynching that was on the way," Ames recalled. "The Negro had escaped and the mob was chasing him. The chairman of the Tennessee Association was not at home but I finally got hold of her in a small town north of Memphis. She went to work immediately . . . funny how a woman could stir up things if she wanted to. And she kept it stirred up until the Negro got over into Arkansas, and he was out of their hands."[25]

In Georgia, Ames was able to act with even more efficiency. On Christmas Day, 1934, an Associated Press correspondent informed her that a black man had killed an officer in Schley County and that a mob was forming. She rushed to her office and called Mary Addie Mullino, head of the South Georgia Conference of the Methodist Woman's Missionary Society and loyal ASWPL supporter. Mullino stopped in the middle

of Christmas dinner and telephoned the sheriff, his deputies, and everyone she knew in Schley County, urging them to
use their influence to prevent a lynching. Until mid-afternoon,
when the man was captured, she stayed at her telephone.
"That Christmas Day," Ames reported, "was not blackened by
a lynching in Georgia."[26]

This campaign of petitions, publicity, and personal contacts
was aimed at law enforcement officials. At the same time, in
significant if less explicit ways, the ASWPL sought to affect the
consciousness and actions of potential lynchers themselves. If
the ASWPL succeeded in forcing sheriffs and governors to
uphold the law, would-be lynchers might be deterred by fear
of failure or armed resistance. But in addition, by "working
through Baptist and Methodist missionary societies, organizations which go into the smallest communities when no other
organizations will be found there," Jessie Daniel Ames hoped
to reach the "mothers, sisters, wives of the men who
lynched."[27] Once persuaded to the ASWPL's point of view, such
women could exercise their time-honored function as moral restraints on masculine violence.

When addressing a "first audience," Ames explained, the
task of ASWPL leaders was to undermine the confidence of
their female audience in the veracity of their own husbands
and fathers. We had to "ask them to accept for truth what we
said even though we contradicted the stories of men whom
they loved and trusted."[28] In this attempt to subvert male authority, the ASWPL stood in a long historical tradition. Assuming a sisterhood of believers, a church within a church fostered
by women's autonomous missionary societies, association
leaders appealed to women's traditional self-concepts while at
the same time subtly challenging the male monopoly over the
definition of public events.

An earnest exchange of letters between Montie B. Greer, Methodist chairman of Christian Social Relations for the North Mississippi Conference, and one of her constituents illustrates this dynamic at work. "I am quite sure [the leaders of the Woman's Missionary Council] are overdoing this phase of our church work," a member of a local auxiliary under Mrs. Greer's jurisdiction complained; "they seem to have a Negro Complex. . . . But as long as there are certain crimes committed by Negro men against white women and there is a drop of southern manhood left, there will be lynching." Greer's reply set forth the religious basis of her own commitment as well as her belief in the efficacy of feminine influence:

> In this anti-lynching work, I think you are doing what I did, what others over the South are doing, namely, refusing to look an un-pleasant fact in the face. I am all Southern and fully understand. The Council did not change me; it cannot change you. I had a con-ference with God about this thing and came out a changed woman. And I warn you and all of the women with convictions like yours, that if you want to hold these convictions, do NOT hold a confer-ence with God, for He has some very plain things to say about giv-ing one man a trial and refusing another.

She then went on to place the responsibility for masculine error on women themselves. "Now, my dear," she ad-monished, "of course your men are fine and they think they are doing right in lynching, for they have not given it serious thought. I never censure men; I censure women. Men think we want them to do it; when they find we do not they will stop." In conclusion, Greer asked her correspondent to read this letter aloud to her local auxiliary. "I want them to know what I stand for as you do, so that when election comes around . . . they will know whether to elect me again. . . . " In urg-ing her followers to declare their independence from male opinion, Mrs. Greer spoke from her own experience, for she herself was forced to conduct investigations of lynchings with-out her husband's knowledge or permission and to hide from her husband and son the threatening letters she received.[29]

The exact nature of the private influence the ASWPL sought

to exert on lynchers remains somewhat obscure. At times the women's literature seems to assume that the men who lynched belonged to a lower economic station than themselves. In that case, the association's leadership may have imagined that local women could use their husband's class position to threaten lynchers with retribution from their creditors, landlords, or employers. [30] For the most part, however, they stressed the white caste solidarity that made lynching such an effective method of repression. Whether ministers' daughters, mayors' wives, or mothers of unemployed young men, ASWPL members from all walks of small-town life might have occasion to register their disapproval of mob violence within their own family circles. Indeed, the ASWPL does seem to have reached women for whom lynching was far from an abstract moral issue. "Auxiliary members have sat in bitter mortification," Bertha Newell, Methodist leader and ASWPL secretary, reported, "when lynchings have involved friends and kinsmen." A correspondent from Tyler, Texas, wrote that "to her certain knowledge" many of the women involved in her mission study course on race relations had relatives who lynched. [31]

Although the threatrical (and patronizing) image of "Southern ladies in white gloves and navy silks" facing down lynch mobs that appears in later treatments of the ASWPL had little basis in reality, women apparently influenced by the movement did find themselves in explosive situations. [32] When a black mill worker was accused of killing a white man in Waxham, North Carolina, the wife of the mill owner instructed the sheriff to remove the prisoner from the county jail and continued to "suppress every suggestion of a lynching" until the threat of violence subsided. In 1936, the seven-year-old daughter of an Alabama ASWPL woman was assaulted by a black man. "The mother," according to Texas journalist Lewis Nordyke, "clinging tenaciously to her . . . principles . . . prevented mob violence by her appeal that law take its course." In another incident, two elderly sisters in Texas who had signed the anti-lynching pledge at a Methodist women's missionary society pleaded with a posse not to lynch a black man who had allegedly attacked them.[33] "Women went into communities in which there had been lynchings," Ames recalled. "Many of the people were surly, belligerent. When we take into consideration the fact that some of the lynchings had grown out of politics and crooked business deals, we can understand that the women were by no means safe at all times. They knew of the constant danger, and they didn't forget to pray."[34]

Whether mobilizing a personal network to prevent a lynching, or leading a delegation of church women to the sheriff's office, or driving across the state to uncover the facts behind an accusation of interracial rape, the women of the ASWPL exhibited a mobility and self-assertiveness that contradicted the stereotype of the southern lady. White women in the South had opposed demon rum, worked for a living, and demanded the vote. But not until the advent of the ASWPL did they forthrightly intervene in the politics of racial violence. "Certainly," Ames asserted, "investigations of lynchings in person was about the most contrary act they could have committed."[35] Yet despite this cultural breakthrough, the fact remains that the ASWPL chose its reform methods within a context of narrowly limited options. Members may have threatened a sheriff with the opposition of female voters at the next election or with social ostracism, but they could not conceive of running for local office themselves. They hoped that the publication of their findings might encourage the indictment of mob members and conniving officials, but they left to their male counterparts in the Interracial Commission or the NAACP the actual task of gathering depositions, hiring attorneys, and initiating legal action. The theme of domestic influence—for which Jessie Daniel Ames had exhibited such scorn in the days of the suffrage campaign—took second place to a view of women as community leaders in their own right, individual citizens with a direct relationship to the social order.[36] Yet most ASWPL women lacked the resources, the skills, and the self-concepts that would have enabled them to intervene directly in political and judicial affairs, and they remained petitioners

Figure 2

Lynchings and Prevented Lynchings, 1914-1942

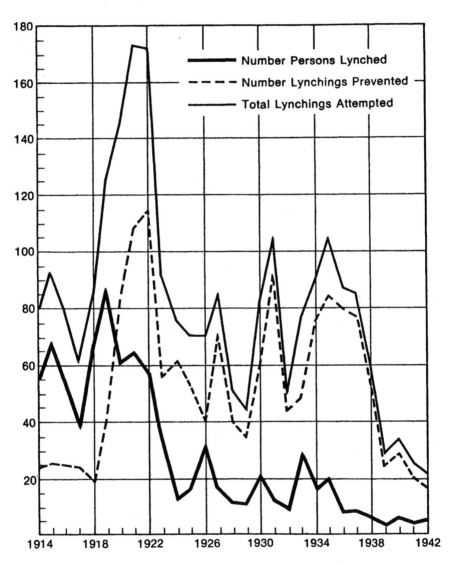

Source: *Data from Monroe N. Work, ed., *Negro Year Book,* 1937-1938, p. 157 and 1941-1946. p. 309.

rather than practictioners of the political game Jessie Daniel Ames loved so well.

Given these limitations, ASWPL women made skillful use of informal modes of social control whose potency in the small town and rural South should not be underestimated. Jessie Daniel Ames would not have claimed major responsibility for the decline in lynching that did in fact take place over the decade of the ASWPL campaign. Nor would she have rested her case for the significance of the ASWPL's efforts, meant to be broadly educational, on such numerical changes alone. Nevertheless, even within this most stringent definition of success—the actual reduction of lynching incidents—empirical evidence can be marshaled to support Ames's conviction of the effectiveness of the social action program she led.

In 1968, the sociologist John Shelton Reed tested the hypothesis that "during the period of the Association's activities, there were fewer lynchings in the counties where it was active than would otherwise have been expected." To do so, he classified all counties where lynchings occurred in the period 1919 to 1942 according to the amount of "treatment" they received from the ASWPL. He found that in the decade before the association's formation, lynching had been declining at approximately the same rate in counties that would later receive major treatment, minor treatment, or no treatment at all from the association. During the organization's twelve-year history, however, southern counties untouched by the anti-lynching campaign had 35 percent as many lynchings as they had had in the previous decade, while counties where the association was most active had only 26 percent as many incidents of mob violence. Moreover, he discovered a particularly dramatic decrease in the number of lynch victims taken from the hands of the law in counties where the association made its presence strongly felt. In conclusion, he suggested that the ASWPL program was indeed able to subject sheriffs to powerful, legitimate demands that they protect their prisoners and to create a climate of disapproval that deterred potential lynchers.[37]

3

While Jessie Daniel Ames and the Anti-Lynching Association searched for ways to prevent mob violence, the NAACP continued its parallel campaign of public exposure and legal action. Walter White, who became NAACP executive secretary in 1930, developed an increasingly close working relationship with the Interracial Commission; when he decided to take up the drive for federal legislation, which had been abandoned ten years before with the defeat of the Dyer Anti-Lynching Bill, he looked to Will Alexander and Jessie Daniel Ames to galvanize southern liberal support. Ames, however, proved a stubborn opponent of the NAACP's new strategy. Sponsored by Edward P. Costigan of Colorado and Robert F. Wagner of New York in the Senate and by Harlem Congressman Joseph A. Gavagan in the House, the Costigan-Wagner Act and its successors became an escalating source of tension between Ames and her allies in the anti-lynching movement. [38]

Like Jessie Daniel Ames, Walter White had forged his career in the anti-lynching struggle. One of his earliest memories was of the 1906 Atlanta race riot when his family had armed themselves with rifles to protect their home from invasion. He had graduated from Atlanta University, and then had risen to national prominence as an intrepid investigator and chronicler of mob violence. In 1933, when lynching once more soared to a record high after dipping to a low of 10 the year before, he determined to channel the NAACP's piecemeal efforts into a concerted federal lobbying campaign. [39]

Before White could carry out his plan, however, he had to overcome strong opposition within the NAACP. In the early years of the Depression, when John L. Lewis of the United Mine Workers began his drive to "organize the unorganized" and reform the moribund AFL, younger NAACP staff members agitated for an emphasis on interracial unionism as a means of addressing the economic needs of the black masses.

As hope for an integrated union movement faded, W.E.B. Du Bois came forward with a plan for racial solidarity and self-help through producers' and consumers' cooperatives and economic boycotts. Despite these pressures to shift NAACP attention to economic issues, Walter White and his chief lieutenant Roy Wilkins held fast to their traditional concern with civil liberties and anti-lynching reform. Du Bois charged White with initiating the federal lobbying effort because of its appeal to white liberals and its usefulness as a fund-raising tool. White, on the other hand, maintained that a rising tide of liberalism in the South as well as in national politics offered an unprecedented opportunity for striking a final blow at terrorism. The responsiveness of local chapters to the anti-lynching campaign confirmed his feeling that no issue so surely touched the heart of black frustration and rage. Moreover, White reasoned that even if he were unable to push an anti-lynching bill through Congress, national publicity and the fear of federal legislation would prompt southern states to take preventive action. Unwilling to carry on a protracted internecine battle, Du Bois resigned from the staff; with his chief opponent gone, White made federal legislation the main thrust of the NAACP's program in the thirties and a major test of the New Deal's commitment to black civil rights. [40]

The Costigan-Wagner Act spoke directly to the chief weakness in the anti-lynching efforts of southern interracialists: their inability to bring lynchers to trial or to punish conniving officials. [41] The measure proposed federal trials for mob members where local authorities refused to act, fines or jail terms for officers who failed to discharge their duties, and damage claims against counties where lynchings occurred. Defining lynching as a breach of Fourteenth Amendment rights, the bill offered not only a means of federal intervention in local judicial processes but also an incentive to action on the part of what Walter White termed "the taxpaying, property-owning classes, who could if they wished stop lynching at its inception." [42]

In order to overcome the major obstacle to passage—the power of southern committee chairmen and the threat of a southern filibuster—Walter White set out to marshal evidence of favorable opinion in the South and to enlist the aid of FDR. Each, he believed, would reinforce the other. Proof that southern voters favored the measure might forestall a filibuster; if the President were convinced that the bill would not meet violent opposition from the southern congressmen on whom the passage of his economic program depended, he would be more likely to lend his name to the campaign. [43]

In his opening move, then, White sought to head off the charge that the Costigan-Wagner Act was a punitive sectional measure—a latter-day "force bill"—by bringing a group of distinguished southerners to Washington to testify in its behalf. High on White's list of such potential witnesses was Jessie Daniel Ames. Inviting her to appear at the Senate Judiciary Hearings scheduled for February 20–21, 1943, he also approached her with an ambitious plan: a nationwide radio broadcast featuring his friend and intermediary in the White House, Eleanor Roosevelt, the NYA official Mary McLeod Bethune, and, speaking for white southern womanhood, Jessie Daniel Ames. [44]

Ames responded cautiously to White's overtures. Confident of her own experience as a lobbyist and her expertise on the issues involved, she refused to endorse the Costigan-Wagner Act until she had studied its provisions carefully. Although she declined White's invitation to testify, she did travel to the Capitol to observe the hearings. She was not, however, pleased with what she learned. Returning to Atlanta, she submitted a report on the bill's shortcomings to association members. At the same time, she wrote to the bill's sponsor, Senator Costigan, suggesting specific changes. "We would like some Federal measure to control and prevent lynchings," she concluded, "but we want the measure to be one that can and will be enforced." [45]

Despite her personal objections, Ames forebore public criticism of the bill and encouraged the ASWPL to maintain a policy of neutrality. Indeed, at the annual meeting of 1934, the Central Council issued a statement that the ASWPL "regards with favor any legal measure that promises sure and permanent eradication of lynching" which was widely construed as support for federal intervention. [46] When Senator "Cotton Ed" Smith of South Carolina defended lynching as a vindication of "the sanctity of our firesides and the virtue of our women" during a successful six-day filibuster the following year, Ames instructed South Carolina ASWPL members, whatever their stand on the measure, to write letters of protest to their representatives. "There can be no time lost if we are to protect ourselves from this humiliating publicity," she urged. [47]

As the NAACP campaign picked up speed, Ames's position hardened, and she began to take behind-the-scenes steps to thwart Walter White's plans. Invited to lunch with Eleanor Roosevelt at the White House, she explained the educational approach of the ASWPL, presented her objections to the bill, and argued for a modified plan of cooperation between state and federal officials. [48] White, whose only hope for reaching the President lay in Eleanor's intercession, counterattacked by questioning Ames's claim to leadership of the southern women's anti-lynching forces. Convinced by White's arguments, Eleanor Roosevelt secured an interview for him with the President and urged upon Ames a more favorable view of the NAACP's strategy. [49]

The most important challenge to Ames's leadership—and Walter White's greatest breakthrough in his search for southern white support—came from the Southern Methodist Woman's Missionary Council. Meeting in Birmingham on March 13, 1934, the 1,000-member convention, representing 250,000 members, voted unanimous approval of federal legislation. [50] Methodist ASWPL leaders Louise Young, Estelle Haskin, and Mrs. J. W. Downs had just emerged from a futile attempt to punish the murderers of a young black man named Cordie Cheek. Kidnapped in full view of witnesses near the Fisk University campus in Nashville, Cheek had been taken to a neighboring county, castrated, and hanged. "This Cheek case," concluded a Scarritt College professor, illustrates perfectly the futility of orderly procedure through state courts. There is no doubt about the meaning of the law and no lack of convincing evidence, and a group of highly respected citizens with the assistance of an excellent criminal lawyer has stuck by the case using every device available to get something done. Thus far we have accomplished exactly nothing except to convince ourselves that we have no legal recourse under the existing system. Of course we could turn "Communist" and use our shot-guns! and maybe that is the way out. [51]

After this experience, the three women had driven together to Washington in February to observe the Senate Judiciary Hearings. There they watched the attorney general of Maryland, appearing under subpoena, testify to a similar example of the "complete impotence of state and county governments." In an "electric stillness," they reported, he read the names of nine leaders of a Princess Anne County lynch mob. Under questioning from the committee he admitted that despite the sworn statements of officers who identified each man, it had been impossible to obtain action from the local prosecuting attorney or indictments from a grand jury. Their long involvement in the Interracial Commission and the ASWPL, their frustration in the Cordie Cheek case, and the evidence presented at the hearings convinced the Methodist representatives that "the crime of lynching is too terrible in its implications to wait on the slow process of education alone." Accordingly, they led first the Woman's Missionary Council and then its constituent conferences in Tennessee and Alabama in endorsing the remedy of federal action. [52] This decision, Walter White claimed in letters to Franklin and Eleanor Roosevelt and statements to the press, represented a "revolutionary change of attitude in the South itself. Once again women have taken the lead in a great social reform." Their backing, he continued, has "materially lessened opposition by southern members of Congress." [53]

Although only the Methodist women, among southern women's groups, gave official support to the NAACP, other ASWPL endorsing organizations and a number of its most ac-

tive members also drifted toward the solution of federal legislation. The national YWCA, the Women's Division of the Federal Council of Churches, and the National Council of Jewish
Women quickly joined the lobbying effort. Under the direction
of Elizabeth Yates Webb and Frances Williams, who had
served together as student interracial secretaries in the South
in the 1920s, the "Y" testified in the bill's behalf and instructed
public affairs chairmen all over the country to organize letter-
writing campaigns to their congressmen. [54]

Soon ASWPL members began to follow the lead of such
regional and national groups, and Jessie Daniel Ames found
herself confronted for the first time with significant internal
dissension. "Personally," admonished Mrs. J. W. Downs, "I
cannot see that a Federal law would handicap us in any way.
Certainly we would not be any *worse off than we are.*" She had
begun, she concluded, to doubt the efficacy of the ASWPL's
methods. "Talk, agitate [*sic*], signatures and speeches" did not
necessarily bring about social change. [55] In response to a
request from the women of the Federal Council of Churches,
Alabama chairman Mary J. McCoy urged President Roosevelt
in the name of the ASWPL to promote the anti-lynching bill.
When she was reprimanded by Ames, McCoy severed her
relationship with the association. [56] Jane Cornell of Florida, one
of Ames's strongest state council chairmen, became increasingly distressed by her leader's intransigence. After the lynching of Claude Neal in Marianna, Florida, in 1934, the subsequent failure of legal authorities to hand down indictments,
and the refusal of the federal government to intervene despite
the fact that Neal had been taken across state lines, she became
more and more pessimistic about reliance on education and
state action. Finally she resigned the Florida chairmanship, unable to reconcile her convictions with her loyalty to Ames. "I
have not a bit of faith in our men in handling this question,"
she wrote, "and I cannot conscientiously continue to voice feelings of the Association which are not mine." [57]

Faced with these defections, Ames poured her time and
energy into shoring up her stance. She found pitfalls in each

new bill introduced in the House or the Senate. More generally, she argued that federal legislation would not touch the
causes of mob violence: only political education could affect attitudes and values. A bill containing "threats and gratuitous insults" would inflame southern sectionalism. While mob action
might wane, courts would be prostituted before community
demands for vengeance. Lynching would be driven underground, and racial violence would in reality increase. Most
importantly, she believed that association endorsement would
offend the deeply held tradition of localism among the organization's constituency and alienate its support in the rural
South.[58] "We were trying to reach the women in those little
rural towns," she recalled, "and I don't believe they would
have gone along with us if we had endorsed a federal anti-
lynching bill. They'd say we were following the Yankees and
doors would have been closed to us."[59]

By the ASWPL annual meeting of 1934, the black women of
the Interracial Commission had begun to voice their dissatis-
faction with the silence of their white allies, and divisions
within the association itself had become too obvious to ignore.
Deciding to meet the issue head on, Ames told the gathering
that

> A very prominent Negro leader . . . called my attention to the
> fact that we today, as Southern white women, had the opportunity
> of performing an act that would make history; that with a Demo-
> cratic Congress and President and a group of Southern white
> women meeting, we should go on record as endorsing this bill in
> Congress. We would be doing more than any one thing that could
> be done.[60]

Should the ASWPL be swayed by the opinion of such black
leaders? Ames asked. To resolve this question, she organized a
conference between the association's executive committee and
black CIC representatives, many of whom were adamant supporters of the NAACP campaign.

Daisy Lampkin, NAACP field secretary, opened this meeting in Atlanta on January 11, 1935, with a plea for ASWPL ap-

proval of the anti-lynching bill. Congressional opponents, Lampkin pointed out, "take new courage and they use it to their advantage when they can stand on the floor and say that the . . . Southern white women did not endorse the Costigan-Wagner bill." Lampkin's argument was reinforced by Charlotte Hawkins Brown: "Southern women, you can do more . . . to bring about . . . freedom for the Negro race than a million from the North. . . . Congress is controlled by Southerners. . . . I would not have expected you to have done it if the South was not in the saddle."[61]

As the discussion proceeded and it became apparent that the ASWPL leaders were not to be convinced, Lugenia Hope expressed her weary disappointment. "My heart is so sick and so weak . . . that I don't know whether I can say anything. I do think that the stand that the Southern women took will retard everything. You may not think so, but it will hold back our interracial work and everything else in the South."

Finally, Nannie Burroughs moved the debate to a new level. The bill would be passed whether the ASWPL helped or not, she asserted. Since black women had been excluded from the organization, they could do nothing to change its course. "I am not a member of [this] association. [But] I am going to be a member of it some of these days." Meanwhile, she concluded that the ASWPL was justified in continuing its educational campaign. Lynching was no "superficial thing. . . . it is in the blood of the nation. And the process of eradicating it will be difficult and long." Mary McLeod Bethune underscored this closing note of conciliation: "I think you have been cautious and wisely so. . . . I, for one, come again with my heart . . . full of appreciation . . . for . . . the daring stand taken by this group of women. I have only gratitude for what you have done."

The effort of black women to influence ASWPL policy won over some individual members but did nothing to sway Jessie Daniel Ames. She remained convinced that endorsing organizations like the Baptists, the Presbyterians, and the women's clubs would withdraw their support if the ASWPL undertook a

federal lobbying effort and that sympathy for federal intervention represented only the "top crust" of southern opinion. As a
regionally based women's organization, the ASWPL had "a
special piece of work to do that no one else can do." As insiders
in local communities, they—and only they—could penetrate
the "morass of fear" and prepare the way for the "complete
eradication of lynching." [62] The force of Ames's personality, her
control over the definition of issues within the organization,
and the personal loyalty she commanded carried the day. Reaffirming its policy of neutrality, the ASWPL dedicated itself to
continuing its own methods of reform. [63]

Despite this decision, however, the issue of federal action
would not subside. Indeed, the events of the next several years
made Ames's position increasingly difficult to maintain. Although black CIC members had been unable to change the
policy of the ASWPL, they did succeed three months later in
winning unanimous endorsement for federal legislation from
the CIC itself. [64] In April 1937, the revelation of a particularly
atrocious lynching in Duck Hill, Mississippi, in which two
black men were tortured with an acetylene torch, helped proponents release an anti-lynching measure from Hatton W.
Summers' Judiciary Committee and push it through the
House. By that time, federal action had been endorsed by
leading daily papers throughout the South, and by many small-
town weekly papers as well. A Gallup poll conducted in January indicated that 70 percent of the national population and 65
percent of southerners believed that Congress should enact a
law making lynching a federal crime. Moreover, 75 percent of
the women in the nation favored such a measure. Whatever
the merits of Ames's argument about the proper role of the
ASWPL, by 1937 she had clearly been bypassed by the southern liberal mainstream. [65]

In 1938, when Senator Costigan introduced the bill in the
Senate for the second time, Ames's convictions led her into
an error of judgment that had serious consequences for her
own career as well as for the movement she led. Southern
senators, under Texas Congressman Tom Connally, met the

bill with the most protracted filibuster since the currency disputes of the 1890s. The refusal of Franklin Roosevelt to intervene shocked and angered the black community, and the fervid oratory of the filibustering southerners helped reverse the trend of public opinion across the country. After "the statesmen from Dixie had shaken the Capitol rafters for two weeks with apostrophes to the fair name of Southern womanhood," commented the Richmond *Times-Dispatch* editor Virginius Dabney, "there were alarms from Harper's Ferry to Eagle Pass, and the excitement hasn't fully subsided yet."[66] On January 28, three weeks into the filibuster when the first attempt at cloture had just gone down in defeat, Jessie Daniel Ames took the opportunity to further her own strategy of state action. In a letter to her old acquaintance Tom Connally, she wrote:

> You are just about to win the fight to defeat the antilynching bill by having it laid aside, It will be a great relief to the public to have that measure laid on the shelf in order that the Senate may go about important and far-reaching legislation.
>
> In the meantime, as you know, this fight has centered attention upon the South and upon lynching itself in a way that has never been done in the past. You also know that our Association is the only regularly functioning body that has made any effort by way of an educational program to eradicate this evil. We have contributed, I believe, quite considerably to the improved conditions.
>
> It is my judgment that we will be somewhat on the spot when the first lynching takes place after the lynching bill is laid aside. News stories will be carried not only in all this country's papers, but in papers all over the world. It is going to be up to us to do something about lynching through an aroused public opinion. It would give impetus to our program of education if, after the bill is laid on the shelf, you and other Southern Senators would make a statement to the press indicating that you intend to help us make good the claim—which I honestly believe to be true—that the South can and will stop lynchings.[67]

On January 30, 1938, Connally released this letter to the press as evidence of widespread southern support for his position. "Dixie Women's Anti-Lynch Society Urges Shelving of Filibuster Bill," a *New York Times* headline read. The women's anti-lynching campaign, Connally concluded, demonstrated that the South "will wipe out lynching without federal legislation."[68]

Roy Wilkins of the NAACP responded to this revelation with an angry press release and letters to black CIC women asking them to take action against the ASWPL director:

> In the course of this hard-fought campaign for a federal anti-lynching law we have come upon many kinds of sentiment, but we have not had from any person in a key position in the interracial movement, an expression as harmful as that of Mrs. Ames. There have been those who have opposed the anti-lynching bill, who have felt that it was not wise, but none who has defended the type of fili-buster that has been carried on.[69]

Despite the furor it aroused, Ames made no apology for her statement. She reiterated her position on federal legislation in a long letter to Mary McLeod Bethune and defended her sincerity and integrity. Her letter to Senator Connally had been "private and personal," meant to encourage him to use his popular following to make good his claim that the southern states "could and would stop lynching":

> We are seeking the same goal, I am sure. Our methods differ. I cannot bring myself to support Federal methods because I cannot see anything but disaster for Southern rural negroes in that way. . . . My integrity forces me to stand on this ground. Pressure of great force, with poorly concealed threats, has been brought to bear on me. But this is politics, something with which I am all too familiar. . . . I am keenly conscious that agitation for a Federal law is focusing Southern attention on the crime of lynching, which is desirable. [But] a lynching is not to me a political argument for a Federal law, but it is a notification that conditions of white and Negro people in a lynching community are bad, economically, edu-cationally, and politically—and that work must be done to improve such conditions out of which lynchings grow.[70]

In reply, Bethune assured her ally of the continuing support of southern black women: "Enough said. I understand you thoroughly. We should all press forward, doing our best. I have unswerving confidence in your interest and cooperation and sincerity." [71]

4

Ames's approach to the most controversial issue faced by the Anti-Lynching Association sheds a critical light on her presumptions and on the quality of her leadership style. White women, she believed, were strategically placed to counteract both the conscious rationalizations for lynching and the subterranean tensions that erupted in mob violence. "During these seven years of conferences," she noted, "I have tried—and in part succeeded—in convincing leading Southern women that lynching is a result of causes which are deeply buried in our political and economic system which find nourishment in our doctrine of white supremacy, which in its nature is tied in to a sex warfare between white and Negro men." [72] To rechannel her carefully built organization would halt this process of internal consciousness raising, shift attention from underlying psychosexual dynamics to legislative panaceas, and obviate the anti-lynching campaign's function as a means of liberation for white women as well as for blacks.

The federal lobbying campaign thus found Jessie Daniel Ames and Walter White vying for control of the image of the southern lady. "We have a number of southerners lined up to testify," Walter White reported to H. L. Mencken before the Senate Judiciary hearings of 1934, "including several personable young ladies who have accents so thick that one can cut them with a knife. I do wish you were going to be there for the show." [73] Both as a southerner and as a woman, Jessie Daniel Ames would have been profoundly insulted by such an exchange. Although her own approach to political education was not without an undertone of condescension, she took herself and her constituency with the utmost seriousness. Seeking to rescue the image of the lady from the ideologues of white supremacy and the pornographers of lynching, she built her campaign on the revised concept of woman as citizen and evangelical reformer. While she herself manipulated rather than directly challenged the symbolism of white southern womanhood, she had no intention of giving over this hard-won power of self-definition to her male allies in the anti-lynching coalition.

Ames's choice of practical methods grew out of her commitment to a particular female constituency. She had long before rejected the notion that women should limit themselves to indirect modes of influence; yet in her arguments against a federal lobbying campaign, she seemed to revert to just such traditional assumptions. In part, this contradiction arose from a sense of her own superiority: while she valued her own coolly analytical approach to issues and her expertise in electoral politics, she sometimes saw women in general as sentimental and inexperienced in the ways of a masculine world. Thus, she maintained, ASWPL members—even those who favored federal legislation—were neither ideologically nor organizationally prepared to play the role Walter White and the NAACP asked of them. Her account of an exchange with an ASWPL member in Dallas who was "rabid for Federal antilynching," clearly illustrates this attitude. The woman had urged her to provide leadership in the lobbying campaign since she "had the experience."

I assured her that I could tell her what to do, and I did forthwith. Hatton Sumners is Chairman of the Judiciary Committee of the House to which this Bill must be referred before it can be considered. He is the Congressman from Dallas County. . . . I told her that if she would go back and work intensely in Dallas County to get at least one-third of the qualified voters of that County to take this up with Hatton Sumners and force his hand, it would do more for the passage of the bill than the work of a hundred women of the Association. She said that she could not do that. It is an emotional attitude on the part of most of the women who want lynching stopped but who are not willing to do any of the intensive work involved in education, let alone the more intensive work involved in political action.[74]

Ames did not see herself as rejecting "political action" outright; on the contrary, a major thrust of her anti-lynching strategy was to urge upon women participation in local political and judicial processes. But the key to this strategy lay in its regional orientation. Partly because of the decline of feminism and the evisceration of the women's movement, partly as an unintended consequence of her decision to join the Interracial Commission staff, she found herself at the helm of an organization of local church women, unschooled in party politics but confident of their roles as the moral arbiters of community life. Accordingly, she urged them to use their personal influence in their own localities in behalf of racial peace and social order. Disappointed in the effects of the Eighteenth and Nineteenth amendments, she refused to direct her constituency's attention to "distant evils" or to encourage their reliance on what she regarded as federal paternalism. By holding the association to its original course, she hoped to encourage women—and through them white southerners in general—to take on the responsibilities of citizenship in local community life.

Ames's stance toward federal legislation also reveals her own paternalistic attitudes toward the victims of racial violence. Her outrage at the cruelty and injustice of lynching is undeniable: "Wanting lynching eradicated is an obsession with me," she wrote to Mary McLeod Bethune in a rare expression of feeling. "The news of one sickens me physically and casts me into depression mentally."[75] Her relationships with individual black women like Bethune seem to have been based on mutual, if distant, respect. Yet it is equally clear that Ames seldom saw blacks as equals even in the struggle against their own oppression. She devoted her life to the protection of those too weak to protect themselves, even while rejecting and fearing such guardianship for herself. Uneasy among her equals, fearful of her own vulnerability, and unwilling to accept the claims of intimacy, she found confirmation of her own strength in promoting the welfare of men and women who were comfortably unequal and safely separate. Without a second thought, she had eliminated blacks from the women's anti-lynching movement;

when a question of strategy arose she felt no obligation to be responsive to black agendas for reform.

The manner in which Ames pursued her control over ASWPL policy demonstrates the effects of her temperament and her situation as a woman on her leadership style. As executive director, she assumed major responsibility for the ongoing program of the ASWPL. She issued statements to the press "whenever necessary," traveled extensively as ASWPL spokesman, decided at her own discretion who would be invited to ASWPL gatherings. At these meetings, she circumvented rival tendencies, guided discussions, and achieved the adoption of her plans. [76] She maintained a careful distance from most of her co-workers, reinforcing her authority by resisting their overtures of friendship. Her closest confidants were her loyal lieutenants. Women of the rank and file were often awed by her "analytical mind"; they saw her very much as an "admired LEADER" and themselves as inadequate and faltering in comparison. "Liquid ore eventually becomes rigid steel," one admiring follower wrote, "so perhaps you can make something out of me sometime." [77] And Ames boasted of her ability to manage "all kinds of people in all conditions. . . . My long years of practice," she wrote, "have taught me how to get what I want without the other fellow knowing that I am getting it or he is giving it." [78]

Under ordinary circumstances, Ames's methods worked remarkably well. Heading a purely voluntary organization, she relied on persuasion for the implementation of her plans. She made certain that the duties of state chairmen were broadly defined and did not seem overwhelming, and then helped the women "develop the details according to [their own] minds and the needs of their states." [79] But she was determined that the "policy and philosophy" of the anti-lynching campaign would remain firmly under her control. "The inception of the movement and the whole program," she informed Julian Harris of the Chattanooga Times, "has had its birth in my mind." [80] When her leadership was challenged in the federal legislation dispute, her ability as a diplomatic administrator and organizer gave way to autocracy. "When I lost a fight," she reflected, "I tried to stand back and view the elements involved, to decide whether after all my earnestness was not . . . the result of a very human determination to have things come my way." [81] But she was seldom capable of such objectivity in the heat of battle. Ames's personal control over the ASWPL meant that there could be little dynamic interplay of values, political ideologies, and tactical conceptions within the organization. No younger generation of women joined and altered the association in response to changing social conditions. In the last analysis, the association would remain, as it had begun, circumscribed by the abilities and perceptions of its leader.

In the anti-lynching movement, Ames had carved out for herself an area of competence and a professional identity. When the Depression and New Deal shifted the terms of political discourse to the left, Ames's male colleagues moved into the national arena. Will Alexander, for example, became head of the Farm Security Administration. He worked comfortably with the urbane, ambitious Walter White and traveled with ease in Washington social circles. The informal channels through which potential members of a national liberal elite made such a transition, however, were closed to all but the most exceptional women, and Ames's career remained tied to a regional infrastructure of women's organizations. As her male co-workers advanced to bigger things, Ames was left in Atlanta to carry out her projects with almost complete autonomy but without the authority and recognition commensurate with her responsibilities. She felt that Alexander provided no encouragement for her work, that he ignored the efforts of women until he wanted to use their network of contacts to elicit a show of support for some project of his own or to take credit for their successes. "Frankly," she wrote, "up until a crisis, it never occurs to Dr. Alexander that there is anything that could be done through the women." [82] Denied access to the philanthropic, political, and economic sources of social power, she resisted a shift toward federal and black initiatives and sought to maintain at all costs her own authority within the southern interracial movement.

The possibility that federal legislation, rather than Ames's own laboriously built association, held the key to effective anti-lynching reform posed an intolerable personal threat. Her position would be undermined, and she would lapse into the obscurity that had marked her childhood and her married life. Having decided upon a course of opposition to the Costigan-Wagner Act, she lacked the flexibility to change her mind. Provided with such psychological space neither by her private experience as a woman nor by a society which recognized her abilities and supported her aspirations, she could not supply the imaginative leadership demanded by changing times. The necessity of "fighting every step of the way" meant, in the end, that she could never risk an admission of error or a moment of deference. [83] Under her leadership, the practice of the ASWPL remained static, a force for social order but not for fundamental social change.

Chapter 9
Quietly but Definitely Allowed to Die

Jessie Daniel Ames died on February 21, 1972, at the age of eighty-eight. She had watched the civil rights movement of the 1960s with approval and satisfaction, confident that the anti-lynching campaign had played its part by undermining the white South's will toward the use of overwhelming physical force. But in the shadow, first of the male-dominated liberalism generated by the Depression decade, then of the black-led direct-action assault on segregation, the courage and dedication of her generation of women reformers seemed to shrink to insignificance. Ames's death passed virtually unnoticed; she had not become part of the folklore of southern struggle. With the rebirth of feminism, however, a different climate of opinion emerged. As women in the 1970s confronted legal, political, and economic issues left unresolved by the women's rights movement a half-century before, intergenerational continuities became clearer; Jessie Daniel Ames's story could be recovered and the implications of her career better understood.

1

The message of the women's anti-lynching campaign reached its widest audience just as the ASWPL's viability as an organization was coming to an end. In 1939, for example, a *Reader's Digest* condensation of an article entitled "Ladies and Lynchings," written by Texas journalist Lewis T. Nordyke, was featured in newspapers across the country. The ASWPL had evolved from a small band of church women pledged to "stand under fire" to a socially acceptable expression of an emerging consensus. At first, Jessie Daniel Ames told an ASWPL gathering, they had been called "sob sisters" and worse; now they had become thoroughly respectable. [1]

At the same time, the accomplishment of the ASWPL's goals seemed almost in sight. In 1930, lynch mobs had claimed 22 victims; two years later the number climbed to 28. But since 1933, mob violence had steadily declined. In May 1940, Ames released to the press a statement that, for the first time in her career, the South could boast of a "lynchless year." [2] Ames harbored no illusions that the decline of lynching signaled the end of covert racial violence. But by the end of the decade, she was convinced that community-sanctioned ritual murders were becoming a thing of the past. Most importantly, she maintained that lynching, when it did occur, had ceased to be justified as a necessity for the protection of white women. In 1942, believing that the purpose of the women's campaign had been fulfilled, she allowed the Association of Southern Women for the Prevention of Lynching to pass quietly from the scene.

Meanwhile, she turned her attention back to her duties as Director of Woman's Work for the Commission on Interracial Cooperation. As she did so, however, she found herself increasingly alienated from the thrust of modern liberalism. Her self-conscious feminism had become an anomaly within the southern left. The Southern Conference for Human Welfare, founded in 1938, had effected a coalition of labor leaders, New Dealers, and black activists concerned with economic democracy and impatient with the tactics of interracial cooperation. While her former allies looked to the federal government to open the doors to regional change, Ames held aloof from the Southern Conference and viewed with distrust the "starry-eyed blueprint designers in Washington." Publicly, she supported administration policies and welcomed the CIO organizing drives in the South. But privately she joined the ranks of veterans of the progressive movement who defected from the New Deal.[3]

Ames's political isolation was mirrored and magnified by the attrition of her institutional base. With its director, Will Alexander, in Washington as head of the Farm Security Administration, the CIC fell into a deepening malaise. In 1938, its major foundation grants were terminated and its budget cut to one-fifth its former size. Two years later, Alexander resigned from the FSA, but rather than return to Atlanta he accepted an appointment in Chicago as vice-president of the Rosenwald Fund. Jessie Daniel Ames was left to carry on her work with almost complete autonomy but without the official recognition she craved. Her greatest handicap, she complained, had always been "the feeling that as Director of Woman's Work, I was occupying a position created to placate women, but without value or importance to the whole Commission." She requested that her title be changed to "Director of Field Work," and in the closing years of the decade she traveled through the region attempting to revitalize state interracial committees. In addition, she launched a publication called the *Southern Frontier*, meant to become the regular voice of the CIC. But even as Ames labored to keep the organization alive, Will Alexander, together with CIC president Howard Odum, Rosenwald chief Edwin R. Embree, and Fisk University president Charles S. Johnson, had concluded that the Interracial Commission had outlived its usefulness and, in Ames's bitter words, "should be quietly but definitely allowed to die."[4]

Ironically, Jessie Daniel Ames herself provided the means for accomplishing their goal. For southern reformers like Ames, schooled in the politics of interracialism, the outbreak of World War II seemed to present both threat and opportunity. Black expectations soared; demanding democracy at home as the price of national solidarity, they used the rhetoric of antifascism to telling effect. A. Philip Randolph's 1941 March on Washington Movement presaged the tactics of mass-based direct action. Black organizations and newspapers united in a militant demand for full participation in the defense effort. By

1941, however, white backlash and black frustration seemed to portend an era of racial conflict like that which had spawned the Interracial Commission after World War I.[5] Ames responded to these tensions with a characteristic mixture of dedication to racial equity and desire to assert the influence of southern interracialists over the course of rapidly unfolding events.

In 1941, she seized upon an article written by Gordon Blaine Hancock, dean of Virginia Union University in Richmond, as an opening for action. In an essay entitled "Interracial Hypertension," released to the Associated Negro Press, Hancock called on "the better-class whites and Negroes" to join in deflecting a "dangerous phase of the interracial conflict." Hancock then went on to chastise militant blacks who ignored the "growing spirit of justice and fair play in the heart of the New South." Struck by the compatibility between Hancock's ideas and her own, Ames contacted him with a plan. Why not, she urged, bypass northern radicals and forestall white reaction by agreeing with other southern black leaders on a unified agenda for reform. In turn, she pledged to organize a white reply to their challenge. Together these two manifestos would prepare the way for interracial cooperation in the postwar South.[6]

Hancock acted eagerly on Ames's suggestion. With P. B. Young of the Norfolk *Journal and Guide,* he called a conference in Durham for October 20, 1942. The exclusion of northerners from the gathering attracted harsh criticism from the black press. But contrary to the expectations of such observers, the Durham Conference issued a forthright and detailed proposal for voting rights, employment opportunities, trade union organization, and access to public services. Although conference representatives declared themselves "fundamentally opposed to the principle and practice of compulsory segregation in our American society," they refrained from demanding the immediate abolition of Jim Crow.[7]

Reaction to the Durham statement stressed the message white moderates wanted to hear. Southern Negroes, commented Ralph McGill of the Atlanta *Constitution,* had repudiated northern spokesmen whose "prejudice and intolerance is every bit as dangerous and as violent as that which they protest against." Moreover, they had wisely accepted the fact that segregation "will be retained for a long time." Satisfied by this interpretation, 113 white business, professional, and religious leaders met in Atlanta on April 8, 1943, to approve, in general terms, the principles of the Durham Conference. At the same time, the group took the opportunity to caution that "the ultimate solution will be found in evolutionary methods and not in ill-founded revolutionary movements." The fragility of this style of interracial communication became apparent at a meeting of a collaboration committee in Richmond two months later. At the end of Gordon Hancock's keynote address, in which he warned of the "grave danger in going too slow," a white elder statesman of the CIC rebuked him "for going too far." Only the intervention of Howard Odum, who proposed the creation of a council on southern regional development as a basis for implementing the Durham proposal, prevented a black walk-out.[8] On August 4, 1943, a second meeting of the collaboration committee voted to replace the Interracial Commission with a new organization to be called the Southern Regional Council (SRC). Odum was to serve as its president; Guy B. Johnson, a young sociologist from the University of North Carolina, was to become its executive director.[9]

Throughout this series of conferences and negotiations, Jessie Daniel Ames worked quietly behind the scenes, assuming responsibility for organizational details and prodding her male co-workers to take public leadership roles. Both Hancock and Young were careful to acknowledge her contribution. "When the final story is written as it most surely will be some day, your name will stand out in bold relief high on the roll of honor," wrote Hancock. "You have fought the good fight and kept the faith." But at the Richmond meeting, the initiative passed to Odum and Alexander. Ames was not included in the discussions leading to the creation of the SRC.[10] Her association with the old organization, her compromising behavior in the debate over federal anti-lynching legislation, and her long-standing personality conflicts with her male colleagues jeopardized her chances of going on with the new organization. As the SRC staff assembled, it became obvious that Jessie Daniel Ames's services would no longer be required.

Although she could read the handwriting on the wall, Ames refused to admit defeat. "I cannot go on into this new period, as a hangover," she announced, "I must go on, if I do, as a new member of the staff, in full knowledge of what is planned and why and what part I am to be responsible for. I have earned a full partnership, if only as a junior partner, and only as a partner can I continue." Far from offering her a "full partnership," Ames recalled, SRC leaders put her in "a humiliating situation. My salary was to be cut in half. My name was not to be on the letterhead. I was to have no identity at all." Guy Johnson—who had seen his own wife's academic career stifled by sex discrimination at the University of North Carolina— seemed willing to have Jessie Daniel Ames continue as editor of the *Southern Frontier*. Alexander, however, insisted that SRC should begin with a clean slate. Believing that when he arrived in Atlanta Ames would be gone, Johnson found her still at her post. Finally, one Saturday morning, Ames asked the incumbent director to meet her for lunch. "We went to a little place nearby," Johnson recalled, "probably sat there for two hours. It became quite late and there was nobody in the place, so we had plenty of privacy." At last Ames spoke: "Now, I know that I have been a great problem to you, that you were no doubt told that I was going and then you've come down here and found that I haven't resigned. But I want you to know that I don't blame you for this. . . . I am resigning and I'll attend the charter meeting and then I will step aside."[11]

A few weeks later, on February 16, 1944, Ames delivered a moving farewell oration to the interracial movement. Fighting to maintain her composure, she made a final plea to black and white women to take the lead in the postwar movement.[12] Immediately afterward, she retired to a cottage called the "Wren's Nest" in the tiny village of Tryon in western North Carolina. She was replaced as Director of Woman's Work by an eminently genteel Methodist church leader named Dorothy Rogers Tilly.[13]

2

In the foothills of the Blue Ridge Mountains, Ames set about at once to rebuild her life. To her co-workers in the women's anti-lynching movement, she announced not that she had been forced to resign but that she had changed her status from "a professional basis to a free lance." The Wren's Nest, she assured them, "will not be occupied by a 'wren.'"[14] Indeed, Tryon had never seen anyone quite like her. "Things just didn't stay still when she was around," her new friends recalled. She lined the walls of her cottage with books, subscribed to magazines and newspapers, and from the sidelines kept up a running commentary on the times. Gathering about her a women's study group on world affairs, she reconstructed her familiar role as teacher, organizer, and gadfly to a female constituency. Elected Superintendent of Christian Social Relations for the Western North Carolina Conference of the Methodist Church, she welcomed the opportunity to "get back into public life and to be remembered." And in the early fifties, from her base in local women's groups, she helped register black voters and plan a precinct organizing campaign modeled on her first victory in the Texas suffrage movement thirty years before.[15]

Perhaps no story better captures Jessie Daniel Ames's style of female reform than that of the day her little band of supporters showed up unexpectedly at the Polk County precinct meeting to wrest control of the Democratic Party away from the courthouse gang. "Jessie had pretty well spearheaded it," recalled one participant.

> I mean, she told us how to go about it and what to expect when we got there. And Jessie arrived all dressed up in a white linen suit,

and had on a little straw hat, sort of a bonnet-like hat, with tiny red roses under the brim. She had on white gloves and a reticule over her arm, looking as though she'd just wandered by on her way to a tea party. And she had masterminded the whole thing! I just had to go behind a tree and laugh.[16]

For one last time, Ames was in her element: ensconced in the protective guise of the southern lady, manipulating local political events, basking in the admiration and loyalty of a network of organized women.

Just as she had asserted control over her own destiny and over the definition of womanhood in southern society, so now Ames looked ahead to the historical interpretation of her career. She lobbied successfully for a congressional resolution recognizing her husband's contributions to yellow fever research. She used the opportunity of arranging and annotating her public correspondence to confound her enemies and explain her own positions. She lived to see the first study of the Interracial Commission published—and to express her annoyance at what she viewed as its inaccuracies and misinterpretations. She particularly resented the condescension and sentimentality with which the women's anti-lynching campaign was treated. "I do hope," she wrote to an inquiring journalist, "that you will confine yourself to facts and not attempt to romanticize the work of Southern women in the field of race relations."[17]

To her friends, Jessie Daniel Ames appeared "animated, positive, and full of determination."[18] In her reluctant retirement, the qualities of independence, wit, and resiliency—forged in a lifetime of striving against inner doubts and external circumstances—stood her in good stead. Yet no amount of "determination" could mask the fact that she had lost the work in which she had achieved her greatest sense of authenticity, in which she had been most fully herself.[19] Her productive middle years had been relatively conflict-free as she channeled her passion, intellect, and formidable physical energy into regional reform. But forced out of the public arena and into the private world of family life, she found herself vulnerable once more to the emo-

tional dilemmas that had blighted her youth and young womanhood.

She proved as temperamentally unsuited to the role of be-
nign grandmother as she had to those of daughter and wife.
Her relationships with her children became increasingly
strained; her correspondence vacillated between demands for
attention, angry denunciations, and abject self-doubt. An intense need for "sympathy and understanding" spilled out onto
page after page of unmailed—but carefully preserved—messages she called her "WAILING WALL" letters. "I have spent too
many years, almost all that I have lived, building up a stone
wall between me and the people whom I love," she concluded.
"My actions produce corresponding reactions to which I react
and so on in a vicious circle. And I am . . . so conscious, now,
that I cause all the hurt I get, unconscious flagellation, that I
have come to the conclusion that I am at present, unfit for family association."[20]

At the same time, history itself dealt her a staggering blow.
As she watched the civil rights movement gather strength and
topple barrier after barrier, she could rest secure in the knowledge of her historic contribution to race relations. But she
could find no parallel confirmation that her struggle for sexual
emancipation had been worth the price. On the contrary, by
the early fifties antifeminist reaction seemed to have won an
overwhelming cultural victory. Following the renewed debate
on "woman's place" among popular psychologists, she found
herself under devastating attack. The women's movement,
wrote Ferdinand Lundberg and Marynia Farnham, in *Modern
Woman: The Lost Sex*, had represented a neurotic reaction to
the erosion of women's traditional home-centered functions
under the impact of industrialization. By encouraging women
to emulate male achievements, it had given rise to a host of
contemporary ills.[21] Ames had easily survived the antisuffrage
polemics of her youth, but she had neither the emotional nor
social support to fend off this far more subtle ideological offensive. As a result, she sometimes looked back on her contraven-

tion of sex-role prescriptions with sharp misgivings. Reading Lundberg and Farnham, she remarked, is like "rereading the story of part of my own life."[22] This is not to say that Ames surrendered to the antifeminist concensus. An interview conducted in the mid-sixties found her proud and undaunted, recounting her battles against the patriarchy with amused delight. Yet the anguish confided to her private journals serves as a measure of the cultural losses suffered by the movement that had so profoundly shaped her life.

Alienated from her children, deprived of her public work, and shaken by the implications of popular Freudianism, Jessie Daniel Ames turned to autobiography in search of justification and personal transcendence. The Ames women, commented her youngest daughter Lulu, are "prima donnas . . . they're troublemakers . . . and they all write their autobiographies in their latter years." Indeed, in her "latter years" Ames reportedly turned out 85 versions of her personal history. This conscious shaping of the material of her life, however, had started long before. In 1894, while a freshman in college, she had written an essay which offered an eerie foreshadowing of the burden of her private experience of womanhood. "It is not common for people to tell the story of their life, nor is it pleasant," wrote Jessie Daniel Ames as a thirteen-year-old schoolgirl. "But since we have such things to do, we might as well do it and be done." Through all her self-revelations ran a central theme: her failure to love and to be loved—to fulfill her culture's expectations of the feminine purpose—had left her with a deep sense of shame that her public accomplishments had never been quite able to erase. "My task now," she concluded in 1951, "is to break the habits" of a lifetime. "There is nothing unworthy or discreditable about me. . . . Now if I can come to accept this emotionally as well as intellectually, I shall have fairly happy and peaceful years ahead of me."[23]

In 1968, as the social upheavals of the sixties climaxed in the announced retirement of Lyndon B. Johnson and the assassinations of Martin Luther King and Robert F. Kennedy, Jessie Daniel Ames succumbed to crippling arthritis. Returning to Texas with Lulu, she lived four more years in an Austin nursing home. Lulu devoted herself to her mother's care, at the cost of her own precarious health and emotional equilibrium. "It got to where it was just mother and me," she recalled. As Jessie clung tenaciously to life, the two women experienced a profoundly unsettling role reversal. "I wasn't her mother," Lulu observed, "but I was—as they say at the hospital—'the responsible person.' " In the end, Jessie turned to Lulu for the physical comfort she had always denied herself. "This business of hugging," Lulu reflected, "there was none of that in our family. And after I brought mother back in 1968, she couldn't get enough loving. . . . My feeling is that what you do is you go back to what you were before the world starts working you over." Whatever Lulu might do, however, she could not ease the pain of mortality. "I knew mother wasn't happy. I knew why she wasn't happy. I knew I couldn't do anything about that because I couldn't make her young and in her prime again." [24]

By the time the women's liberation movement emerged from the crucible of the civil rights campaign in the late 1960s, Jessie Daniel Ames was too old and too ill to understand its implications. Neither her childhood nor her culture had offered models for balancing the drive to achieve in the world with the need for intimate and meaningful relationships with others. For Ames, the road out of the female condition had lain in harnessing emotion to work and reform. It remained for a new generation to develop a critique of the politics of personal life, a demand for the fundamental alteration of sex roles, and a vision of fulfillment in the private as well as the public sphere. [25] As the new feminism propelled women into public political battles and confronted them with the exigencies of coalition-building across class and racial lines, however, the issues faced by the transitional generation of the 1930s took on new significance. Indeed, even as Ames lay dying, such continuities were beginning to be discerned. On February 12, 1972, nine days before Ames's death, a southern women's political caucus assembled at Scarritt College in Nashville, Tennessee, home base for the women leaders of Southern Methodism. Exhorting her audience to a broad conception of their political responsibilities, the keynote speaker, Congresswoman Bella Abzug of New York, could find no closer analogy for such an effort than the Association of Southern Women for the Prevention of Lynching. Jessie Daniel Ames would have wanted no better tribute.

Jessie Daniel Ames in Atlanta, 1937. Courtesy of the Lulu Daniel Ames Papers, Southern Historical Collection, University of North Carolina at Chapel Hill.

Epilogue

They're prima donnas . . . they're troublemakers . . . and they all write their autobiographies in their latter years.
— Lulu Daniel Ames, speaking of the women in her family (1972)

I advance, therefore, the perfectly accepted theory that cases of dual personality do exist, in which the feminine and the masculine elements alternately preponderate. I advance this in an impersonal and scientific spirit, and claim that I am qualified to speak with the intimacy a professional scientist could acquire only after years of study and indirect information, because I have the object of study always to hand, in my own heart, and can gauge the exact truthfulness of what my own experience tells me. However frank, people would always keep back something. I can't keep back anything from myself.
— Vita Sackville-West, in Nigel Nicolson, *Portrait of a Marriage* (1973)

I did not set out to make Jessie Daniel Ames so central to this book. But as I inched my way through the papers of the Antilynching Association, I became aware of its marked dependence on the mind and will of a single, dynamic leader. I could not understand the organization Ames led, it seemed to me, without a close look at her temperament and motivations. That conviction was, and was not, congruent with the times in which

I wrote. If, as the women's movement would have it, the personal was political, a study of a women's voluntary association would have to be concerned with the nexus between private experience and public activity. Yet most historians of women steered clear of biography, with its focus on unique, individual lives. They saw the genre not as a means of learning why individuals occupying similar social locations make different choices—and thus of exploring issues of contingency, agency, and identity—but as replicating the elitism of traditional scholarship.

Now, twenty years after I began the research for *Revolt Against Chivalry*, I find myself influenced by a different intellectual surround. Feminist biography has come into its own.[1] Early formulations of the distinction between the private and the public spheres have given way to more subtle understandings of how social and historical conditions produce our most private sense of self and of how, conversely, we challenge and revise society's prescriptions. Postmodern notions of gender identities as perpetually unstable have drawn renewed attention to the questions of how individuals come into and subvert those identities and of the links between that process and political action.[2]

Together, feminism and postmodernism have also raised fresh questions about the boundary between the researcher and the subject of research. Biographers writing today can hardly avoid self-reflection. Nor can they fall back on totalizing theories or reductive social scientific categories, dedicated as they are to building "causeways between the facts" of a particular person's life as it unfolds over time.[3] Increasingly they speak in the first person, probing their relationship to their subjects, acknowledging their standpoints, and making clear that while we can empathize with others, we can never really walk in their shoes.

Indeed, biography attracts us as writers and readers in part because of qualities it shares with literature. In biographies as in novels, we puzzle out the narrative of other people's lives, recognizing dimensions of their subjectivity to which they themselves are blind and consequently discovering new dimensions and possibilities in our own. That project of self-discovery is open-ended, for just as we "remain a mystery to ourselves," so the biographies we write remain provisional and thus incomplete.[4]

Looking back at *Revolt Against Chivalry*, I wondered how context and consciousness had shaped my rendition of Ames's story. What new narrative might emerge under different times and circumstances? How might I now formulate the public/private, masculine/feminine dynamics that I saw as her life's major themes?

The answers called for introspection. But they also called for an understanding of the collaborative nature of the biographical enterprise, for *Revolt Against Chivalry* was not fashioned by me alone. It was also produced by a circle of women who refused to let Ames and her antilynching campaign disappear into "the twilight zone that lies between living memory and written history."[5] Those women ranged from Ames herself, who saved the documents that made my project possible, to her daughters and coworkers, to the feminist historians who helped to create the discursive context in which my book made sense. Closing the circle, but also setting it in motion, was a postpublication encounter with Ames's niece, Laura Hardy Crites, whose writings, inspired in part by my book, encouraged me to take a second look at some of the key documents on which *Revolt Against Chivalry* depends.[6]

When I began reconstructing Ames's story, she and the Antilynching Association had found their way into history books mainly as footnotes to the saga of southern liberalism. I first encountered them in a biography of Will Alexander, a circumstance that would not have pleased Ames at all. She had blamed Alexander for shunting her aside, and she had been highly annoyed by what she regarded as his biographers' off-hand and sentimental treatment of her role in the Interracial Commission. Anne Firor Scott's *The Southern Lady*, by contrast, placed the Antilynching Association more firmly in the context of women's history.[7] As I pursued my research, a generation of feminist scholars was developing an increasingly dialectical understanding of the link between middle-class women's culture—the values, rituals, and networks formed under a system of sex segregation—and their efforts at reform. That understanding underlay my view of the Antilynching Association as an important manifestation of the female reform tradition.

Unfortunately, there was a wild card in this interpretation: Jessie Daniel Ames, the founder, leader, and chief ideologue of the movement. The Antilynching Association, for all its racial daring, appeared to be a late-blooming variation on what were essentially nineteenth-century themes. Updating the "cult of true womanhood"—the belief in women's passionlessness and moral superiority—many of Ames's colleagues saw their influence as radiating outward from the home. But Ames seemed to be cut from a different cloth. She sometimes used the rhetoric and methods of earlier reformers, but she had much in common with the breakaway generation of single women who sought not indirect influence but professional opportunities and political power. Her career depended on a constituency of small-town churchwomen whose courage she admired but whose piety she did not fully share. She wore ladyhood as a mask, employed evangelical language for reformist ends, and remained an outsider even in the organizations she ran.

At the time Ames's marginality sometimes made me feel victimized by my subject. Why was I writing about such an anomalous figure? Why not Jane Addams or Eleanor Roosevelt, who seemed to epitomize their times?

In retrospect I can see that Ames's refusal to fit comfortably into conventional categories was part of what drew me to her. Feminist biographers are often engaged in acts of rescue, trying to restore to their rightful place foremothers who have been ignored, misunderstood, or forgotten. Ames suffered triple invisibility: as a woman in a region whose history has been written by and about men; as a southerner in a women's movement that has been understood from the perspective of the urban Northeast; and as an individual whose talents and sensibilities were in some ways out of step with her circumstances and her times. I too was a product of the small-town Southwest, the first in my family to go to college, and for me as for Ames race and gender issues were always intertwined. I was not fully conscious of this at the time, but writing Ames into history was surely a way of asserting a view of feminism and of women's experience, indeed of the American experience, that was expansive enough for me and the women I knew.

In any case my interpretation of the Antilynching Association evolved relatively smoothly out of the counterpoint between my own research and the cumulative efforts of other scholars. But when it came to *Revolt Against Chivalry*'s biographical theme, I stumbled over problems of evidence and timing. Ames's correspondence was rigorously impersonal; it told little about the private experiences that shaped her public choices. And I gained access to the sources that revealed her personal story only after I had drafted the history of the movement she led.

The collaboration that made biography possible began when I arrived at the Austin home of Ames's youngest daughter, Lulu Daniel Ames, tape recorder in hand, intent on asking personal questions about a woman who had already become a rather formidable figure in my mind. I knew from her mother's records that Lulu had suffered from infantile paralysis, but I was unprepared for the apparent frailty of the wheelchair-bound woman who met me at the door. Luckily there was no time for diffidence. Lulu Ames summoned me in to a supper of homemade soup and fresh-baked bread, brought out a bottle of Jack Daniels, and started to talk. The story she told me was compounded of family tradition, her own observations, and her reading of the letters, diaries, and autobiographical fragments that her mother left behind. From her I first heard about the "tragedies" in Jessie Daniel Ames's life: her father's open preference for her older sister Lulu Daniel Hardy; her own short, unhappy marriage; the agonizing search for her daughter's cure. In the months that followed, Lulu Ames continued to go over her mother's papers, sending them to me with her own commentary, box by box, and calling at all hours to compare insights and interpretations. Those papers enabled me to add to my portrait of a reformer whatever psychological depth it contains.[8]

Several years later, after the book came out, one of Ames's coworkers gave me a letter Lulu Ames had written at a critical juncture, a letter that reminded me of the contingency and fragility of the historical enterprise. Written just before Lulu decided to turn her mother's papers over to me (except, heartbreakingly, those she had destroyed the summer before), the letter sought to explain her motivations.

> I do not mean that I didn't love Mother, that she didn't do a tremendous job, that she wasn't magnetic and creative and brilliant, that all her public life and work weren't remarkable. . . . But . . . the whole . . . person isn't known and the whole person was human and real and good and bad. And if Jackie writes a thing on Mother, I want it to be on all of Mother.[9]

Lulu Ames's desire to honor her mother without simplifying her complex life made biography possible. Yet the very factors that made the daughter's testimony so valuable also made it problematic. Lulu's father died before she was born. She spent her early life in and out of hospitals; in later years her mother was always on the road. Like her brother and sister, she sometimes felt neglected. Yet there was no denying the strength of the mother-daughter bond. Lulu and Jessie kept up a steady correspondence throughout their lives. Until she was well into her twenties, Lulu filled her letters with a private language of endearment, mixing professions of love and dependency with news of progress or backsliding in her efforts to please. Ames reserved a special tenderness for her "sweetest . . . gentlest . . . most sensitive child." But mainly she dispatched instructions about what Lulu should eat, do, and wear. "I have no lectures for you," she might begin—and then proceed with detailed instructions about diet, exercise, money, and school.[10] As an adult Lulu shared Jessie's sense of irony, her taste for introspection, and her commitment to politics and reform. And she never ceased to view her mother with compassion and respect. But she also blamed Ames for holding her to impossible standards of "normality," for pushing her too hard. When Lulu tried to work out those conflicts through autobiography, Ames responded with a literary critique. End the story with your graduation from college, she advised. "I am the antagonist from this point on and overcoming that hatred for me which is akin to love and becoming close friends with me marks the end in fact of your psychological struggle."[11]

Ames, for her part, may have seen her own psychic injuries embodied in her child. "I must destroy my wall of self-protection and take chances . . . even though I may be shot at, wounded, crippled," she once wrote.[12] At other moments, she gallantly (if unrealistically) likened her daughter's accomplishments to her own. "I'll tell you right now," she admonished an interviewer when she was eighty-two and already suffering from the arthritis and osteoporosis that would soon make it impossible for her to manage on her own, "being on crutches is not a handicap—either for her or for me."[13]

When I met Lulu Ames, her mother had died only nine months before. Lulu had had a heart attack; a few years later she too would die. Her willingness to help me was entangled with a process of life review: she was sorting out for the last time where her personality ended and her mother's began.[14] No wonder Lulu seemed to have been waiting for my arrival, preparing herself for exactly the project I had in mind.

It is difficult to describe the feelings this alliance with Ames's daughter evoked in me. There were gratitude and excitement, to be sure, but also trepidation. How could I do justice to such intensely lived lives? How could I maintain my intellectual independence against the force of Lulu's interpretations? Mindful of the dangers, I circled around her testimony, supplementing it with other interviews and comparing it to written sources. All in all I concluded that Lulu Ames was a remarkably reliable witness. And I would, for the most part, stand by the interpretations that grew out of our encounter.

Yet even as the story fell together, gaps remained. Chief

among them was the private dimension of Jessie Daniel Ames's middle years. By and large the documents that shed light on Ames's inner life had been written either before her antilynching career began or after she had retired. Other diaries had been destroyed, and I had only the public record of her forties, fifties, and early sixties, when she was at the height of her career.

But evidence was not the only problem. In hindsight I would say that the intellectual context in which I worked was less helpful here than elsewhere. I would also say that although my own life experience made me sensitive to certain aspects of Ames's personal history, it may have hindered my understanding of other dimensions. Indeed, these two factors were closely related—my own consciousness and the state of feminist scholarship at the time.

The problems with the literature are fairly obvious. The nineteenth-century preoccupations of women's history told us little about the modern era. The periodization that grew out of studies of the urban, industrial Northeast obscured the nature of generational change in other regions. Perhaps most important was the inadequacy of available psychological tools. Developmental psychology, to which a biographer might naturally turn, was premised almost entirely on studies of men. Object relations theorists such as Nancy Chodorow had gone a long way toward modifying Freudian biases. Yet they remained focused on the Oedipal romance, especially on the child's early identification with the mother, and had little to say about other identifications or about unconventional developmental histories or sexual identities. Their celebration of androgyny—the reintegration of a personality split apart by the imposition of hierarchical sexual distinctions in infancy—struck me at the time as particularly liberating. But it could also become a normative ideal: a dream of psychic unity that neither we nor our foremothers could ever quite achieve.[15]

Among my own limitations was an unrealistic belief in the promise of female solidarity, nurtured by an idealistic view of the women in my own family, by the early women's liberation movement, and by the scholarship on the nineteenth-century female world. I was not surprised by the racial hierarchies and hostilities that hobbled women's interracial activities. On the contrary what surprised me were the moments of frank discussion and mutual effort I found. By contrast I did expect to see "bonds of womanhood" within class- and race-limited circles. Once I discovered Ames's conflicted relationships with men, I looked for evidence that she relied for support and intimacy on women instead. But I found that even as she devoted herself entirely to a female *public* world, her private relationships with women were often marked either by distance and reserve or by stormy competition. The question then was what to do with these unwelcome signs of ambivalence where I had hoped to find connection.

Nineteenth-century biographers often went to great lengths to prove the femininity of their heroines by suppressing traces of ambition, anger, or passion. With the popularization of Freudianism after World War I, scholars turned to portraying successful women as aberrations from a healthy feminine norm. In either case, where a man might be assessed wholly on the basis of his public accomplishments, a woman also had to prove herself in the private sphere. Was she a good mother? A loving wife?[16] Given this double standard, it occurred to me that writing about Ames's difficulties with men would reinforce sexist stereotypes. But that fear was allayed by confidence that the women's movement had created an audience that would not reduce public striving to a compensatory flight from private failure. Ames's attitudes toward other women, along with her political rigidity and her devotion to intellect at the expense of the emotions and the body, were something else again. Here I had to struggle not just with concern about discrediting an admirable woman, but with my own feelings of disappointment—even, perhaps, dislike.

In the end I argued that Ames's relationships with her father and her husband taught her the risks of intimacy and denied her a secure sense of self-worth. At the same time those experiences were a source of her insight and power. They mobilized her resistance, her distrust of paternalism, and her desire for autonomy. Had all this occurred under other circumstances, Ames might have found her place within a separate, nurturing female world. As it was, she could neither wholeheartedly adopt the values of her mother's generation nor reject those values in exchange for such new ideals as sexual liberation or assimilation. She was trapped between Victorianism and modernism, finding neither fulfillment in women's networks nor success in male-dominated institutions. She resolved her dilemma by immersing herself in practical activity that bound her to other women in pursuit of political goals. But because she equated womanhood with weakness, dependency, and competition for men, she kept her distance from her coworkers, viewing them as followers to be influenced or dominated and not, for the most part, as equals and friends.

In response to this interpretation, a few reviewers gently suggested that I treated Ames's relationships with other women too negatively or that I placed too much emphasis on her personal limitations.[17] My own feeling is that the problem lay rather in my tendency to posit too sharp a distinction between the realm of intimacy and affection, from which she fled, and the realm of competence, in which she found satisfaction. Having assumed this dichotomy, I tended to underestimate the emotional significance of Ames's relationships with women and, paradoxically, to judge her against an unstated androgynous ideal.

If I were writing *Revolt Against Chivalry* today I would look harder at Ames's middle years. I would focus more sharply on her involvement with her sister, Lulu Daniel Hardy. Above all I would amend my view of Ames's rejection of conventional femininity, stressing instead the ways in which she handled the gender ambiguities that haunt—and animate—all our lives.

Such a reframing would be commensurate with postmodern notions of the flux of self. It would also reflect my own passage through time. Since I wrote *Revolt Against Chivalry*, the women in my family have grown up or grown old; we didn't turn out to

Jessie Daniel Ames's husband, Roger Post Ames, Guatemala, 1914. Courtesy of the Lulu Daniel Ames Papers, Southern Historical Collection, University of North Carolina at Chapel Hill.

be a latter-day version of *Little Women* (plus one loved brother) struggling through life in perfect unity. Instead we have had to come to grips with difference and distance and, over the years, to discover a new basis for solidarity that takes those realities into account. I have also gained a sense, which I could not have had when I started out, of what it means to survive—from one identity to another, from one era to the next—and to combine, over time and in daily life, ways of feeling and behaving that I was raised to believe must be split apart.

Most immediately, this revision would draw on the insights I gained from an encounter with a final member of the remarkable Daniel-Ames clan. I never met Ames or her older sister Lulu. My sources reflected primarily Jessie's side of their story. But after the book came out, Lulu's daughter, Laura Hardy Crites, came to see me in Chapel Hill, bringing with her an essay about Jessie and Lulu she had written in response to my book. Entitled "The Sisters," it confirmed my book's basic conclusions, but it also encouraged a second reading of my critical texts. In light of "The Sisters," I saw subthemes in Ames's autobiographical writings I had not noticed before. Or rather, I took seriously comments that I had seen and not seen, read but in effect dismissed.

Looking back, Jessie Daniel Ames portrayed her marriage as a series of painful partings and reconciliations, in which she was always being sent away to live, a Cinderella in exile, in her beautiful, well-to-do sister's home. By contrast, in her sister's account, Ames experienced sex as violation and sought asylum in her sister's home at every opportunity. Ames's first two children were born there, rather than with her husband in Central America or her parents in Texas, and she gave her last-born daughter her sister Lulu's name. This is how "The Sisters" described those days:

> Lulu surrounded her sister with constant care and attention, understanding and love. Her home was Jess's home. The two young women sewed together, read aloud, cared for their children, played cribbage, went for long afternoon buggy rides, planned the exten-

sive entertaining that was called for by Lulu's Position as wife of the
commandant of [a military academy] and mistress of a large staff.[18]

Ames's father died in 1911; her husband's death occurred
three years after that. Only then did she establish her own
household, settling in Georgetown within walking distance of
her mother, then moving into her mother's larger home. She
and her children continued to spend summers with her sister's
family. When Lulu's husband died, Jessie took care of her
sister's children while Lulu returned to school; Jessie's daughter, in turn, lived with Lulu during the Ames's move from Texas
to Georgia in 1929. Clearly theirs was an intergenerational
extended family in which Jessie, her mother, and her sister
relied upon one another's support and raised two sets of children as if they were one.

Critical to this support network—and yet barely mentioned
in Ames's writings—were the African-American women who
labored in all these women's homes. Chief among them was
Louise Kirkland, whose importance leaps out from the pages of
the photograph albums that I discovered shortly after *Revolt
Against Chivalry* appeared. In 1931 Ames published a pamphlet
entitled *What Price Domestic Service?*, and she persistently
tried to turn the attention of the CIC Woman's Committee to
the low wages and poor working conditions of domestic workers. Louise Kirkland had died by the time I began working on
Revolt Against Chivalry, but if I could turn back the clock I
would try harder to find her descendants and to explore the
relationships among these black and white women. How did
Kirkland view her work and the Ames family? How did she
juggle her own family responsibilities? How did Ames's concerns about household workers as a group affect her own behavior as an employer? What impact did women such as Louise
Kirkland have on Ames's thinking and reform career?[19]

Ames's preoccupation with her sister stands in sharp contrast
to her silence about the African-American women on whose
work she relied. In fact, by the time Ames began writing the
surviving versions of her autobiography, her memories hinged

on resentment against a sister whom her father had outrageously adored. This is true of a relatively lighthearted memoir written when she was thirty-nine, as well as of the darker self-scrutinies of later years. Starting out to examine her marriage in an essay called "Daniel-Ames Family Life," she wove back and forth between her husband and her sister, ending with an effort to absolve herself of guilt for "this antagonism, this dislike." Her goal was not reconciliation, but getting "this poison . . . out—and for good and for the last time."

Yet however much she might emphasize her present "antagonism" and "dislike," Ames also acknowledged other, earlier

Jessie Daniel Ames and her sister, Lulu Hardy Daniel, in 1955. Courtesy of the Lulu Daniel Ames Papers, Southern Historical Collection, University of North Carolina at Chapel Hill.

themes, themes more consonant with Lulu's recollections. When Jessie's honeymoon was cut short, "there was one comfort in being sent home that helped me. Lulu . . . wanted me to go back with her. I was delighted, made happy." After a long catalog of her sister's faults, particularly her helplessness and need for constant sympathy and attention, Ames ended with the claim that only by severing the relationship altogether could she avoid being reabsorbed by the "adulation and worship I used to have for her."[20]

I tended to discount such affirmations of sisterly love in part because of the force of Ames's more negative recollections. I also assumed that youthful feelings of "adulation" could even then have been manufactured from converted rage. There was, in any case, little doubt about Ames's later rejection of her sister or of the reverberations of that rejection in her public and private life.

The very rhetoric of the antilynching campaign mirrored Ames's rebellion against a model of femininity she explicitly identified with her sister. Where her sister was protected by men, she would reject protection in the name of autonomy. Where, in her view, her sister got her way through manipulation, she (and the Antilynching Association) would use the franchise to punish and reward. If her sister epitomized the southern lady as beloved wife, lavish hostess, apolitical clubwoman, Ames would use the image of the lady for political ends.

Ames played herself off against her sister in her personal style as well. Photographs show Jessie to have been an attractive, soft-featured young woman with striking, luminous eyes. Yet her sister had occupied the place of beautiful daughter. Jessie had been the "tomboy," learning her first lessons in survival on the back lots of a desolate East Texas town. One game lodged in her memory with particular force. As a girl playing with "less respectable" children in an abandoned brick kiln, she was always the tail in "crack the whip," whirled outward to slam against the brick ovens until she fought her way close to the head of the line. Throughout her life, she prized physical vigor, hid weakness, despised sentimentality, and unnerved her male

coworkers with her "direct way of walking and talking" and her
strength of will. By contrast she portrayed her sister, in later
years, as a seductive hypochondriac and a "clinging vine."[21]

The importance of this motif is underlined by the frequency
with which it crops up in writings on subjects with which it
seems to have little to do. In a journal kept while her son
Frederick was dying of cancer in 1958, Ames returned from the
hospital to title that day's entry "Memories," devoting it to her
sister and their childhood games. Sixteen years earlier, in a
letter written to Frederick during World War II, she followed a
familiar logic that linked her feminism, her self-image, and her
sister's contrasting personality and views:

> Women in war work are demonstrating without a doubt that this
> ancient idea that women are delicate, fragile . . . creatures is being
> so fast exploded that soon a woman who can't do things will be as
> obsolete as the women who used to faint around and have the
> vapours [sic]. Your auntie thinks it is a shame and that women will
> be degraded by working in steel mills and boiler factories and other
> heavy industry. . . . If I were younger I would certainly be doing
> physical war work of some [kind] but the old gal at nelly bout sixty
> is not what she used to be. Though I still think I can do anything I
> really have to do at whatever the price. [22]

To a certain extent, Ames's relationship with her mother
echoed the ambivalence of this sibling bond. In contrast to her
comments about her sister, her writings acknowledged only
minor conflicts with her mother. Laura Daniel fully supported
her daughter's reform career, and Ames attributed to her mother
the qualities she most valued in herself: devotion to principle
and to keeping one's "chin up, fighting thro."[23] As a child, she
had sided with her evangelical mother against her agnostic
father, and she went on to build the Antilynching Association
primarily on a base of Methodist missionary societies. Yet Ames
wrote of her own conversion experience with an irony that was
echoed in her stance toward the evangelical women she led.
And she remembered her mother as remote and preoccupied,
too busy to notice the loneliness of a little girl.

One might expect that Ames's rejection of the models provided by her sister and her mother would lead her to abandon
the conventional feminine domestic role, and to a certain extent
I drew that conclusion. But nothing could be further from the
truth. Ames had three children to raise; she could employ
household workers but she could not avoid domesticity. Moreover, it was through her ability to take care of her children, to
support them without a husband's help (thus combining masculine and feminine roles), that she achieved the personal competence upon which she built her public success. Her public and
private lives were joined in another way as well. The respect
and allegiance accorded her by coworkers in the Antilynching
Association was based in part on their perception of her as an
effective and heavily burdened mother.

Two incidents that occurred during Ames's middle age under-
line the depth of her investment in this nurturing role. In 1937
her mother died of cancer; in 1951 her niece Verona (Lulu
Daniel Hardy's oldest daughter) succumbed to the same disease. Both women chose Ames, rather than her sister, to nurse
them through their final days. Verona had already, from childhood, shifted her allegiance from her mother to her aunt, whom
she took as a model of worldliness and political commitment. It
is significant, I think, that Ames viewed nursing the sick and
caring for the old not as burdens to be avoided but as privileges
to be fought for, as opportunities to prove that she could blend
the competence and control on which she staked her career
with the ability to nurture, to take care. Emotional need thus
merged with altruism; Ames saw these moments as victories
over her sister, a vindication of her brand of womanhood, proof
that she loved and was loved.

Ames wrestled all her life with these two dimensions of the
self: the instrumental and the affective, each coded as masculine or feminine, each associated with other hierarchical oppo-
sitions. In Ames's case those voices warred against one another
more painfully than they do in the lives of most of us. As a child
she played with boys but saved her affection for other girls. As
a wife she felt herself to be an impostor, a substitute for the

womanly woman her husband might have had. As a mother she played a double role. She was shadowed to the end by the ghosts of her father and her husband, but her existence turned on relationships with women. And the difficulty of those relationships did not detract from their emotional power. Beneath coolness, there was passion; difficulty was not the antithesis of love but rather its occasion. Alongside Ames's more visible self-assertion in the public realm ran an abiding desire to reclaim and express an affective life that she associated with weakness and rejection. Thus her lifelong obsession with her sister reflected more than sibling rivalry. She saw her sister not just as a negative prototype of femininity but also as an alter ego, an embodiment of a side of herself she could neither abandon nor fully express.

How this inner struggle affected Ames's sexual life remains a mystery. Was her reserve toward women rooted in an ambivalence about same-sex relationships born of repressed desire? Was she a lesbian? There are indications that, by some definitions, she might have been. Among these are her friendship with Frank King, the Texas suffragist who ran a ranch and dressed as a man; her love for her niece Verona, who, according to Ames's daughter Lulu, was a lesbian; and her immersion in a close-knit female world. Yet I could find no love letters, no hint of eroticism in her adult relationships with either men or women. Except for family members, she always lived alone. The only mention of sexual experience in her writings concerned her marriage, where sex was a failed promise, one of many sources of despair. I was faced with a dilemma astutely limned since by Leila Rupp: how to deal with the complexities of relationships between women in the twentieth century, after sexologists had medicalized—and stigmatized—romantic, same-sex friendships and a lesbian subculture had emerged. Given the absence of evidence, I drew no conclusions about Ames's sexual orientation, speculating that whatever the nature of her desires, they found little overt expression—or at least none whose traces were not repressed or destroyed. If I were writing *Revolt Against Chivalry* today, I might not change that interpretation, but I would certainly expand upon it. I would emphasize the emotional centrality of her relationships with women without imposing inappropriate categories on the "devices and desires" of her heart.[24]

What is clear is that Ames's emotional suffering intensified in the 1950s, and the reasons are not hard to find. Political fashions had shifted, leaving her stranded, a relic of a silenced feminist past. Her mother was dead; she had broken with her sister and left the church. She was dependent on her children for financial support, and she could be vicious in demanding her due. She concealed much and, of course, was misunderstood. In earlier times she would have saved herself through work. Alone in retirement in the North Carolina mountains, she turned to autobiography, seeking to conquer depression through self-knowledge. "My task now," she wrote, is to break the habit [of a lifetime, to discover] what, if anything, I can do . . . to attain peace within for the years that may remain to me."[25] Of all the distances she had traveled, perhaps none took more courage than this inward journey.

That said, I would reaffirm, and even emphasize more strongly, my original perception of the satisfaction Jessie Daniel Ames won from her public role. If the spiritual quest of the 1950s reveals her private pain, an oral history interview constructed fourteen years later attests to her resilience. Conducted by a journalist in Atlanta about 1966, this interview was initiated by a friend named Josephine Wilkins, who had shared and admired Ames's work. Just as Lulu Ames was responsible for salvaging the evidence of her mother's private life, so it is to Josephine Wilkins that we owe our most vivid glimpse of Jessie Daniel Ames's public persona.[26] Here grievance and self-doubt give way to serene self-possession. Ames minced no words about the shortcomings of her former colleagues or the importance of her own contributions. She voiced no regrets. Had the board members of the Interracial Commission disliked her? "They would have liked me if I had been submissive." Had their successors in the Southern Regional Council sent her packing? "They were blotting me out of existence—but I kept on breathing just the same." What, in the end, had motivated her? "It was my sense of justice and fair play and it was the only thing that ever moved me and it always has."[27] The autobiographies of nineteenth-century women often stressed self-denial and played down achievement.[28] By contrast, when asked to order her life's meaning for posterity, Ames did so in structure, language, and detail that conveyed a triumphant conviction of self-worth. Yet public performance and introspection must be read side by side. Together they constitute more than evidence of a divided life. They are bids for transcendence and for immortality.

Jessie Daniel Ames, in Austin, Texas, May 24, 1965. Courtesy of the Lulu Daniel Ames Papers, Southern Historical Collection, University of North Carolina at Chapel Hill.

Notes

Preface

1. Jacquelyn Dowd Hall, " 'The Mind That Burns in Each Body': Women, Rape, and Racial Violence," in *Powers of Desire: The Politics of Sexuality*, ed. by Ann Snitow, Christine Stansell, and Sharon Thompson (New York: Monthly Review Press, 1983), pp. 328–49. Earlier versions of the epilogue were delivered as a paper at a 1983 workshop on "New Approaches to Women's Biography and Autobiography,"sponsored by the Smith College Project on Women and Social Change, and published as "Second Thoughts: On Writing a Feminist Biography," *Feminist Studies* 13 (Spring 1987), 19–37, and as "Lives Through Time: Second Thoughts on Jessie Daniel Ames," in *The Challenge of Feminist Biography: Writing the Lives of Modern American Women*, ed. by Sara Alpern, Joyce Antler, Elisabeth Israels Perry, and Ingrid Winther Scobie (Urbana: University of Illinois Press, 1992), pp. 139–58. I am grateful to Christine Stansell and Joyce Antler for inviting me to contribute to these volumes and for their careful readings of my work.

Introduction

1. For this battle, in which women's groups won a notable victory, see Eleanor Holmes Norton, ". . . And the Language Is Race," *Ms.* 2, no. 4 (January/February 1992), 43–45; and Judith Resnik, "Hearing Women," *Southern California Law Review* 65 (March 1992), 1333–45.

2. Rosemary L. Bray, quoting Cornel West, in "Taking Sides Against Ourselves," *New York Times Magazine*, Nov. 17, 1991, p. 94. For a sampling of the written commentary on the hearings, see *The Black Scholar* 22 (Winter 1991–Spring 1992), 1–156 (reprinted as Robert Chrisman and Robert L. Allen, eds., *Court of Appeal: The Black Community Speaks Out on the Racial and Sexual Politics of Clarence Thomas vs. Anita Hill* [New York: Ballantine, 1992]); *Ms.* 2, no. 4 (January/February 1992), 32–45, 70–71; "Sexuality After Thomas/Hill," *Tikkun* 7 (January/February 1992), 17–18, 20–30, 96–97. The following appeared after this essay was completed: Toni Morrison, ed., *Racing Justice, En-gendering Power: Essays on Anita Hill, Clarence Thomas, and the Construction of Social Reality* (New York: Pantheon Books, 1992); Paul Simon, *Advice and Consent: Clarence Thomas, Robert Bork, and the Intriguing History of the Supreme Court's Nomination Battles* (Washington, D.C.: National Press Books, 1992); Timothy M. Phelps and Helen Winternitz, *Capitol Games: Clarence Thomas, Anita Hill, and the Story of a Supreme Court Nomination* (New York: Hyperion, 1992); and Geneva Smitherman, ed., *Reflections on Anita Hill: Race, Gender, and Power in the United States* (Detroit: Wayne State University Press, forthcoming).

3. Alan K. Simpson, *Congressional Record-Senate*, 102d Cong. 1st sess., 1991, 137, pt. 143:14546.

4. "Second Statement From Judge Clarence Thomas, Oct. 11, 1991," *Washington Post,* Oct. 12, 1991, p. A12; reprinted in *The Black Scholar,* p. 12.

5. Ibid. Indeed, white liberals had been reluctant to subject Thomas's views to scrutiny from the beginning—because of his race and the story of his rise from rural poverty. A similar ambivalence marked the response of the black community. For this point, see Kimberlé Crenshaw's comments in "Roundtable: Doubting Thomas," *Tikkun* 6 (September/October 1991), 24–25.

6. Roger Wilkins made this point eloquently at the time: Wilkins, quoted by Tom Shales, *Washington Post,* Oct. 14, 1991, p. D8.

7. Dan Dervin, "Testimony of Silence: A Psychohistorical Perspective on the Thomas-Hill Hearings," *The Journal of Psychohistory* 19 (Winter 1992), 258, 265.

8. For these stereotypes on both sides of the Atlantic, see Vron Ware, *Beyond the Pale: White Women, Racism and History* (London/New York: Verso/Routledge, Chapman and Hall, 1992); see also Joan Didion, "Sentimental Journeys," in *After Henry* (New York: Simon and Schuster, 1992), pp. 253–319.

9. I thank Della Pollock for this formulation.

10. Nancy Fraser, "Sex, Lies, and the Public Sphere: Some Reflections on the Confirmation of Clarence Thomas," *Critical Inquiry* 18 (Spring 1992), 604.

11. For this point, see Crenshaw's comments in "Roundtable: Sexuality After Thomas/Hill," p. 26; and Elsa Barkley Brown, " 'What Has Happened Here': The Politics of Difference in Women's History and Feminist Politics," *Feminist Studies* 18 (Summer 1992), 302. For earlier instances of white women converting black women into universal symbols of oppression, see Phyllis Marynick Palmer, "White Women/Black Women: The Dualism of Female Identity and Experience in the United States," *Feminist Studies* 9 (Spring 1983), 151–70; and Jean Fagan Yellen, *Women and Sisters: The Antislavery Feminists in American Culture* (New Haven: Yale University Press, 1989). Quotations are from Bray, "Taking Sides Against Ourselves," pp. 56, 94.

12. Martha R. Mahoney, "Exit: Power and the Idea of Leaving in Love, Work, and the Confirmation Hearings," *Southern California Law Review* 65 (March 1992), 1283–1319. Fraser makes a similar point in "Sex, Lies, and the Public Sphere," pp. 607–609.

13. Susan Brownmiller and Dolores Alexander, "From Carmita Wood to Anita Hill," *Ms.,* p. 71; Felicity Barringer, "Hill's Case Divisive to Women," *New York Times,* Oct. 18, 1991, p. A12; Orlando Patterson, "Race, Gender and Liberal Fallacies," *New York Times,* Oct. 20, 1991, p. E15, reprinted in *The Black Scholar,* pp. 77–80.

14. Barbara Smith, "Ain't Gonna Let Nobody Turn Me Around," *Ms.,* p. 38; Vicki Crawford, "On the Clarence Thomas Hearings," *The Black Scholar,* pp. 15–17; "African American Women in Defense of Ourselves," advertisement, *New York Times,* Nov. 17, 1991, p. Y19, reprinted in *The Black Scholar,* p. 155.

15. "Alchemy" is Patricia J. Williams's evocative term: Williams, *The Alchemy of Race and Rights* (Cambridge: Harvard University Press, 1991).

16. For a reflection of this phenomenon in the cinema of the 1930s, see Elizabeth Young, "Here Comes the Bride: Wedding, Gender, and Race in *Bride of Frankenstein*," *Feminist Studies* 17 (Fall 1991), 403–437.

17. Quotation is from Dykeman and Stokely, *Seeds of Southern Change*, p. 143.

18. Sara M. Evans, *Born for Liberty: A History of Women in America* (New York: The Free Press, 1989), p. 211. Evans sees the Antilynching Association as "one of the last opportunities for women to generate organized power outside the corridors of public political life by drawing on traditional women's networks."

19. Martha Elizabeth Hodes, "Sex Across the Color Line: White Women and Black Men in the Nineteenth-Century American South" (Ph.D. diss., Princeton University, 1991); Victoria E. Bynum, *Unruly Women: The Politics of Social and Sexual Control in the Old South* (Chapel Hill: University of North Carolina Press, 1992); Laura F. Edwards, "Sexual Violence, Gender, Reconstruction, and the Extension of Patriarchy in Granville County, North Carolina," *North Carolina Historical Review* 68 (July 1991), 237–60, and "The Politics of Manhood and Womanhood: Reconstruction in Granville County, North Carolina" (Ph.D. diss., University of North Carolina at Chapel Hill, 1991).

20. Edwards, "Politics of Manhood and Womanhood."

21. Hodes, "Sex Across the Color Line"; and Glenda Elizabeth Gilmore, "Boss Liars, Soft Women, And Peanut Galleries: The Politics of Gender As a Tool of Racial Repression," (paper presented at the annual meeting of the Organization of American Historians, Chicago, Ill., April 1992).

22. Carter, *Scottsboro: A Tragedy of the American South*, p. 297.

23. Quotation is from Cash, *The Mind of the South*, p. 117. Historians of the South have told us much more about sexual/racial oppression than about the meaning of sexuality from the perspective of nondominant groups. This approach stands in sharp contrast to the emphasis on the sexual revolution in the urban North and Midwest. Thus, as is often the case, southern history is written as tragedy while United States history generally is written as romance. The consequences can be seen in the treatment of the South in John D'Emilio and Estelle B. Freedman, *Intimate Matters: A History of Sexuality in America* (New York: Harper & Row, 1988), an exemplary synthetic work necessarily limited by the available literature. For a critique of D'Emilio and Freedman's work, see Ann duCille, " 'Othered' Matters: Reconceptualizing Dominance and Difference in the History of Sexuality in America," *Journal of the History of Sexuality* 1 (July 1990), 102–127. See "Commentary: A Response to Ann duCille's 'Othered' Matters," *Journal of the History of Sexuality* 1 (July 1990), 128–30, for D'Emilio and Freedman's reply.

24. Jacquelyn Dowd Hall, "Disorderly Women: Gender and Labor Militancy in the Appalachian South," *Journal of American History* 73 (September 1986), 354–82; "Private Eyes, Public Women: Images of Class and Sex in the Urban South, Atlanta, Georgia, 1913–1915," in *Work Engendered: Toward a New History of American Labor*, ed. by Ava Baron (Ithaca: Cornell University Press, 1991), pp. 243–72; and "Sex, Lies, and Southern History," Somers Memorial Lecture, Georgia State University, Atlanta, Georgia, October 10, 1991. See also Jacquelyn Dowd Hall, James Leloudis, Robert Korstad, Mary Murphy, Lu Ann Jones, and Christopher B. Daly, *Like a Family: The Making*

of a Southern Cotton Mill World (Chapel Hill: University of North Carolina Press, 1987), pp. 226–88. For a conservative response to the anxieties stirred up by the emergence of this new sexual order, see Nancy MacLean, "The Leo Frank Case Reconsidered: Gender and Sexual Politics in the Making of Reactionary Populism," *Journal of American History* 78 (December 1991), 917–48.

25. For more recent treatments, see Rosalyn Terborg-Penn, "African-American Women's Networks in the Anti-Lynching Crusade," in *Gender, Race, and Reform in the Progressive Era,* ed. by Noralee Frankel and Nancy S. Dye (Lexington, Ky.: University Press of Kentucky, 1991), pp. 148–161 and Jacquelyn Dowd Hall, "Antilynching Movement," in *Black Women in America: An Historical Encyclopedia,* ed. by Darlene Clark Hine (Brooklyn, N.Y.: Carlson Publishing, 1992, 38–41).

26. See Christina Brooks Whitman, "Feminist Jurisprudence (Review Essay)," *Feminist Studies* 17 (Fall 1991), 493–507, for the response of feminist legal theorists to the problem of differences among women. Seeking an alternative to the formal equality model that guided litigation in the 1970s, they have concentrated less on doctrinal arguments and more on creating "partial narratives" and analyzing underlying judicial assumptions about the world.

27. This discussion is drawn from Hall, " 'The Mind That Burns in Each Body.' " See that essay for full documentation.

28. Accounts of how many African-American women were executed by lynch mobs vary. According to White, *Rope and Faggot,* p. 67, 4,951 people were lynched in the United States between 1882 and 1927. Of these, 3,513 were black and 76 were black women. The circumstances and significance of these lynchings of women deserve more historical attention. This does not mean, however, as Leslie Ann Schwalm has cogently argued, that the freedwomen withdrew from field work. Rather, they pursued a variety of labor arrangements that allowed them to meet their double duty as wives and workers while participating with men in struggles to shape the terms of their own and their families' labor: Schwalm, "The Meaning of Freedom: African-American Women and Their Transition from Slavery to Freedom in Lowcountry South Carolina" (Ph.D. diss., University of Wisconsin-Madison, 1991).

29. Sander L. Gilman, "Black Bodies, White Bodies: Toward an Iconography of Female Sexuality in Late Nineteenth-Century Art, Medicine, and Literature," *Critical Inquiry* 12 (Autumn 1985), 204–42 (quotation p. 209), finds an association between the covert sexuality of white women and the overt sexuality of blacks throughout the eighteenth and nineteenth centuries. For an earlier work that places more emphasis on the preoccupation with black *men's* sexuality, see Jordan, *White Over Black.*

30. "Appendix F. Digest of Discussion," n.d. (Nov. 20, 1931), Ames Papers.

31. Michael W. Agopian, Duncan Chappell, and Gilbert Geis, "Black Offender and White Victim: A Study of Forcible Rape in Oakland, California," in *Forcible Rape: The Crime, The Victim, and the Offender,* ed. by Duncan Chappell, Robley Geis, and Gilbert Geis (New York: Columbia University Press, 1977); Dianne F. Herman, "The Rape Culture," in *Women: A Feminist Perspective,* ed. by Jo Freeman (Mountain View, Calif.: Mayfield Publishing Co., 1989, 4th ed.), pp. 36–37; Gary D. LaFree, "The Effect of Sexual Stratification by Race on Official Reactions to Rape," *American Sociological*

Review, 45 (October 1990), 847–48, and *Rape and Criminal Justice: The Social Construction of Sexual Assault* (Belmont, Calif.: Wadsworth Publishing, 1991), 114–47. These assumptions also underlie the stereotype of the sexually irresponsible welfare mother, who, along with the young black criminal, dominates the conservative imagination of our times. As Kimberlé Crenshaw and other African-American feminists were quick to point out, Clarence Thomas himself reinforced such stereotypes by contrasting his own bootstrapping rise from Pin Point, Georgia, with his sister's supposed dependence on welfare. See Crenshaw, "Roundtable: Doubting Thomas," p. 27.

32. Charles R. Lawrence III, "Cringing at Myths of Black Sexuality," *Los Angeles Times*, October 16, 1991, p. B7. Alice Walker's novel, *The Color Purple* (New York: Pocket Books, 1982), is perhaps the most controversial and widely read treatment of this subject.

33. *Revolt Against Chivalry* scrutinized the politics of protection only where whites were concerned. Laura Edwards, however, has suggested that when poor men in the postbellum South based their claim to manhood on their right to exercise control over their own families, they built gender hierarchy into the struggle to equalize class and race relations, thereby limiting the egalitarian impulse of the day: Edwards, "Sexual Violence, Gender, Reconstruction." In a study of twentieth-century club work, on the other hand, Deborah Gray White has argued that black women activists were critical of black men in part because of their failure to defend them from sexual slander. Fannie Williams, for instance, argued that black women had to rely on themselves for protection because there were "too many colored men who hold the degrading opinions of ignorant white men, that all colored girls are alike. . . . How rare are the reported instances of colored men resenting any slur or insult upon their own women": Williams, "The Colored Girl," *Voice* 2 (1905), 403. Quoted in White, "The Cost of Club Work, The Price of Black Feminism," in *Visible Women: An Anthology*, ed. by Nancy Hewitt and Suzanne Lebsock (Urbana: University of Illinois Press, 1993). For yet another dimension of the politics of protection, see Nancy MacLean, "White Women and Klan Violence in the 1920s: Agency, Complicity, and the Politics of Women's History," *Gender and History* 3 (Autumn 1991), 285–303. MacLean shows how poor white women, unable to depend on the state for protection against wife beating and other forms of domestic violence, turned to the Ku Klux Klan. In the process they simultaneously used their limited resources to secure decent treatment and helped to justify vigilante activity against other groups.

34. A notorious example is Eldridge Cleaver's claim that he raped black women with impunity, as practice for more risky attacks on white women: Cleaver, *Soul on Ice*, p. 14. Thanks to Robert Korstad for helping me to clarify this point.

35. Darlene Clark Hine, "Rape and the Inner Lives of Black Women in the Middle West: Preliminary Thoughts on the Culture of Dissemblance," *Signs* 14 (Summer 1989), 912–20; White, "The Cost of Club Work."

36. Among the early published commentaries were Bray, "Taking Sides Against Ourselves"; Crenshaw, "Roundtable: Sexuality After Thomas/Hill"; Nell Irvin Painter, "Who Was Lynched?" *The Nation*, Nov. 11, 1991, p. 577; and "African-American Women in Defense of Ourselves."

37. For recent surveys of this literature, see Evelyn Brooks Higginbotham,

"Beyond the Sound of Silence: Afro-American Women's History," *Gender and History* 1 (Spring 1989), 50–67; Jacquelyn Dowd Hall, "Partial Truths," *Signs* 14 (Summer 1989), 902–11; Chana Kai Lee, "African-American Women," in *Unequal Sisters: A Multicultural Reader in U.S. Women's History*, ed. by Ellen Carol DuBois and Vicki L. Ruiz (New York: Routledge, 1990), pp. 447–50; and Anne Firor Scott, "Most Invisible of All: Black Women's Voluntary Associations," *Journal of Southern History* 56 (February 1990), 3–22.

38. Especially important was Brown, *Homespun Heroines*. Hallie Quinn Brown served as president of the National Association of Colored Women and as director of the Colored Women's Republican National Committee in the 1920s.

39. Gerda Lerner, *Black Women in White America*; Sharon Harley and Rosalyn Terborg-Penn, eds., *The Afro-American Woman: Struggles and Images* (Port Washington, N.Y.: National University Publications, 1978).

40. Elsa Barkley Brown, "Womanist Consciousness: Maggie Lena Walker and the Independent Order of Saint Luke," *Signs* 14 (Spring 1989), 610–33; Jacqueline Anne Rouse, *Lugenia Burns Hope: Black Southern Reformer* (Athens: University of Georgia Press, 1989); Glenda Elizabeth Gilmore, "Gender and Jim Crow: Women and the Politics of White Supremacy in North Carolina, 1896–1920" (Ph.D. diss., University of North Carolina at Chapel Hill, 1992); White, "The Cost of Club Work"; Elizabeth Lasch-Quinn, *Black Neighbors: Race and the Limits of Reform in the American Settlement House Movement, 1890–1945* (Chapel Hill: University of North Carolina Press, forthcoming); Evelyn Brooks Higginbotham, *Righteous Discontent: The Women's Movement in the Black Baptist Church, 1880–1920* (Cambridge: Harvard University Press, forthcoming).

41. Gilmore, "Gender and Jim Crow"; Higginbotham, *Righteous Discontent;* Mary E. Frederickson, " 'Each One Is Dependent On the Other': Southern Churchwomen and Visions of Progress," in Hewitt and Lebsock, *Visible Women*. For an original and illuminating look at the pre-World War I roots of interracial and antilynching reform, see David Fort Godshalk, "In the Wake of Riot: Atlanta's Struggle for Order, 1899–1919" (Ph.D. diss., Yale University, 1992). Godshalk, however, focuses on male business and religious leaders, and he emphasizes the conservative nature of their efforts.

42. Cott, *The Bonds of Womanhood*; "Background [of Memphis Conference]," Jessie Daniel Ames papers, Southern Historical Collection, University of North Carolina, Chapel Hill.

43. Gail Bederman, " 'Civilization,' the Decline of Middle-Class Manliness, and Ida B. Wells's Antilynching Campaign (1892–1894)," *Radical History Review* 52 (Winter 1992), 5–30; Hazel V. Carby, " 'On the Threshold of Woman's Era': Lynching, Empire, and Sexuality in Black Feminist Theory," *Critical Inquiry* 12 (Autumn 1985), 262–77, and *Reconstructing Womanhood: The Emergence of the Afro-American Woman Novelist* (New York: Oxford University Press, 1987).

44. Ann Laura Stoler, "Carnal Knowledge and Imperial Power: Gender, Race, and Morality in Colonial Asia," in *Gender at the Crossroads of Knowledge: Feminist Anthropology in the Postmodern Era*, ed. by Micaela di Leonardo (Berkeley: University of California Press, 1991), pp. 51–101.

45. Stoler, "Carnal Knowledge," p. 71. But see Nupur Chaudhuri and Margaret Strobel, eds., *Western Women and Imperialism: Resistance and Complicity* (Bloomington, Ind.: Indiana University Press, 1992), for the ways in which imperialism offered individual women opportunities to pursue unconventional lives.

46. See, for example, Herbert Shapiro, *White Violence and Black Response: From Reconstruction to Montgomery* (Amherst: University of Massachusetts Press, 1988), pp. 283–86, and Alan Dawley, *Struggles for Justice: Social Responsibility and the Liberal State* (Cambridge: Belknap Press of Harvard University Press, 1991), p. 162. For exceptions to this rule, see Neil R. McMillen, *Dark Journey: Black Mississippians in the Age of Jim Crow* (Urbana: University of Illinois Press, 1989), pp. 200, 239, 246, 249, 314, and Evans, *Born for Liberty*, pp. 210–13.

47. Joel Williamson, *The Crucible of Race: Black-White Relations in the American South Since Emancipation* (New York: Oxford University Press, 1984), pp. 306–10; Ware, *Beyond the Pale*, p. 254 (quotation).

48. "Bush Emphasizes He Backs Thomas in Spite of Uproar," *New York Times*, 10 Oct. 1991, pp. A1, B14.

49. The following is drawn in part from " 'The Mind That Burns in Each Body.' " That essay, however, does not deal with the legal breakthroughs regarding sexual harassment.

50. Rosalind Pollack Petchesky, "Reproductive Freedom: Beyond 'A Woman's Right to Choose,' " *Signs* 5 (Summer 1980), 661–85. For the notion of "coming to voice," see bell hooks, *Talking Back: Thinking Feminist, Thinking Black* (Boston: South End Press, 1989), p. 10.

51. Herman, "The Rape Culture"; Adrienne Rich, "Taking Women Students Seriously," in Rich, *On Lies, Secrets, and Silences: Selected Prose, 1966–1978* (New York: W. W. Norton, 1979), p. 242 (quotation); Fred Strebeigh, "Defining Law on the Feminist Frontier," *New York Times Magazine*, Oct. 6, 1991, 28–31, 52–56.

52. Sharon Marcus, "Fighting Bodies, Fighting Words: A Theory and Politics of Rape Prevention," in *Feminists Theorize the Political*, ed. by Judith Butler and Joan W. Scott (New York: Routledge, 1992), pp. 385–403.

53. This is not to suggest that black political opinion was responsible for Thomas's confirmation. As Eleanor Holmes Norton has pointed out, while blacks "did not squarely veto Thomas," it was whites who "carried Thomas over." A *New York Times* poll conducted three days after the publication of Hill's revelations showed that only 36 percent of African-Americans favored Thomas's confirmation. That percentage had risen to 40 percent by the time the Senate voted for confirmation: Norton, ". . . And the Language Is Race," pp. 44–45.

54. MacKinnon quotations are from Ellen Rooney, " 'A Little More than Persuading': Tess and the Subject of Sexual Violence," in *Rape and Representation*, ed. by Lynn A. Higgins and Brenda R. Silver (New York: Columbia University Press, 1991), pp. 87, 89. The "reasonable woman" argument was established in January 1991 in *Ellison v. Brady*, 924 F. 2d 872–885 (9th Cir. 1991). See Carol Sanger, "The Reasonable Woman and the Ordinary Man," *Southern California Law Review* 65 (March 1992), 1411–17.

55. Lauren Berlant, "The Queen of America Goes to Washington City: Harriet Jacobs, Frances Harper, and Anita Hill" (lecture sponsored by the Curriculum in American Studies, University of North Carolina at Chapel Hill, April 13, 1992).

Chapter 1: Beginnings

1. Dabney White, "Observations in Old Anderson County, Texas," *Farmer and Ranch* (Oct. 27, 1900), 1. See also Avera, *Wind Swept Land*, and R. E. Riegel, *The Story of the Western Railroads* (New York: Macmillan, 1926), pp. 109, 135 ff., 177 ff.

2. Williamson County (Tex.) *Sun*, Feb. 8, 1911; [Laura Leonard Daniel], "Nathaniel and Martha Malinda Leonard," autobiographical MS, 1933; [Jessie Daniel Ames], "The Story of My Life," Feb. 27, 1922; [Lulu Daniel Hardy], "In the Fullness of Time," autobiographical MS., 1946; Lulu Daniel Ames Family papers, Private Collection in possession of author, hereinafter cited as Priv. Coll.

3. [JDA], "Story." See also Dorman Hayward Winfrey, *A History of Rusk County, Texas* (Waco: Texian Press, 1961) and Garland Roscoe Farmer, *The Realm of Rusk County* (Henderson, Texas: Henderson Times, 1951); Jessie Daniel, "Story of My Life," Oct. 23, 1897, Priv. Coll.

4. [Hardy], "Fullness."

5. [JDA], "Story"; [Hardy], "Fullness."

6. [Hardy], "Fullness."

7. Between 1889 and 1893, only the incidence of lynching in the Deep South states of Alabama, Mississippi, and Louisiana exceeded that of Texas. In the thirty years between 1900 and 1929, when Ames left the state, there were more lynchings in East Texas in proportion to the black population than in any other part of the southern black belt. NAACP, *Thirty Years of Lynching*, pp. 30, 34–35, 95–99. See also Raper, *Tragedy of Lynching*, pp. 27, 483, and Wells-Barnett, *On Lynchings*, pp. 25–32.

8. JDA Interview.

9. Ames, "Whither Leads the Mob?," p. 20.

10. [JDA], "Story"; [JDA] "Death of James Malcom Daniel, Jr., 14 July 1904" and "Last Days of James Malcom Daniel"; James Malcom Daniel to Mrs. Roger P. Ames. Apr. 23, 1910, Mar. 8, 1910, May 14, 1910, and June 11, 1910; Williamson County (Tex.) *Sun*, Feb. 8, 1911; [Hardy], "Fullness," Priv. Coll.; Lulu Daniel Ames Interview. For an illuminating portrait of a contemporaneous Texas family, see Doris Kearns, *Lyndon Johnson and the American Dream*.

11. [JDA], "Story"; [Hardy], "Fullness."

12. Lulu Daniel Ames Interview; [JDA], "Memories," Nov. 11, 1958; [JDA], "Story," Priv. Coll. Jessie's belief that her father preferred her sister to herself was expressed in autobiographical writings and in numerous letters

to and conversations with her friends and relatives. Little evidence remains of James Daniel's point of view, nor did his wife ever comment directly on these intrafamily relationships. This account reflects Jessie's perspective, as corroborated by less direct evidence in her sister's autobiography and her daughter's recollections. For the purposes of this study, of course, what matters most is what Jessie remembered.

13. [Hardy], "Fullness." Both women recalled the same major incidents in their common history and were quite aware that their interpretations of these incidents were sometimes sharply contradictory. See [JDA], "Memories."

14. [JDA], "Story."

15. [JDA], "Story"; [Hardy], "Fullness"; Lulu Daniel Ames Interview.

16. [Hardy], "Fullness."

17. Laura Daniel, "Dr. John C. Granbery," n.d., Priv. Coll.

18. [JDA], "Story."

19. Brown, *Strain of Violence*, pp. 237–87.

20. [JDA], "Story"; [Hardy], "Fullness"; Scarbrough, *Land of Good Water; Williamson County Sun*, July 21, 1904.

21. [Hardy], "Fullness"; J. M. Daniel to Mrs. Roger P. Ames, June 11, 1910, Priv. Coll.

22. [JDA], "Story"; Lulu Daniel Ames Interview.

23. [JDA], "Story"; Lulu Daniel Ames Interview; [Hardy], "Fullness." Both sisters agree that Lulu was responsible for James Daniels's restrictions. But Lulu claimed to have been motivated by protectiveness; in Jessie's version Lulu did not want attention drawn to her own unmarried state by having a younger sister old enough to go out with boys.

24. Quotations are from JDA to Frederick, Aug. 30, 1943, and JDA to Mary Daniel Ames, Sept. 11, 1930, Priv. Coll. See also, [JDA], "Lesson XIII," a short story written for a University of Chicago Extension Division course, n.d. Priv. Coll.; Edward T. James, et al., eds., *Notable American Women, 1607–1960: A Biographical Dictionary* (Cambridge: Harvard University Press, 1971), I, 429–30.

25. [JDA], "Story"; Kate Chopin, "The Awakening," in *The Awakening and Other Stories*, ed. by Lewis Leary (New York: Holt, Rinehart and Winston, 1970), pp. 199–341.

26. Laredo *Daily News*, July 16, 1904; [JDA], "Death of James Malcom Daniel, Jr."

27. See Filene, *Him/Her/Self*, pp. 77–130, for a persuasive discussion of this pre–World War I crisis of manliness.

28. [Hardy], "Fullness"; [JDA], "Last Days"; Georgetown (Tex.) *Commercial*, Feb. 9, 1911, Priv. Coll.

29. [JDA], "Post-Ames Family" and "Daniel-Ames Family Life" [1950–51]; Roger Ames to Jessie Ames, Feb. 9, 1911, Priv. Coll. On July 19, 1959, after long years of effort on Jessie's part, Roger received a posthumous congressional award for his contribution to Reed's yellow fever experiments. See H.R. 1952, 75th Cong. 1st sess., 1937.

30. [JDA], "Daniel-Ames"; JDA Interview; Lulu Daniel Ames Interview; [JDA], "Lesson XIII"; Charley L. Daniel to Frederick Daniel, Oct. 11, 1929, Priv. Coll.; Private letter to author from Lulu Daniel Ames, n.d.

31. JDA to Mary Ames, Sept. 11, 1930, Priv. Coll.

32. JDA to Lulu Ames, Oct. 15, 1945 and Jan. 1, 1941; [JDA], "Daniel-Ames," Priv. Coll.

33. [JDA], "Daniel-Ames"; JDA to Frederick Ames, Nov. 30, 1952; Roger Ames to [?], Aug. 23, 1913, Priv. Coll. JDA to Jane Cornell, Sept. 11, 1938, ASWPL Papers; JDA Interview.

34. JDA to Frederick Ames, Nov. 30, 1952; [JDA], "Last Days," Priv. Coll.

35. JDA to Hope Ames, Feb. 21, 1939, Priv. Coll.

36. [JDA], "Daniel-Ames"; Lulu Hardy to JDA, Dec. 2, 1914; JDA to Frederick Ames, Mar. 21, 1953, Priv. Coll.

37. JDA to Mrs. W. A. Newell, Jan. 30, 1934 and Christmas, 1937, Jessie Daniel Ames Papers, Southern Historical Collection, University of North Carolina at Chapel Hill, hereinafter cited as Ames Papers (NC).

38. JDA to Mrs. W. A. Newell, Oct. 4, 1938, Ames Papers (NC).

39. JDA to Mrs. W. A. Newell, Oct. 8, 1939, Ames Papers; JDA Interview; [Daniel], "Leonard."

40. Ames was, of course, a product of an era in which sex role prescriptions and the dangers of pregnancy combined to inhibit the expression of female sexuality. Laura Daniel, for example, warned her daughter that "your wedding gown may be your winding sheet" ([Hardy], "Fullness"). Yet when Jessie spoke of herself as "frigid" she seemed to be expressing more than conventional Victorian attitudes. Her daughter Lulu speculated that her sexual feelings were directed toward other women. My own interpretation is that she remained troubled all her life by what Erik Erikson terms the conflict between "intimacy" and "isolation." Whatever her sexual orientation might have been, it found little overt expression. Instead, as we shall see, she channeled her passion into the external world of work and reform and found in large public forums and the loyalty of faithful followers the reassurance and satisfaction her private life could not provide. For discussions of nineteenth-century female sexuality, see Alfred C. Kinsey, et al., *Sexual Behavior in the Human Female* (Philadelphia: Saunders, 1953); Katharine B. Davis, *Factors in the Sex Life of Twenty-Two Hundred Women* (New York: Harper and Brothers, 1929); Robert Latou Dickinson and Laura Beam, *A Thousand Marriages: A Medical Study of Sex Adjustment* (Baltimore: Williams and Wilkins, 1931); and Degler, "What Ought to Be and What Was." For Erikson's developmental model of personality formation, see Erikson, *Identity and the Life Cycle*, pp. 50–100, and *Childhood and Society*, pp. 247–69. Also helpful to my understanding of Ames's life were Erikson's applications of this model to the careers of two historically significant reformers and ideological innovators: *Gandhi's Truth: On the Origins of Militant Nonviolence* (New York: Norton, 1969) and *Young Man Luther: A Study in Psychoanalysis and History* (New York: Norton, 1958).

41. JDA to Frederick Ames, Jan. 1, 1941, Aug. 1, 1949, and Feb. 28,

1953; Lulu Ames to JDA, June 11, 1940, Priv. Coll.; Lulu Ames Interview; JDA to Mr. W. A. Newell, Aug. 5, 1938, Ames Papers (NC); JDA to Jane Cornell, May 26, 1937 and Mar. 6, 1934, ASWPL Papers.

42. This view assumes that psychoanalytic theory offers important insights into the way women internalize patriarchal values. As a female child is incorporated into society through the acceptance of the incest taboo, elements of a social structure that devalues women are embedded in her personality. Shifting from an active to a passive sexual mode, retaining her identification with a powerless mother and her desire for a powerful father, she remains psychologically bound within the family. A "successful" resolution of the Oedipus complex within a patriarchal society requires an acceptance of a position of subordination and the transfer of desire for the father to sexual intimacy with another man. In "The Flight from Womanhood: The Masculinity Complex in Women as Viewed by Men and by Women," reprinted in *Psychoanalysis and Women*, ed. by Jean Baker Miller (Baltimore: Penguin Books, 1974), pp. 3–20, Karen Horney argues that the "masculinity complex" is a result not of penis envy but of a "flight from womanhood" occurring when a girl, forced to renounce her libidinal wishes toward the father, abandons the feminine role altogether. This rejection of femininity is reinforced by the girl's exposure from birth onward to the suggestion of female inferiority. In Ames's case, her father's coldness and her husband's seeming abandonment combined to force her out of the mold of conventional womanhood. The penalty may have been feelings of inadequacy and inferiority. But, within limits, she was also able to transcend those feelings, reject passivity and subordination, and use that "flight from womanhood" as a springboard for accomplishment. For a contrasting view of an exceptional feminist who, in the context of an earlier Victorian culture, was able to combine self-love and an affirmation of femininity with a militant demand for equality, see Elizabeth Cady Stanton, *Eighty Years and More*. For feminist interpretations of the insights of Sigmund Freud, see Juliet Mitchell, *Woman's Estate* (New York: Vintage, 1973) and Nancy Chodorow, "Family Structure and Feminine Personality."

43. [JDA], "Story"; [JDA], "Daniel-Ames"; JDA to Mary, Mar. 25, 1960, Priv. Coll. For examples of the sisters' lifelong sibling rivalry, see JDA to Miss Miriam Rogers, Aug. 28, 1936; JDA to Mrs. W. A. Newell, n.d.; JDA to Mrs. J. E. Bagwell, Feb. 6, 1940, CIC Papers; JDA to Mrs. L. W. Alford, Feb. 28, 1936, ASWPL Papers; JDA to Lulu Ames, July 11, 1965, Priv. Coll.; JDA Interview. From one point of view, Lulu could be seen as breaking the ground for Jessie's accomplishments. Her academic performance set the standard against which Jessie measured herself. She eventually pursued graduate study, led a statewide organization of women's clubs, and, after her husband's death, taught school. Yet she was married to a man who would scarcely allow her to carry out the ordinary tasks of housekeeping, which he considered unsuitable for a lady, much less work for a living. And Jessie acknowledged only her sister's negative qualities.

44. JDA to Mrs. W. A. Newell, Aug. 25, 1938, Ames Papers (NC); JDA, "Copied from Mama's Diary—1934–35–36," [1966]; [JDA], "Story," Priv. Coll.

45. Simone de Beauvoir persuasively argues that, for a woman, such a rejection of identification is the *sine qua non* of human liberty and transcen-

dence: "In the sense in which the psychoanalysts understand the term, 'to identify onself' with the mother or with the father is to *alienate oneself* in a model, it is to prefer a foreign image to the spontaneous manifestation of one's own existence, it is to play at being. Woman is shown to us as enticed by two modes of alienation. Evidently to play at being a man will be for her a source of frustration; but to play at being a woman is also a delusion: to be a woman would mean to be the object, the *Other*—and the Other nevertheless remains subject in the midst of her resignation. The true problem for woman is to reject these flights from reality and seek self-fulfillment in transcendence. To paint, to write, to engage in politics—these are not merely 'sublimations'; here we have aims that are willed for their own sakes. To deny it is to falsify all human history." *The Second Sex*, p. 46.

· 46. JDA to Mrs. W. A. Newell, Sept. 13, 1938; JDA to Carrie Parks Johnson, Sept. 8, 1924, Ames Papers (NC).

Chapter 2: Out of Obscurity

1. Parker, ed., *The Oven Birds*, introduction; Barbara Welter, "The Cult of True Womanhood: 1820–1860," *American Quarterly*, 17 (Summer 1966), 151–74.

2. Taylor, *Cavalier and Yankee*; Scott, *The Southern Lady* and "Women's Perspective on the Patriarchy in the 1850's"; Lerner, *The Grimké Sisters of South Carolina*; Eaton, *The Freedom-of-Thought Struggle in the Old South*; Gay, "The Tangled Skein of Romanticism and Violence in the Old South" (Ph.D. diss.).

3. Kraditor, *Ideas of the Woman Suffrage Movement*, pp. 138 ff. For a recent survey of the suffrage campaign, see Scott and Scott, *One Half the People*.

4. Fuller, *Laura Clay and the Woman's Rights Movement*; K. R. Johnson, "Kate Gordon and the Woman Suffrage Movement in the South."

5. For the origins and significance of black disfranchisement, see Kousser, *Shaping of Southern Politics*, and Goodwyn, *Democratic Promise*. We have no study of the racial attitudes and practices of southern suffragists on the state and local level. Anne Firor Scott has taken issue with Aileen Kraditor's contention that southern suffragists were motivated by a desire to ensure a white voting majority. Their motives, Scott claims, were mixed, but their primary concern was justice for women rather than supremacy for whites. Paul E. Fuller's study of Laura Clay seeks to exonerate her from the charge of racism by characterizing her early advocacy of an educational requirement that would restrict the political participation of both blacks and whites as "liberal" for the times and accepting at face value her states' rights explanation of her later opposition to ratification of the Nineteenth Amendment. In fact, as

Kousser and Goodwyn have shown, the stance of southern progressives like Laura Clay toward the restriction of the electorate was part of a profoundly antidemocratic response to Reconstruction and Populism. A full-scale analysis of the social origins, ideas, and actions of southern suffragists would provide a needed shift in emphasis from the study of national leadership and strategy to the nature of the suffrage campaign as a social movement with significant regional variations.

6. For a case study of the suffrage movement on the state level similar to the one attempted here, see Strom, "Leadership and Tactics in the American Woman Suffrage Movement."

7. See Goodwyn, *Democratic Promise*, pp. 25–33, and Webb, *The Great Plains*, for the social consequences of the great migration to Texas.

8. C. Richard King, ed., *A Victorian Lady on the Texas Frontier: The Journal of Ann Raney Coleman* (Norman: University of Oklahoma Press, 1971); William Forrest Sprague, *Women and the West: A Short Social History* (New York: Arno Press, 1972); Nancy W. Ross, *Westward the Women* (New York: Knopf, 1944); Potter, "American Women and the National Character."

9. Lebsock, "Radical Reconstruction and the Property Rights of Southern Women," p. 206; Stanton, et al., eds., *The History of Woman Suffrage*, III, 804–5.

10. For intriguing studies of women on the frontier, see Faragher and Stansell, "Women and Their Families on the Overland Trail, 1842–1867," and Christine Stansell, "Women on the Plains," *Women's Studies*, 4 (1976), 87–98.

11. Paulson, *Women's Suffrage and Prohibition*, presents a suggestive comparison of the two movements.

12. A. E. Taylor, "The Woman Suffrage Movement in Texas." Other studies of the Texas movement are Vielock, "Texas Women Campaign for Suffrage" (M.A. thesis); Bowles, "History of Woman Suffrage in Texas" (M.A. thesis).

13. Jeffrey, "Women in the Southern Farmers' Alliance." Grimes, in *The Puritan Ethic and Woman Suffrage*, convincingly describes the conservative forces in the West that viewed woman suffrage as a means to social control; however, he underestimates the role of suffragists as actors in history effecting change in their own behalf.

14. The following account of Texas politics during the progressive era relies primarily on Gould, *Progressives and Prohibitionists*.

15. Jane Y. McCallum to Mrs. Harris Masterson, Feb. 15, 1930, McCallum Family Papers; *The Texas Women's Hall of Fame* (Austin: Biographical Press, 1971), pp. 111–12.

16. Cunningham, "Too Gallant a Walk"; *Texas Who's Who* (Dallas: Texian Co., 1937), I, 112–13.

17. See McCallum, "Activities of Women in Texas Politics."

18. A. E. Taylor, "The Woman Suffrage Movement in Texas," p. 204; *Dallas Morning News*, Nov. 11, 1915.

19. U.S. Department of the Interior, Bureau of the Census, *Ninth Census of the United States, 1870; The Statistics of the Wealth and Industry of the*

U.S., III, 808–9; U.S. Department of Commerce, Bureau of the Census, *Fourteenth Census of the United States, 1920: Population,* IV, 54. In a study of prominent women in the progressive era, Richard Jensen found that professional careers were major predictors of pro-suffrage sentiments; however, he also discovered that married women with children and broad career interests were more likely to be supportive of humanitarian causes, including suffrage, than were childless wives or single women with specialized careers. See "Family, Career, and Reform: Women Leaders in the Progressive Era," in *The American Family in Social-Historical Perspective,* ed. by Michael Gordon (New York: St. Martin's Press, 1973), pp. 267–80.

20. Williamson County *Sun,* Jan. 4, 1894.

21. [Lulu Daniel Hardy], "In the Fullness of Time," autobiographical MS, 1946, Priv. Coll.

22. Williamson County *Sun,* June 11, 1920.

23. [JDA], "The Story of My Life," Feb. 27, 1922; J. M. Daniel to JDA, May 8, 1920, Priv. Coll.

24. JDA Interview.

25. JDA to Mary Daniel Ames, Dec. 25, 1949, Priv. Coll.

26. J. M. Daniel to JDA, May 8, 1910, Priv. Coll.; JDA Interview.

27. Williamson County *Sun,* June 29, 1916; Laura Leonard Daniel, "Women," n.d., Priv. Coll. Born in 1874, Granbery received a divinity degree from Vanderbilt University and a Ph.D. from the University of Chicago. After a dozen years in the ministry, he began teaching at Southwestern in 1913. During World War I, he served with the YMCA in France and in the French and Greek armies. During his career he was associated with the Socialist Party, the CIO, and the Congress on Racial Equality (CORE). He became a staunch supporter of the interracial movement and, after World War II, of the struggle against segregation. In 1938, he began publishing a crusading newspaper called *The Emancipator* with his wife who, in the early twenties, had edited the Texas League of Women Voters publication, *The New Citizen.*

28. For a study of the function of such female networks see Smith-Rosenberg, "The Female World of Love and Ritual." Williamson County *Sun,* Aug. 6, 1937; Dallas *Morning News,* Aug. 7, 1937.

29. JDA, "Copied from Mama's Diary—1934–35–36," [1966], Priv. Coll.; Reba McKeithen Interview; JDA to Mrs. [Edith Hinkle] League, June 20, 1918, Cunningham Papers.

30. Williamson County *Sun,* Jan. 3, 1918, Jan. 3, Apr. 11, May 9, 1919; McKeithen Interview.

31. JDA Interview.

32. McKeithen Interview.

33. Williamson County *Sun,* June 12, 1913.

34. JDA Interview.

35. JDA to Mary Daniel Ames, Dec. 25, 1949, Priv. Coll. See also JDA Interview.

36. JDA, "Daniel-Ames Family Life," Priv. Coll.

37. Lulu Daniel Ames Interview; Atlanta *Constitution*, Feb. 25, 1941; JDA to Mrs. W. A. Newell, Oct. 31, 1938, Ames Papers (NC).

38. JDA Interview; Williamson County *Sun*, Apr. 6 and Apr. 27, 1916.

39. Cornelia T. Teasbey to Mrs. Cunningham, May 6, 1916 and May 26, 1916, McCallum Family Papers.

40. John C. Granbery to Jane Y. McCallum, Nov. 26, 1921, McCallum Family Papers; Williamson County *Sun*, June 16, 1916, Feb. 15, Feb. 22, and May 17, 1917.

41. Broadside, Jessie Daniel Ames Papers, Texas State Library, Austin, Texas, hereinafter cited as Ames Papers (Austin).

42. Williamson County *Sun*, June 7, 1917.

43. Quoted in Lash, *Eleanor and Franklin*, p. 262.

44. Williamson County *Sun*, May 3 and May 17, 1917. Quotation is from Jane Y. McCallum Diary, March 17, 1926, McCallum Family Papers.

45. Williamson County *Sun*, Sept. 6 and Aug. 23, 1917.

46. McKeithen Interview, Waco *Daily Times-Herald*, n.d. [May 17, 1917], Jessie Daniel Ames Papers, Dallas Historical Society, Hall of State, Dallas, Texas, hereinafter cited as Ames Papers (Dallas).

47. Waco *Daily Times-Herald*, May 6, 1917, with notation by JDA, Ames Papers (Dallas), Williamson County *Sun*, June 14, 1917.

48. McCallum, "Activities," p. 477. For the women's anti-vice campaign see the Cunningham Papers, Container 25, Folder no. 1 and Container 37, Folder no. 2.

49. Williamson County *Sun*, Sept. 6, 1917, Feb. 21 and May 31, 1918. See also Williamson County *Sun*, June 7, June 14, June 21, July 19, and Aug. 23, 1917.

50. Gould, *Progressives and Prohibitionists*, pp. 129–32, 219–20.

51. Ibid., p. 172; J. C. Granbery to Mrs. Jane Y. McCallum, Nov. 25, 1921; Dallas *Morning News*, May 25, 1916; Houston *Daily Post*, May 27, 1916, McCallum Family Papers; McCallum, "Activities," pp. 469–70.

52. Morgan, *Suffragists and Democrats*, p. 109; Harper, ed., *History of Woman Suffrage*, VI, 633.

53. Gould, *Progressives and Prohibitionists*, p. 206; McCallum Diary, October 15 or 16, 1916, McCallum Family Papers.

54. Harper, ed., *Woman Suffrage*, VI, 632.

55. McCallum, "Activities," pp. 474–76.

56. Ibid.; Gould, *Progressives and Prohibitionists*, p. 218. See Strom, "Leadership and Tactics," pp. 306–11, for a discussion of the influence of English militancy on the tactics of the American movement and of the adoption of the open-air meeting in Massachusetts in 1909.

57. McCallum, "Activities," p. 477.

58. Gould, *Progressives and Prohibitionists*, pp. 228–33.

59. McCallum, "Activities," p. 475; Harper, ed., *Woman Suffrage*, VI, 634; Minnie Fisher Cunningham to Thomas B. Love, Feb. 10, 1918, Love Papers.

60. Taylor, "Woman Suffrage," pp. 194–215; Harper, ed., *Woman Suffrage*, VI, 630–37. See Kousser, *Shaping of Southern Politics*, p. 208, for the history and significance of the Terrell Election Law.

61. Harper, ed., *Woman Suffrage*, VI, 639; Edith Hinkle League to JDA, June 7, June 22, and July 2, 1918; Minnie Fisher Cunningham to JDA, June 10, 1918, Cunningham Papers.

62. Williamson County *Sun*, June 28, 1918; JDA to Mrs. League, June 13, 1918, Cunningham Papers. See also Williamson County *Sun*, June 21 and July 12, 1918; Georgetown *Commercial*, July 12, 1918.

63. JDA to Cunningham, July 3, 1918, Cunningham Papers.

64. Williamson County *Sun*, Sept. 6, 1917.

65. Austin *American-Statesman*, May 24, 1965; JDA to Mrs. League, July 29, ·1918, Cunningham Papers. Williamson County *Sun*, July 19 and Aug. 2, 1918. "I am," wrote Minnie Fisher Cunningham, "as close to all of the women of the state as it is possible for one woman to get, or will ever again be possible for any woman to get." Cunningham to Senator [Morris] Sheppard, Apr. 11, 1918, Cunningham Papers.

66. *New York Times*, July 29 and July 31, 1918: McCallum, "Citizens for Twenty Years," p. 2, quoted in Anastatia Sims, "The Woman Suffrage Movement in Texas," unpublished MS, Apr. 1974.

67. Georgetown *Commercial*, Aug. 9, 1918.

68. Gould, *Progressives and Prohibitionists*, p. 247; Grimes, *Puritan Ethic and Woman Suffrage*.

69. Cunningham, "Too Gallant a Walk," p. 12; Minnie Fisher Cunningham to Maude Wood Park, Feb. 16, 1919, Cunningham Papers; Minnie Fisher Cunningham to Carrie Chapman Catt, June 5, 1919, McCallum Family Papers.

70. Minnie Fisher Cunningham to Charles Fowler, Feb. 21, 1919; Minnie Fisher Cunningham to Mrs. E. B. Reppert, Dec. 23, 1918, McCallum Family Papers.

71. Minnie Fisher Cunningham to Carrie Chapman Catt, June 5, 1919; Carrie Chapman Catt to JDA, Jan. 3, 1919; Minnie Fisher Cunningham to Jane Y. McCallum, January 19, 1919 and January 20, 1919, McCallum Family Papers.

72. R. E. Thomason to Minnie Fisher Cunningham, Jan. 21, 1919, McCallum Family Papers.

73. Minnie Fisher Cunningham, 1940, quoted in Sims, "Woman Suffrage in Texas," introduction. Scott and Scott, *One Half the People*.

74. See for example, "The Suffrage Amendment, Statement by Senator Sheppard," McCallum Family Papers.

75. Carrie Chapman Catt to Mrs. Edith Hinkle League, July 17, 1918, McCallum Family Papers, quoted in Sims, "Woman Suffrage in Texas," p. 42.

76. Seneca Falls "Declaration of Sentiments," reprinted in Scott and Scott, *One Half the People*, pp. 56–59; Stanton, *Eighty Years and More*, p. xii; Wiebe, *Search for Order*.

77. Elizabeth H. Potter to Woodrow Wilson, Mar. 7, 1918, Woodrow Wilson Papers, Manuscripts Division, Library of Congress, quoted in Gould, *Progressives and Prohibitionists,* p. 234; Minnie Fisher Cunningham to All County Chairmen of the Democratic Party in Texas, May 17, 1919. See also Jane Y. McCallum to My dear Sir, Mar. 13, 1919; McCallum to Charles M. Dickson, May 14, 1919, McCallum Family Papers; Williamson County *Sun,* June 7 and June 14, 1917.

78. "Many Factors Contributed to the Apparent Defeat of Suffrage," McCallum Family Papers. See also Jane Y. McCallum to Hugh Nugent Fitzgerald, Mar. 12, 1919; Minnie Fisher Cunningham to R. E. Thomason, May 28, 1919; Cunningham to Carrie Chapman Catt, June 2, 1919; Cunningham to M. Eleanor Brackinridge, June 4, 1919; Cunningham to Catt, June 5, 1919; M. M. Brane to Cunningham, June 11, 1919; Jane Y. McCallum to Marin Fenwich, June 16, 1919, McCallum Family Papers.

79. McCallum, "Activities," p. 486; Catt and Schuler, *Woman Suffrage and Politics,* p. 349.

80. See E. DuBois, "The Radicalism of the Woman Suffrage Movement."

81. Chafe, *American Woman,* pp. 34–35; Scott, "After Suffrage," pp. 302–3; JDA, "Texas League of Women Voters, 10 October, 1919–6 December, 1923," Ames Papers (Austin); Peck, *Carrie Chapman Catt,* pp. 235 ff.; JDA Interview.

82. Quotation is from JDA, "Texas League of Women Voters," Ames Papers (Austin); JDA to Mrs. Lily W. Thompson, Aug. 27, 1940, ASWPL Papers. Ames seems to have supported the poll tax law because it linked payment with property taxes and made it mandatory for both husband and wife, thus forcing husbands who were opposed to woman suffrage to pay poll taxes for their wives. JDA, "The Negro and the White Primary" [1940], Priv. Coll.; JDA to Mrs. J. Morgan Stevens, Feb. 12, 1941, ASWPL Papers.

83. Pickens, "The Woman Voter Hits the Color Line." See also Tindall, *Emergence of the New South,* pp. 165–66.

84. W. E. B. Du Bois, *Darkwater,* pp. 163–86; [Du Bois], "Votes for Women"; Pickens, "Woman Voter." *The Nation* sent Pickens's article to the members of the National Advisory Committee of the National Woman's Party, asking their opinions on "the attempt to nullify the Nineteenth Amendment in regard to colored women." For their replies, see "The White Woman's Burden."

85. JDA, "Texas League of Women Voters," Ames Papers (Austin); Lewinson, *Race, Class, and Party,* pp. 112–13. Paulson, in *Women's Suffrage,* makes a useful distinction between the nativist goal of exclusion and the progressive goal of assimilation. Texas suffragists were paternalistic and ethnocentric in their attitudes toward the foreign-born, but their program of "Americanization" assumed that immigrants would be incorporated into, not excluded from, Texas society. See for example, *The Woman Citizen,* June 30, 1917, Cunningham Papers. There is some evidence that Jessie Daniel Ames's sojourns in Latin America gave her a more sympathetic and sophisticated perspective on Texas' Mexican-American population than that evinced by her co-workers. For example, in 1923, she attended the First Congress of the North American League of Women. In her report on the gathering, she sup-

ported its controversial stance on birth control and common-law marriages and recommended that in the future North American women's organizations should send Spanish-speaking delegates more familiar with Mexican conditions. [JDA], "Report of First Congress of the North American Section of the Pan-American League of Women, May 20th–30th, 1923"; Carrie Chapman Catt to JDA, Sept. 29, 1923; JDA to Catt, Oct. 8, 1923; Catt to JDA, Oct. 16, 1923, Ames Papers (Dallas). See also Williamson County *Sun*, June 14, 1917.

86. Waskow, *From Race Riot to Sit-In*, pp. 16–20.

87. Gould, *Progressives and Prohibitionists*, pp. 253, 266. For a discussion of the uses of this analogy, see Chafe, *Women and Equality*, pp. 43–114.

88. JDA, "Texas League of Women Voters," Ames Papers (Austin).

89. Ibid.; [JDA], "Daniel-Ames," Priv. Coll.; Lulu Daniel Ames Interview; Dallas *Morning News*, Apr. 11, 1920; *New York Times*, Feb. 18, July 29, and July 30, 1920; JDA, "White Primary," Priv. Coll.

90. Quotation is from JDA to Mrs. Maude Park, Aug. 14, 1920, National League of Women Voters Papers, Library of Congress, hereinafter cited as LWV Papers; JDA to Mrs. Percy V. Pennybacker, Dec. 26, 1919, Mrs. Percy V. Pennybacker Papers, Archives Collection, University of Texas Library, Austin, Texas; [ASW] to Hon. A. S. Burleson, May 29, 1920, McCallum Family Papers. JDA, "Women Voters of Texas Attention," Dallas *Home and State*, May 1, 1920; JDA to Hon. Clyde A. Sweeton, April 19, 1920; Beaumont *Enterprise*, July 26, 1920, Ames Papers (Dallas).

91. Houston *Post*, Apr. 30, 1920, Ames Papers (Dallas).

92. Quotation is from Dallas *Morning News*, May 4, 1920, Ames Papers (Dallas). Press coverage of this first venture of women into national party politics ranged from amused praise to ridicule. Headlines in the Austin *American-Statesman*, May 25, 1920, read: "Power of Woman Very Apparent at Dallas Convention . . . Mere Man Just Stepped to One Side and Cleared the Skirted Track." See also Dorothy Dix, "Beauty Parlor is Meeting Place for Women Delegates," Fort Worth *Record*, June 27, 1920; Austin *American-Statesman*, July 11, 1920; *Comanche Chief*, Dec. 11, 1920 [?]; Waco *Daily News*, June 6, 1920, Ames Papers (Dallas).

93. Quotation is from Gould, *Progressives and Prohibitionists*, pp. 266–67. *New York Times*, Feb. 18, July 29, and July 30, 1920. Upon her selection as a delegate to the national convention, Ames enjoyed the triumph of a public reception in Georgetown, presided over by the town mayor. Williamson County *Sun*, June 11, 1920.

94. Dallas *Morning News*, June 30, 1920, Ames Papers (Dallas). Harper, ed., *Woman Suffrage*, VI, 640–41; JDA, "Texas League of Women Voters," Ames Papers (Austin); Report, Gertrude Watkins, Jan. 1921 [?], LWV Papers.

95. Ruth Spence to author, Dec. 30, 1973.

96. JDA to Mrs. Richard Edwards, Nov. 11, 1921; Edwards to JDA, Nov. 8, 1921, LWV Papers.

97. McCallum, "Activities," p. 487.

98. Dallas *Morning News*, Dec. 24, 1922, quoted in Jane Y. McCallum, "Eve in the New Era," Austin *American-Statesman*, Sept. 29, 1946.

99. McCallum, "Activities," p. 489; Jane Y. McCallum, "Women's Joint Legislative Council," in *The Handbook of Texas*, ed. by Walter Prescott Webb (Austin: Texas Press Association, 1952), II, 929.

100. McCallum, "Eve in the New Era," Austin *American-Statesman*, Oct. 6, 1946.

101. For the role of Texas women in passage of the federal bill, see collection of letters in Texas File, LWV Papers, and JDA to Senator Morris Sheppard, Feb. 11, 1928, Priv. Coll.

102. Williamson County *Sun*, Aug. 10, 1923; JDA to Mrs. Roberta C. Lawson, July, 1935, ASWPL Papers; *New York Times*, Jan. 23, and Jan. 24, 1921; Louise Moyer Jackson to author, n.d.

103. Louise Moyer Jackson to author, n.d.; Gould, *Progressives and Prohibitionists*, pp. 286–87; Edwards, "Texas"; Dallas *Morning News*, Dec. 15, 1920; Williamson County *Sun*, June 3, 1921; Charles W. Pipkin, "Social Legislation," in *Culture in the South*, ed. by W. T. Couch (Chapel Hill: University of North Carolina Press, 1934), pp. 657–58, 664–66; Lucy Randolph Mason, *Standards for Workers*. Included in the petitions to the Industrial Welfare Commission advocating a minimum wage for women was a missive from Georgetown in behalf of the telephone operators employed by the Ames women. Dallas *Morning News*, Dec. 15, 1920.

104. Sullivan and Blair, *Women in Texas Industries*. Women employed in telephone exchanges, like that owned by the Ames women in Georgetown, enjoyed the highest industrial wages in the state.

105. Quotation is from JDA Interview. See also JDA to Judge Sarah T. Hughes, Feb. 3, 1937, ASWPL Papers; Ralph W. Steen, *Twentieth Century Texas* (Austin: Steck Co., 1942), pp. 255–57; Ocie Speer, "Woman and the Law in Texas," *The Texas Monthly*, 5 (May 1930), 406–11; Wooten, "Status of Women in Texas" (Ph.D. diss.), pp. 299–346.

106. JDA to *Collier's National Weekly*, Dec. 27, 1927, Priv. Coll.; Houston *Chronicle*, Apr. 26, 1926; Dallas *Morning News*, Oct. 9, 1926. Under Ames's guidance, the Texas AAUW also supported a range of other social welfare reforms. These included prison reform, extension of the Sheppard-Towner appropriation, and improvement of rural schools. "State Convention, Texas Branch, American Association of University Women," Oct. 8–9, 1926, Dallas, Texas, Priv. Coll.

107. O'Neil, *Everyone Was Brave*. The best survey of the political activities of southern women in this period are Scott, "After Suffrage," pp. 298–318 and Scott, *The Southern Lady*, pp. 185–211. For the context of "business progressivism" in which women reformers operated, see, Tindall, *Emergence of the New South*, pp. 219–53. The range of Jessie Daniel Ames's legislative concerns can be traced in: JDA to Miss Lelia Bridges, Nov. 11, 1922; JDA to Miss Reynolds, Apr. 8, 1928, LWV Papers; JDA to Louis Dietrich, Feb. 10, 1928; JDA to Mrs. Noyes Smith, Feb. 10, 1928; "Joint Legislative Council Rules," Spring 1928, Priv. Coll.

108. Austin *American-Statesman*, May 5, 1965; Nannie Hite Winston to JDA, Nov. 9, 1931, ASWPL Papers.

109. Quoted in Chafe, *American Woman*, p. 34.

110. JDA to Lillian Smith, Dec. 30, 1941, Ames Papers (NC). See also JDA Interview; Minutes, Second Annual Meeting, May 17, 1923, Texas

Woman's Committee, Dallas, Texas; JDA to Mrs. W. A. Newell, May 5, 1938, Ames Papers (NC); Gould, *Progressives and Prohibitionists*, pp. 262–63; Marquerite Owen to Miss Evelyn S. Logen, Dec. 17, 1924, LWV Papers.

111. Quotation is from JDA Interview. Mims, *The Advancing South*, pp. 265–66; Williamson County *Sun*, Nov. 14 and Dec. 24, 1919; JDA to Mrs. L. A. Sanders, March 9, 1934, ASWPL Papers; JDA to Mrs. W. A. Newell, July 7, 1938, Ames Papers (NC).

112. JDA Interview. As early as 1917, the Methodist women's missionary society, led by Ames's mother, was discussing Atticus G. Haygood's *Our Brother in Black: His Freedom and His Future* (New York: Phillips and Hunt, 1881). The first contemporary evidence of Ames's growing interest in racial issues occurred in 1921, when the president of the Texas Federation of Women's Clubs appointed her chairman of the federation's Committee on the Condition of Our Colored People. Williamson County *Sun*, May 17 and June 7, 1917, Oct. 6, 1922; JDA to Elizabeth Ring, Nov. 3, 1922, Mrs. Henry [Elizabeth R.] Ring Papers, Archives Collection, University of Texas Library, Austin, Texas.

113. Typewritten notation by JDA, Nov. 25, 1953, attached to Frederick Ames to JDA, July 28, 1922, Priv. Coll. JDA opposed the Klan from its inception. JDA to R. M. Dudley, July 3, 1924, Ames Papers (Dallas).

114. Alexander, *Crusade for Conformity*, pp. 40–53; Jackson, *Ku Klux Klan in the City*, pp. 66–80, 235–49; Dallas *Morning News*, Sept. 6–20, 1921.

115. Kirby, *Darkness at the Dawning*, pp. 4, 179.

116. Neal R. Peirce, "Texas: Land of the Monied Establishment," in Peirce, *Megastates of America*, pp. 489–500; Edwards, "Texas"; Gould, *Progressives and Prohibitionists*, pp. 285–87.

117. JDA to Louise Dietrich, Apr. 28, 1936, CIC Papers. See also JDA to Mrs. W. A. Newell, Jan. 30, 1934 and Christmas, 1937, Ames Papers (NC).

118. JDA to Mrs. L. W. Alford, Dec. 30, 1935; Minutes, Georgia ASWPL Institute, Nov. 29, 1938, ASWPL Papers; JDA Interview. Ames was quite contemptuous of those who were "naive . . . as far as bills and legislatures go." She vigorously criticized women's organizations that passed resolutions endorsing legislation without doing the kind of painstaking study pioneered by her own Texas Joint Legislative Council. JDA to Mrs. Brevard Jones, May 24, 1935, ASWPL Papers; JDA to Lucy Randolph Mason, July 22, and July 30, 1931, CIC Papers; Dallas *Morning News*, Oct. 10, and Oct. 12, 1926.

119. JDA to Mr. Wainwright D. Black, Oct. 24, 1952, Priv. Coll.; Spence Interview.

120. Smith-Rosenberg, "Female World of Love and Ritual"; Christopher Lasch, *The New Radicalism in America, 1889–1963* (New York: Random House, 1967), pp. 3–37.

121. JDA to Johnson, Aug. 5, and Sept. 8, 1924, Ames Papers (NC).

122. For a perceptive statement of this feminist dilemma, see Filene, *Him/Her/Self*, pp. 54–60.

123. JDA to Mary Ames, Mar. 18, 1946, Priv. Coll.; Spence Interview; Mary Ryan, *Womanhood in America: From Colonial Times to the Present*

(New York: New Viewpoints, 1975), p. 137. Gerda Lerner, in "Women's Rights and American Feminism," p. 236, offers a useful definition of feminism. American feminism, she argues, embraces "any struggle designed to elevate [women's] status, socially, politically, economically, and in respect to their self concepts," while the term "women's rights movement" refers more narrowly to the demand for legal rights. The ideological position of individual women, of course, is much more difficult to categorize, particularly when one is dealing with an organizer rather than a writer or theorist. Jessie Daniel Ames, like Texas suffragists generally, belonged to the women's rights wing of the feminist movement. I would argue, on the other hand, that the emotional logic of her personal revolt embraced the broader feminist goals of psychological and economic autonomy.

124. For similar expressions of this exhilarating sense of an escape from the prison of self, of losing "the personal in the great impersonal," see Scott, *One Half the People*, p. 38, and Fuller, *Laura Clay*, p. 50.

Chapter 3: A Bond of Common Womanhood

1. JDA Interview.

2. For the best study of these events, see Waskow, *From Race Riot to Sit-In*. Estimates of the number of riots in 1919 run as high as 25; 7 major clashes occurred that evoked national attention. See Claude McKay's poem "If We Must Die" in Kerlin, ed., *Voice of the Negro*, p. 186.

3. Frazier, *Negro Family in the United States*, p. 225. For an account of this prewar population movement see Gilbert Osofsky, *Harlem: The Making of A Ghetto* (New York: Harper and Row, 1966), pp. 17–34. For a discussion of the Great Migration see Allen H. Spear, *Black Chicago: The Making of a Negro Ghetto, 1890–1920* (Chicago: University of Chicago Press, 1967), pp. 129–46.

4. Mary White Ovington, "Is Mob Violence the Texas Solution," p. 320. For a similar NAACP offensive and white backlash in South Carolina, see Newby, *Black Carolinians*, pp. 192–93.

5. Will Alexander to J. E. McColloch, July 2, 1921, Neighborhood Union Papers, Atlanta University, hereinafter cited as NU Papers; Torrence, *Story of John Hope*, p. 227.

6. James K. Vardaman, quoted in Tindall, *Emergence of the New South*, p. 151.

7. Waskow, *From Race Riot to Sit-In*, p. 182; Kerlin, ed., *Voice of the Negro*, p. 128.

8. For the creation and history of the CIC, see Dykeman and Stokely, *Seeds of Southern Change;* Burrows, "Commission on Interracial Cooperation" (Ph.D. diss.), Ellis, "The Commission on Interracial Cooperation, 1919–1944" (Ph.D. diss.); and Tindall, *Emergence of the New South,* pp. 177–83. For southern white accommodationist thought and racial liberalism, see Frederickson, *Black Image in the White Mind,* pp. 283–319, and Sosna, *In Search of the Silent South.*

9. There is some evidence that the rise of the CIC may have undermined the financial base of older interracial organizations. For example, gifts from the Laura Spelman Rockefeller Memorial and from John D. Rockefeller, Jr., accounted for more than 25 percent of the National Urban League's annual income in 1925–29; yet during a period when their pledges to the Urban League ranged from $4,000 to $20,000 annually, they gave $40,000 a year to the Interracial Commission. Moreover, in the late twenties, Alfred K. Stern, the son-in-law of Julius Rosenwald, launched a scheme to consolidate the NAACP and the Urban League into one large race relations agency under the leadership of Will Alexander and the Interracial Commission. When the two northern-based groups resisted merger, Stern convinced the Rosenwald Fund (a major supporter of the CIC) to reduce drastically its commitment to the Urban League. See Parris and Brooks, *Blacks in the City,* pp. 196–204, and Weiss, *National Urban League,* pp. 156–61.

10. The CIC at one time or another had state committees in thirteen southern states, some of which were appointed by the governor. Its original goal was to set up local interracial committees in 805 counties where blacks made up at least 10 percent of the population. Most committees, however, met only during crises and disintegrated rapidly. By 1932, only 23 such groups were listed for the whole South, and the organization turned increasingly from fieldwork to information and research. Membership on the various levels of organization was constantly changing, and the CIC programs depended heavily on the work of the professional staff at the central office. Financial support continued to come from the YMCA until 1922; after that a large proportion of CIC funds came from northern foundations. Burrows, "Commission on Interracial Cooperation," pp. 79–109, 146–49.

11. Dykeman and Stokely, *Seeds of Southern Change,* p. 65; O'Brien, "C. Vann Woodward." For an expression of the new self-confidence and assertiveness of the white southern bourgeoisie, see Mims, *The Advancing South,* esp. pp. 257–78.

12. Quoted in Waskow, *From Race Riot to Sit-In,* p. 198.

13. "When a total ruling community is determined that a law shall not be enforced, or that justice shall not be done," despaired a neo-abolitionist in 1903, "they are sure to nullify any laws." Quoted in McPherson, *Abolitionist Legacy,* p. 355.

14. Quoted in McPherson, *Abolitionist Legacy,* pp. 364–65.

15. W.E.B. Du Bois, "The Newer South."

16. W.E.B. Du Bois, "Inter-Racial Comity" and "The Liberal South."

17. W.E.B. Du Bois to R. B. Eleazer, Mar. 12, 1926; Report of the Findings Committee, Annual Meeting, CIC, Apr. 8–10, 1926, CIC Papers. See also, W.E.B. Du Bois, "Inter-Racial Comity," p. 6, and Dykeman and Stokely, *Seeds of Southern Change,* p. 68. These suspicions obviously were not

without foundation. For example, Thomas Jackson Woofter divided the causes of black migration into two categories: economic conditions and "treatment." He then went on to suggest that the best way to alleviate black grievances, and thus halt the black exodus "which has so severely handicapped planters, mill owners and landlords in recent years" was through the formation of local committees of the CIC. "Negro Migration," *Missionary Voice*, 11 (Mar. 1921), 88.

18. Torrence, *Story of John Hope*, pp. 227–29.

19. W.E.B. Du Bois, "The Newer South," p. 164; Ovington, "Revisiting the South," p. 43.

20. Reporting on a presentation of interracial work at a pastor's conference in Richmond, Virginia, Durham described the response of the women present: "They are far more difficult to work with than men on this proposition. Their faces were liken unto graven images to me. [But] I gave them first the principle and description of our program and they gave every emphasis of applause and came afterward to give themselves to the movement," Minutes, CIC Meeting, Mar. 23, 1920, CIC Papers; Dykeman and Stokely, *Seeds of Southern Change*, p. 83.

21. Reminiscences of Will W. Alexander.

22. M. Ashby Jones, a Baptist minister whose father was a former chaplain to Robert E. Lee, believed the relationship between black and white women was "the most delicate and difficult point of contact." John J. Eagan, wealthy businessman and chairman of the CIC, believed that "while men might make a little dent on this problem," it would take generations to achieve "the conversion of the women." Dykeman and Stokely, *Seeds of Southern Change*, p. 88; "Background [of Memphis Conference]," Ames Papers (NC), Continuation Committee Meeting, Nov. 16, 1920, CIC Papers; Robert Russa Moton, *What the Negro Thinks* (Garden City, N.Y.: Doubleday, Doran, 1929); Logan, ed., *What the Negro Wants*.

23. I am indebted to Donald G. Mathews' study *Religion in the Old South* for this view of southern evangelicalism. Scott, "Women, Religion, and Social Change," is the best treatment of southern women and religion in the postbellum period.

24. Mathews, *Religion in the Old South*, preface and pp. 101–24.

25. For social change in sex roles in this period, see Scott, *Southern Lady*, pp. 105–63, and Filene, *Him/Her/Self*, pp. 7–76.

26. Welter, "Feminization of American Religion"; Douglas, *Feminization of American Culture*. For the contradictory elements in the ideal of the evangelical woman, and for the contrast between ideal and reality, see Mathews, *Religion in the Old South*, pp. 112–13, 115, 117–20, 123, 243.

27. Quotation is from *Report of Commission on Woman's Place*, p. 50. Hageman, "Women and Missions," pp. 168–69, 176. Hageman's provocative essay views the role of women in the missionary movement as "a tale of contradictions." Middle-class women, suffering from internal domination by male standards and structures, found in foreign missions an opportunity for interesting and responsible work. In the foreign mission field they offered an image of women's spiritual equality and worked with great dedication to improve health and educational conditions. At the same time, they acted as agents of American cultural imperialism. Their presence functioned to divert

attention from the colonialist roots of social conditions and to develop among converts ties of dependency on patrons in the United States. Similar paradoxes appear in the relationship between the city missions and settlement houses of the Home Mission Society and the black and white working-class communities they served. See also, R. Pierce Beaver, *All Loves Excelling: American Protestant Women in World Missions* (Grand Rapids, Mich.: William B. Eerdmans, 1968) and Elaine Magalis, *Conduct Becoming to a Woman: Bolted Doors and Burgeoning Missions* (New York: Women's Division, Board of Global Ministries, The United Methodist Church, 1973).

28. "Our Outlook," *Our Homes*, 7 (May 1898), 4: Howell, *Women and the Kingdom*, p. 20; Dunn, *Women and Home Missions*, p. 9.

29. MacDonell, *Belle Harris Bennet*, p. 38. See also Edward T. James, et al., eds., *Notable American Women: A Biographical Dictionary* (3 vols.; Cambridge: Harvard University Press, 1971), I, 132–34; Baker, *Following the Color Line*, p. 56; Mathews, *Religion in the Old South*, pp. 104–5, 123.

30. Haskin, *Women and Missions*, pp. 232, 239. See also Louise Young Interview; Thelma Stevens Interview; Alice Cobb Interview; Sue Thrasher, personal communications.

31. C. S. Johnson, et al., *Into the Main Stream*, pp. 163, 238. The other was the University of North Carolina.

32. For this new cultural image, see Virginia A. Shadron's excellent study, "Out of Our Homes" (M.A. thesis), pp. 39–41, 75–82. What is striking here is the degree to which women were appropriating for themselves the qualities traditionally associated with the "evangelical man." See Mathews, *Religion in the Old South*, pp. 113, 120–23, for these nineteenth-century images.

33. Dunn, *Women and Home Missions*, pp. 16, 40; Hammond, "A Lover of All Races," p. 304; "What a Deaconess Is and What She Is Not," p. 1.

34. Belle H. Bennett, "The President's Message," *Our Homes*, 18 (Dec. 1909), 9, quoted in Shadron, "Out of Our Homes" (M.A. thesis), p. 116. See Mathews, *Religion in the Old South*, pp. 238–39.

35. MacDonell, *Belle Harris Bennett*, pp. 89, 94; MacDonell, *Shifts of Emphasis*, pp. 4, 7.

36. Dunn, *Women and Home Missions*, p. 74; MacDonell, *Belle Harris Bennett*, p. 167; Haskin, *Women and Missions*, pp. 206–7; *Reports of the . . . Woman's Missionary Council*; Eleanor Copenhaver Report, 1930–31, YWCA Industrial Department, YWCA Papers; Taylor, "Southern Social Awakening"; Fish, "Southern Methodism in the Progressive Era" (Ph.D. diss.), pp. 78–109. This is not to argue that the political attitudes of Methodist women in general necessarily differed from those of men of their own class; it is to say rather that a combination of organizational autonomy and cultural assumptions that allowed women to participate in public life only under the rubric of "service" or "benevolent action" encouraged a distinctive *corporate* response to social issues.

37. For the racial attitudes of the southern Protestant churches, see Newby, *Jim Crow's Defense*; Miller, *American Protestantism and Social Issues*; Miller, "Attitudes of American Protestantism"; Eighmy, *Churches in Cultural Captivity*; Loescher, *Protestant Church and the Negro*; and Bailey, *Southern White Protestantism*.

38. Tatum, *Crown of Service*, p. 349.

39. MacDonell, *Belle Harris Bennett*, pp. 121–40. For the industrial education movement, see McPherson, *Abolitionist Legacy*; Burns, "Industrial Education Myth" (Ph. D. diss.); and Woodson, *Mis-education of the Negro*.

40. Shadron, "Out of Our Homes" (M.A. thesis), pp. 41–47; Helm, "The Negro Problem," p. 3; Mrs. R. W. MacDonell, "Sophie," *Our Homes*, 11 (Mar. 1902), 3; "The Hand on the Cradle," p. 1.

41. Tatum, *Crown of Service*, p. 355; Helm, *The Upward Path*, p. 214. See also, Helm, *From Darkness to Light*; "Paine College and Its Annex."

42. Mary De Bardeleben to Louise Young, Aug. 31, 1963, Louise Young Papers. See also Hammond, *In Black and White*, p. 197.

43. De Bardeleben to Young, Aug. 31, 1963; Tobias, "Two Southern Women Pioneers," p. 29; "Can We Do Less," *Missionary Voice*, 10 (Mar. 1920), 92.

44. MacDonell, *Shifts of Emphasis*, pp. 6–7. The impetus for the Nashville settlement house came from Sallie Hill Sawyer. Sara Estelle Haskin, who had opened a settlement house in Dallas and taught social work at Scarritt, answered Sawyer's appeal to aid her work in the black community. Sawyer became housemother for the Nashville Bethlehem House, and in 1923, its first permanent building was named in honor of the two women. Dunn, *Women and Missions*, pp. 64–65. Weiss, *National Urban League*, pp. 74–76; James R. Anderson, "Co-operation for Community Betterment," *Southern Workman*, 46 (Feb. 1917), 77–78.

45. Dykeman and Stokely, *Seeds of Southern Change*, pp. 84–85; Will Alexander to Parker, May 4, 1921, CIC Papers.

46. Hammond, *In Black and White*, pp. 43–98, 124–25, 152. Hammond also wrote *In the Vanguard of a Race*, and both have been reprinted as *Race and the South: Two Studies, 1914–1922*. See also Hammond, "Negro Boys Make Good," and Kellogg, *NAACP*, p. 216. For the response to Hammond's book, see Mary White Ovington review, *Survey*, 32 (May 16, 1914), 201; Villard, "The Race Problem."

47. *Report of Commission on Woman's Place*, p. 20; MacDonell, *Belle Harris Bennett*, p. 86.

48. Shadron, "Out of Our Homes" (M.A. thesis), pp. 66–83; Hageman, "Women and Missions," pp. 178–79.

49. Virginia Shadron demonstrates a considerable overlap between the personnel of the suffrage and laity rights movements. Among Home Mission Society leaders, Belle Bennett, Mrs. R. W. MacDonell, Mable K. Howell, and Nellie N. Somerville were also active in the southern suffrage campaign. A survey of Southern Methodist women in *Who's Who of American Women, 1914–1915* reveals that of 50 women listed as active in women's missionary societies, 30 favored women's suffrage; only 5 were opposed, and 15 expressed no opinion. Shadron, "Out of Our Homes" (M.A. thesis), pp. 96–98.

50. *Report of Commission on Woman's Place*, pp. 107, 92, 118. Mitchell, in "From Social to Radical Feminism," notes that as late as 1975 women still comprised only 13 percent of the delegates to the General Conference. Although Methodist women consistently demonstrated a sense of collective identity as women, they confined the expression of their grievances to peti-

tions and study commissions. Mitchell argues, however, that when changes in the larger society gave rise to the women's movement of the 1960s, organized Methodist women quickly moved from petitions to protest activity.

51. _Report of Commission on Woman's Place_, pp. 9, 29, 32, 26.

52. Ibid., pp. 30, 8, 33.

53. For example, in 1928, Mrs. R. W. MacDonell, Belle Bennett's closest ally in the early days of the movement, admonished the younger generation: "Recapture the social spirit of your pioneers; reclaim the creative faith that led them to stupendous tasks with 'the passion that left the ground to lose itself in the sky.' Count, as they did, your God-given power, your equipment. Victory is yours." MacDonell, _Shifts of Emphasis_, p. 8.

54. This verbal distinction between women's activities and "the man's church" recurs in the writing and conversation of Methodist women. See, for example, Louise Young Interview.

55. Most studies of the genesis of the interracial women's movement have ignored the role of these southern black women. See, for example, Dykeman and Stokely, _Seeds of Southern Change_, pp. 82–96; Smith, _Killers of the Dream_, pp. 124–31.

56. Quoted in Raper and Reid, _Sharecroppers All_, p. 105.

57. Tanner, "Matrifocality"; Lewis, "A Response to Inequality"; Lerner, ed., _Black Women in White America_; Ladner, _Tomorrow's Tomorrow_. For rich literary evidence, see the works of Margaret Walker, Zora Neale Hurston, Toni Morrison, and Alice Walker.

58. The following account of Wells's career is taken from Lerner, "Early Community Work," and Wells, _Crusade for Justice_. Quotations are from Wells, _Crusade for Justice_, pp. 52, 62–66, and Wells-Barnett, _On Lynchings_, pp. 4–5.

59. Walter R. Chivers, untitled biographical sketch of Lugenia Hope, NU Papers; Torrence, _Story of John Hope_, p. 127; Shivery, "History of Organized Social Work among Atlanta Negroes" (M.A. thesis). John Hope, like his wife, had been protected from the full brunt of racial injustice. His Scottish father had been the wealthiest cotton mill owner in Augusta and had lived openly and faithfully with Hope's mother, a free black woman. In 1905, Hope, W.E.B. Du Bois, and a coterie of their friends organized the Georgia Equal Rights Convention and fought to maintain the foothold of political power blacks had gained during Reconstruction. Hope worked with Du Bois on his social study of blacks at Atlanta University, participated in the Niagara movement, and traveled throughout the country defending the concept of liberal education for blacks against what both men regarded as Booker T. Washington's capitulation to "Negro submission and slavery." Du Bois to Hope, Jan. 22, 1910, quoted in Torrence, _Story of John Hope_, p. 162.

60. Documents reflecting the activities of the Neighborhood Union can be found in Lerner, ed., _Black Women_, pp. 497–509. See also, Torrence, _Story of John Hope_, pp. 138–40, and Lerner, "Early Community Work."

61. Atlanta _Constitution_, Feb. 1911, NU Papers.

62. The work in progress of Dan Durrett on Atlanta University as an urban land user, for example, indicates that the school acted as a land bank, selling property at low prices to desirable neighbors. The institution thus served as a

community builder by controlling property ownership and residence. At the same time, its interests did not necessarily coincide with those of the urban poor in the area. I am indebted to Darlene Roth White for bringing Durrett's research to my attention.

63. During their campaigns, the women of the Neighborhood Union sometimes appealed for and got the support of white women's groups. They worked closely with Rosa Lowe's Anti-Tuberculosis League. In a campaign to improve black public schools in 1913, they visited "every influential white woman in the city that could be reached. . . . Some met with us and pledged their cooperation," Hope reported. "They could scarcely believe the facts we presented them, but they visited those schools themselves and saw conditions just as we had pictured." As a result, the chairman of the "board of lady visitors" supported the union's petition and denied the charge that it grossly exaggerated conditions in black schools. Lerner, *Black Women*, p. 503; "Survey of Colored Public Schools 1913–1914;" Petition to Board of Education, Aug, 19, 1913, NU Papers; Atlanta *Constitution*, Oct. 24, 1913, and Dec. 3, 1913.

64. Edward T. James, et al., eds., *Notable American Women: A Biographical Dictionary* (3 vols.; Cambridge: Harvard University Press, 1971), II, 365–67; Mary Jackson McCrorey, "Lucy Laney," *Crisis*, 41 (June 1934), 161.

65. For biographies of Bethune see Peane, *Mary McLeod Bethune*, Holt, *Mary McLeod Bethune*, and Lerner, *Black Women*, pp. 135–46.

66. James, ed., *Notable American Women*, I, 96–97. See also W. R. Hall, "Janie Porter Barrett" (M.A. thesis). Other members of this network were: Mrs. M. L. Crosthwaite, Registrar of Fisk University in Nashville; Juliette Derricotte, leader of interracial work in the National Student Council of the YWCA and Dean of Women at Fisk University; Mrs. H. A. Hunt, President of the Georgia Federation of Colored Women's Clubs; Mary Jackson McCrorey, president of the Baptist Division of Missions for Colored People and pioneer YWCA worker; Jennie B. Moton, wife of Robert R. Moton, Booker T. Washington's successor as head of Tuskegee Institute, and editor of the *Woman's National Magazine*; Margaret Murray Washington of Tuskegee; Marion Raven Wilkinson, president of the South Carolina Federation of Colored Women's Clubs and wife of the president of the Colored Normal, Industrial, Agricultural and Mechanical College of South Carolina in Orangeburg; and Mrs. Nettie Langston Napier, a president of NACW, whose husband, James Carroll Napier, was a register of the treasury and a member of the Board of Trustees of Fisk University.

67. Sims, *The YWCA*, pp. 5, 78–79; Grace L. Coyle, "A Historical Outline of the Work of the Industrial Department," Nov., 1923, YWCA Papers; Miller, *American Protestantism*, pp. 31–35. See also Mary S. Sims, *The Natural History of a Social Institution–The Y.W.C.A.* (New York: Woman's Press, 1936) and Elizabeth Hendee, *The Growth and Development of the Young Women's Christian Association: An Interpretation* (New York: Woman's Press, 1930).

68. Katharine Du Pre Lumpkin Interview; Frederickson, "Southern Summer School for Women Workers." These generalizations are based on a wide range of interviews with southern women reformers undertaken by the Southern Oral History Program. See especially, Alice Spearman Wright Interview, August 8, 1976.

69. James, ed., *Notable American Women*, I, 214–15; Lerner, *Black Women*, pp. 428–500; Gladys Gilkey Calkins, "The Negro in the YWCA: Historical Outline of Interracial Education and Race Relations in the National Student Council of the YWCA," Grace Towns Hamilton Papers, Atlanta University; Mrs. Cordelia Winn, "Historical Account of Colored Work" [1928]; "The Young Women's Christian Association Among Colored Girls and Women," 1928, YWCA Papers; Calkins, "The Negro in the YWCA" (M.A. thesis).

70. From the point of view of black participants, the Louisville conference failed to make "Colored work . . . an integral part of the Association." Instead it left the administration of the southern field entirely in the hands of southern white women, set up distinctive by-laws for the governance of black branches, and provided no machinery for bringing blacks into the National Student Council. "Suggestions from the Committee on Findings at the Conference on Colored Work, Louisville, Ky., October 14 and 16, 1915," NU Papers.

71. Josephine Pinyon Holmes, "Youth Cannot Wait," *Crisis*, 28 (July 1924), 128.

72. Olcott, comp. *Work of Colored Women*, p. 122.

73. In her usual thorough way, Hope divided the city into zones and the zones into neighborhood units with a committee of volunteers in each unit. The War Work Council also raised $1,800 to build a YMCA for the recreational use of black soldiers and their families. Eva Bowles to Lugenia Hope, July 30, 1931, NU Papers.

74. Chafe, *American Woman*, pp. 51 ff.; Olcott, *Work of Colored Women*, p. 132; Eva Bowles to [?], Jan. 5, 1920, NU Papers.

75. Eva Bowles to Lugenia Hope, Mar. 19, 1920, NU Papers.

76. Eva Bowles to Lugenia Hope, Apr. 29, 1919 and Nov. 10, 1919, NU Papers.

77. Their positions as paid professional staff members representing a black constituency that had no voice in selecting them nor in formulating the policies they carried out prevented the black national staff from presenting a united and effective defense. Receiving little support for her stand for equal accommodations for black staff members at national conventions and refusing to work under a southern white woman, Lealtad eventually "became so disgusted with the whole crowd and their 'milk and water' policies that [she] resigned" to become Associate Secretary of the New York Urban League. Eva Bowles to [?], Jan. 25, 1930; Eva Bowles to Lugenia Hope, Jan. 17, 1920 and Jan. 25, 1920; Catherine D. Lealtad to Lugenia Hope, Mar. 5, 1920, NU Papers.

78. Lerner, *Black Women*, pp. 479–97; Lugenia Hope, n.d., NU Papers.

79. "The National Board of the Young Women's Christian Association," NU Papers. In addition, under Hope's leadership, the Atlanta Federation of Colored Women's Clubs petitioned the National YWCA Board not to put a southern white woman in charge of student affairs: "First because of barriers which have been built up by her own race, she . . . knows absolutely nothing of our student life. . . . We beseech you not to turn this work over to people who know nothing of our life and aspirations." Draft letter, Lugenia Hope to Eva Bowles, Jan. 13, 1920, NU Papers.

80. "We are women together," Eva Bowles assured the black caucus, "and I seem to see light ahead where all has been dark." Wiring her encouragement, Mrs. Nettie Langston Napier bolstered their stand: "There is but one standard for Americanism the colored woman aspires to. In the name of our boys who fought and died for it, we demand all that it encompasses. This we ask for the people north and south alike and will never be satisfied with one whit less." Eva Bowles to Lugenia Hope, Apr. 10, 1920; Napier to Hope, Apr. 13, 1920, NU Papers.

81. Mary McCrorey to Hope, May 7, 1920, NU Papers. "The Cleveland meeting," wrote Lucy Laney, "was a page in history or it will be—but the stand taken by our women must be held. We must agitate a little more." Laney to Hope, May 4, 1920, NU Papers. In Cleveland, Public attention was focused on the black women's struggle by hard-hitting editorials in the Cleveland *Advocate*, Apr. 24 and May 1, 1920.

82. McCrorey to Hope, Jan. 27, 1921; Hope to Katherine Hawes, Aug. 4, 1920, NU Papers. For a more positive view of the Richmond meeting, see "Minutes of the meeting held in the office of the SAFC, Richmond, Va., July 3, 1920," YMCA Papers.

83. For example, petitions were secured from the National Association of Colored Women and from a group of Atlanta clergymen. Janie Porter Barrett to Hope, Feb. 8, 1921; petition, n.d., NU Papers.

84. Eva Bowles to Hope, Mar. 8, 1921; Mrs. Lewis H. Lapham to Charlotte Hawkins Brown, June 21, 1921; Brown to Hope, June 16, 1921; Ruth [?] to Hope, Nov. 1921, NU Papers.

85. Hope to Eva Bowles, Mar. 15, 1922, NU Papers. Hope was chagrined, in part, because she had expected to receive the appointment offered to Charlotte Hawkins Brown.

86. Mary McCrorey to Lugenia Hope, July 6, 1931, NU Papers.

87. Newell, *Handbook for Interracial Committees;* Tatum, *Crown of Service,* pp. 31, 356; "Background [of Memphis Conference]," Ames Papers (NC); *Eleventh Annual Report of the Woman's Missionary Council of the M.E. Church, South, for 1920–1921, Nashville, Tennessee.*

88. Because the general church press dropped the issue from its pages, the final educational campaign for laity rights was conducted primarily through the *Laity Rights Advocate*. No copies of the publication appear to have survived. Shadron, "Out of Our Homes" (M.A. thesis), pp. 131–33. Quotation is from Dunn, *Women and Home Missions,* pp. 68.

89. Reminiscences of Will Alexander; Mary J. McCrorey to Lugenia Hope, July 6, 1931; handwritten note, Louise Shivery, n.d.; Estelle Haskin to Lugenia Hope, May 8, 1920; Carrie Parks Johnson to Lugenia Hope, June 3, 1920, NU Papers; "Background [of Memphis Conference]," Ames Papers (NC).

90. See Cayton, *Long Old Road,* pp. 189–206 for a view of Tuskegee by a northern black scholar.

91. Quotations are from *Eleventh Annual Report of the Woman's Missionary Council;* Minutes of Inter-Racial Commission, Nov. 17, 1920, CIC Papers. See also Dykeman and Stokely, *Seeds of Southern Change,* p. 89.

92. Quotations are from "Background [of Memphis Conference]" and Charlotte Hawkins Brown Address, CIC Annual Meeting, Oct. 7, 1926,

Ames Papers (NC). See also Findings Committee, CIC Annual Meeting, Apr. 8–10, 1926, CIC Papers.

93. Carrie Parks Johnson, "The Business of Peace," National Convention, Young Women's Christian Association, Hot Springs, Arkansas, Apr. 24, 1922, CIC Papers.

94. Charlotte Hawkins Brown, "Mrs. Hope in the National Scene" [1947], Charlotte Hawkins Brown Papers; Mary J. McCrorey to Lugenia Hope, July 6, 1931, NU Papers. "We saw the shadows were lifted," said Charlotte Hawkins Brown, "and we stood as Christian women to discuss face to face the hard problems that were eating at our hearts. We were surprised to find the same thing that interested us, the things we so desired, so much wanted, were the things the white women desired and wanted today." Brown Address, CIC Annual Meeting, Oct. 7, 1926, Ames Papers (NC).

95. Johnson, "The Business of Peace." Johnson was quoting the black leader Nannie H. Burroughs.

96. Ibid. See also Minutes of the Interracial Commission, Atlanta, Georgia, Nov. 17, 1920, CIC Papers.

97. JDA Interview.

98. "The Memphis Conference," October 6–7, 1920; "List of Women Present at the Woman's Inter-Racial Conference, Memphis, Tennessee, October 6–7, 1920," Ames Papers (NC).

99. "Memphis Conference"; Reminiscences of Will Alexander; Dykeman and Stokely, *Seeds of Southern Change,* p. 92.

100. Hallie Brown, *Homespun Heroines.* In 1896, Washington merged the Afro-American Federation of Colored Women, of which she was president, with the NACW; from 1914 to 1915, she served as president of NACW and, until her death in 1925, edited its publication, *National Notes.* As founder and president of the International Council of Women of the Darker Races of the World, she sought to develop among "peoples of color the world over . . . a larger appreciation of their history and accomplishments that . . . they may have a greater degree of respect for their own achievement, and a greater pride in themselves. . . ." In pursuit of this end, she organized a campaign, led by Hope in Georgia, "to get into every school, private, public, or otherwise, Negro literature and history." See Minutes, International Council of the Women of the Darker Races of the World, Washington, D.C. [1923]; Margaret Washington to Lugenia Hope, Sept. 15, 1922, NU Papers; Lerner, *Black Women,* pp. 443–47, and "Early Community Work," pp. 159–60.

101. Margaret Washington Address, Memphis Conference, Oct. 6–7, 1920, Ames Papers (NC). Jennie B. Moton was the second black speaker of the conference.

102. Elizabeth Ross Haynes, "Negroes in Domestic Service in the United States," *Journal of Negro History,* 8 (Oct. 1923), 384–442.

103. Stanton, *Woman Suffrage,* I, 115–17. The dialect recorded in this source has been dropped.

104. Brown's grandmother was a descendant of the English navigator John D. Hawkins, whose children settled in Vance County, North Carolina, and became great slaveholders and traders. Brown proudly described her, a house slave in the home of a railroad magnate who was her blood brother, as

"fair with blue eyes, an aristocrat to the manor born." In addition to her role as an educator, Brown was a leader in the black women's club movement: vice-president of the NACW and president of the North Carolina Federation of Colored Women's Clubs. See Bardolph, *The Negro Vanguard*, pp. 123, 130; Lerner, *Black Women*, pp. 125–32; "Some Incidents in the Life and Career of Charlotte Hawkins Brown Growing Out of Racial Situations, At the Request of Dr. Ralph Bunche," Brown Papers; Sylvia Dannett, *Profiles of Negro Womanhood* (New York: Educational Heritage, 1966), II, 61; C. H. Brown, *The Correct Things to Do, to Say, to Wear*.

105. "Try to make friends of those southern white people, for they can make you or break you," Brown's mother advised her when she left New England. Although fund-raising was a constant struggle, Brown did enjoy some success in gaining the patronage of wealthy North Carolinians. The goal of her school was to "prepare Negro youth to fit into society with the rough edges removed." Yet Brown was aware of the ambivalence of her role as a spokesman for her race, and along with her effort to integrate blacks into white cultural traditions went a strong commitment to black civil rights. For example, resisting the counsel of northern financial supporters who would "tie my hands so I can't speak out when I am being crushed," she fought back through the courts every time she was forced to use inferior Jim Crow transportation facilities. W.E.B. Du Bois to R. B. Eleazer, Mar. 12, 1926, CIC Papers; Frazier, *Black Bourgeoisie*; Lerner, *Black Women*, p. 130; Brown, "Some Incidents," Brown Papers; Charlotte Hawkins Brown Address, CIC Meeting, Oct. 7, 1921; Charlotte Hawkins Brown Address, Memphis Conference, Oct. 6–7, 1920, Ames Papers (NC); JDA to Mrs. Charles S. E. Mason, Apr. 23, 1940, CIC Papers.

106. Brown, "Some Incidents," Brown Papers; Brown Address, CIC Meeting Oct. 7, 1921, Ames Papers (NC); Brown, "My Theory of Public Speaking," Brown Papers.

107. Brown Address, Memphis Conference, Ames Papers (NC).

108. Lerner, *Black Women*, p. 130; Brown Address, Memphis Conference; Minutes of CIC Administrative Committee, Oct. 12, 1932, Ames Papers (NC).

109. Brown Address, Memphis Conference, Ames Papers (NC).

110. See Pat Watters, *Down to Now: Reflections on the Southern Civil Rights Movement* (New York: Random House, 1971) for a suggestive treatment of the similar ecstatic religious quality of the early civil rights movement, the roots of this phenomenon in the black southern church, and its loss in the movement's later stages.

111. Brown Address, CIC Meeting, Oct. 7, 1921, Ames Papers (NC).

112. Even intransigent opponents of the admission of women to the Interracial Commission were soon calling the Memphis Conference "the most significant meeting . . . that has taken place in the South." CIC Meeting, Nov. 17, 1920, CIC Papers.

113. See Dr. W. A. Shelton, "Mrs. Luke Johnson: An Appreciation"; Mrs. Wallace Rogers, "From the North Georgia Conference: A Tribute to Mrs. Luke Johnson"; Mrs. Robert Moton, "A Pioneer in Inter-racial Work," all in *Missionary Voice* (Feb. 1930), pp. 14–16, 31, 36; Tatum, *Crown of Service*, pp. 30–31, 37–38, 40.

114. [?] to Hope, n.d., NU Papers.

115. *Southern Negro Women and Race Co-operation* (Atlanta: Southeastern Federation of Colored Women's Clubs, 1921); Lugenia Hope to Mrs. Archibald Davis, Mar. 1, 1921, NU Papers. One version of this statement is reprinted in Lerner, *Black Women*, pp. 461–67.

116. Lugenia Hope to Charlotte Hawkins Brown, Feb. 12, 1921; Margaret Washington to Lugenia Hope, July 27, 1920, NU Papers.

117. Lugenia Hope to Charlotte Hawkins Brown, Feb. 12, 1921, NU Papers.

118. Lugenia Hope to Mrs. Archibald Davis, Mar. 1, 1921; Janie Porter Barrett to Lugenia Hope, Apr. 2, 1921; Carrie Parks Johnson to Lugenia Hope, Feb. 13, 1921, Mar. 12, 1927, NU Papers; Minutes, Continuation Committee, Mar. 28, 1921, CIC Papers.

119. Lugenia Hope to Mrs. Archibald Davis, Mar. 1, 1921, NU Papers.

120. "Background [of Memphis Conference]," Ames Papers (NC); Lugenia Hope to Carrie Parks Johnson, June 24, 1921, NU Papers.

121. Lugenia Hope to Carrie Parks Johnson, June 24, 1921, note by Louise Shivery in margin; W. O. Brown, "Interracial Cooperation"; Wilson Record, "Intellectuals in Social and Racial Movements," in Sternsher, ed., *Negro in Depression and War*, pp. 282–95; Lugenia Hope to Carrie Parks Johnson, June 24, 1921, NU Papers.

122. Lugenia Hope to Mrs. Archibald Davis, Mar. 1, 1921, NU Papers.

123. For organizational problems in including black women see: Minutes, Texas Woman's Committee Meeting, Dallas, Texas, Sept. 27, 1922; "High Points," Woman's General Committee, CIC, Nov. 19, 1928; JDA to Mrs. W. A. Newell, Sept. 7, 1929, Ames Papers (NC); Carrie Parks Johnson to Members, Woman's General Committee, Mar. 10, 1925, NU Papers; Woman's Committee Meeting, July 12–14, 1924, CIC Papers. By 1923 there were 800 official CIC local committees in the South. No figures are available on the sexual and racial composition of these groups.

124. Report of Informal Conference of State Leaders, Feb. 18–20, 1924, Ames Papers (NC); Eleazer, "Southern Women Against the Mob," p. 129.

125. Report of Director of Woman's Work, July 15, 1924, NU Papers.

126. Johnson Address, CIC Meeting, Nov. 17, 1920, CIC Papers.

127. "Findings of Women's State Committees on Lynchings and Womanhood," ASWPL Papers.

128. C. H. Brown, "Mrs. Hope in the National Scene," Brown Papers; Murray, *Proud Shoes* and "The Liberation of Black Women." Gutman, in *The Black Family*, pp. 386–402, discusses the analogous efforts of the ex-slaves during Reconstruction to outlaw concubinage while at the same time legalizing interracial marriage.

129. Minutes, CIC Meeting, Oct. 7, 1921, Ames Papers (NC). Typical of black CIC leaders was Marion B. Wilkinson of South Carolina, whom black and white observers alike described as "every inch a lady . . . queenly in her carriage, very very refined." Wright Interview; Modjeska Simkins Interview.

130. Johnson Address, CIC, Nov. 17, 1920; Church Woman's Conference, June 10–11, 1933; Report of the Director of Woman's Work to the CIC An-

nual Meeting, Oct. 1921; For the concept of "tilting up the color line" see Gunnar Myrdal, et al., eds., *An American Dilemma*, II, 689–93; Robert E. Park, "The Bases of Race Prejudice," in *Annals of the American Academy of Political and Social Science*, 40 (Nov. 1928), 20; Powdermaker, *After Freedom*; W.E.B. Du Bois, *Dusk of Dawn*; Frazier, *Black Bourgeoisie*; and Davis, Gardner, and Gardner, *Deep South*. For racial solidarity among organized black women, see Meier, *Negro Thought in America*, p. 135.

131. Minutes, Woman's Committee, Oct. 20–21, 1922, NU Papers; Report to CIC on First Year of Woman's Work, Oct. 7, 1921, Ames Papers (NC). See Charlotte Hawkins Brown, *Mammy: An Appeal to the Heart of the South* (Boston: Pilgrim Press, 1919), for the way in which the appeals of black leaders could reinforce white stereotypes.

132. Janie Porter Barrett, "The Negro Home," Nov. 15, 1921, CIC Papers.

133. Church Woman's Conference, June 10–11, 1933, CIC Papers.

134. For other examples see Minutes, Georgia Committee, Feb. 24, 1925, CIC Papers; Johnson [?] to Maude Henderson, May 5, 1927, Ames Papers (NC); Minutes, Woman's Section, Georgia State Committee, n.d. [1921], CIC Papers; Ralph J. Bunche, "The Problems, Ideologies, Tactics and Achievements of Negro Betterment and Interracial Organizations," Memorandum prepared for the Carnegie-Myrdal Study of the Negro in America, Schomburg Collection, New York Public Library, esp. pp. 461–81. Hoffman, "Genesis of the Modern Movement for Equal Rights," pp. 198–99. See Johnson Address, National Convention, YWCA, Apr. 24, 1922, CIC Papers and Church Woman's Conference, June 10–11, 1933, CIC Papers, for unresponsiveness of white leaders to black criticism.

135. Wright Interview; Simkins Interview.

136. Newell, *Handbook for Interracial Committees*. These efforts can be traced in the *Annual Reports* of the Woman's Missionary Council.

137. Quotations are from Lumpkin Interview. [Carrie Meares], "Historical Outline of Interracial Education and Race Relations in the National Student Council of the Y.W.C.A."; "Memo to the Sub-Committee on Race of the National Student Council From Frances Williams," Hamilton Papers; Winifred Wygal, "Juliette Derricotte, Her Character and Her Martyrdom," *Crisis*, 39 (Mar. 1932), 84–86; James, ed., *Notable American Women*, I, 214–15; Lerner, *Black Women*, pp. 479, 485, 487; Lumpkin, *Making of a Southerner*, pp. 211–29; Elizabeth Ross Haynes to Lugenia Hope, Jan. 26, 1925; Minutes, Apr. 6, 1920, NU Papers; Scott, *Southern Lady*, pp. 191–93.

138. [Meares], "Historical Outline," Hamilton Papers. These developments can be traced in the *Interracial News Bulletins* of the National Student Council, YWCA Papers. Among the young men who, in Frances Williams' words, "hit the sawdust trail" in the southern student movement were Myles Horton, founder of Highlander Folk School, and Howard Kester, a founder of the Southern Tenant Farmers Union and the Fellowship of Southern Churchmen. The autonomy of local YWCA branches makes it difficult to assess the relationship between the attitudes of regional and national leaders and local members. Particularly in the South, national field representatives handpicked delegates to conferences on the basis of their racial and economic attitudes, so that Southern Student Council members were far from represen-

tative of the student groups from which they came. From their own perspective, there is no question of the influence of the YWCA experience on a small cadre of student leaders, but the organization—like other interracial groups—made little headway in affecting racial attitudes and practices in general. After World War II, the "Y" responded to the beginnings of the modern civil rights movement by endorsing the Fair Employment Practices Commission (FEPC) and unanimously adopting an "Interracial Charter" calling for the integration of black women into "the mainstream of association life." Sara Evans, in "Women's Consciousness and the Southern Black Movement," argues that when the direct action movement began in the 1960s, it touched a "chord of moral idealism" among southern white students fostered over the years in student religious groups like the YWCA. See also Bell and Wilkins, *Interracial Practices in Community YWCA's;* "Confidential Report of Meeting to Discuss the Objectives of the Y.W.C.A. considered in Relation to its interracial work," YWCA Papers.

139. Myrdal, *American Dilemma,* II, 847.

140. "Report of Informal Conference of State Leaders . . . ," Feb. 18–20, 1924, NU Papers; Woman's General Committee Meeting, July 10, 1924, CIC Papers; Carrie Parks Johnson to JDA, June 10, 1924, Ames Papers (NC).

141. Quotation is from Church Woman's Conference, June 10–11, 1933, CIC Papers. Minutes, Annual Meeting, Woman's General Committee, Apr. 21, 1925, Ames Papers (NC); "Report of Informal Conference of State Leaders," Feb. 18–20, 1924; Minutes, Woman's Committee, Apr. 8, 1926, NU Papers; JDA Interview.

142. Johnson, "The Business of Peace"; *Fourteenth Annual Report of The Woman's Missionary Council of the Methodist Episcopal Church, South, for 1923–1924, Nashville, Tenn.;* Woman's General Committee Meeting, July, 1924, CIC Papers. For the cultural context formed by the nineteenth-century assignation of feminine virtues to Christ and of Christlike natures to women, see Welter, "Feminization of American Religion," and Douglas, *Feminization of American Culture.*

143. Cott, *Bonds of Womanhood,* p. 1.

144. JDA to Carrie Parks Johnson, Feb. 13, 1924, Ames Papers (NC).

Chapter 4: The Double Role

1. Alva Myrdal and Viola Klein, *Women's Two Roles: Home and Work* (London: Routledge and Paul, 1956).

2. Quotations are from JDA to Carrie Parks Johnson, Dec. 4, and Sept. 17, 1924, Ames Papers (NC). See also JDA to Mrs. Newell, Apr. 8, 1929, Ames Papers (NC). Among Ames's readings in this period were the NAACP's jour-

nal, *The Crisis; The Negro in Chicago; A Study of Race Relations and a Race Riot by the Chicago Commission on Race Relations* (Chicago: University of Chicago Press, 1922); George E. Haynes, *The Trend of the Races* (New York: Council of Women for Home Missions, 1922); and Woofter, *The Basis of Racial Adjustment.* Her library was eventually donated to the Cody Memorial Library, Southwestern University, Georgetown, Texas.

3. Virginia Kelly to JDA, May 14, 1927; Jessie Daniel Ames, "Report," n.d. [Oct. 1924]; E. M. Castleberry to JDA, May 10, 1923, Ames Papers (NC); Dallas *Morning News,* Dec. 17 and Nov. 29, 1926.

4. Ibid.; Dallas *Morning News,* Nov. 2, 1929. See also JDA to Virginius Dabney, Apr. 2, 1942, quoted in Morton Phillip Sosna, "In Search of the Silent South: White Southern Racial Liberalism, 1929–1950" (Ph.D. diss., University of Wisconsin, 1972), p. 6. Significantly, the press, in reporting Ames's speech, elevated her passing disavowal of the goal of "amalgamation" to headline status.

5. Quotations are from JDA to Lillian Smith, Dec. 30, 1941; undated, unsigned MS written by Ames [1940]; and JDA to Carrie Parks Johnson, Feb. 13, 1924, Ames Papers (NC). In 1929, at least one member of the CIC Woman's Committee objected to Ames's appointment as Director of Woman's Work on the grounds that she was not sufficiently pious. Nevertheless, in the secondary literature on the Anti-Lynching Association, Ames is often referred to as a "church woman." JDA Interview; Minutes, Membership Committee, Woman's Committee, CIC, Sept. 21, 1929, NU Papers.

6. Quotations are from JDA to Carrie Parks Johnson, Dec. 4 and Jan. 31, 1924. See also, Minutes, Texas Woman's Committee Meeting, Dallas, Sept. 27, 1922, Ames Papers (NC).

7. Ames received $200 a month plus expenses for her work. JDA Interview; Carrie Parks Johnson to JDA, Jan. 26, 1924; JDA to Johnson, Jan. 31, 1924; Minutes, Woman's General Committee, CIC, July 12–14, 1924; Report of Director of Woman's Work, July 15, 1924, CIC Papers; JDA to Johnson, Aug. 25, Sept. 8, and Sept. 17, 1924, Ames Papers (NC).

8. Minutes, Committee on Woman's Work, Texas CIC, Oct. 23, 1924; Johnson to JDA, Aug. 8, 1924; JDA to Johnson, Aug. 25, and Sept. 8, 1924, Ames Papers (NC); Minutes, Woman's General Committee, CIC, Asheville, North Carolina, July 12–14, 1924; Report of Director of Woman's Work, July 15, 1924, CIC Papers.

9. JDA to Carrie Parks Johnson, Apr. 24, 1924; JDA to Johnson, Feb. 22, 1924, Ames Papers (NC).

10. JDA to Carrie Parks Johnson, Apr. 24, 1924, Ames Papers (NC).

11. Jackson, *Ku Klux Klan,* pp. 244–45; JDA to Will Alexander, Sept. 24, 1924; JDA, "Report," n.d., Ames Papers (NC).

12. Dallas *Journal,* May 5, and May 9, 1925; Dallas *Morning News,* Oct. 28, 1926; JDA, "Report" n.d.; Carrie Parks Johnson to JDA, Oct. 2, 1924, Ames Papers (NC).

13. "Legislation," [1927]; JDA to Mrs. W. A. Newell, Apr. 8, 1929, Ames Papers (NC). The interest of CIC women in homes for delinquent black girls

represented a drive for social control that could have repressive effects. See David Rothman, *The Discovery of the Asylum: Social Order and Disorder in the New Republic* (Boston: Little, Brown, 1971) for a discussion of the development of such institutions in the nineteenth century. For Ames's (and the CIC's) continuing concern for "training schools," see JDA to Eleanor Roosevelt, Mar. 28, 1941; Miss Malvina C. Thompson to JDA, Apr. 1, 1941; JDA to Thompson, Apr. 1, 1941, Eleanor Roosevelt Papers. Other projects undertaken by Ames were the building of a tuberculosis hospital, reorganization of the state Department of Health to provide more services for blacks, and the adoption of black history textbooks. M. E. O'Neill to JDA, Apr. 26, 1929; Minutes of the Inter-Racial Commission, Dallas, Texas, Apr. 29, 1929, Ames Papers (NC).

14. Quotations are from Williamson County *Sun,* July 1, 1915, Aug. 5, 1915, June 30, 1922, and Aug. 26, 1921. See also Williamson County *Sun,* Mar. 28, 1918. Oct. 14, 1921, Nov. 4, 1921, Jan. 6, 1922, Mar. 3, 1922, Jan. 27, 1922, June 30, 1922 and Aug. 17, 1923.

15. McKeithen Interview; Anonymous, n.d. [1926], Priv. Coll.; JDA to Mary McLeod Bethune, Mar. 6, and Mar. 9, 1938, ASWPL Papers.

16. JDA Interview; JDA to Rev. Joseph Patrick Lynch, May 31, 1926, Ames Papers (NC).

17. "Legislation," [1927], Ames Papers (NC).

18. Williamson County *Sun,* July 28, 1922, May 27, 1921, July 15, 1921, July 29, 1921, Aug. 12, 1921, Aug. 26, 1921, Sept. 2, 1921, Oct. 7, 1921, Oct. 14, 1921, May 12, 1922, Dec. 15, 1922, Jan. 19, 1923, and Feb. 2, 1928.

19. Alexander, *Crusade for Conformity,* pp. 21–26; [JDA], "Moody-Beaumont," 1928, Ames Papers (Austin).

20. Alexander, *Crusade for Conformity,* pp. 55–56; Dallas *Morning News,* June 26, and June 30, 1924. Fort Worth *Star-Telegram,* June 26, 1924; Frank King to JDA, July 9, 1924, Priv. Coll.

21. Alexander, *Crusade for Conformity,* p. 63.

22. JDA Interview. See also JDA to V. O. Key, n.d., ASWPL Papers.

23. JDA to Dan Moody, Mar. 5, 1926, Dan Moody Papers, Texas State Library, Austin, Texas; JDA to Will Alexander, Oct. 4, 1924, Ames Papers; McCallum Diary, Mar. 13, 1926, McCallum Family Papers. See also Louise Moyer Jackson to author, n.d.

24. A. B. Wilson to Dan Moody Headquarters, Austin, July 13, 1926, Moody Papers.

25. The candidacy of Alfred E. Smith posed a dilemma for dry progressives like Jessie Daniel Ames. At the state convention in Beaumont on May 24, she tried to steer a middle path: on the one hand she pushed for a resolution calling for a reaffirmation of the Democratic Party's support for prohibition; on the other, she sidetracked a WCTU effort to censure Al Smith outright. She was dubious about Dan Moody's proposal for a "harmony Democrats" strategy for holding the state party together and opposed his favorite son candidacy. She believed that Moody had betrayed the principles of the progressive coalition and that the women who supported him were pawns in a game of political expediency. She backed Moody in the governor's race.

But when his prediction that the Texas delegation would vote as a unit for prohibition proved inaccurate and Al Smith won the nomination, she bolted the Democratic Party and campaigned for Herbert Hoover.

26. McCallum Diary, Dec. 21, 1926, McCallum Family Papers; Gould, *Progressives and Prohibitionists*, p. 281. There is some indication that Ames considered running for the state legislature herself at this time. See Williamson County *Sun*, Feb. 12, 1926.

27. Ruth Potts Spence Interview; Cunningham, "Too Gallant a Walk."

28. Austin *American-Statesman*, Oct. 3, 1971; JDA to Mrs. League, June 13, 1918, Cunningham Papers; Minnie Fisher Cunningham to Jane Y. McCallum, n.d. [1921], McCallum Family Papers; JDA to Cunningham, July 13, 1918, Cunningham Papers.

29. Spence Interview; Minnie Fisher Cunningham to Jane Y. McCallum, n.d. [1921], McCallum Family Papers.

30. Frank King to My Dear General, July 9, 1924; [JDA], "Daniel-Ames Family Life," Priv. Coll.

31. JDA to Carrie Parks Johnson, Nov. 8, 1924; JDA, "Report," n.d.; JDA to Johnson, June 19, 1924; JDA to Will Alexander, Oct. 4, 1924, Ames Papers (NC); JDA Interview; JDA to Johnson, Mar. 18, 1924, Ames Papers (NC).

32. Minutes, Texas CIC Meeting, Nov. 6, 1925; JDA to Carrie Parks Johnson, Dec. 23, 1924, Ames Papers (NC).

33. JDA Interview; Williamson County *Sun*, June 11, 1920.

34. McKeithen Interview; JDA to Miss Louise Dietrich, Mar. 10, 1934; JDA to [?], Nov. 20, 1936, ASWPL Papers. JDA to Frederick Ames, June 30, 1936 and Feb. 22, 1939, Priv. Coll. Quotations are from JDA to Frederick Ames, June 28, 1945 and [JDA], "Memories," Priv. Coll.

35. JDA to Carrie Parks Johnson, Jan. 31, 1924, Ames Papers (NC). See also JDA to Johnson, Oct. 31, 1924, Ames Papers (NC).

36. JDA to Lulu Ames, Aug. 15, 1949, Priv. Coll.; Mary Ames Raffensperger Interview. See also JDA to Mrs. Alex W. Spence, Nov. 27, 1935; JDA to Mrs. T. B. Neblett, Dec. 4, 1935, ASWPL Papers; JDA to Mrs. W. A. Newell, Dec. 4, 1935 and Nov. 20, 1936, Ames Papers (NC); JDA to Mrs. Fath, Apr. 9, 1940, CIC Papers.

37. JDA to Frederick Ames, June 15, 1945, Priv. Coll. Ames's children did, in fact, live up to her high expectations of accomplishment; despite these tensions, Ames felt she had "succeeded" as a mother. Her son Frederick was graduated from Harvard Medical School and practiced medicine in Houston, Texas, until his death from cancer in 1956. Her daughter Mary was graduated from the University of Pennsylvania Medical School and became Professor of Pediatrics and Director of Ambulatory Services of the Children's Hospital of Philadelphia. She is a feminist and feels that the "current women's movement ties me much closer to mother than any of the other of her activities." Mary Ames Raffensperger to Lulu Ames, Mar. 5, 1973, Priv. Coll. Lulu Ames was graduated from Agnes Scott College, became a freelance newspaper reporter, and owned and managed the *Capital Report Service* in Austin. The extremely conflictive relationship between Ames and her three children is documented in voluminous family correspondence. See for example, Lulu Ames Interview; JDA to Frederick Ames, June 25, 1927, Oct. 29, 1951, Oct. 16, 1945,

Oct. 16, 1945 (not sent), Oct. 28, 1945, Oct. 30, 1945, Nov. 12, 1945, Priv. Coll.

38. Lulu Ames Interview; JDA Interview.

39. JDA to Mrs. W. A. Newell, Apr. 8, 1929, Ames Papers (NC). It is typical of Ames's rigorous separation of her public from her private life that the emotional and physical trials of these years left no trace in the public record of her career. Two remarkably complementary sets of personal documents, however, provide glimpses into the anguish of family life. A series of contemporary letters reflect Ames's desperate search for the key to her daughter's recovery. In a lengthy autobiography written twenty years later, Lulu Ames sought to capture the perspective of a crippled child and to come to terms with the impact of her illness both on her mother and on herself.

40. Quotations are from Lulu Ames interview; JDA to Dr. W. B. Carroll, June 9, 1923, Priv. Coll. See also JDA to Dr. John McCelvey, Dec. 28, 1920; JDA to Dr. J. Spencer Davis, Jan. 31, 1921; Davis to JDA, Feb. 2, 1921; JDA to Aunt Annie [Dr. Annie Sturges Daniel], Mar. 18, 1921, Priv. Coll; JDA to Mrs. Rex Forster, May 7, 1940, CIC Papers.

41. J. M. Woodson to JDA, May 19, 1921; JDA to Dr. Claude C. Cody, July 15, 1921; JDA to Woodson, May 17, 1921; JDA to Cody, Mar. 7, 1921; JDA to Aunt Annie, Mar. 10, 1921; Cody to JDA, Mar. 19, 1921; JDA to Cody, Apr. 8, 1921; JDA to Mr. Devore, Aug. 6, 1923; JDA to Dr. W. B. Carroll, Aug. 16, 1922; Carroll to JDA, Aug. 9, 1922; JDA to Carroll, Aug. 21, 1922, Priv. Coll.

42. JDA to Aunt Annie, Mar. 18, 1921; JDA to Claude C. Cody, Nov. 29, 1921, Priv. Coll.

43. Quotation is from JDA to Dr. W. B. Carroll, Nov. 6, 1923, Priv. Coll. Carroll to JDA, Nov. 5, 1923; JDA to Carroll, Nov. 7, 1923; Hella Tempel Children's Hospital, Information and Instructions, n.d., Priv. Coll.

44. JDA to Dr. W. B. Carroll, Jan. 5, 1924, Priv. Coll.

45. Lulu Ames, untitled, undated autobiography; JDA to Aunt Annie, Sept. 8, 1924, Priv. Coll.

46. Lulu Daniel Ames Interview.

47. Lulu Ames autobiography, Priv. Coll.; Lulu Ames Interview. Lulu sought to rationalize her feelings for her mother under the rubric of John Dollard's concept of "frustration and aggression." Frustrated in her attempt to achieve complete normality, she became aggressively hostile toward her mother. See for example, Lulu Ames to JDA, June 15, 1940, [June 28], 1940, June 30, 1940, July 2, 1940, Priv. Coll. Later, she came to believe that her mother in fact had been the source of much of her frustration. In psychoanalytic terms, Lulu seems to have been troubled all her life by a radical confusion of ego-boundaries, an inability to differentiate herself from her mother. The result was an unresolved combination of dependence and hostility. For a discussion of the prevalence of this issue of ego-boundaries in mother-daughter relationships, see Chodorow, "Family Structure and Feminine Personality," pp. 43–66.

48. Quotations are from Rebecca Gershon Interview; Lulu Ames Interview. Lash, *Eleanor and Franklin*, pp. 259–64, 265–76. For a sensitive exploration of the power and oppressiveness of motherhood, see Adrienne

Rich, *Of Woman Born: Motherhood as Experience and Institution* (New York: Norton, 1976).

49. Quotation is from JDA to Mrs. Julia [Collier] Harris, Sept. 17, 1935, ASWPL Papers. JDA to Mrs. J. W. Mills, Oct. 30, 1935, ASWPL Papers.

50. Alexander Interview; Dykeman and Stokely, *Seeds of Southern Change*, p. 116.

51. JDA to Carrie Parks Johnson, Sept. 8, 1924, Ames Papers (NC).

52. JDA Interview; Dykeman and Stokely, *Seeds of Southern Change*, p. 116.

53. Raper Interview; Dykeman and Stokely, *Seeds of Southern Change*, p. 116; Ruth Spence to author, Dec. 30, 1973; Gershon Interview; Alice Spearman Wright Interview. No direct written evidence of Alexander's and Eleazer's attitudes toward Ames seems to have survived. This account of intrastaff friction reflects primarily Ames's point of view, as confirmed by interviews with both her supporters and detractors, including the only surviving male CIC staff member, Arthur F. Raper.

54. JDA Interview. See also Juanita Brown to JDA, Jan. 3, 1944; JDA to Brown, Jan. 6, 1944, CIC Papers; JDA to Mrs. W. A. Newell, Sept. 7, 1929, Ames Papers (NC). Under Ames's direction, the Texas Interracial Commission had eliminated separate men's and women's committees and had conducted its annual meetings as an integrated group.

55. JDA Interview; Minutes, Membership Committee, Committee on Woman's Work, CIC, Sept. 21, 1929, NU Papers.

56. "High Points," 1928, NU Papers.

57. Mrs. W. C. Winsborough to JDA, Oct. 14, 1929, CIC Papers. See also Minutes, Woman's General Committee, CIC, Oct. 19, 1928, Ames Papers (NC). The Federal Council Commission had its genesis in a conference of southern church leaders in Blue Ridge, North Carolina, sponsored by the CIC and in the CIC Woman's Conference in Memphis in 1920. Formed in 1921 and headed by the black sociologist George E. Haynes, its purpose was "to promote the cause of better race relations in the denominations represented in the Federal Council." Focusing its activities chiefly on the North, the Federal Council also worked with church groups in the South, particularly in the larger cities, thus potentially overlapping and competing with the CIC both in program and constituency. Baker, *Negro-White Adjustment*, pp. 24–27.

58. Mary McLeod Bethune to JDA, Oct. 18, 1929; JDA to Mrs. W. C. Winsborough, Oct. 14, 1929; Mrs. W. A. Newell to JDA, Oct. 19, 1929; Mrs. C. P. McGowan to JDA, Oct. 19, 1929, CIC Papers; JDA to Mrs. John Hope, Oct. 15, 1929, NU Papers.

59. *Twentieth Annual Report of the Woman's Missionary Council of the Methodist Episcopal Church, South, 1920–1930, Nashville, Tenn.; Twenty-Third Annual Report of the Woman's Missionary Council of the Methodist Episcopal Church South, 1933, Nashville, Tenn.*

60. [Meanes], "Historical Outline of Interracial Education."

61. JDA, "Whither Leads the Mob," p. 20.

Chapter 5: A Strange and Bitter Fruit

1. This account of the incident is from Raper, *Tragedy of Lynching*, pp. 319–55.

2. Cutler, *Lynch-Law*, p. 29. Other historical studies of vigilantism and lynching include: Richard Maxwell Brown, *South Carolina Regulators* (Cambridge: Harvard University Press, 1963); Shay, *Judge Lynch;* Myrdal, et al., eds., *American Dilemma*, II, 529–34, 558–69, 676–83; Baker, *Following the Color Line*, pp. 175–215; White, *Rope and Faggot*. For bibliographical information, see D. T. Williams, comp., *Eight Negro Bibliographies*, pp. 16–39.

3. For the concept of "establishment violence," see H. Jon Rosenbaum and Peter C. Sederberg, "Vigilantism: An Analysis of Establishment Violence," in Rosenbaum and Sederberg, eds., *Vigilante Politics*, pp. 3–29. The authors offer a typology of vigilantism, which they define as "the use of violence by established groups to preserve the status quo at times when the formal system of rule enforcement is viewed as ineffective or irrelevant." They differentiate between "crime control," "social group control," and "regime control" vigilantism and offer a number of hypotheses about the conditions likely to produce vigilante action, as well as about the effects of vigilantism on the creation and maintenance of a stable sociopolitical order.

4. Anti-abolitionist mobs, whose victims were primarily white men, increased markedly after 1830. See Leonard L. Richard, *"Gentlemen of Property and Standing": Anti-Abolition Mobs in Jacksonian America* (New York: Oxford University Press, 1970), pp. 7, 13–14; Eaton, *Freedom-of-Thought Struggle*, pp. 376–78, and "Mob Violence in the Old South." No statistics are available on the lynching of blacks in the antebellum period, although several authors suggest that they composed approximately 10 percent of mob victims. Cash, *Mind of the South*, p. 45; Eaton, "Mob Violence," p. 369. See also, Kenneth M. Stampp, *The Peculiar Institution: Slavery in the Ante-Bellum South* (New York: Random House, 1956), pp. 190–91; Jordan, *White Over Black*, pp. 121, 473; Ulrich Bonnell Phillips, *American Negro Slavery* (New York: Peter Smith, 1952), pp. 460–63.

5. Carter, "Anatomy of Fear." There is a wealth of literature on slave revolts and slave conspiracy scares, but little comparable work has been done on the post-emancipation panics that gave rise to lynchings and pogroms against the black community.

6. Quotation is from John Hope Franklin, *From Slavery to Freedom: A History of Negro Americans* (New York: Random House, 1969), p. 327. The thirteen-volume record of an 1871 congressional investigation contains thousands of instances of physical violence perpetrated against the freedmen and their white Republican allies by such terrorist groups as the Ku Klux Klan, the Knights of the White Camellia, and the Red Shirts. U.S. Congress, House, Joint Select Committee to Inquire into the Condition of Affairs in the Late Insurrectionary States, *Affairs in the Late Insurrectionary States*, H. Rept. 22, 42d Cong., 2d Sess., 1872. The first full-scale, scholarly study of

this white supremacist reaction to growing black power was not published until one hundred years later. See Trelease, *White Terror*. See also, W. E. B. Du Bois, *Black Reconstruction, 1860–1880* (New York: Harcourt Brace, 1935); Otis Singletary, *Black Militia and Reconstruction* (Austin: University of Texas, 1957); Williamson, *After Slavery*.

7. This account of the Populist movement is based on Goodwyn, *Democratic Promise*. For the transitional period, see also Woodward, *Origins of the New South*.

8. Goodwyn, *Democratic Promise*, pp. 292, 657; William H. Chafe, "The Negro and Populism: A Kansas Case Study," *Journal of Southern History*, 34 (Aug. 1968), 402–19, reprinted in Robert C. Twombly, ed., *Blacks in White America since 1865: Issues and Interpretations* (New York: David McKay, 1971), pp. 139–55.

9. Work, ed., *Negro Year Book*, p. 293. Of this number, 100 were white and 155 were black. In 1893, the total number of lynch victims declined to 201, but the number of black victims remained constant.

10. Inverarity, "Populism and Lynching in Louisiana." For a critique of Inverarity's thesis, see Whitney Pope and Charles Ragin, "Mechanical Solidarity, Repressive Justice, and Lynchings in Louisiana: Comment on Inverarity," *American Sociological Review*, 42 (Apr. 1977), 363–68. For examples of explicitly political antiblack violence, see William Holmes, "The Arkansas Cotton Pickers' Strike of 1891 and the Demise of the Colored Farmers' Alliance," *Arkansas Historical Quarterly*, 32 (Summer 1973), 107–19 and "The Leflore County Massacre and the Demise of the Colored Farmers' Alliance," *Phylon*, 34 (Sept. 1973), 267–74; Goodwyn, "Populist Dreams and Negro Rights"; Woodward, *Origins of the New South*, p. 63.

11. Goodwyn, *Democratic Promise*, p. 306; McLaurin, *Paternalism and Protest*, pp. xvi, xviii, 61–67; Holmes, "Whitecapping."

12. Van den Berghe, *Race and Racism*, pp. 25–37, offers this "typology of racism." Under slavery, he argues, role and status were sharply and securely defined along racial lines. As paternalism gave way to competition between the subordinate race and the working class of the dominant race, the latter joined the upper class in a "Herrenvolk democracy" in which the exercise of power was restricted, de facto, and increasingly de jure, to whites only.

13. O'Malley, "The Salisbury Lynching" (M.A. thesis), pp. 24–34, 44; Dew, "Lynching of 'Boll Weevil.' " George Hughes, for example, was an itinerant laborer who had been in the community only a few months. Five of the persons lynched in 1930 were considered "outsiders" by local Negroes. Raper, *Tragedy of Lynching*, pp. 3–4, 329. Quotation is from Ralph Ellison, "Richard Wright's Blues," in Ellison, *Shadow and Act*, p. 100.

14. For racist ideology, see Frederickson, *Black Image in the White Mind*, pp. 256–83.

15. Raper, *Tragedy of Lynching*, pp. 25, 480–83; and Gutman, *Black Family*, pp. 531–38; Hofstadter and Wallace, eds., *American Violence*, p. 20; Woodward, *Origins of the New South*, p. 252. Yearly rates for lynchings since 1882 are available in Work, *Negro Year Book*, published annually from 1912 to 1956. No editions appeared for 1920–21, 1923–24, 1927–28, 1928–29, 1929–30. Cumulative statistics through 1968 can be found in Williams, *Eight Negro Bibliographies*, pp. 6–15. The other major source for the period

1889–1946 is the NAACP's *Thirty Years of Lynching* and "Supplements." Incidents cited by Tuskegee and by the NAACP vary somewhat. The earliest systematic attempt to collect lynching statistics was that of the Chicago *Tribune*, 1882–1903. All such statistics are approximate at best, since southern newspapers and court records often made no distinction between homicides and lynchings.

16. Harris, "Culture of Catastrophe" (unpublished paper). According to a black anti-lynching tract published in 1892: "The Associated Press, that agent so powerful for the enlightenment of the public and the formation of public opinion, gives its assent to murder by branding the victims [of lynching] with vile epithets, and many sleep in bloody graves, stigmatized as 'black fiends,' 'negro monsters' and the like, who with fair trials might have gone free." "To the Colored People of the United States," Mar. 1892, Albion W. Tourgée Papers, quoted in Gerber, "Lynching and Law and Order," p. 41.

17. In his critique of Robert William Fogel and Stanley L. Engerman, *Time on the Cross: The Economics of American Negro Slavery* (Boston: Little, Brown, 1974), Herbert G. Gutman makes an illuminating comparison between the significance of whippings on antebellum plantations and of lynchings in the post–Civil War period. Fogel and Engerman claim that on a given plantation an average slave received only 0.7 whippings per each year, and they use this calculation to support their thesis regarding the relative mildness of slave treatment. The more important figure, Gutman points out, is that slaves *observed* someone being whipped on the plantation every four and one half days. If one expressed the rate of lynchings in Fogel and Engerman's form, only 0.00002 lynchings per black occurred in 1893. Such a statistical formulation, Gutman emphasizes, would completely obscure the import of the 155 lynchings of blacks that occurred in that year. Thomas L. Haskell, "The True and Tragical History of 'Time on the Cross,' " *New York Review of Books*, Oct. 2, 1975, pp. 33–39. Quotation is from Wright, *Black Boy*, p. 190.

18. See, for example, Butterfield, *Black Autobiography in America;* Fiedler, *Love and Death in the American Novel;* Levine, *Black Culture and Black Consciousness*, pp. 206–319; W.E.B. Du Bois, *Dusk of Dawn*, pp. 29, 55–56, 67–68, 95, 223, 241, 251, 264–66.

19. Van den Berghe, *Race and Racism*, pp. 34–41; Goodwyn, *Democratic Promise*, pp. vii–xxvii, 515–56; Rosenbaum and Sederberg, *Vigilante Politics*, pp. 3–4. Recent studies of American violence, inspired for the most part by the civil disorders of the 1960s, include: Brown, *Strain of Violence;* T. Rose, ed., *Violence in America;* Hofstadter and Wallace, eds., *American Violence;* and Hugh Davis Graham and Ted Robert Gurr, eds., *Violence in America: Historical and Comparative Perspectives, A Report to the National Commission on the Causes and Prevention of Violence* (Washington, D.C.: U.S. Government Printing Office, 1969).

20. Steelman, "A Study of Mob Action in the South" (Ph.D diss.); Young, "The Relation of Lynching to the Size of Population Areas"; Wimpy, "Mob Lynching Lynches the Law" and "Lynching: An Evil of County Government." A study done by T. J. Woofter for the CIC's Southern Commission on the Study of Lynching found a high correlation between the per acre value of cotton and lynching during the period 1900 to 1930. Omitting the three years of high racial violence during World War I, his data indicated an increase in

lynchings during periods of agricultural depression and a decrease during periods of prosperity. See Raper, *Tragedy of Lynching*, pp. 30–31, for Woofter's thesis. More recent quantitative studies have tended to bear Woofter out. Carl Iver Hovland and Robert R. Sears, using data for 14 states during the period 1882 to 1930, found an even higher correlation between declines in per acre value of cotton and rises in lynching than Woofter had indicated; "Minor Studies of Aggression: VI Correlations of Lynchings with Economic Indices," in Grimshaw, ed., *Racial Violence*, pp. 344–49. But criticizing Hovland and Sears for using deviations from trends in their correlations rather than actual numbers of lynchings or the value of cotton, Alexander Metztz found a much lower correlation than either Woofter or Hovland and Sears; "A Re-Examination of Correlations Between Lynchings and Economic Indices," in Grimshaw, *Racial Violence*, pp. 349–53. Tannenbaum, *Darker Phases of the South*, pp. 20–27; White, *Rope and Faggot*, pp. 19–21, 304. For "percent black" as an explanatory variable, see Hubert Blalock, *Toward a Theory of Minority-Group Relations* (New York: Wiley, 1967), p. 159, and John Shelton Reed, "Percent Black and Lynching: A Test of Blalock's Theory," *Social Forces*, 50 (Mar. 1972), 356–60.

21. T. W. Adorno, et al., *The Authoritarian Personality* (New York: Harper, 1950); Gordon W. Allport, *The Nature of Prejudice* (Cambridge, Mass.: Addison-Wesley, 1954); Dollard, et al., *Frustration and Aggression;* Cantril, *Psychology of Social Movements;* Goldstein, *Roots of Prejudice.* As Pierre van den Berghe, *Race and Racism*, points out, the problem with these hypotheses is that within a society in which racism is the official norm, personality factors such as "authoritarianism" lose their predictive value. There is, he argues, "unquestionably a psychopathology of racism but in racist societies most racists are not 'sick.' "

22. Raper, *Tragedy of Lynching*, pp. 3–13, 27–30. See also Raper, "Race and Class Pressures" (unpublished MS.), for a study of the lynchings that occurred between 1929 and 1940; Southern Commission on the Study of Lynching, *Lynchings and What They Mean*, p. 31; Chadbourn, *Lynching and the Law*, p. 4. Similarly, the notoriously high homicide rate in the region varies inversely with the proportion of blacks in the population.

23. Cutler, *Lynch Law*, p. 276. In 1937, the major anti-lynching reform organizations agreed upon a revised definition of lynching as "death . . . at the hands of a group acting under the pretext of service to justice, race, or tradition." Ames, *Changing Character of Lynching*, p. 29.

24. Durkheim, *Division of Labor*, pp. 70–133. In Durkheim's formulation, repressive justice consists of ritual punishments "in which the whole society participates in some measure." It is characteristic of preindustrial societies, in which solidarity is maintained by the subordination of the individual to the collectivity. In heterogeneous, modern societies, law enforcement is delegated to one segment of the population and assumes the function of restitution rather than repression. The late nineteenth-century South may have been more homogeneous and less "modern" than the non-South, but it was far from Durkheim's preindustrial ideal type; on the contrary, it was undergoing the early stages of industrialization and was characterized by class and racial conflict. Moreover, lynching was perpetrated by one group against another, not by the entire biracial society against one of its members. Nevertheless, lynching was an expression of the *ideal* of white communal solidarity. An

anomaly in a modernizing society, it functioned to obscure class divisions and to demonstrate that the will toward white supremacy was indeed, as U. B. Phillips maintined, the "central theme" of southern history.

25. Ethridge, "Salesmen of Violence"; Kearney, *Slaveholder's Daughter*, pp. 95–96; Carter, *Scottsboro*, p. 114; Atlanta *Constitution*, Jan. 16, 1931.

26. Raper, "Race and Class Pressures" (unpublished MS), p. 275; Raper, *Tragedy of Lynching*, pp. 13–14, 338; Miller, "Protestant Churches and Lynching."

27. Tindall, *Emergence of the New South*, p. 618; O'Malley, "Salisbury Lynching," pp. 73–75; Gerber, "Lynching and Law and Order," p. 44; Dew, "Lynching of 'Boll Weevil,' " p. 152. See also, "Tennessee Mobilizing for Law and Order," and "Missouri Leads 1931 Lynching Parade."

28. Pickens, *Lynching and Debt Slavery*; Grant, *Anti-Lynching Movement*, pp. 6–7; Carter G. Woodson, *A Century of Negro Migration* (Washington, D.C.: Association for the Study of Negro Life and History, 1918), p. 155; Daniel, *Shadow of Slavery*.

29. Quotations are from Minutes, Association of Southern Women for the Prevention of Lynching Conference, Jan. 13–14, 1936, and untitled, undated typescript of speech by Jessie Daniel Ames [1939], ASWPL Papers. See also Ames, *Toward Lynchless America*; Raper, *Tragedy of Lynching*, pp. 56–57. Steelman, "Study of Mob Action," found the highest incidence of lynching during the summer months, especially in July.

30. Peter R. Teachout, "Louisiana Underlaw," in Friedman, ed., *Southern Justice*, p. 60; Berry, *Black Resistance/White Law*; Newby, *Black Carolinians*, pp. 65–75; O'Malley, "Salisbury Lynching," pp. 52, 63, 73.

31. Grant, *Anti-Lynching Movement*, pp. 186–95; Tannenbaum, *Darker Phases*, pp. 156–57; W.E.B. Du Bois, "A Mild Suggestion," in *Seventh Son*, II, 29–32; Tippett, "Short Cut to a Lynching."

32. Carter, "Anatomy of Fear," p. 356; Richard Wright, "The Ethics of Living Jim Crow," in *Uncle Tom's Children*, pp. 7–17; Myrdal, *American Dilemma*, II, 559; Chicago *Defender*, Apr. 5, 1919; St. Louis *Argus*, Nov. 9, 1923, reprinted in Ginzburg, *100 years of Lynching*.

33. A. Rose, *The Negro in America*, p. 185; ASWPL, *This Business of Lynching*, p. 5; Ames, *Changing Character*, p. 57.

34. Wright, "The Ethics of Living Jim Crow"; Ellison, "Richard Wright's Blues," p. 95; Wright, *Black Boy*.

35. Jessie Daniel Ames, untitled, undated MS., ASWPL Papers; Ames, *Changing Character*, p. 53. See also, Lacy, *White Use of Blacks in America*, p. 128.

36. Quotation is from Professor Lawrence Jones to JDA, July 12, 1935, ASWPL Papers. See, for example: Albert Murray, *Train Whistle Guitar* (New York: McGraw-Hill, 1974) and *Stomping the Blues* (New York: McGraw-Hill, 1976); Levine, *Black Culture*; Alice Walker, "In Search of Our Mothers' Gardens," *Southern Exposure*, 4 (Winter 1977), 60–65; W.E.B. Du Bois, *The Souls of Black Folk* (Chicago: A. C. McClurg, 1903); Hurston, *Their Eyes Were Watching God*.

37. Ellison, "Richard Wright's Blues," p. 94. For discussions of the psychology of oppression, resistance, and rebellion, see Frantz Fanon, *The*

Wretched of the Earth (New York: Grove Press, 1968) and George P. Rawick, *From Sundown to Sunup: The Making of the Black Community* (Westport, Conn.: Greenwood, 1972), pp. 95–121.

38. "Lynching at Vienna, Georgia, Sept. 28, 1935," JDA Report, ASWPL Papers. This analogy is drawn by Levine, *Black Culture*, p. 418. See also Ellison, "Richard Wright's Blues," p. 100. For a discussion of the historical tendency of both black and white southerners toward a high rate of violence against persons, see Hackney, "Southern Violence."

39. Rosengarten, *All God's Dangers*, pp. xxii, 318, 355, 571.

40. William Archer, *Through Afro-America* (London: Chapman and Hall, 1910), pp. 234 ff.; J. W. Johnson, *Autobiography of an Ex-Colored Man*, pp. 433–34; Charles Spencer Smith, *A History of the African Methodist Episcopal Church* (New York: Johnson Reprint, 1968), p. 70; Davis, et al., *Deep South*, pp. 48–49; Ames, *Changing Character*, p. 53; Interview with Richard Wright in Abraham Chapman, ed., *Black Voices: An Anthology of Afro-American Literature* (New York: New American Library, 1968), p. 542. For work in progress on black initiatives in this struggle to define the shape of southern society, see Vincent Harding, "The Black Struggle for Freedom, 1875–1914, Reflections on the Post-Reconstruction South" (unpublished paper presented at the annual meeting of the Association for the Study of Afro-American Life and History, Chicago, Ill., Oct. 30, 1976).

41. Estelle J. Humphries to [?], Oct. 27, 1934, ASWPL Papers.

42. Wascow, *From Race Riot to Sit-In* and "Public and Private Violence: 1919," in Rose, ed., *Violence in America*, pp. 158–67. For the theoretical relationship between violence and the state, see H. H. Gerth and C. Wright Mills, eds., *From Max Weber: Essays in Sociology* (New York: Oxford University Press, 1958), pp. 77–78.

43. For this distinction between culture and society, see Herbert G. Gutman, "Work, Culture, and Society in Industrializing America, 1815–1919," *American Historical Review*, 78 (June 1973), esp. 541–43. Ralph Ellison, "An American Dilemma: A Review," in Ellison, *Shadow and Act*, pp. 290–302, provides a trenchant discussion of the consequences of the growing discontinuity between the South's ideological superstructure and its economic base.

44. W.E.B. Du Bois, *Dusk of Dawn*, p. 264.

45. Frederickson, *Black Image*, p. 174. For the role of sexual tensions in American race relations, see: Jordan, *White Over Black*, p. 156; Young, *Eros Denied*; Johnston, *Race Relations . . . and Miscegenation*; Myrdal, *American Dilemma*, I, 140, II, 1213; Calvin Hernton, *Sex and Racism in America* (Garden City, N.Y.: Doubleday, 1965); Goldstein, *Roots of Prejudice*, pp. 79–93; Thorpe, *Eros and Freedom*; Dollard, *Caste and Class in a Southern Town*, pp. 134–72. Sanctions for rape have continued, to the present, to be much more severe for blacks than for whites. For example, a comparison of the punishment meted out to men convicted or rape in eleven southern states between 1945 and 1965 found that blacks were seven times more likely to be sentenced to death than whites and that a black man was eighteen times more likely to be executed for raping a white woman than a black woman. Of the national total of 455 persons executed for rape in the period 1930–68, 405 were black. Marvin E. Wolfgang and Bernard Cohen, *Crime and Race* (New York: Institute of Human Relations Press, 1970), cited

in Brownmiller, *Against Our Will*, p. 215. *National Prisoner Statistics*, no. 45 (Aug. 1969), "Capital Punishment, 1930–1968," p. 7. See also O. C. Johnson, "Is the Punishment of Rape Equally Administered to Negroes and Whites in the State of Louisiana?"; Partington, "The Incidence of the Death Penalty for Rape in Virginia."

46. Mrs. E. S. Cook to Frederick Sullens, Editor, Jackson *Daily News*, May 25, 1937, ASWPL Papers; Williamson County *Sun*, Sept. 8, 1904; Conyers (Ga.) *Times*, Nov. 27, 1931, quoted in Jessie Daniel Ames, "The Lynchers' View on Lynching," typescript of speech, 1937, Ames Papers (NC); Wells-Barnett, *On Lynchings*, pp. 10, 8–15. See also, Douglass, "Lynch Law in the South."

47. Tindall, *South Carolina Negroes*, p. 245; Gutman, *Black Family*, pp. 531–44; Wood, *Black Scare*, pp. 53–79, 130–55; Frederickson, *Black Image*, pp. 276–82; Bruce, *Plantation Negro as a Freeman*, pp. 15–28, 77–92.

48. Simkins, "Ben Tillman's View of the Negro"; Bruce, *The Plantation Negro*, pp. 83–84; Graves quoted in Dabney, *Liberalism in the South*, pp. 241–42.

49. *Forum*, 76 (Dec. 1926), 813; Jackson *Daily News*, May 27, 1937; Powdermaker, *After Freedom*, 54–55, 389. See also Williamson County *Sun*, June 23, 1922 and June 30, 1922.

50. See Fiedler, *Love and Death*, for a discussion of this theme in American literature.

51. Quoted in Rogin, *Fathers and Children*, p. 7. I am particularly indebted to Michael Paul Rogin's provocative study of Indian-white relations in the Jacksonian era for this conception of the conflict between savagery and civilization.

52. Ibid., pp. 5–9; Rawick, *Sundown to Sunup*, pp. 125–47; Jordan, *White Over Black*, pp. 3–43; Barker-Benfield, *Horrors of the Half-Known Life*; Norman O. Brown, *Life Against Death: The Psychoanalytical Meaning of History* (New York: Vintage, 1959).

53. Filene, *Him/Her/Self*, pp. 88–104; Paul Robinson, *The Modernization of Sex* (New York: Harper Colophon, 1977).

54. Dixon, *The Clansman*; Ellison, *Shadow and Act*, pp. 265–66.

55. Cash, *Mind of the South*, p. 117; Rose, ed., *Negro in America*, p. 117; NAACP, *Thirty Years of Lynching*, pp. 9–10; Raper, *Tragedy of Lynching*, p. 37.

56. Myrdal, *American Dilemma*, II, 972–73; Amir, *Patterns in Forcible Rape*. Moreover, recent studies have shown white assumptions about black family disorganization and sexual criminality to be unfounded. See, for example: Gutman, *Black Family*, pp. 382–402, 432–75; Rawick, *Sundown to Sunup*; Eugene Genovese, *Roll, Jordan, Roll: The World the Slaves Made* (New York: Random House, 1974); Carol Stack, *All Our Kin: Strategies for Survival in the Black Community* (New York: Harper and Row, 1974).

57. My reading of lynching as a "cultural text" is modeled on Clifford Geertz, "Deep Play: Notes on the Balinese Cockfight," in *The Interpretation of Cultures: Selected Essays by Clifford Geertz* (New York: Basic Books, 1973), pp. 412–53. Neil Smelser, in *Theory of Collective Behavior*, pp. 74–75, corroborates this notion of the multiple significance of lynching. On

the borderline between collective behavior and ceremonial behavior, lynching could range from a quasi-institutional form of justice to a ritualistic reaffirmation of values to a release for sexual and social tensions. Thus, he argues, its analytic definition depends on the context in which it occurs.

58. Waldemar Hille, ed., *The People's Songbook* (New York: Boni and Gaer, 1948), pp. 124–25. Billie Holiday recounts a suggestive anecdote about the reaction of white audiences to her best-selling record. The death of Holiday's father in Dallas, Texas, when he was refused medical treatment by white hospitals provided the inspiration for "Strange Fruit." The song affected her deeply, and she used its performance as a means of "flailing that audience." Nevertheless, "Strange Fruit" became one of her most popular recordings. An incident in a Los Angeles nightclub provides a glimpse into the dynamics of white audience reaction: "Billie," requested a patron, "why don't you sing that sexy song you're so famous for? You know, the one about the naked bodies swinging in the trees." "Needless to say," Holiday recalled, "I didn't." Holiday, *Lady Sings the Blues*, pp. 70–71, 86–88.

59. Conyers (Ga.) *Times*, Nov. 27, 1931. For contemporary feminist analyses of rape as a mode of masculine aggression and intimidation, see Ruth Herschberger, *Adam's Rib* (New York: Pellegrini and Cudahy, 1948), pp. 15–27; Kate Millett, *Sexual Politics* (Garden City, N.Y.: Doubleday, 1970), pp. 43–46; Brownmiller, *Against Our Will*; E. M. Curley, "Excusing Rape," *Philosophy and Public Affairs*, 5 (Summer 1976), 325–60; Marilyn Freye and Carolyn Shafer, "Rape and Respect," and Pamela Foa, "What's Wrong With Rape," in *Feminism and Philosophy*, ed. by Mary Vetterling, Frederick Elliston, and Jane English (Totowa, N.J.: Littlefield, Adams, in press). For a discussion of male hostility toward women and fear of female sexual powers, see Lederer, *Fear of Women*.

60. "Just a Floridia [*sic*]" to Mrs. W. P. Cornell, Oct. 29, 1934, ASWPL Papers. See also, Bruce, *Plantation Negro*, p. 84.

61. Geertz, "Deep Play," p. 7.

62. See, for example, Gerber, "Lynching and Law and Order," p. 42; Howard Kester, "The Lynching of Claude Neal," NAACP report, Nov. 30, 1934, Howard Kester Papers; Braden, "A Second Open Letter to Southern White Women"; Seligmann, "Protecting Southern Womanhood"; Smith, *Killers of the Dream*, pp. 83, 97–119, 167.

63. Fox, " 'Nice Girl' "; Erikson, *Identity and the Life Cycle*, pp. 36–38.

64. Thomas R. Dew, "On the Characteristic Differences between the Sexes, and on the Position and Influence of Woman in Society," *Southern Literary Messenger*, 1 (May 1835), 493–512; (July 1835), 621–23; (August 1835), 672–91. Quoted in Taylor, *Cavalier and Yankee*, pp. 148–51.

65. Fiedler, *Love and Death*, pp. 320–24. For the sexual antagonism revealed by the decline of gallantry, see Christopher Lasch, "The Flight from Feeling: Sociopsychology of Sexual Conflict," *Marxist Perspectives*, 1 (Spring 1978), 74–95.

66. George T. Winston, "The Relation of the Whites to the Negroes," *Annals of the American Academy of Political and Social Science*, 17 (July 1901), 108–9; Kearney, *A Slaveholder's Daughter*, p. 96; Avary, *Dixie After the War*, pp. 377–90. Rebecca Latimer Felton of Georgia represents an extreme example of the confluence of southern feminism with racial terrorism.

As a popular newspaper columnist and speaker, Felton advocated a variety of causes, including abolition of the convict lease system, prison reform, and women's suffrage. In 1922, she was appointed to fill Tom Watson's unexpired seat in the U. S. Senate, becoming the first woman to hold that office. She died in her ninety-first year, on the eve of the founding of the ASWPL. Like Watson, Felton used her considerable public influence to exacerbate a climate of racial violence in middle Georgia. In the summer of 1897, in a widely reported address to the State Agricultural Society, she announced that the gravest problem farm women faced was the threat of black rapists. If the law could not put a stop to the crime, the men of Georgia should lynch these "ravening beasts a thousand times a week if necessary." Two years later, when a black man named Sam Horse became the object of a massive manhunt, Felton urged his pursuers to shoot him on sight. On the day her editorial appeared in the Atlanta *Constitution*, a mob took Horse from a Newnan jail and burned him alive. Talmadge, *Rebecca Latimer Felton*, pp. 98–124.

67. Sylvia Metcalf to George Fort Milton, Sept. 21, 1930, ASWPL Papers. For other statements of the theme that southern white women lived in fear of sexual attack, see: Minutes, ASWPL Meeting, Nov. 1, 1930; Report, Jessie Daniel Ames, Director, ASWPL, Jan. 10, 1935; Mrs. E. S. Cook to Editor, Jackson *Daily News*, May 25, 1937; Ames, "Southern Women and Lynching," reprinted as *Southern Women and Lynching* (Atlanta: ASWPL, 1936); Mrs. S. L. Hollingsworth to Mrs. Lester Greer, Feb. 27, 1931, ASWPL Papers. For accounts of the socialization of southern women, see Boyle, *The Desegregated Heart*; Lumpkin, *Making of a Southerner*; Virginia Foster [Durr], "The Emancipation of Southern, Pure, White Womanhood"; Smith, *Killers of the Dream*.

68. Ames, "Southern Women and Lynching." See also JDA to Mrs. J. W. Mills, Dec. 2, 1935, ASWPL Papers; Ames, "The Lynchers' View," Ames Papers (NC).

69. Anonymous from LX, Maryland, ASWPL Papers. See also: J. P. Kelly to Mrs. Lester Greer, July 19, 1934; A. B. Newitz to Jane Cornell, Apr. 20, 1935; "Just a Florida [sic]" to Mrs. W. P. Cornell, Oct. 29, 1934; T. O. Richards to Dear Ladies, Dec. 15, 1934; Cordele (Ga.) *Dispatch*, Jan. 25, 1931; Charleston (S.C.) *Evening Post*, Nov. 12, 1930; Conyers (Ga.) *Times*, Nov. 27, 1931, ASWPL Papers. Similarly, white female abolitionists were accused of going to the "shocking extremity of unnatural, legal prostitution, known as miscegenation." New York *Daily News*, Apr. 9, 1864, quoted in Wood, *Black Scare*, p. 63. For the continuing impact of such cultural preoccupations on the civil rights movement, see Evans, "Women's Consciousness."

70. JDA to Lulu Daniel Ames, July 3, 1965, Priv. Coll. For statements of this theme, see Wilmington *Daily Record*, Aug. 18, 1898; Jackson *Daily News*, Feb. 1931; Galveston (Tex.) *Tribune*, June 21, 1934; Memphis *Commercial Appeal*, Jan. 14, 1922.

71. The relationship between black men and white women has been a recurring theme in American literature. See, for example, Fiedler, *Love and Death*, pp. 412–13, on the Gothic novel of miscegenation. Doris Lessing's *The Grass Is Singing*, however, set not in the American South but in South Africa in the 1950s, provides a rare evocation of such an affair from the point of view of a white woman. Mary Turner, the lonely wife of an ineffectual farmer, finds herself locked in silent struggle with an enigmatic servant for

whom she feels a mounting attraction, mixed with repulsion and despair. When the psychic tension between them erupts in murder, the white community closes ranks against both the murderer and his victim.

72. Thomas, "The Double Standard." For a contemporary discussion of legal proscriptions against rape, see "Forcible and Statutory Rape."

73. Bilbo, *Take Your Choice*, pp. 57–58; Cash, *Mind of the South*, p. 87; Jordan, *White Over Black*, p. 150. Ellison's *Invisible Man*, pp. 21–24, embodies this symbolism in the surrealist image of a white prostitute dancing before a group of terrified black boys.

74. Douglass, "Lynch Law in the South," p. 22; Hernton, *Sex and Racism*; Frantz Fanon, *Black Skin, White Masks: The Experiences of a Black Man in a White World* (New York: Grove Press, 1967). Eldridge Cleaver, in *Soul on Ice*, pp. 10–14, claims that the lynching of Emmett Till in Mississippi in 1955 "turned him inside out" and set him on a course of aggression toward white society in general and white women in particular.

75. See for example, Bruce, *The Plantation Negro*, p. 84. The Negro rapist, writes Bruce, "is not content merely with the consummation of his purpose, but takes that fiendish delight in the degradation of his victim which he always shows when he can reek [*sic*] his vengeance upon one whom he has hitherto been compelled to fear, and here, the white woman in his power is, for the time being, the representative of that race which has always overawed him."

76. Carl Carmer, in *Stars Fell on Alabama* (New York: Hill and Wang, 1934), pp. 14–15, recounts a fraternity ritual called the "Key-Ice" practiced at University of Alabama dances in the 1920s. During an intermission, while the lights were turned out, the young men wheeled in a cart of ice. The leader, mounted on a table in the center of the gymnasium, lifted a glass of water and offered a toast that ran: "To Woman, lovely woman of the Southland, as pure and chaste as this sparkling water, as cold as this gleaming ice, we lift this cup, and we pledge our hearts and our lives to the protection of her virtue and chastity." See also, Smith, *Killers of the Dream*, pp. 120–38; Virginia Foster Durr Interview.

77. "Appendix F. Digest of Discussion," n.d. [Nov. 20, 1931], ASWPL Meeting, Ames Papers (NC); Minutes, ASWPL, Jan. 13–14, 1936, ASWPL Papers.

78. Lerner, *Black Women*, p. 173. See section, "The Rape of Black Women as a Weapon of Terror," pp. 172 ff., for examples of rape of black women during Reconstruction, lynching of black women, and lynching of black men who tried to protect their women and children from sexual assault. For the black response to these sexual stereotypes, see Levine, *Black Culture*, pp. 332–41; Du Bois, *Darkwater*, pp. 163–86; and Dollard, *Caste and Class*, pp. 134–72.

79. Dollard, *Caste and Class*, pp. 134–72; Woodward, *American Counterpoint*, p. 89.

80. Woodward, *American Counterpoint*, p. 76.

Chapter 6: A Movement of
Southern White Women

1. JDA Interview; *Literary Digest*, 105 (May 24, 1920), 8; Miller, "Protestant Churches and Lynching," 2.

2. Burrows, "Commission" (Ph.D. diss.), p. 171; Parris and Brooks, *Blacks in the City*, pp. 196–204; "A Survey and Plan of Fund-Raising for the Commission on Interracial Cooperation," prepared by the John Price Jones Corporation, New York, N. Y., June 25, 1929, CIC Papers.

3. *Lynchings and What They Mean: General Findings of the Southern Commission on the Study of Lynching* (Atlanta, Ga.: CIC, n.d.), p. 6; Milton, "Impeachment of Judge Lynch."

4. *Lynchings and What They Mean*, pp. 5–7; Minutes, Southern Commission on the Study of Lynching, Sept. 5, 1930, Dec. 22, 1930, ASWPL Papers. Other members of the southern commission were: Julian Harris, Benjamin F. Hubert, W. P. King, W. J. McGlothlin, Howard W. Odum, and Alex W. Spence.

5. Mrs. J. W. Downs to JDA, Nov. 15, 1930, ASWPL Papers.

6. JDA Interview; Minutes, ASWPL Annual Meeting, Jan. 13, 1936, ASWPL Papers. Jessie Daniel Ames, "The Commission on Interracial Cooperation, 1933–1938"; JDA to Mrs. George Davis, May 1, 1935; JDA to Will Alexander, July 31, 1931, CIC Papers; Burrows, "Commission" (Ph.D. diss.), p. 171; Bunche, "Tactics and Achievements" (unpublished MS), p. 460.

7. Dykeman and Stokely, *Seeds of Southern Change*, p. 146; Minutes, Administrative Committee on Women's Activities, CIC, Oct. 4, 1930, NU Papers; [JDA] to Mrs. Julian McKey, Jan. 3, 1931, ASWPL Papers; "Future Program" [1928], CIC Papers. Invitations had been extended to carefully chosen representatives of middle-class women's organizations, rather than to the kind of prominent individuals represented on the Southern Commission on the Study of Lynching. Public announcement of such a conference was virtually unthought of: throughout the history of both the CIC and the ASWPL, members were carefully chosen and self-perpetuating, seldom recruited from the public at large.

8. Jessie Daniel Ames, "History of Movement," n.d., ASWPL Papers; Atlanta *Constitution*, Nov. 5, 1930; Minutes, Organizational Meeting, Nov. 1, 1930, Ames Papers (NC); Ames, "Southern Women and Lynching"; Minutes, Second Conference of Southern White Women, Nov. 6, 1930, Dallas, Texas, ASWPL Papers. Earlier studies of the ASWPL include: Yandle, "A Delicate Crusade" (M.A. thesis); Barber, "The Association of Southern Women for the Prevention of Lynching, 1930–1942" (M.A. thesis) and "The Association of Southern Women for the Prevention of Lynching," *Phylon*, 24 (Dec. 1973), 378–89; Crites, "A History of the Association of Southern Women for Prevention of Lynching, 1930–1942" (M.A. thesis); Ames, *Associ-*

ation of Southern Women for the Prevention of Lynching; Ames, *Southern Women Look at Lynching;* [JDA], "Southern Women and Lynching, Beginning of the Movement," 1932, ASWPL Papers.

9. Ethridge, "Southern Women Attack Lynching"; Dalton (Ga.) *Citizen,* Dec. 11, 1930; Cordele (Ga.) *Dispatch,* Dec. 10, 1930; Macon (Ga.) *Telegraph,* Nov. 4, 1930 and Jan. 26, 1931, ASWPL Papers.

10. Atlanta *World,* Dec. 12, 1932; Philadelphia *Tribune,* Dec. 5, 1933; Pittsburgh *Courier,* Dec. 22, 1933, ASWPL Papers. For favorable reaction from the white southern press see: Dallas *Times-Herald,* Jan. 7, 1932; Hattiesburg (Miss.) *American,* Nov. 11, 1930 and Jan. 22, 1931; Macon (Ga.) *Evening News,* Dec. 4 and Nov. 4, 1930, ASWPL Papers. For historical evaluations of the significance of the founding of the ASWPL see Smith, *Killers of the Dream,* pp. 121, 122–23, 125–26 and Scott, *Southern Lady,* p. 194.

11. For the black-led anti-lynching movement, see Grant, *Anti-Lynching Movement;* Kellogg, *NAACP,* esp. pp. 216–21; and Degler, *The Other South,* p. 361.

12. Lerner, *Black Women,* pp. 211–14; NAACP, Minutes of the Meeting of the Board of Directors, Sept. 11, 1922; "One Million Women Crusade Against Lynching," Foreign Press, n.d.; Mary B. Talbert to [white women], Oct. 21, 1922, NAACP Papers; Ovington, *Walls Came Tumbling Down,* p. 154; U. S. Congress, Senate, Committee on the Judiciary, *To Prevent and Punish the Crime of Lynching, Hearings,* before a subcommittee of the Committee on the Judiciary, Senate, on S. 121, 29th Cong., 1st sess., 1926, pp. 7, 42–43.

13. *Woman's Voice,* 4 (Jan. 1923), quoted in Lerner, *Black Women,* p. 215.

14. Zangrando, "Efforts of the NAACP" (Ph.D. diss.), p. 118; Kellogg, *NAACP,* pp. 235–46; Report of Mary B. Talbert, Director, n.d. [May 14, 1923]; Walter White to Mrs. Helen Curtis, July 20, 1922; Memorandum to Mesdames Mary B. Talbert, Butler Wilson, and Helen Curtis from Herbert J. Seligman, June 27, 1922, NAACP Papers; JDA to Will Alexander, July 31, 1931, CIC Papers. Three black Anti-Lynching Crusaders state directors were active CIC participants: Mrs. Nettie L. Napier (Tennessee), Nannie Burroughs (Washington, D.C.), and Mrs. M. L. Crosthwaite (Missouri).

15. James Weldon Johnson to Mrs. Lillian A. Alexander, May 21, 1923; Alexander to Johnson, May 22, 1923, NAACP Papers. See also Mary Talbert to Lugenia Hope, Sept. 20, 1922, NU Papers.

16. Tindall, *Emergence of the New South,* pp. 208–28; Cash, *Mind of the South,* pp. 311–12, 382–83. For example, Julian and Julia Collier Harris purchased the Columbus (Ga.) *Enquirer-Sun* with the "avowed purpose of fighting intolerance and bigotry" in 1923. Their attack on the KKK and lynching earned them a Pulitzer prize but finally lost them their paper. See Mims, *Advancing South,* pp. 185–89 and Dabney, *Liberalism in the South,* pp. 401–2. For other indications of southern disapprobation of lynching see Dabney, *Liberalism in the South,* p. 252; Kellogg, *NAACP,* p. 30; Davis, "A Substitute for Lynching," pp. 12–13. On the other hand, on the eve of the ASWPL's founding, Howard Odum described a pervasive climate of fear that continued to suppress indigenous white anti-lynching sentiment; see "Lynchings, Fears, and Folkways."

17. For example, Governor Thomas W. Bickett of North Carolina claimed to have personally fended off one lynch mob and called out federal troops to prevent another. *Public Letters and Papers of Thomas Walter Bickett, Governor of North Carolina 1917–1921* (Raleigh: Edwards and Broughton Printing Co., 1923), pp. 72–73. Bickett's wife was a founding member of the CIC Woman's Committee.

18. JDA to Mary McLeod Bethune, Mar. 9, 1938, ASWPL Papers; Dykeman and Stokely, *Seeds of Southern Change*, p. 143.

19. Tindall, *Emergence of the New South*, pp. 1–5, 53–70, 287.

20. The impact of industrialization on women's lives constitutes one of the major themes in recent women's history. For discussions of this process, see Gerda Lerner, "The Lady and the Mill Girl: Changes in the Status of Women in the Age of Jackson," *Mid-Continent American Studies Journal*, 10 (1969), 5–15; Douglas, *Feminization of American Culture*, pp. 44–79; Cott, *Bonds of Womanhood;* Joan Scott and Louise Tilly, "Women's Work and the Family in Nineteenth-Century Europe," *Comparative Studies in Society and History*, 17 (Jan. 1975), 36–64.

21. Tindall, *Emergence of the New South*, pp. 70–99.

22. For a discussion of the social transformation undergone by succeeding generations of American industrial workers, see Gutman, "Work, Culture, and Society."

23. Ellison, *Shadow and Act*, pp. 297–99.

24. Louisville *Courier-Journal*, Nov. 29, 1939.

25. Vance and Demerath, eds., *Urban South*, pp. 68–70, 74; U. S. Department of Commerce, Bureau of the Census, *Thirteenth Census of the United States, 1910: Population Occupation Statistics*, IV, 48–49; U. S. Department of Commerce, Bureau of the Census, *Sixteenth Census of the United States, 1940: The Labor Force, III;* U. S. Department of Commerce and Labor, Bureau of Statistics, *Statistical Abstract of the United States, 1910* (Washington, D.C., 1911), pp. 104–5; U. S. Department of Commerce, Bureau of the Census, *Statistical Abstract of the United States, 1942* (Washington, D.C., 1943), pp. 142–43; idem., *Historical Statistics of the United States, Colonial Times to 1970* (Washington, D.C., 1975), p. 54.

26. Will Alexander had readily agreed to underwrite the expenses of the founding conferences, but treasurer R. H. King was strongly opposed to pouring more money into the women's project. Jessie Daniel Ames recalled: "Mr. King hit the ceiling. He was a South Carolinian and should have been a gentleman. But he said some very rough things to me." JDA Interview.

27. JDA to Edna Fuller, Dec. 7, 1931; Minutes, ASWPL Meeting, Jan. 10–11, 1938, AWPL Papers; Burrows, "Commission" (Ph.D. diss.), pp. 146, 158.

28. Ames, *Toward Lynchless America*, p. 60.

29. Ames, "Southern Women and Lynching"; *"With Quietness They Work": Report of the Activities of Southern Women in Education Against Lynching During 1937* (Atlanta: ASWPL, 1938); Ames, *Southern Women Look at Lynching;* JDA to Mrs. W. A. Martin, Oct. 20, 1931; JDA to Senator Tom Connally, June 23, 1937; Questionnaires on ASWPL Annual Meeting, 1935, ASWPL Papers.

30. JDA to Mrs. R. S. Crichlow, Nov. 2, 1931, ASWPL Papers; Mississippi Plan of Action, 1932, Ames Papers (NC); Hattiesburg *American*, Apr. 6, 1936; JDA to Mrs. Elizabeth Wells Harrington, Oct. 30, 1935; Mrs. L. W. Alford to JDA, Nov. 7, 1931; Minutes, ASWPL Meeting, Nov. 20, 1931; JDA to Mrs. Margaret Yost, Dec. 7, 1931, ASWPL Papers; Ames, "The Shame of a Christian People."

31. Ranked according to absolute numbers of lynchings, Georgia was second only to Mississippi; Texas was third; Louisiana was fourth. However, ranked according to incidence of lynching per 10,000 black population, Florida had the highest lynching rate in the country. For the progress and strength of state councils see: Abigail Curlee to Miss Alia Henry, Apr. 17, 1931, ASWPL Papers; "Report," 1937, Priv. Coll.; JDA to Mrs. James H. McCoy, Mar. 3, 1937; JDA to Mrs. L. A. Sanders, Jan. 30, 1931; Margaret Yost to JDA, May 23, 1931; JDA to Yost, May 26, 1931; JDA to Mrs. Neal Spahr, Oct. 7, 1931, ASWPL Papers.

32. For the interracial movement in South Carolina during this period, see Hoffman, "Genesis of the Modern Movement for Equal Rights in South Carolina."

33. JDA to Mrs. W. J. Piggott, Oct. 7, 1931; JDA to Clara Cox, Oct. 10, 1931, ASWPL Papers.

34. Blanche Sydnor White to JDA, Oct. 20, 1931, ASWPL Papers. See also JDA to White, Oct. 22, 1931, and White to JDA, Oct. 26, 1931, ASWPL Papers.

35. [?] to JDA, Jan. 28, 1935; JDA to Mrs. E. M. Bailey, Feb. 5, 1935; JDA to Mrs. Arch Trawick, March 26, 1935; JDA to Mrs. George Davis, Feb. 5, 1935, ASWPL Papers.

36. Ames, *Southern Women Look at Lynching*, pp. 10–11; Jessie Daniel Ames, "Report to the Delegates to the Sixth Conference and First Biennial Conference" [1937], ASWPL Papers; *Organizations Committed to a Program of Education to Prevent Lynching* (Atlanta: ASWPL, 1941).

37. Montie B. Greer to JDA, Feb. 22, 1934, and Oct. 25, 1935; JDA to Miss Janie McGaughey, Dec. 1, 1937; Minutes, ASWPL Conference, Jan. 13–14, 1936, ASWPL Papers; ASWPL, *Death by Parties Unknown*, p. 26.

38. Born in Wisconsin in 1867, Newell was one of a number of southern women of northern heritage who played important roles in the anti-lynching movement. She received a Ph.B. from the University of Chicago in 1909, where she evidently came under the influence of Jane Addams, and served as head of the Department of Kindergarten Education in the University's School of Education from 1901 to 1909. Married to a Southern Methodist minister in 1909, she moved to North Carolina and took an increasingly prominent part in the affairs of the Woman's Missionary Council. She was a founding member of the CIC Woman's Committee in 1920. "Neither the eighteenth nor the nineteenth amendment to the Constitution," she commented, "carries any greater moment than the movement you have begun. . . . I found long ago that it did not further my usefulness to speak my exact and entire opinions on the subject of color; and even at this date I do not publish them without reservations; setting that limitation aside I have done all I could for the 11 years that I have been a Tar Heel to create an atmosphere of fairness to the colored sisters. Now I go into the long march with better courage and

great hope." As a member of such organizations as the National Child Labor Committee, the National Consumers' League, the American Association for Labor Legislation, the Women's Trade Union League, the Women's International League for Peace and Freedom, and the North Carolina Legislative Council, she participated in the full range of social feminist concerns. Mrs. W. A. Newell to Commission on Interracial Cooperation, Oct. 15, 1920, CIC Papers; Excerpt from Biennial Report for 1928 and 1929 by Eleanor Copenhaver, YWCA Papers.

39. Born in 1892, Louise Young was educated at Vanderbilt, the University of Wisconsin, and Bryn Mawr. In 1919, she shocked her family by returning to the South to accept a position as Dean of Women at Paine College at Augusta, Georgia, where Mary De Bardeleben had established Southern Methodism's first black settlement house. It was, she recalled, "a disgraceful thing to do. One young man told me he would rather see me in the penitentiary, he'd rather see me in prisoner's garb than to see me go down there." She viewed herself, however, simply as putting into practice the implicit values of her upbringing. Her father, dispossessed of his family's plantation wealth by the Civil War, "had been thrown with new Italian immigrants and poor people and knocked around in that wholesale farm market of Memphis. And he really had seen all kinds of peple. And he had respect for them all." She perceived "not a shadow of a difference" between what she learned in church and what she learned at home: "If you read the Bible . . . all men were brothers." At Paine she found herself "literally living in a Negro world." Disoriented and lonely after her brother's death, she moved to Hampton Institute in Virginia, run by Boston Congregationalists who had initiated the industrial education movement. In 1926, she began teaching at Scarritt College, where she inaugurated one of the earliest black history courses in the region. Working with Charles S. Johnson, the sociologist and first black president of Fisk, she helped nourish an atmosphere of student inquiry and racial liberalism that made Nashville, along with Atlanta, a center of student civil rights activities in the 1960s. Young Interview; Stevens Interview; personal communications from Sue Thrasher.

40. "In Memoriam—Sara Estelle Haskin," The Methodist Woman, Nov. 1940, 5, 29; J. Brown, "Sara Estelle Haskin"; [Haskin], "Southern Women and Mob Violence"; Ames, "The Shame of a Christian People." Estelle Haskin to JDA, Nov. 25, 1931, ASWPL Papers. In addition to serving as "woman editor" of the Board of Mission's publication, World Outlook, and authoring several books, Haskin created and distributed missionary literature to a constituency of approximately 300,000 young people and adults.

41. Quotation is from Twenty-Third Annual Report, Woman's Missionary Council, Methodist Episcopal Church, South, 1933 (Nashville, Tenn.: Publishing House of the Methodist Episcopal Church, South, 1933), p. 107. See also Twenty-Fourth Annual Report, Woman's Missionary Council, Methodist Episcopal Church, South, 1934 (Nashville, Tenn.: Publishing House of the Methodist Episcopal Church, South, 1934); Report, Association of Southern Women for the Prevention of Lynching, Jan.–Apr. 30, 1931; Mrs. L. A. Sanders to JDA, Nov. 9, 1931, ASWPL Papers; Parrott, "Seven Thousand Women Pledge to Eradicate Mob Violence"; Twenty-Fourth Annual Report, Woman's Missionary Society, Tennessee Conference (Apr. 9, 11, 1935), pp. 62, 65; Winfrey, "The Organized Activities of the Women of Southern Methodism in the Field of Negro-White Relationships" (M.A. thesis); Correll,

"North Carolina Baptist and Methodist Women's Missionary Organizations" (M.A. thesis).

42. *"With Quietness They Work"; Southern Baptist Convention Bulletin,* May 14, 1937; Mrs. Una Roberts Lawrence to JDA, Jan. 4, 1935; JDA to Mrs. Paul Arrington, July 6, 1939, ASWPL Papers; Thompson, *Presbyterians in the South,* III, 384–402; *Baptist History and Heritage,* 22 (Jan. 1977), special issue on "The Role of Women in Baptist History." Ames described Presbyterian women as "a conservative group who cling rather tenaciously to the paternal attitude not only toward Negroes but to all disadvantaged groups." JDA to Mary J. McCoy, Mar. 3, 1937; Janie McGaughey to JDA, Oct. 7, 1937, and Dec. 15, 1937, ASWPL Papers.

43. Jane Cornell to JDA, Dec. 3, 1935; Minutes, ASWPL Annual Meeting, Jan. 11, 1935, ASWPL Papers; James Thayer Addison, *The Episcopal Church in the United States, 1789–1931* (New York: Scribner's, 1951), pp. 192–99.

44. See, for example, Nell R. Jones to Presidents of YWCA's, Nov. 13, 1934, ASWPL Papers.

45. Minutes, ASWPL Executive Committee, 1936, ASWPL Papers.

46. Ames, *Southern Women and Lynching;* JDA to Mrs. Ruth Atkinson, Oct. 1, 1931; JDA to Clara Cox, Oct. 10, 1931; JDA to Mrs. W. A. Newell, Dec. 16, 1932, Ames Papers (NC); JDA to Abigail Curlee, Feb. 14, 1931; Kate T. Davis to JDA, May 16, 1936; JDA to Ethel Hilton, June 10, 1931; Nell Battle Lewis to Clara Cox, Mar. 13, 1931, ASWPL Papers.

47. Born in 1866, Georgia May Martin was the daughter of a Louisville, Kentucky, bookseller and the wife of a wealthy businessman. Privately educated, she published her first book, *The Angel of the Tenement,* in 1897. She followed this tale of immigrant life with a series of mildly feminist books about the Victorian education of characters named "Emmy Lou" and "Selina." After World War I, she began writing about other social issues and became active in national Democratic Party politics. Among her many publications were *Children of the Mist,* a collection of sketches about "the virtues and . . . limitations" of the Negro; "American Women and Paternalism," *Atlantic Monthly,* 133 (June 1924), 744–52; "American Women and Public Affairs," *Atlantic Monthly,* 133 (Feb. 1924), 169–71; and "American Women and Representative Government," *Atlantic Monthly,* 135 (Mar. 1925), 363–67. Described as "intensely feminine" by the members of her Louisville literary club, she always chose male parts in club plays and wrote under a masculine pen name. See Evelyn Snead Barnett, "George Madden Martin," in *Library of Southern Literature,* ed. by Edwin Alderman and Joel C. Harris (Atlanta: Martin and Hoyte, 1907), pp. 3413–15; *Nation,* 99 (Dec. 14, 1914), 774. For Mason and Ethridge, see Mason, *To Win These Rights;* Mason Papers; Ethridge Interview.

48. JDA to Mrs. W. A. Newell, Dec. 16, 1932; Jessie Daniel Ames Speech, Southern Presbyterian Church Women, Montreat, N. C., 1935, Ames Papers (NC); Ames, *Toward Lynchless America.*

49. Minutes, Executive Committee, Jan. 14, 1936, ASWPL Papers; *Tenth Annual Conference Planning Committee, Association of Southern Women for the Prevention of Lynching* (Jan. 1935); Nordyke, "Ladies and Lynchings."

50. JDA to Margaret Prescott Montague, Dec. 16, 1931, ASWPL Papers.

51. JDA to Lewis T. Nordyke, May 30, 1939, ASWPL Papers. See also Nordyke, "Ladies and Lynchings"; JDA to Tom Brady, Jr., June 5, 1931, ASWPL Papers; JDA to Harold Lasswell, Feb. 8, 1937, CIC Papers.

52. JDA to Mrs. Alex Spence, July 6, 1931; Minutes, ASWPL Meeting, 1933; JDA to Ethel Hilton, June 10, 1931; Mrs. Ruth W. Atkinson to JDA, June 11, 1931; JDA to Mrs. Ruth W. Atkinson, Oct. 1, 1931; JDA to Mrs. W. J. Piggott, Oct. 7, 1931; JDA to Clara Cox, Oct. 10, 1931; Mrs. Ruth W. Atkinson to JDA, Nov. 4, 1931, ASWPL Papers.

53. JDA to Ethel Hilton, June 10, 1931, ASWPL Papers. See also JDA to W. L. Hutchuson, Mar. 13, 1931; JDA to J. Max Bond, Feb. 13, 1931; JDA to Blanche White, Oct. 22, 1931; JDA to Mrs. Henry Peabody, Nov. 2, 1931; Mrs. Ruth Atkinson to JDA, Mar. 4, 1931; Jane Cornell to JDA, Dec. 3, 1935, ASWPL Papers.

54. JDA to Nannie Burroughs, Oct. 24, 1931; Burroughs to JDA, Oct. 30, 1931, ASWPL Papers. Burroughs frequently editorialized against lynching in her column in the Pittsburgh *Courier*, was chairman of the Anti-Lynching Committee of the National Association of Colored Women, and had been a charter member of the Anti-Lynching Crusaders.

55. Executive Committee Meeting, Council, ASWPL, Feb. 5, 1941; Ludie Andrews to JDA, Feb. 21, 1931; JDA to Andrews, Feb. 26, 1931; JDA to Mrs. Moton, Oct. 3, 1931; Mrs. Sallie W. Steward, president of National Association of Colored Women, to JDA, Oct. 26, 1931; JDA to Mrs. Steel, Mar. 6, 1935; Janie Porter Barrett to JDA, Mar. 3, 1933; JDA to Barrett, Mar. 6, 1933, AWSPL Papers.

56. JDA to Mrs. L. A. Sanders, Jan. 30, 1931, ASWPL Papers; Mrs. Luke Johnson to JDA, Mar. 24, 1924; JDA to Johnson, Oct. 9, 1924; JDA "Report," n.d., Ames Papers (NC).

57. The 115 women included in this social profile served over a period of years as members of the ASWPL Central Council or as chairmen or members of the executive committees of state councils. In addition, a small number of women are included who did not hold these offices but who were listed as members of the state councils *and* whose correspondence with Jessie Daniel Ames indicated that they were more than members in name only. In most cases, ASWPL records provided only the official positions these women held in other women's organizations and their city of origin. Other biographical information was gleaned from chance references in ASWPL correspondence, state and regional biographical dictionaries, church histories, interviews, obituaries, correspondence with living ASWPL members, city directories, and local libraries and historical associations. ASWPL women did not, in general, achieve "notable" distinction or notoriety. Only a small number appear in Edward T. James, et al., eds., *Notable American Women: A Biographical Dictionary* (3 vols.; Cambridge: Harvard University Press, 1971); a few more are included in *Who's Who in the South and Southwest*. More helpful were Durward Howes, ed., *American Women: The Standard Biographical Dictionary of Notable Women* (Los Angeles: American Publications, 1939), III, and Elmer T. Clark, *Who's Who in Methodism* (Chicago: A. N. Marquis, 1952). The excellent records maintained by the United Methodist Publishing House in Nashville, Tennessee, were invaluable, as was the aid and interest of local librarians throughout the region.

58. The South's urban population in 1930 was 32.1 percent of the total; there were 19 cities with a population of 100,000 or more. Arthur Raper, in *The Tragedy of Lynching,* pp. 28–29, observes that an inhabitant of the South's most sparsely populated 250 counties was in sixty times as much danger of mob death as a person living in or near one of the region's half-dozen largest cities.

59. Tindall, *Emergence of the New South,* pp. 99–100.

60. JDA to Mrs. J. Morgan Stevens, June 9, 1935; JDA to Mrs. J. W. Mills, Aug. 7, 1934; JDA to Mrs. Neblett, Dec. 7, 1937, ASWPL Papers.

61. JDA to Miss Doris Loraine, Mar. 5, 1935, ASWPL Papers. See also Minutes, ASWPL Meeting, Jan. 13–14, 1936, ASWPL Papers.

62. Inquiries to surviving ASWPL members turned up little information concerning husbands' positions, and several replied, with some indignation, that such questions were beside the point. See, for example, Arlene R. Park to author, Dec. 30, 1973.

63. Data from U. S., Department of Commerce, Bureau of the Census, *Religious Bodies: 1936,* vol. I, *Summary and Detailed Tables* (Washington, D.C., 1941).

64. Emily Maclachlan Interview. See also Mrs. L. W. Alford to JDA, May 27, 1931, ASWPL Papers, and Helena H. Smith, "Mrs. Tilly's Crusade."

65. Young Interview. For a similar story, see Shankman, "Dorothy Tilly and the Fellowship of the Concerned" (unpublished MS).

66. Mrs. L. W. Alford to JDA, May 31, 1937; Mrs. C. C. Alford to Mrs. Lester Greer, Sept. 9, 1935, ASWPL Papers. See also Eurie M. Weston to Mrs. L. W. Alford, Jan. 5, 1936; Mrs. H. R. Whiteside to JDA, Apr. 30, 1935, ASWPL Papers; JDA Interview.

67. JDA to Mrs. L. W. Alford, July 30, 1935, ASWPL Papers; JDA Interview.

68. Eurie M. Weston to JDA, Jan. 6, 1935, ASWPL Papers.

69. JDA to Nannie Hite Winston, Oct. 15, 1931, ASWPL Papers. See also Mrs. Neal Spahr to JDA, Aug. 26, 1936, ASWPL Papers.

70. Martin to Will Alexander, Jan. 24, 1934; JDA to Martin, Feb. 7, 1934, ASWPL Papers.

71. Mrs. L. W. Alford to JDA, Aug. 11, 1934, Aug. 17, 1934, Oct. 13, 1934, Aug. 11, 1935, ASWPL Papers.

72. Estelle Haskin to JDA, Nov. 12, 1931; Ruth W. Atkinson to JDA, Oct. 13, 1931, ASWPL Papers; JDA Interview; Burrows, "Commission" (Ph.D. diss.), pp. 158–59.

73. Ruth Atkinson to JDA, Feb. 19, 1931, Oct. 13, 1931; JDA to Miss Hannah E. Reynolds, Nov. 2, 1931, ASWPL Papers.

74. Despite the fact that she worked for an Episcopal bishop who was a CIC member, Cornell got "no support from my superior officer." Cornell to JDA, Dec. 3, 1935, Feb. 8, 1936, ASWPL Papers.

75. Trawick to Mrs. Robert O'Neal, Feb. 8, 1936, ASWPL Papers; Miss Earle Chambers to JDA, Aug. 8, 1936, CIC Papers.

76. Julia Collier Harris to JDA, Sept. 8, 1935, ASWPL Papers. See also Harris to JDA, n.d. [1937–38]. Among Harris's publications are *The Foundling Prince* (Boston: Houghton Mifflin, 1917) and *Joel Chandler Harris: Editor and Essayist* (Chapel Hill: University of North Carolina Press, 1931). Julian Harris seems to have been remarkably supportive of his wife's aspirations. For her career as a crusading journalist, her self-image as an unselfish, nurturing woman, and her progressive psychological deterioration, see her correspondence in the Julian LaRose Harris Papers, Emory University.

77. Louise Young to JDA, Apr. 24, 1931, ASWPL Papers. See also Young Interview.

78. Telegram re: Mrs. O. I. Woodley, n.d. [1931]; JDA to Mary M. McCoy, Mar. 3, 1937, ASWPL Papers.

79. Jane Cornell to Forest A. Lord, Jan. 2, 1935; Jane Cornell to JDA, Oct. 11, 1935, ASWPL Papers.

80. JDA to Frederick Ames, Feb. 22, 1939, Priv. Coll.

Chapter 7: Deeply Buried Causes

1. JDA to Julian Harris, Jan. 14, 1938, ASWPL Papers.

2. See JDA to Frederick Ames, Feb. 22, 1939, Priv. Coll.

3. Quotations are from JDA to Theodore Dreiser, July 30, 1931, ASWPL Papers; ASWPL, *A New Public Opinion on Lynching*. See also, JDA, "Lynchers' View on Lynching"; "Call to a Conference on the Prevention of Lynching," ASWPL Papers.

4. Ethridge, "Southern Women Attack Lynching."

5. Hoffman, "Genesis of the Modern Movement"; Cash, *Mind of the South*, p. 253; Columbia *State*, July 8, 1930; Columbia *Record*, Sept. 25, 1930; Spartanburg *Journal*, Dec. 30, 1930, ASWPL Papers; "Southern Women Fight Lynching Evil."

6. Dykeman and Stokely, *Seeds of Southern Change*, p. 148.

7. Hattiesburg *American*, Nov. 11 and Jan 22, 1931; Macon *Evening News*, Dec. 4, 1930.

8. Smith, *Killers of the Dream*, pp. 126–27.

9. Atlanta *Constitution*, Nov. 22, 1931; ASWPL, *New Public Opinion*; Ames, *Southern Women Look at Lynching*; JDA Interview.

10. "Suggested Points in Presenting the Purpose of the Association of Southern Women for the Prevention of Lynching," n.d., ASWPL Papers. See also, Ames, *Changing Character*, p. 58.

11. Will Alexander to George Fort Milton, Aug. 19, 1933, ASWPL Papers. See also JDA to Frederick Ames, Feb. 25, 1946, and Sept. 18, 1950, Priv. Coll.

12. News Bulletin, no. 2 (Dec. 1, 1930), ASWPL Papers. See also, Carter, Scottsboro, p. 127.

13. "Resolutions," Conference of Southern White Women, Atlanta, Georgia, Nov. 1, 1930; Pronouncement, Tennessee Association of Southern Women for the Prevention of Lynching, ASWPL Papers.

14. D. Amis to George Fort Milton, Nov. 13, 1931, CIC Papers. For the black-led struggle against judicial discrimination, see Carter, Scottsboro, pp. 103, 115–16; Jack Greenberg, Race Relations and American Law (New York: Columbia University Press, 1959); Berry, Black Resistance/White Law, pp. 139–88.

15. The following account is based primarily on Dan T. Carter's excellent study of the Scottsboro case.

16. Carter, Scottsboro, p. 116.

17. Mrs. J. F. Hooper to JDA, Apr. 28, 1931; Mary M. McCoy to JDA, Apr. 21, 1931, ASWPL Papers.

18. JDA to [nine Alabama women], Apr. 16, 1931; Mary M. McCoy to JDA, Apr. 21, 1931; Mrs. W. J. Adams to JDA, Apr. 30, 1931; Mrs. L. P. Donovan to JDA, July 7, 1931, ASWPL Papers.

19. JDA to Louise Young, May 22, 1931; JDA to Mrs. Kendall Emerson, Feb. 5, 1936; JDA to Mrs. George E. Davis, Feb. 11, 1936, ASWPL Papers.

20. "Minutes, Executive Session, Southern Commission on the Study of Lynching," July 20 [1931], Harris Papers. Younger southern liberals, less reluctant to ally themselves with Popular Front organizations like Dreiser's committee, urged Interracial Commission leaders to adopt a stance of "public agitation and outspoken, militant protest." See for example, C. Vann Woodward to W. W. Alexander, Oct. 15 and 19, 1933; Howard Odum to Will Alexander, Oct. 17, 1933, ASWPL Papers.

21. Theodore Dreiser to JDA, July 13, 1931; JDA to Dreiser, July 30, 1931, ASWPL Papers.

22. JDA to Carter Taylor, Aug. 5, 1931; JDA to Judge George W. Tedder, Oct. 18, 1935; JDA to Mrs. George E. Davis, Feb. 11, 1936, ASWPL Papers.

23. Ames, "Editorial Treatment of Lynching." See also, T. O. Richards to Dear Ladies, Dec. 15, 1934; JDA to O. W. Riegel, Nov. 5, 1937; Minutes, Executive Committee, ASWPL, Feb. 8, 1940, ASWPL Papers.

24. Quotations are from Ames, Changing Character, p. 51, and the Law Enforcement Club to JDA, Nov. 30, 1933, ASWPL Papers.

25. JDA to Arthur Raper, Jan. 19, 1939, ASWPL Papers; Ames, Whither Leads the Mob?

26. Ames, Changing Character, pp. 12–14; Ames, Whither Leads the Mob?

27. ASWPL, Are the Courts to Blame?; JDA to Eleanor Roosevelt, Apr. 20, 1934, Eleanor Roosevelt Papers; ASWPL Semi-Annual Report, Jan.–June, 1936, ASWPL Papers.

28. "Minutes, Anti-Lynching Conference of Southern White Women, Atlanta, Georgia, November 1, 1930," Ames Papers (NC).

29. "Report of Activities, 1933," ASWPL Papers.

30. Theodore Dreiser, July 13, 1931, ASWPL Papers; Mrs. E. F. Reid to Mrs. W. A. Newell, Jan. 5, 1934, Ames Papers (NC).

31. JDA, "Lynchers' View on Lynching," ASWPL Papers.

32. A white youth appeared in court and testified that he and a friend had had intercourse with the women the night before the freight train incident. One of the doctors who examined them told the judge that they had not been assaulted (though he refused to testify in court). Finally, Ruby Bates appeared in court and denied her earlier story. Carter, *Scottsboro*, p. 83.

33. She reported, for example, that 1934 lynchings in Newton, Texas, and Marianna, Florida, and a 1936 lynching in Danielsville, Georgia, all had involved interracial affairs. Ames, *Changing Character*, p. 58; JDA to Eleanor Roosevelt, Jan. 26, 1935, Eleanor Roosevelt Papers.

34. Quoted in Dollard, *Caste and Class*, pp. 169–70.

35. Jackson *Daily News*, Feb. 1931; Minutes, Executive Committee, ASWPL, Feb. 8, 1940, ASWPL Papers.

36. Carter, *Scottsboro*, pp. 295–96; Daisy T. Morris to JDA, Apr. 27, 1931, ASWPL Papers.

37. JDA to Mrs. W. J. Adams, May 1, 1931, ASWPL Papers.

38. Mrs. George E. Davis to JDA, May 11, 1935, ASWPL Papers. In contrast, another ASWPL member, Lucy Randolph Mason, helped defeat a segregation statute in her home town of Richmond, Virginia. See Norfolk *Journal and Guide*, Feb. 2, 1929, Mason Papers.

39. Minutes, Executive Committee, ASWPL, Feb. 8, 1940, ASWPL Papers.

40. JDA to Nannie Burroughs, Oct. 24, 1931; Burroughs to JDA, Oct. 30, 1931, ASWPL Papers.

41. "Appendix F, Digest of Discussion," n.d. [Nov. 20, 1931], Ames Papers (NC).

42. Ibid. See also, Minutes, Administrative Committee, Oct. 12, 1932, Ames Papers (NC).

43. JDA to Jane Cornell, July 16, 1935, ASWPL Papers; "Appendix F," Ames Papers (NC).

44. JDA to Charlotte Hawkins Brown, Mar. 20, 1930, CIC Papers.

45. ASWPL Annual Meeting, Nov. 19, 1932, Ames Papers (NC); "Report," Jessie Daniel Ames, Executive Director, Jan. 10, 1935, ASWPL Papers.

46. Ames, *Changing Character*, p. 16.

47. Homicide rates for southern blacks rose steadily. No figures are available to indicate how much of this homicide was interracial, but the lenient treatment of white murderers of blacks in courts indicates that cultural values and legal practices combined to permit such crimes. No outcry over this phenomenon ever approached the public opposition to lynching. See Hackney, "Southern Violence," and Davis, "Substitute for Lynching," pp. 12–14.

48. For support for Ames's contention that quiet murder without the formation of a mob gradually replaced lynching see: Myrdal, *American Dilemma*, II, 566; Raper, *Tragedy of Lynching*, pp. 56–58, and "Race and Class Pressures" (unpublished paper). Cantril, in *Psychology of Social Movements*, also discusses the distinction between "Bourbon" and "proletarian" lynchings. For accounts of the two types of violence see Caughey, ed. *Their Majesty the Mob*, and James Street, *Look Away: A Dixie Notebook* (New York: Viking, 1936). Allison Davis and John Dollard in *Children of Bondage: The Personality Development of Negro Youth in the Urban South* (Washington, D.C.: American Council on Education, 1940), p. 248, discuss another substitute for lynching: the killing of black suspects by police officers. By means of detailed accounts in the newpapers, they conclude, these symbolic . . . 'lynchings' were made known to the colored population and served as a means of further intimidation." C. S. Johnson, in *Growing Up in the Black Belt*, p. 5, quotes an interviewee as saying: "lynchings often happen. They are different to what they used to be though. They used to be big mobs hunting for a nigger, but now you just hear about some nigger found hanging off a bridge."

49. Minutes, ASWPL Annual Meeting, Jan. 13–14, 1936, ASWPL Papers.

50. JDA to Miss Doris Loraine, Mar. 5, 1935, ASWPL Papers.

51. Norfolk (Va.) *Journal and Guide*, Jan. 20, 1934.

52. Ibid.

53. Smith, *Killers of the Dream*, p. 128.

54. Nordyke, "Ladies and Lynching"; ASWPL, *Are the Courts to Blame?*; Yandle, "A Delicate Crusade" (M.A. thesis), pp. 31–34; Bulletins, 1933–38, ASWPL Papers.

55. Walter White to JDA, Jan. 7, 1936, NAACP Papers; JDA to Mrs. Una Roberts Lawrence, Mar. 3, 1937; Minutes, ASWPL Annual Meeting, Jan. 13–14, 1937; "Lynching 1882–1936," ASWPL Papers.

56. Ames, *Southern Women and Lynching*.

57. Dykeman and Stokely, *Seeds of Southern Change*, p. 145; Ames, *Changing Character*; Nordyke, "Ladies and Lynchings."

58. JDA to Jane Cornell, Dec. 4, 1934, ASWPL Papers.

59. JDA to Janie Porter Barrett, Mar. 6, 1933; Report of the Committee on Methods, Jan. 10–11, 1938; Minutes, ASWPL Annual Meeting, Jan. 13–14, 1937, ASWPL Papers.

60. Minutes, ASWPL Annual Meeting, Jan. 13–14, 1936; Report of Director of Woman's Work, Apr. 18, 1933; [JDA], unsigned, undated MS. [1923]; Onilee R. Brown to JDA, Feb. 21, 1934; Minutes, ASWPL Annual Meeting, Jan. 13–14, 1937, ASWPL Papers.

61. Report of CIC, American Missionary Association, 1936, CIC Papers; JDA Interview.

62. Minutes, ASWPL Annual Meeting, Jan. 13–14, 1937, ASWPL Papers.

63. See, for example, Odum, "Lynchings, Fears, and Folkways"; JDA to Mrs. J. W. Mills, Feb. 14, 1934; JDA to Dr. L. M. Bristol, Dec. 11, 1936; JDA to Mrs. James A. Richardson, Aug. 5, 1936; Minutes, ASWPL Meetings, Jan. 13–14, 1936, ASWPL Papers; JDA to Harold Lasswell, Feb. 8, 1937, CIC Papers; Myrdal, *American Dilemma*, II, 1032–34.

64. Ames, *Changing Character*, p. 12; JDA Interview.

65. Address to Southern Presbyterian Church Women, Montreat, N.C., 1935, Ames Papers (NC).

66. [JDA], unsigned, undated typescript in ASWPL Papers. See also, Report, JDA, Executive Director, ASWPL, Jan. 10, 1935, ASWPL Papers, and JDA, "Lynchers' View on Lynching," Ames Papers (NC).

67. Alice Spearman Wright Interview.

68. Oklahoma City *Times*, Nov. 16, 1935; Austin *Statesman*, Nov. 14, 1935; Unattributed newsclips, Ames Papers (NC).

69. JDA to Mrs. J. W. Mills, Dec. 2, 1935, ASWPL Papers.

70. Ames, *Southern Women Look at Lynching*; Minutes, Annual Meeting, Jan. 13–14, 1936; JDA to Miss Henrietta Roelofs, Dec. 4, 1935; Minutes, Biennial ASWPL Conference, Jan. 13, 1937; Jackson, Miss., Institute, May 27, 1937, ASWPL Papers; JDA to Mrs. B. J. Reaves, Sept. 21, 1936, CIC Papers.

71. Mrs. L. W. Alford to JDA, Nov. 9, 1935, ASWPL Papers.

72. Mrs. L. W. Alford to JDA, Apr. 28, 1933. Alford's speeches to women's missionary societies in small towns became increasingly hard-hitting and gained favorable press coverage. Lynching, she told a group in Hattiesburg, was not simply due to disrespect for law and order; it was deeply rooted in racial prejudice and economic greed. Hattiesburg *American*, Apr. 6, 1935.

73. Mrs. L. W. Alford to JDA, Nov. 26, 1936, and Feb. 21, 1939, ASWPL Papers.

74. Jane Cornell to JDA, May 9, 1935; Mrs. J. D. Lawhorn to JDA, Nov. 24, 1934; Mrs. Ruth Knox to JDA, Dec. 29, and May 26, 1934, ASWPL Papers.

75. Ames, *Southern Women Look at Lynching*.

76. Quotations are from JDA to Miss Doris Loraine, Mar. 5, 1935, and JDA to Mrs. W. A. Newell, Sept. 19, 1935, ASWPL Papers. See also Dallas *Gazette*, July 29, 1933; Minutes, ASWPL Annual Meeting, Jan. 13–14, 1936; JDA to Mrs. J. W. Mills, Aug. 7, 1934, ASWPL Papers; JDA Interview. On a trip to Texas in 1933, Ames's passion for intelligence-gathering led her to stop at a filling station every time she could squeeze in another gallon of gasoline in order to talk to people along the way. "I think filling stations must be as fruitful with public opinion as livery stables used to be before the days of suffrage," she commented. "At any rate, I learned a great deal." JDA to Mrs. R. R. Moton, Sept. 29, 1933, ASWPL Papers.

77. JDA to O. W. Riegel, Nov. 5, 1937, ASWPL Papers; Ames, *Changing Character*, p. 7.

78. See, for example, JDA to Arthur Raper, Jan. 19, 1939; Mrs. L. W. Alford to JDA, Aug. 11, 1934, and Oct. 13, 1934, ASWPL Papers.

79. Walter Spearman, *Country Sunday* (Atlanta, 1936); Seymour, "Lawd, Does You Undahstan'?"; Minutes, ASWPL Conference, Jan. 13–14, 1936; "Skeleton Outline of the Work of the Women of the Association of Southern Women for the Prevention of Lynching," ASWPL Conference, Jan. 13–14,

1936; JDA to Play Committee, Feb. 18, 1936; JDA to Miss Ann Seymour, July 14, 1936, ASWPL Papers.

80. Mrs. George E. Davis to JDA, Jan. 21, 1937, ASWPL Papers.

81. JDA Interview. See also JDA to Mrs. Frank Burns, Jan. 19, 1937; JDA to Dr. R. W. Burns, Feb. 16, 1937, ASWPL Papers.

82. JDA to Mrs. J. D. McKay, Mar. 9, 1934, ASWPL Papers.

83. See, for example, Chattanooga *Times*, Dec. 2, 1932, and Oct. 18, 1936.

84. Jessie Daniel Ames, "Can Newspapers Harmonize Their Editorial Policy on Lynching and Their News Stories on Lynching?," Speech at the Southern Newspaper Publishers' Association Convention on May 18, 1936, reprinted in Ames, *Changing Character*, pp. 55–58; Bulletin of the Southern Newspaper Publishers' Association, Chattanooga, Tenn., July 1, 1936, ASWPL Papers.

85. ASWPL members were particularly incensed by the press coverage of the Claude Neal lynching of 1934. In this Marianna, Florida, case a "Committee of Six" issued a timetable for the lynching that was carried as front-page news across the country. Headlines such as "All White Folks Invited to Party" summoned onlookers from miles away. See, for example, Macon (Ga.) *Telegraph*, Savannah (Ga.) *News*, and Marianna *Daily Times-Courier*, all for Oct. 26, 1934; Kester, *Lynching of Claude Neal*.

86. JDA to editors and publishers of newspapers, Mar. 5, 1936; JDA to Tom Wallace, editor, Louisville *Times*, March 10, 1937, ASWPL Papers.

87. Ames read and was influenced by the research of the political scientist Harold D. Lasswell of the University of Chicago's Institute for Propaganda Analysis. She shared with other members of her generation a conviction that Allied propaganda against the Germans had swept the United States into the First World War, and she drew analogies between this experience and the ideological underpinnings of racial violence. "The surest method to follow in developing hate and fear to the point of violence, whether in precipitating a lynching or a war," she wrote, "is the use of stories of sex crimes. . . . In both, a whole people lose for the benefit of the few." Through the ASWPL, she proposed to counter the "propaganda" of chivalry with her own brand of "education" based on a combination of documented facts, moral suasion, and the symbolism inherent in the image of the southern lady. Ames, *Changing Character*, pp. 55–56; JDA to Mrs. James A. Richardson, Aug. 5, 1936, ASWPL Papers; JDA to Harold Lasswell, Feb. 8, 1937, CIC Papers; Lasswell, *Propaganda Technique in the World War*; Irwin, *Propaganda and the News*.

88. JDA to Willie Snow Ethridge, Mar. 10, 1937, ASWPL Papers.

89. Ames, "Can Newspapers Harmonize Their Editorial Policy?"

90. JDA Interview; JDA to O. W. Riegel, Nov. 5, 1937, ASWPL Papers. For support for Ames's observation, see Mrydal, *American Dilemma*, II, 565, and Dabney, *Liberalism in the South*, p. 380.

91. Women who attended ASWPL meetings, for example, heard speeches by Arthur Raper and W.E.B. Du Bois and were urged to read the works of John Dollard and Charles S. Johnson.

92. Ames, *Southern Women Look at Lynching*. The ASWPL's impulse toward "realism"—its attention to the sexual and racial tensions beneath the genteel surface of middle-class life—found parallel expression in the literature of the southern renaissance. In the 1880s and '90s, southern women writers played a central role in the outpouring of sentimental plantation literature that refurbished the romantic legend of the Old South. By the 1920s and '30s, however, they could be found in the forefront of a new literary realism. Ellen Glasgow, a gentlewoman from Richmond, Virginia, led the move from gentility to "blood and irony." Julia Peterkin of South Carolina, Elizabeth Maddox Roberts of Kentucky, Katherine Ann Porter of Texas, Lillian Hellman of Louisiana, Lillian Smith of Georgia, and Carson McCullers of Tennessee tackled subjects and characters with a frankness unthinkable to earlier generations. Their focus on violence, sexuality, and racial and class oppression provides a measure of deep-going cultural change.

Chapter 8: A Choice of Tactics

1. Reed, *Enduring South*, pp. 33–43.

2. Jessie Daniel Ames, "Women and Lawlessness," p. 31; Ames, *Southern Women Look at Lynching*, p. 3.

3. Dalton (Ga.) *Citizen*, Dec. 11, 1930, Ames Papers (NC).

4. Chadbourn, *Lynching and the Law*, pp. 58–67; ASWPL, *Where Were the Police Officers?*; Macon (Ga.) *News*, Apr. 23, 1931, Ames Papers (NC); "Some Examples of How Sheriffs Prevent Lynchings," n.d., ASWPL Papers.

5. Minutes, Institute, Georgia Council, Nov. 29, 1938, ASWPL Papers; "The Lynching Record for 1938 as Compiled in the Department of Records and Research," Tuskegee Institute, Tuskegee, Alabama.

6. Ames, *Changing Character*, p. 19; Minutes of Discussion, ASWPL Annual Meeting, Jan. 10, 1935.

7. ASWPL, *"White Primary."*

8. JDA to Mrs. F. M. Burkhead, Feb. 18, 1936, ASWPL Papers.

9. Tindall, *Emergence of the New South*, p. 618; Reed, "Ladies and Lynching, In Retrospect" (working paper), p. 175.

10. JDA to Miss Doris Loraine, Mar. 5, 1935, ASWPL Papers.

11. Ames, "Women and Lawlessness," 31, 47–48.

12. Brownmiller, *Against Our Will*, p. 225; Ames, *Southern Women Look at Lynching*, p. 3.

13. Ames, *Toward Lynchless America*.

14. ASWPL, *This Business of Lynching;* Mrs. William P. Cornell to The Sheriffs of Florida, n.d., ASWPL Papers.

15. Mrs. Ruth Knox to JDA, May 13, 1934; CIC Press Service, "Louisiana Peace Officers Ask Anti-Lynching Law," May 19, 1934, ASWPL Papers; Savannah *Tribune*, May 24, 1934, Ames Papers (NC). Similarly, Jane Cornell of Florida convinced the state attorney general to present an anti-lynching address to a Florida School for Peace Officers, and Texas women were instrumental in placing anti-lynching statements in the Texas Sheriffs' Association's monthly magazine. Cornell to JDA, July 13, 1934, ASWPL Papers.

16. ASWPL, *A New Public Opinion;* JDA to ASWPL Members, July 20, 1938, ASWPL Papers; Nordyke, "Ladies and Lynchings."

17. Brownmiller, *Against Our Will*, pp. 225–26.

18. Atlanta *Constitution*, Nov. 5, 1930; JDA to Lucy Randolph Mason, Nov. 3, 1931; Elizabeth Head to Mrs. W. A. Turner, Nov. 3, 1931; JDA to Estelle Haskin, n.d., ASWPL Papers.

19. JDA to ASWPL Chairmen, June 12, 1934; JDA to Mrs. J. W. Mills, Aug. 7, 1934; JDA to Mrs. B. J. Reaves, Apr. 16, 1935; JDA to Mrs. J. Morgan Stevens, June 10, 1935, ASWPL Papers. The effort to secure governors' endorsements was in part designed to gain credibility among moderates and conservatives, and the ASWPL was criticized for placing so much stress on cultivating relationships with state officials. For example, Governor Laffoon of Kentucky attended the 1933 meeting of the Kentucky ASWPL and introduced resolutions calling upon political and civic leaders to build up anti-lynching sentiment in the state. In an open letter published in the Louisville *Courier Journal*, May 14, 1933, John W. Taylor called the governor's action a "pitiful gesture towards 'covering up' and an inadequate substitute for official action" and castigated the Kentucky ASWPL for allowing the governor to dominate its meeting.

20. See, for example, JDA to Gov. David Sholtz, Jan. 30, 1934; Jane Cornell to JDA, Mar. 26, 1935; JDA to Mrs. J. Morgan Stevens, June 10, 1935, ASWPL Papers. These women claim not to be "political," commented Gov. Sholtz of Florida in reference to his experience with ASWPL lobbyists at the Southern Governor's Conference of 1935, "but don't get them crawling your neck or you will never hear the end of it." JDA to Jane Cornell, July 16, 1935, ASWPL Papers.

21. Ames, *Southern Women and Lynching*, p. 11; "What Can A Woman Do?" in *With Quietness They Work: Report of the Activities of Southern Women in Education Against Lynching During 1937* (Atlanta: ASWPL, 1938), pp. 9–10; Jane Cornell to JDA, Jan. 3, 1934; Minutes, Informal Meeting of North Georgia District Secretaries, Sept. 4, 1935, ASWPL Papers. In the Hinds case, a change of venue was granted, but the defendant was convicted of rape by a circuit court jury in Tallahassee and given the death penalty. Cornell's report ends noncommittally: "Robert Hinds was electrocuted on July 31." See also Jane Cornell to JDA, Mar. 26, 1935, ASWPL Papers.

22. Mrs. L. W. Alford to JDA, July 18, 1939, ASWPL Papers.

23. JDA to Mr. W. F. Caldwell, Jan. 12, 1940, ASWPL Papers.

24. JDA Interview.

25. Ibid.

26. Nordyke, "Ladies and Lynchings"; Dykeman and Stokely, *Seeds of Southern Change*, p. 147. See Bessie O'Neal to JDA, Nov. 12, 1935, ASWPL Papers, for a less successful effort of another local woman.

27. Minutes, ASWPL Meeting, Jan. 13–14, 1936; Minutes, ASWPL Annual Conference, Nov. 29, 1938, ASWPL Papers. See also, "Future Program," n.d. [1928], ASWPL Papers.

28. Ames, *Southern Women Look at Lynching*, p. 8.

29. Mrs. S. L. Hollingsworth to Mrs. Lester Greer, Sept. 27, 1933; Greer to Hollingsworth, Sept. 29, 1933; Greer to JDA, July 17, 1934; JDA to Mrs. L. W. Alford, June 30, 1935, ASWPL Papers.

30. Reed, "Evaluation of an Anti-Lynching Organization," p. 176.

31. Report of Mrs. W. A. Newell to Woman's National Committee for Law Enforcement, n.d., Ames Papers (NC); [?] to JDA, n.d. [1937], Ames Papers (NC). See also *Twenty-Sixth Annual Report, Woman's Missionary Council, Methodist Episcopal Church, South, 1935–36* (Nashville, Tenn.: Publishing House of the Methodist Episcopal Church, South, 1936), p. 124.

32. Dykeman and Stokely, *Seeds of Southern Change*, pp. 136, 142, 146.

33. Mrs. L. E. (Onilee R.) Brown to JDA, Mar. 5, 1934, ASWPL Papers; Nordyke, "Ladies and Lynchings"; JDA Interview.

34. Nordyke, "Ladies and Lynching."

35. JDA to Julian Harris, Jan. 14, 1938, ASWPL Papers; Ames, *Toward Lynchless America*.

36. For the role of the suffrage campaign in establishing this new concept of women's relation to the social order, see Ellen DuBois, "The Radicalism of the Woman Suffrage Movement."

37. Reed, "An Evaluation," pp. 172–82. See also, John Shelton Reed, "A Note on the Control of Lynching," *Graduate Sociology Society Journal*, Columbia University, 6 (Sept. 1966), 6–11. For county-by-county analyses of anti-lynching pledges, see "Executive Committee Meeting, Feb. 5, 1941," ASWPL Papers.

38. The best studies of the NAACP campaign for federal anti-lynching legislation are Zangrando, "Federal Anti-Lynching Law," a summary of which appears as Robert L. Zangrando, "The NAACP and a Federal Anti-Lynching Bill, 1934–1940," in Sternsher, ed., *Negro in Depression and War*, pp. 182–83; Wolters, *Negroes and the Great Depression;* and Grant, *Anti-Lynching Movement*. A helpful summary can be found in Tindall, *Emergence of the New South*, pp. 551–56.

39. Wolters, *Negroes and the Great Depression*, pp. 338–39. See also, White, *A Man Called White;* Walter White to Edward P. Costigan, Nov. 27, 1933, Edward P. Costigan Collection.

40. Wolters, *Negroes and the Great Depression*, pp. 221–352.

41. In the 84 lynchings that occurred between 1931 and 1935, indictments were returned in only one lynching out of twelve, and convictions in scarcely one in thirty. Commission on Interracial Cooperation, *The Mob Still Rides*.

42. Walter White to Edward P. Costigan, May 8, 1934, Costigan Collection. See also, Walter White to Drew Pearson, Dec. 26, 1933; Ludwell

Denny to Walter White, Dec. 27, 1933, NAACP Papers; *Crisis*, 42 (Jan. 1935), passim.

43. Albert E. Barnett to Walter White, Jan. 16, 1934; Walter White to Edward P. Costigan, May 8, 1934, Costigan Collection; Walter White to Eleanor Roosevelt, Apr. 20, 1934, Eleanor Roosevelt Papers.

44. Walter White to Hon. Thomas F. Ford, Jan. 13, 1934, Costigan Collection; Walter White to JDA, Jan, 18, 1934 and Oct. 30, 1934; Walter White to Albert E. Barnett, Feb. 8, 1934; Walter White to Will Alexander, Jan. 30, 1934, NAACP Papers.

45. JDA, Report on the Costigan-Wagner Bill Hearings, Feb. 20–21, 1934, ASWPL Papers; JDA to Edward P. Costigan, Feb. 28, 1934, Costigan Collection.

46. Minutes, ASWPL Annual Meeting, Jan. 10, 1935, ASWPL Papers; Edward P. Costigan to JDA, Mar. 7, 1935, Costigan Collection; *World Telegram*, Jan. 18, 1934; *New York Times*, Jan. 14, 1934; Pittsburg *Courier*, Jan. 27, 1934; Walter White to Ludwell Denny, June 19, 1934, NAACP Papers.

47. JDA to "Dear Friend," Apr. 18, 1935, ASWPL Papers; Katherine Gardner to Editor, *New York Times*, Apr. 22, 1935, Costigan Collection.

48. Eleanor Roosevelt to Jane Hoey, Jan. 17, 1934; Roosevelt to JDA, Apr. 20, 1934; JDA to Roosevelt, Jan. 29, 1935, Eleanor Roosevelt Papers; JDA to Walter White, Nov. 3, 1934; White to JDA, Nov. 6, 1934, ASWPL Papers.

49. Lash, *Eleanor and Franklin*, pp. 512–19; Walter White to Eleanor Roosevelt, Apr. 4, 1934, Apr. 20, 1934, May 7, 1934, and May 29, 1934; Roosevelt to White, Nov. 23, 1934, Eleanor Roosevelt Papers; Zangrando, "Federal Anti-Lynching Law" (Ph.D. diss.), p. 329; Walter White to Eleanor Roosevelt, Apr. 29, 1934; White to Edward P. Costigan, May 8, 1934; Costigan to Sen. Joseph T. Robinson, June 11, 1934; "Memorandum on Interview of the NAACP With the President at the White House on January 2, 1935, From 12:15 to 12:50 P.M.," Costigan Collection.

50. "Woman's Missionary Society Denounces Lynching," Birmingham *Age-Herald*, Mar. 13, 1934, Costigan Papers; *Twenty-Fourth Annual Report of the Woman's Missionary Council*, p. 34; *Twenty-Fifth Annual Report of the Woman's Missionary Council of the Methodist Episcopal Church, South, 1934–1935* (Nashville, Tenn.: The Publishing House of the Methodist Episcopal Church, South, 1935), pp. 62–63, 135.

51. Albert E. Barnett to Will Alexander, Oct. 27, 1934; Barnett to Franklin D. Roosevelt, Oct. 27, 1934, ASWPL Papers.

52. Ina Corinne Brown, "Hearings on the Costigan-Wagner Bill," *World Outlook*, 24 (Apr., 1934), 21, 34; U.S. Congress, Senate, Committee on the Judiciary, *Punishment for the Crime of Lynching, Hearings* before a subcommittee of the Committee on the Judiciary, Senate, on S. 1978, 73d Cong. 2d sess., 1934; Walter White to Mr. William Rosenwald, Nov. 1, 1934; White to Will Alexander, Jan. 26, 1934; Albert E. Barnett to White, Jan. 27, 1934, "Alphabetical List of Witnesses to Appear at Hearings on the Costigan-Wagner Anti-Lynching Bill, before the Senate Sub-Committee on the Judiciary," Feb. 20–21, 1934, NAACP Papers; Barnett to Will Alexander, Jan. 27, 1934, ASWPL Papers.

53. Walter White to Eleanor Roosevelt, Apr. 14 and Apr. 20, 1934, Eleanor Roosevelt Papers; Walter White to Mr. Marvin H. McIntyre, May 1, 1934, NAACP Papers.

54. Minutes, Atlanta Conference, Nov. 1, 1930, Ames Papers; JDA to Julian Harris, Jan. 24, 1938; Questionnaires [Dec. 1934]; Katherine Gardner to JDA, Mar. 18, 1934, ASWPL Papers; Frances Williams to Walter White, Jan. 23, 1934, Jan. 24, 1934, and Jan. 30, 1934; Elizabeth S. Harrington to Walter White, Jan. 29, 1934, NAACP Papers.

55. JDA to Mrs. J. W. Downs, Feb. 4, 1934; Downs to JDA, Feb. 8, 1934; Louise Young to Members, Woman's Missionary Council, Mar. 29, 1934; JDA to Mrs. W. A. Newell, Dec. 21, 1934; Mrs. R. P. Neblett to Will Alexander, Nov. 1, 1934, ASWPL Papers; Mrs. W. A. Newell to JDA, Dec. 18, 1934; JDA to Newell, Feb. 22, and Mar. 17, 1938, Ames Papers (NC).

56. Mary J. McCoy to Will Alexander, Jan. 4, 1933; McCoy to JDA, Dec. 3, 1937, ASWPL Papers.

57. Jane Cornell to JDA, Nov. 24, 1934; Cornell to Katherine Gardner, Jan. 4, 1935; Cornell to JDA, Mar. 1, and Mar. 11, 1938, ASWPL Papers. For another active supporter who left the association over this issue, see JDA to O. O. McCollum, Mar. 7, 1938, ASWPL Papers.

58. New York Times, Jan. 11, 1934, and Nov. 1, 1934; JDA to "Dear Friend," Nov. 13, 1934; George Madden Martin to Will Alexander, Jan. 23, 1934; JDA to George Foster Peabody, Nov. 21, 1934, ASWPL Papers; JDA to Emily Newell Blair, Feb. 14, 1934, CIC Papers, JDA Interview; JDA to Eleanor Roosevelt, Apr. 20, 1934; Walter White to Eleanor Roosevelt, Apr. 20, 1934, Eleanor Roosevelt Papers. For support for Ames's view that legislation would result in "farcical 10 minute trials" from a reluctant proponent of federal action, see Gordon B. Hancock, Norfolk Journal and Guide, Feb. 16, 1935, Ames Papers (NC).

59. JDA Interview.

60. Minutes, ASWPL Annual Meeting, Jan. 9, 1934, ASWPL Papers.

61. All quotations are from Minutes, ASWPL Annual Meeting, Jan. 11, 1935, ASWPL Papers. An abridged version of this debate is reprinted in Lerner, Black Women, pp. 473–77.

62. JDA to Henrietta Roeloffs, Apr. 18, 1935, JDA to Julian Harris, Jan. 24, 1938; "Report, Jessie Daniel Ames, Executive Director, Jan. 10, 1935," ASWPL Papers. Ames's assessment of the attitudes of the ASWPL's constituent organizations was probably accurate. In 1938, for example, the Presbyterian Committee on Woman's Work warned her that if the Association did anything to "link it up to the political world," they would withdraw their support. Committee on Woman's Work, Presbyterian Church in the U.S. to JDA, Jan. 10, 1938, ASWPL Papers.

63. While the Methodist leader Sara Estelle Haskin responded to the black women's arguments with a strong affirmation of support, a number of ASWPL members took offense at the tone of the meeting. "An all-day session with the Negro and white women," Ames commented, "has a tendency to drag itself out into recriminations—which are never wholesome." Nevertheless, Ames continued to invite black representatives to meet with the white

women in order to undercut "the radical criticism that is being directed toward us in the present hysteria connected with Federal anti-lynching legislation" and in order to inspire confidence in the ASWPL's work. JDA to Mrs. J. A. Richardson, May 9, 1935; JDA to Mrs. Ben Knox, Jan. 21, 1935; Knox to JDA, Jan. 31, 1935; JDA to Mrs. Steel, Mar. 6, 1935; JDA to Mrs. W. A. Newell, Dec. 4, 1935; Minutes, ASWPL Annual Meeting, Jan. 13–14, 1936; JDA to Kate Davis, Feb. 2, 1937, ASWPL Papers; "Joint Meeting of the Central Council of the ASWPL and a Special Committee of Negro Women of the Interracial Commission," Tuskegee, Alabama, 1938, Ames Papers (NC).

64. Will W. Alexander to Mr. Harold Evans, Mar. 27, 1935; Kate Davis to JDA, Apr. 27, 1935; [JDA], "Anent Commissions Stand on Federal Lynching Law," [1935]; JDA to Mrs. Gertrude Orendoff, May 9, 1935, ASWPL Papers; Walter White to Will Alexander, May, 7, 1935, NAACP Papers; Charles H. Houston to Edward P. Costigan, Apr. 26, 1935, Costigan Collection.

65. JDA to ASWPL Council Members, July 1, 1937, CIC Papers; Hadley Cantril, ed., *Public Opinion, 1935–1946* (Princeton: Princeton University Press, 1951), pp. 151–52; Dabney, "Dixie Rejects Lynching." For southern liberal sentiment, see: Clark Foreman to Clark Howell, Dec. 6, 1933; Mark Ethridge to Will Alexander, Jan., 1934; Alexander to Senator Van Nuys, Feb. 16, 1934, ASWPL Papers; Walter White to Julian Harris, Jan. 12, 1934; Albert E. Barnett to White, Jan. 31, and Feb. 3, 1934; White to Barnett, Jan. 8, 1934; Harris to White, Jan. 6, 1934; George Fort Milton to White, Jan. 30, 1934; White to Will Alexander, Feb. 2, 1934; "What the South Thinks of the Federal Anti-Lynching Bill," NAACP Papers; Julian Harris, "Federal Anti-Lynching Law," Nov. 6, 1934, Harris Papers; Pittsburgh *Courier*, Jan. 20, 1934; Birmingham *Post*, Feb. 22, 1934; Macon *Telegraph*, Feb. 6, 1934 and Feb. 15, 1934; Knoxville *News Sentinel*, Jan. 11, 1934; Newport News (Va.) *Star*, Jan. 11, 1934; Charlottesville (Va.) *Progress*, Dec. 13, 1933; Atlanta *Constitution*, Dec. 9, 1933, Ames Papers (NC); U.S. Congress, Senate, Committee on the Judiciary, *Punishment for the Crime of Lynching, Hearings* before a subcommittee of the Committee on the Judiciary, Senate, on S. 24, 74th Cong., 1st sess., 1935.

66. "Houston Plays Roosevelt Silence on Anti-Lynching Bill," Apr. 27, 1935; Walter White to Franklin D. Roosevelt, May 6, 1935, Costigan Collection. According to Walter White, FDR explained his failure to endorse the bill vigorously in terms of political expediency: "The Southerners by reason of the seniority rule in Congress are chairmen or occupy strategic places on most Senate and House committees. If I come out for the anti-lynching bill now, they will block every bill I ask Congress to pass to keep America from collapsing. I just can't take that risk." White, *A Man Called White*, pp. 167–70. See also Frank Freidel, *F.D.R. and the South* (Baton Rouge: Louisiana State University Press, 1965); Fuller, "The Ring Around the President." Franklin L. Burdette, *Filibustering in the Senate* (Princeton: Princeton University Press, 1940), pp. 179–80. Dabney quoted in Tindall, *Emergence of the New South*, p. 554. By January 1938, during the filibuster, a majority in the South, together with the Rocky Mountain and Coast regions, were opposed to federal legislation.

67. JDA to Sen. Tom Connally, Jan. 28, 1938, Tom Connally Papers; Zangrando, "Federal Anti-Lynching Bill" (Ph.D. diss.), pp. 187–88; JDA to

Bertha Newell, Jan. 28, 1938, Ames Papers (NC). Ames instructed other ASWPL leaders to send similar messages to their governors and senators. Cornell to JDA, Mar. 1, 1938; JDA to Mrs. W. A. Newell, Jan. 28, 1938; Jacksonville *Journal*, Feb. 24, 1938; Jacksonville *Times Union*, Feb. 26, 1938, ASWPL Papers.

68. Atlanta *Constitution*, Jan. 30, 1938; *New York Times*, Jan. 30, 1938. For other instances in which opponents of federal legislation used the ASWPL as evidence of a new morality below the Mason-Dixon line, see *Christian Science Monitor*, Jan. 22, 1935; Augusta (Ga.) *Chronicle*, Feb. 10, 1940; and Pensacola (Fla.) *Journal*, Dec. 15 and Dec. 31, 1939, Feb. 12, 1940. Connally's justification of the filibuster can be found in Tom Connally, as told to Alfred Steinberg, *My Name is Tom Connally* (New York: Crowell, 1954), pp. 169–71. For his continuing role as a powerful opponent of the measure, see U.S. Congress, Senate, Committee on the Judiciary, *Crime of Lynching, Hearings*, before a subcommittee of the Committee on the Judiciary, Senate, on H. R. 801, 76th Cong., 3d sess., 1940.

69. Roy Wilkins to Mrs. Marian Wilkinson, Feb. 3, 1938; Mary McLeod Bethune to Roy Wilkins, Feb. 14, 1938, ASWPL Papers. Arthur Raper, former Research and Field Secretary for the CIC, believed that Ames also gave Connally information that helped him discredit Raper's pro-legislation testimony at congressional hearings in 1940. Ames allegedly provided Connally with details of prevented lynchings that had occurred after the termination of Raper's investigations. Connally used such details to challenge Raper's knowledgeability about the current situation. Raper Interview. For the exchange between Raper and Connally, see U.S. Congress, Senate, Committee on the Judiciary, *Crime of Lynching, Hearings* before a subcommittee of the Committee on the Judiciary, Senate on H.R. 801, 76th Cong., 3d sess, 1940.

70. JDA to Mary McLeod Bethune, Mar. 9, 1938, ASWPL Papers.

71. Mary McLeod Bethune to JDA, Mar. 24, 1938, ASWPL Papers. See also Bethune to Roy Wilkins, Feb. 14, 1938, and "Excerpt From Letter of Mrs. M. R. Wilkinson to Mrs. George Davis," n.d. [1938], ASWPL Papers.

72. JDA to Julian Harris, Jan. 14, 1938, ASWPL Papers.

73. Walter White to H. L. Mencken, Feb. 5, 1934, NAACP Papers.

74. JDA to Una Roberts Lawrence, Dec. 17, 1934, ASWPL Papers, in reference to Texas YWCA leader Mrs. John Hanna.

75. JDA to Mary McLeod Bethune, Mar. 9, 1938, ASWPL Papers.

76. JDA to Edna Giles Fuller, Dec. 7, 1931; Mrs. L. W. Alford to Eurie M. Weston, Jan. 6, 1936, ASWPL Papers; JDA to Mrs. W. A. Newell, Feb. 8, 1938, Feb. 22, 1938, and Mar. 17, 1938, Ames Papers (NC).

77. Mrs. Addie Mullino to JDA, Jan. 15, 1936, Eurie M. Weston to JDA, Jan. 6, 1936, Jane Cornell to JDA, April 23, 1936, Mrs. Sager to JDA, May 12, 1936, JDA to Jane Cornell, May 26, 1937, ASWPL Papers; Gershon Interview; Mrs. W. A. Newell to JDA, June 29, 1938, Ames Papers (NC); Stevens Interview; Young Interview; Margie Groome to author, Dec. 26, 1973.

78. JDA to Mrs. Luke Johnson, Feb. 13, 1924; JDA to Mrs. W. A. Newell, Sept. 7, 1929, Ames Papers (NC).

79. JDA to Mrs. Attwood Martin, Feb. 1, 1939. See also JDA to Jane Cornell, July 24, 1936, and Minutes, Annual Meeting, Jan. 13–14, 1937, ASWPL Papers.

80. JDA to Julian Harris, Oct. 25, 1935; JDA to Miss Doris Loraine, Mar. 5, 1935, ASWPL Papers.

81. JDA to Mrs. W. A. Newell, Feb. 8, 1938, Sept. 13, 1938, Ames Papers (NC). For examples of Ames's antagonism toward women she may have viewed as potential rivals, see JDA to Mrs. W. A. Newell, Oct. 27, 1932, and June 15, 1934; JDA to Emily Clay, Dec. 30, 1962; Emily Clay to JDA, Feb. 2, 1960, Ames Papers (NC); [JDA], "Daniel-Ames Family Life," Priv. Coll.

82. JDA to Mrs. W. A. Newell, July 8, 1935, CIC Papers. For further evidence of the conflict between Ames and Alexander, and for Ames's view of her situation, see: JDA to Mrs. W. A. Newell, July 23, 1937; JDA to Olive Newell, Apr. 9, 1936 and Apr. 22, 1936; JDA to Mrs. Ruth Spence, Oct. 20, 1936; JDA to Mrs. W. A. Newell, Nov. 30, 1936 and July 23, 1937, ASWPL Papers; JDA to Mrs. W. A. Newell, Sept. 1, 1938, and July 27, 1940, Ames Papers (NC); Will Alexander memorandum, May 23, 1936; "Brief Summary of Cooperation Between Church Women and CIC," [1920–40], CIC Papers.

83. JDA to Carrie Parks Johnson, Sept. 8, 1924, Ames Papers (NC).

Chapter 9: Quietly but Definitely Allowed to Die

1. "The Ladies and the Lynchers," *Readers Digest*, 35 (Nov. 1939), 110–13. See, for example, Mobile *Press*, Feb. 2, 1940; Gadsden (Ala.) *Times*, Feb. 2, and Feb. 7, 1940; Birmingham *Age-Herald*, Feb. 3, 1940; Louisville *Times*, Dec. 9, and Nov. 4, 1939; Asheville *Citizen*, Dec. 11, 1939; Kansas City *Call*, Nov. 10, 1939; Chattanooga *Times*, Nov. 7, 1939; Charlotte *News*, Dec. 12, 1939, Ames Papers (NC). Quotations are from Ames, *Southern Women Look at Lynching*, p. 5, and Minutes, ASWPL Annual Meeting, Jan. 26–27, 1939, ASWPL Papers.

2. Ames's "lynchless year" statement—which ran counter to the NAACP's effort to broaden the definition of lynching—proved to be another incident in her running battle with Walter White. For this controversy, see Anna Damon to JDA, May 14, 1940; Walter White to Will W. Alexander, May 15, 1940; Alexander to White, May 17, 1940; "Mrs. Ames Speaks for Self Alone, Says Head of Southern Interracial Commission," Press Service of the NAACP, May 17, 1940, ASWPL Papers; Emily H. Clay to Alexander, May 22, 1940, Southern Regional Council Papers, Southern Regional Council, Atlanta, Georgia, herinafter cited as SRC Papers.

3. For the growth of southern liberalism and the attrition of progressive support for the New Deal, see Krueger, *Promises to Keep;* Grubbs, *Cry From the Cotton;* and Graham, *Encore for Reform.* Quotation is from JDA to Virginius Dabney, July 26, 1943, Ames Papers (NC). See also, JDA to Bertha Newell, Aug. 25, Sept. 13, Oct. 31, 1938, and Mar. 31, 1940; JDA to Mrs. Eason, Apr. 1, 1940, Ames Papers (NC). In a survey prepared for the Carnegie-Myrdal study, *An American Dilemma,* Ralph Bunche indicted the CIC for its pessimism about the racial prejudices of the white working class, on the one hand, and for its optimism about "interracial accommodation" within the middle class on the other. The organization's tactics, he wrote, were based on the "naïve assumption that when the two races know and understand each other better, the principal incidents of the race problem will then disappear." Gunnar Myrdal's treatment of the CIC in an early draft of *American Dilemma* was also quite critical. But in response to objections from the staff, he tempered his interpretation before publication. See Bunche, "Programs, Ideologies, Tactics and Achievements" (unpublished MS), pp. 451–60; Myrdal, *American Dilemma,* II, 842–50; Myrdal to Arthur Raper, July 24, 1942; [Gunnar Myrdal], "The Commission on Interracial Cooperation," n.d.; Emily H. Clay to Myrdal, Aug. 24, 1942; JDA to Myrdal, Aug. 31, 1942, Ames Papers (NC); Clay to Howard Odum, Aug. 9, 1942; Clay to Arthur Raper, Aug. 11, 1942, CIC Papers. For other criticisms, see William E. Cole, "Report on the Commission on Interracial Cooperation," typed report in the CIC Papers, and Gordon B. Hancock to JDA, July 5, 1943, Ames Papers (NC).

4. [JDA], untitled memorandum, Nov. 11, 1942, SRC Papers. See also, Reminiscences of Will W. Alexander, and Alexander to CIC Members, June 20, 1940, CIC Papers.

5. For World War II as a watershed in black history, see Richard M. Dalfiume, "The 'Forgotten Years' of the Negro Revolution," and *Desegregation and the U.S. Armed Forces: Fighting on Two Fronts, 1939–1953* (Columbia, Mo.: University of Missouri Press, 1969); Harvard Sitkoff, "Racial Militancy and Interracial Violence"; Herbert Garfinkel, *When Negroes March: The March on Washington Movement in the Organizational Politics for FEPC* (Glencoe: Free Press, 1959); Finkle, "Conservative Aims of Militant Rhetoric"; Jones, "The Editorial Policy of Negro Newspapers of 1917–18 as Compared with That of 1941–42." For the fears of white interracialists, see Dabney, "Nearer and Nearer the Precipice."

6. Mays, *Born to Rebel,* pp. 214–15; JDA to Gordon B. Hancock, Mar. 12, and Apr. 7, 1942; JDA to Mark Ethridge, May 26, 1942; JDA to Virginius Dabney, May 26, 1942; JDA to Will W. Alexander, July 23, 1942; JDA to Gordon B. Hancock, July 24, 1942, Ames Papers (NC).

7. Quotation is from "A Basis for Interracial Cooperation and Development in the South: A Statement by Southern Negroes," *New South,* 19 (Jan. 1944), 3. The dismantling of the CIC and its replacement by the Southern Regional Council can be traced also in George B. Tindall, "The Significance of Howard W. Odum to Southern History: A Preliminary Estimate," *Journal of Southern History,* 24 (1958), 285–307; Houser, "Founding of the Southern Regional Council" (M.A. thesis); and Allred, "Southern Regional Council," (M.A. thesis).

8. Ralph McGill, "One Word More," Atlanta *Constitution*, Dec. 18, 1942; "Statement of Conference of White Southerners on Race Relations," *New South*, 19 (Jan. 1964), 12; Gavins, "Gordon Blaine Hancock," p. 225; Gordon B. Hancock to JDA, June 25, 1943; JDA to P. B. Young, July 12, 1943, Ames Papers (NC). Odum had first proposed that the CIC be transmuted into a broader Council on Southern Regional Development in 1938. Much to his disappointment, however, his plan was undercut by the formation of the Southern Conference for Human Welfare.

9. Odum's grand design for a coordinated attack on regional problems was never implemented, and during its first decade SRC continued in the tradition of the Interracial Commission. After World War II, however, the issue of segregation could not be avoided. Dissenters, led in 1944 by Lillian Smith, plunged the organization into a controversy that was resolved only in 1951, when SRC finally issued a public statement of its opposition to Jim Crow.

10. Quotation is from Gordon B. Hancock to JDA, Feb. 21, 1944, Priv. Coll. See also P. B. Young to JDA, Feb. 29, 1944, Priv. Coll.; JDA to Josephine Wilkins, Apr. 3, 1957, Ames Papers (NC); Josephine Wilkins Interview. For a detailed narrative of these events, see Gavins, *Perils and Prospects of Black Leadership*, pp. 100–60.

11. Quotations are from [JDA], untitled memorandum, Nov. 11, 1942, SRC Papers; JDA Interview; and Guy B. Johnson Interview. See also Howard Odum to William E. Cole, June 25, 1943; Emily H. Clay to Odum, Nov. 30, 1943; Odum to Cole, Dec. 6, 1943; Odum to JDA, Jan. 3, 1944; Odum to Will W. Alexander, Jan. 6, 1944; Alexander to Odum, Jan. 13, 1944, Howard W. Odum Papers.

12. For accounts of this speech, see Guy B. Johnson Interview; Gordon B. Hancock to JDA, Feb. 21, 1944; P. B. Young to JDA, Feb. 29, 1944; Carter H. Wesley to JDA, Mar. 9, 1944; JDA to Wesley, Apr. 10, 1944, Priv. Coll.

13. As Superintendent of Christian Social Relations for the North Georgia Conference of the Methodist Church, Tilly had worked closely with Ames in the ASWPL. Marion Wright, an Interracial Commission leader in South Carolina who later became president of SRC, described the differences between the two women in these words: Mrs. Ames "was the aggressive, forthright, argumentative type of person. . . . Mrs. Tilly, on the other hand, was soft, effeminate, spiritual, constantly quoting scripture and relying on divine aid as she saw it. Mrs. Ames relied more heavily upon her own strength and the strength of such people as she could summon to her side." Marion A. Wright Interview. In the 1940s and 1950s, Tilly organized a network of church women called the Fellowship of the Concerned to monitor the treatment of black defendants in southern courts. After the 1954 Supreme Court decision, the group was instrumental in mobilizing white support for integration. H. H. Smith, "Mrs. Tilly's Crusade"; Eliza Heard, "Who Remembers Willie?" *New South*, 19 (July–Aug., 1964), 3–4; Shankman, "Dorothy Tilly" (unpublished MS).

14. Quotation is from JDA to Thelma Stevens, Feb. 11, 1944, CIC Papers. See also, JDA to Mrs. Attwood Martin, Feb. 11, 1944, CIC Papers.

15. Quotations are from JDA to Frederick Ames, Mar. 26, 1946, Priv. Coll., and Eugenia Walcott and M. L. Preston Interview, Tryon, North Carolina, Apr. 5, 1976. See also, Mason and Frances Merrill, "Jessie Daniel

Ames," typescript in possession of author; JDA to Guy B. Johnson, Aug. 3, 1946, Ames Papers (NC); JDA to Lulu Daniel Ames, June 1, 1952, Priv. Coll.

16. Walcott and Preston Interview.

17. Quotation is from JDA to Joan Titus, Dec. 30, 1962, Ames Papers (NC). See also, JDA to Frederick Ames, Aug. 12, 1959, Priv. Coll.; JDA to Emily H. Clay, Dec. 30, 1962; Clay to JDA, Feb. 2, 1963, Ames Papers (NC).

18. Merrill, "Jessie Daniel Ames."

19. See Filene, Him/Her/Self, pp. xiii, for this notion of "authenticity."

20. Quotations are from [JDA], "Daniel-Ames Family Life," and JDA to "Dear Son," Feb. 28, 1953, Priv. Coll. See also, JDA to Frederick, Jan. 1, 1941, Aug. 9, 1945, Jan. 9, 1953, and Feb. 28, 1953, Priv. Coll.

21. For this antifeminist reaction, see Chafe, American Woman, pp. 199–225; Evans, "Personal Politics" (Ph.D. diss.), pp. 1–47; Philip Wylie, Generation of Vipers (New York: Farrar and Rinehart, 1942); Lundberg and Farnham, Modern Woman: The Lost Sex; Deutsch, Psychology of Women.

22. JDA to Lulu Hardy, Oct. 19, 1947, Priv. Coll. See also, JDA to Frederick, Aug. 9, 1945, Priv. Coll.

23. Lulu Daniel Ames Interview; JDA, "Story of My Life," Oct. 23, 1897; [JDA], "Daniel-Ames Family Life," Priv. Coll.

24. Lulu Daniel Ames Interview.

25. For the new feminism, see Evans, "Personal Politics" (Ph.D. diss.).

Epilogue

1. For comments on feminist biography, see Gerda Lerner, "Placing Women in History: A 1975 Perspective," in Liberating Women's History: Theoretical and Critical Essays, ed. by Berenice A. Carroll (Urbana: University of Illinois Press, 1976), p. 357 (where she suggested that biographies of "women worthies" belonged to an early stage of "compensatory history") and "Priorities and Challenges in Women's History Research," Perspectives: Newsletter of the American Historical Association 26 (April 1988), 17–20 (where she concluded that the "biographical field within women's history remains one of the most promising and challenging for the researcher"); Carolyn G. Heilbrun, Writing a Woman's Life (New York: Ballantine, 1988); Joan W. Scott, "Gender: A Useful Category of Historical Analysis," American Historical Review 91 (December 1986), 1068; Sara Alpern, et al., "Introduction," Challenge of Feminist Biography; "Special Issue on Auto/biography," Gender & History 2 (Spring 1990); "Introduction," in Hewitt and Lebsock, Visible Women; Carol Ascher, Louise DeSalvo, and Sara Ruddick, eds., Between Women: Biographers, Novelists, Critics, Teachers, and Artists Write About Their Work on Woman (Boston: Beacon Press, 1984). See also Samuel H. Baron and

Carl Pletsch, eds., *Introspection in Biography: The Biographer's Quest for Self-Awareness* (Hillsdale, N.J.: Analytic Press, 1985).

2. I am using *postmodernism* here to refer to a variety of theoretical approaches that on the one hand question the norm of objectivity and the existence of a unified subject and on the other emphasize the ways in which experience is constituted through language. On the gendering of the "self" and the instability of gender identity, see Scott, "Gender: A Useful Category," and "Experience," in *Feminists Theorize the Political*, ed. by Joan W. Scott and Judith Butler (New York: Routledge, 1992), pp. 22–40; Judith Butler, "Gender Trouble, Feminist Theory, and Psychoanalytic Discourse,"in *Feminism/Postmodernism*, ed. by Linda J. Nicholson (New York: Routledge, 1990), pp. 324–40. Leora Auslander, in "Feminist Theory and Social History: Explorations in the Politics of Identity," *Radical History Review* 54 (Fall 1992), 158–76, raises the question of individual identity, often ignored in favor of more collective approaches to the "identity problem." For the uneasy relationship between feminism, postmodernism, and African-American thought, see Jane Flax, *Thinking Fragments: Psychoanalysis, Feminism, and Postmodernism in the Contemporary West* (Berkeley: University of California Press, 1990); and bell hooks, *Yearning: Race, Gender, and Cultural Politics* (Boston: South End Press, 1990). My thinking has also been influenced by James Clifford and George E. Marcus, eds., *Writing Culture: The Poetics and Politics of Ethnography* (Berkeley: University of California Press, 1986).

3. This is Diane Middlebrook's phrase.

4. Robin West, "Economic Man and Literary Woman: One Contrast," *Mercer Law Review* 39 (Spring 1988), 870. Thanks to Charles Lawrence for drawing this article to my attention.

5. C. Vann Woodward, *The Strange Career of Jim Crow* (Oxford: Oxford University Press, 1966; 2d revised ed.), p. xii.

6. Laura Hardy Crites, "The Sisters" [1981], 12, in Laura Crites's possession. I am indebted to Della Pollock for the metaphor of a "circle in motion." The following reflections are drawn in part from Hall, "Second Thoughts" and "Lives Through Time."

7. Dykeman and Stokely, *Seeds of Southern Change*; Scott, *The Southern Lady*, pp. 194–99.

8. Lulu Ames, interview by Jacquelyn Hall, Austin, Texas, 11 Nov. 1972, Southern Oral History Program Collection, and Lulu Daniel Ames Papers, both in Southern Historical Collection, Wilson Library, University of North Carolina at Chapel Hill.

9. Lulu Ames to Benjamin Mays, 22 Jan. 1973, Lulu Daniel Ames Papers.

10. JDA to Darling Lulu, 16 Apr. 1929, Lulu Daniel Ames Papers.

11. JDA to Violet Kimberly of Canada, 25 Jan. 1943, Lulu Daniel Ames Papers. Lulu apparently used "Violet Kimberly" as a pseudonym.

12. This reference to a "wall of self-protection" is contained in an autobiographical essay, "Post-Ames-Family," that Ames wrote about 1951 (in Lulu Daniel Ames Papers). It signifies the Berlin Wall and, more generally, the arms race, in an extended metaphor of "Cold War." Jessie Daniel Ames drew on her private experience to understand social life. At the same time she drew on her politics—in this case, an avid interest in international relations—in

introspection. Thanks to Susan Bourque for drawing this aspect of Ames's thought to my attention.

13. JDA Interview by Pat Watters, Atlanta, Georgia [1966], Southern Oral History Program Collection.

14. For the concept of life review, see Paul Thompson, *The Voice of the Past: Oral History* (Oxford: Oxford University Press, 1978), pp. 100–13.

15. Chodorow, "Family Structure and Feminine Personality." For a critique of object relations theory, see Butler, "Gender Trouble."

16. Jill Conway, "Women Reformers and American Culture, 1870–1930," *Journal of Social History* 5 (Winter 1971–72), 164–77; Joyce Antler, "Was She a Good Mother? Some Thoughts on a New Issue for Feminist Biography," in *Women and the Structure of Society: Selected Research from the Fifth Berkshire Conference on the History of Women*, ed. by Barbara J. Harris and JoAnn K. McNamara (Durham: Duke University Press, 1984), pp. 53–66.

17. See, for example, Barbara Melosh in *Oral History in the Mid-Atlantic Region Newsletter* 5 (Summer 1981), 1; Bettina Aptheker in *Science and Society* 45 (Summer 1981), 236–39.

18. Crites, "The Sisters," 12.

19. Jessie Daniel Ames, *What Price Domestic Service?* These photographs can now be found in the Lulu Daniel Ames Papers.

20. JDA, "Daniel-Ames Family Life" [1951], 18, 19, 24, Lulu Daniel Ames Papers.

21. JDA, "The Story of My Life" [27 Feb. 1922], 4–5, Lulu Daniel Ames Papers; Dykeman and Stokely, *Seeds of Southern Change*, 116; Ames, "Daniel-Ames Family Life," 23.

22. JDA to Frederick Daniel Ames, 30 Aug. 1943, Lulu Daniel Ames Papers.

23. JDA to Mrs. W. A. Newell, 25 Aug. 1938, JDA Papers, Southern Historical Collection.

24. Leila J. Rupp, " 'Imagine My Surprise': Women's Relationships in Mid-Twentieth Century America," in *Hidden From History: Reclaiming the Gay and Lesbian Past*, ed. by Martin Bauml Duberman, Martha Vicinus, and George Chauncey, Jr. (New York: NAL Books, 1989), pp. 395–410, 561–66. Quotation is from *The Book of Common Prayer:* "We have erred and strayed from thy ways like lost sheep. We have followed too much the devices and desires of our own hearts."

25. JDA, "Daniel-Ames Family Life," 18, 22. See also "Post-Ames-Family." For an eloquent description of a similar experience, see Elinor Langer, *Josephine Herbst: The Story She Could Never Tell* (Boston: Little, Brown, 1983), pp. 299–331.

26. Josephine Wilkins, interview by Jacquelyn Hall, March 21, 1972, Southern Oral History Program Collection.

27. JDA Interview.

28. Patricia Meyer Spacks, "Selves in Hiding," in *Women's Autobiography: Essays in Criticism*, ed. by Estelle C. Jelinek (Bloomington: Indiana University Press, 1980), pp. 112–32.

Selected Bibliography

The following bibliography includes the works that proved most useful to this study. This list, together with the notes, makes up a complete survey of the sources upon which this book is directly based; full citations are given in the notes for those sources not listed here.

Manuscript Collections

Jessie Daniel Ames Papers, Dallas Historical Society, Hall of State, Dallas, Texas.

Jessie Daniel Ames Papers, Southern Historical Collection, University of North Carolina at Chapel Hill.

Jessie Daniel Ames Papers, Texas State Library, Austin, Texas.

Lulu Daniel Ames Family Papers, Private Collection in possession of author.

Association of Southern Women for the Prevention of Lynching Papers, Trevor Arnett Library, Atlanta University, Atlanta, Georgia.

Mary McLeod Bethune Papers, Amistad Research Center, Dillard University, New Orleans, Louisiana.

Charlotte Hawkins Brown Papers, Arthur and Elizabeth Schlesinger Library, Radcliffe College, Cambridge, Massachusetts.

Commission on Interracial Cooperation Papers, Trevor Arnett Library, Atlanta University.

Tom Connally Papers, Library of Congress.

Edward P. Costigan Collection, Western Historical Collections, University of Colorado Libraries, Boulder, Colorado.

Minnie Fisher Cunningham Papers, University Libraries, University of Houston.

Grace Towns Hamilton Papers, Trevor Arnett Library, Atlanta University.

Joint Legislative Council Papers, Library of Congress, Washington, D.C.

Julian LaRose Harris Papers, Woodruff Library, Emory University, Atlanta, Georgia.

Julius Rosenwald Fund Archives, Fisk University, Nashville, Tennessee.

Howard Kester Papers, Southern Historical Collection, University of North Carolina at Chapel Hill.

Thomas B. Love Papers, Dallas Historical Society, Hall of State, Dallas, Texas.

Jane Y. McCallum Family Papers, Austin Public Library, Austin, Texas.

Lucy Randolph Mason Papers, William Perkins Library, Duke University, Durham, North Carolina.

George Fort Milton Papers, Library of Congress.

Dan Moody Papers, Texas State Library, Austin, Texas.

National American Woman Suffrage Association Collection, Library of Congress.

National Association for the Advancement of Colored Peoples Papers, Library of Congress.

National League of Women Voters Papers, Library of Congress.

Neighborhood Union Papers, Trevor Arnett Library, Atlanta University.

North Carolina Commission on Interracial Cooperation Papers, Southern Historical Collection, University of North Carolina at Chapel Hill.

Howard Odum Papers, Southern Historical Collection, University of North Carolina at Chapel Hill.

Eleanor Roosevelt Papers, Franklin Delano Roosevelt Library, Hyde Park, New York.

Lillian Smith Papers, University of Florida, Gainesville, Florida.

Southern Regional Council Papers, Southern Regional Council, Atlanta, Georgia.

Mary Church Terrell Papers, Library of Congress.

Records of the Women's Joint Congressional Committee, Library of Congress.

Louise Young Papers, Scarritt College Division, Joint Universities Library, Scarritt College, Nashville, Tennessee.

Young Women's Christian Associations Papers, Sophia Smith Collection, Smith College, Northampton, Massachusetts.

Interviews

Reminiscences of Will W. Alexander, Oral History Research Office, Columbia University, New York, New York.

Jessie Daniel Ames Interview, n.d. [1965–66?], Southern Regional Council Papers, Atlanta, Georgia, and Southern Oral History Program, University of North Carolina at Chapel Hill.

Lulu Daniel Ames Interview, private interview, Austin, Texas, November 11, 1972, and May 21, 1973.

Emily Clay Interview, private interview, Chapel Hill, North Carolina, July 1, 1975.

Alice Cobb Interview, February 15, 1972, Southern Oral History Program.

Virginia Foster Durr Interview, March 13–15, 1975, Southern Oral History Program.

Willie Snow Ethridge Interview, December 15, 1975, Southern Oral History Program.

Rebecca Gershon Interview, private interview, Atlanta, Georgia, December 28, 1972.

Grace Towns Hamilton Interview, July 19, 1974, Southern Oral History Program.

Guion Griffis Johnson Interview, April 17, May 17, May 28, June 1, 1974, Southern Oral History Program.

Guy B. Johnson Interview, December 16, 1974, Southern Oral History Program.

Katharine Du Pre Lumpkin Interview, June 4, 1974, Southern Oral History Program.

Lois MacDonald Interview, November 6, 1974, and June 24, 1975, Southern Oral History Program.

Reba McKeithen Interview, private interview, Georgetown, Texas, March 8, 1975.

Emily S. MacLachlan Interview, July 16, 1974, Southern Oral History Program.

Pauli Murray Interview, February 13, 1976, Southern Oral History Program.

Mary Ames Raffensperger Interview, private interview, Philadelphia, Pennsylvania, July 7, 1974.

Arthur Raper Interview, January 30, 1974, Southern Oral History Program.

Modjeska Simkins Interview, July 28–31, 1976, Southern Oral History Program.

Ruth Potts Spence Interview, private interview, Dallas, Texas, March 12, 1975.

Thelma Stevens Interview, February 14, 1972, Southern Oral History Program.

Olive Stone Interview, March 6, June 27, August 13, September 10, October 14, November 4, 1975, Southern Oral History Program.

Eugenia Walcott Interview, private interview, Tryon, North Carolina, April 5, 1976.

Josephine Wilkins Interview, March 21, 1972, Southern Oral History Program.

Alice Spearman Wright Interview, February 28, August 8, 1976, Southern Oral History Program.

Marion A. Wright Interview, March 11, 1976, Southern Oral History Program.

Louise Young Interview, February 14, 1972, Southern Oral History Program.

Other Unpublished Material

Allred, William Clifton, Jr. "The Southern Regional Council, 1943–1961." M.A. thesis, Emory University, 1966.

Barber, Henry Eugene. "The Association of Southern Women for the Prevention of Lynching, 1930–1942." M.A. thesis, University of Georgia, 1967.

Bowles, Willie Dee Worley. "History of Woman Suffrage in Texas." M.A. thesis, University of Texas, 1939.

Bunche, Ralph J. "Extended Memorandum on the Programs, Ideologies, Tactics and Achievements of Negro Betterment and Interracial Organizations." Unpublished Memorandum for the Carnegie Foundation–Gunnar Myrdal Study of the Negro in America, 1940. Schomburg Collection, New York Public Library.

Burns, Elizabeth Jacoway. "The Industrial Education Myth: Character Building at Penn School, 1900–1948." Ph.D. dissertation, University of North Carolina, 1974.

Burrows, Edward Flud. "The Commission on Interracial Cooperation, 1919–1944: A Case Study in the History of the Interracial Movement in the South." Ph.D. dissertation, University of Wisconsin, 1955.

Calkins, Gladys Gilkey. "The Negro in the YWCA." M.A. thesis, George Washington University, 1960.

Correll, Emily Newby. "North Carolina Baptist and Methodist Women's Missionary Organizations." M.A. thesis, University of North Carolina, 1977.

Cole, William C. "Report on the Commission on Interracial Cooperation, 1942–1943." Commission on Interracial Cooperation Papers. (Mimeographed.)

Crites, Laura Hardy. "A History of the Association of Southern Women for Prevention of Lynching, 1930–1942." M.A. thesis, American University, 1965.

Davis, Sidney Thomas. "Woman's Work in the Methodist Church." Ph.D. dissertation, University of Pittsburgh, 1963.

Eleazer, Robert B. "My First Eighty Years: A Brief Account of My Life for Those Who Come After." September 21, 1957. Special Collections, Joint University Libraries, Vanderbilt University, Nashville, Tennessee. (Typewritten.)

Ellis, Ann Wells. "The Commission on Interracial Cooperation, 1919–1944: Its Activities and Results." Ph.D. dissertation, Georgia State University, 1975.

Evans, Sara Margaret. "Personal Politics: The Roots of Women's Liberation in the Civil Rights Movement and the New Left." Ph.D. dissertation, University of North Carolina, 1976.

Fish, John. "Southern Methodism in the Progressive Era: A Social History." Ph.D. dissertation, University of Georgia, 1969.

Gay, Dorothy Ann. "The Tangled Skein of Romanticism and Violence in the Old South: The Southern Response to Abolitionism and Feminism, 1830–1861." Ph.D. dissertation, University of North Carolina, 1975.

Green, Linda Lou. "Nell Battle Lewis: Crusading Columnist, 1921–1938." M.A. thesis, East Carolina University, 1969.

Hall, Jacquelyn Dowd. "Revolt Against Chivalry: Jessie Daniel Ames and the Women's Campaign Against Lynching." Ph.D. dissertation, Columbia University, 1974.

Hall, Winona R. "Janie Porter Barrett, Her Life and Contributions to Social Welfare in Virginia." M.A. thesis, Howard University, 1954.

Harris, Neil. "The Culture of Catastrophe in Nineteenth-Century America." Paper delivered at University of North Carolina at Chapel Hill, November 20, 1975.

Higgins, Ray E., Jr. "Strange Fruit: Lynching in South Carolina, 1900–1914." M.A. thesis, University of South Carolina, 1961.

Hoot, John W. "Lynch Law: the Practice of Illegal Popular Coercion." Ph.D. dissertation, University of Pennsylvania, 1935.

Houser, Henry Paul. "The Founding of the Southern Regional Council." M.A. thesis, University of North Carolina, 1950.

Kirby, John Byron. "The New Deal Era and Blacks: A Study of Black and White Race Thought, 1933–1945." Ph.D. dissertation, University of Illinois, 1971.

Mounger, Dwyn M. "Lynching in Mississippi, 1830–1930." M.A. thesis, Mississippi State University, 1961.

National Student Council, Young Women's Christian Association. "Interracial News Bulletins," 1931–1932. (Mimeographed.)

Neustadt, Margaret Lee. "Miss Lucy of the CIO: Lucy Randolph Mason, 1882–1959." M.A. thesis, University of North Carolina, 1969.

O'Malley, Stephen. "The Salisbury Lynching, 1906." M.A. thesis, University of North Carolina, 1977.

Price, Margaret Nell. "The Development of Leadership by Southern Women Through Clubs and Organizations." M.A. thesis, University of North Carolina, 1945.

Raper, Arthur. "Race and Class Pressures." Gunnar Myrdal Collection, Schomburg Collection, New York Public Library, 1940. (Mimeographed.)

Reed, John Shelton. "Ladies and Lynching, In Retrospect: An Application of Methods of Evaluation." Working paper, Graduate Sociological Society, Columbia University, December, 1966, Association of Southern Women for the Prevention of Lynching Papers, Trevor Arnett Library, Atlanta University.

Shadron, Virginia A. "Out of Our Homes: The Woman's Rights Movement in the Methodist Episcopal Church, South, 1890–1918." M.A. thesis, Emory University, 1976.

Shankman, Arnold. "Dorothy Tilly and the Fellowship of the Concerned." Paper delivered at the Citadel, Charleston, S.C., 1978.

Shivery, Louise D. "History of Organized Social Work Among Atlanta Negroes." M.A. thesis, Atlanta University, 1936.

Steelman, John R. "A Study of Mob Action in the South." Ph.D. dissertation, University of North Carolina, 1928.

Strickland, Scott. "The North Carolina Slave Conspiracy Scare of 1802 and the Great Revival: An Examination of Precipitants of Crisis in Antebellum Southern Society." Paper delivered at North Carolina State University, 1977.

A Survey and Plan of Fund-Raising for the Commission on Interracial Cooperation. Report prepared by the John Price Jones Corporation, June 25, 1929. Commission on Interracial Cooperation Papers, Trevor Arnett Library, Atlanta University. (Mimeographed.)

Vielock, Mamie B. "Texas Women Campaign for Suffrage." M.A. thesis, St. Mary's University, 1949.

Winfrey, Annie Laura. "The Organized Activities of the Women of Southern Methodism in the Field of Negro-White Relationships, 1886–1937." M.A. thesis, Scarritt College, 1938.

Wooten, Mattie Lloyd. "The Status of Women in Texas." Ph.D. dissertation, University of Texas, 1941.

Yandle, Carolyn Devore. "A Delicate Crusade: The Association of Southern Women for the Prevention of Lynching." M.A. thesis, University of Virginia, 1969.

Zangrando, Robert L. "The Efforts of the NAACP to Secure Passage of a Federal Anti-Lynching Law, 1920–1940." Ph.D. dissertation, University of Pennsylvania, 1963.

Government Documents

U.S. Congress. House. Joint Select Committee to Inquire into the Condition of Affairs in the Late Insurrectionary States. *Affairs in the Late Insurrectionary States.* H. Rept. 22, 42d Cong., 2d sess., 1872.

U.S. Congress. Senate. Committee on the Judiciary. *To Prevent and Punish the Crime of Lynching. Hearings* before a subcommittee of the Committee on the Judiciary, Senate, on S. 121, 69th Cong., 1st sess., 1926.

—— *Punishment for the Crime of Lynching. Hearings* before a subcommittee of the Committee on the Judiciary, Senate, on S. 1978, 73d Cong., 2d sess., 1934.

—— *Punishment for the Crime of Lynching. Hearings* before a subcommittee of the Committee on the Judiciary, Senate, on S. 24, 74th Cong., 1st sess., 1935.

—— *Crime of Lynching. Hearings* before a subcommittee of the Committee on the Judiciary, Senate, on H.R. 801, 76th Cong., 3d sess., 1940.

Books, Pamphlets, and Reports

Alexander, Charles C. *Crusade for Conformity: The Ku Klux Klan in Texas, 1920–1930.* Houston: Texas Gulf Coast Historical Association, 1962.

Ames, Jessie Daniel. *Association of Southern Women for the Prevention of Lynching.* Atlanta: Commission on Interracial Cooperation, 1932.

—— *Cast Down Your Bucket Where You Are.* Atlanta: Commission on Interracial Cooperation, 1931.

—— *The Changing Character of Lynching.* Atlanta: Commission on Interracial Cooperation, 1942.

—— *Democratic Processes at Work in the South: Report of the Commission on Interracial Cooperation, 1939–1941.* Atlanta: Commission on Interracial Cooperation, 1941.

—— *Free Schools for All Alike.* Atlanta: Commission on Interracial Cooperation, n.d.

—— *Southern Women Look at Lynching.* Atlanta: Association of Southern Women for the Prevention of Lynching, 1937.

Ames, Jessie Daniel. *Toward Lynchless America*. Reprint. Atlanta: Association of Southern Women for the Prevention of Lynching, December 1940.

—— *What Price Domestic Service?* Atlanta: Commission on Interracial Cooperation, 1931.

—— *Whither Leads the Mob?* Atlanta: Commission on Interracial Cooperation, 1932.

——, comp. *Friends and Neighbors*. Atlanta: Commission on Interracial Cooperation, 1935.

——, ed. *The Future of the Negro in American Life*. Atlanta: Commission on Interracial Cooperation, 1942.

——, and Bertha Payne Newell. *Repairers of the Breach: A Story of Interracial Cooperation Between Southern Women, 1935–1940*. Atlanta: Commission on Interracial Cooperation, 1940.

Amir, Menachem. *Patterns in Forcible Rape*. Chicago: University of Chicago Press, 1971.

Association of Southern Women for the Prevention of Lynching. *Are the Courts to Blame?* Atlanta: Association of Southern Women for the Prevention of Lynching, 1934.

—— *Death by Parties Unknown*. Atlanta: Association of Southern Women for the Prevention of Lynching, 1936.

—— *Feeling Is Tense*. Atlanta: Association of Southern Women for the Prevention of Lynching, 1938.

—— *Lynching Is Wholesale Murder*. Atlanta: Association of Southern Women for the Prevention of Lynching, 1937.

—— *A Lynching Threatens*. Atlanta: Association of Southern Women for the Prevention of Lynching, 1936.

—— *A New Public Opinion on Lynching: A Declaration and a Pledge*. Atlanta: Association of Southern Women for the Prevention of Lynching, 1932–1941.

—— *Organizations Committed to a Program of Education to Prevent Lynching*. Atlanta: Association of Southern Women for the Prevention of Lynching, 1941.

—— *This Business of Lynching*. Atlanta: Association of Southern Women for the Prevention of Lynching, 1935.

—— *What One Woman Can Do to Prevent Lynchings*. Atlanta: Association of Southern Women for the Prevention of Lynching, 1938.

—— *What We Know about Lynchings and Mobs*. Atlanta: Association of Southern Women for the Prevention of Lynching, 1936.

—— *Where Were the Police Officers?* Atlanta: Association of Southern Women for the Prevention of Lynching, 1937.

—— *The "White Primary," An Extra-Legal Institution*. Atlanta: Association of Southern Women for the Prevention of Lynching, January, 1942.

—— *Why We Lynch*. Atlanta: Association of Southern Women for the Prevention of Lynching, 1932.

Avary, Myrta Lockett. *Dixie After the War: An Exposition of Social Conditions Existing in the South, during the Twelve Years Succeeding the Fall of Richmond*. 1906. Reprint, New York: Negro Universities Press, 1969.

Avera, Carl L. *Wind Swept Land*. San Antonio: Naylor Company, 1964.

Bailey, Hugh C. *Liberalism in the New South: Southern Social Reformers and the Progressive Movement*. Coral Gables: University of Miami Press, 1969.

Bailey, Kenneth K. *Southern White Protestantism in the Twentieth Century*. New York: Harper and Row, 1964.

Baker, Paul E. *Negro-White Adjustment: An Investigation and Analysis of Methods in the Interracial Movement in the United States*. New York: Association Press, 1934.

Baker, Ray Stannard. *Following the Color Line: An Account of Negro Citizenship in the American Democracy*. 1908. Reprint, New York: Harper and Row, 1964.

Barker-Benfield, G. J. *The Horrors of the Half-Known Life: Male Attitudes Toward Women and Sexuality in Nineteenth-Century America*. New York: Harper and Row, 1976.

Bardolph, Richard. *The Negro Vanguard*. New York: Rinehart, 1959.

Beam, Lura. *He Called Them by the Lightning: A Teacher's Odyssey in the Negro South, 1908–1919*. New York: Bobbs-Merrill, 1967.

Beard, Mary. *America Through Women's Eyes*. New York: Macmillan, 1933.

Beauvoir, Simone de. *The Second Sex*. 1949. Reprint, New York: Bantam Books, 1961.

Bell, Juliet O., and Helen J. Wilkins. *Interracial Practices in Community YWCA's*. New York: National Board, YWCA, 1944.

Berry, Mary Frances. *Black Resistance/White Law*. New York: Meredith, 1971.

Bilbo, Theodore. *Take Your Choice: Separation or Mongrelization*. Popularville, Miss.: Dream House Publishing Co., 1947.

Boyle, Sarah Patton. *The Desegregated Heart: A Virginian's Stand in Time of Transition*. New York: Morrow, 1962.

Brown, Charlotte. *The Correct Thing to Do, to Say, to Wear*. Boston: Christopher Publishing House, 1941.

Brown, Hallie Quinn. *Homespun Heroines and other Women of Distinction*. Xenia, Ohio: Aldine, 1926.

Brown, Richard Maxwell. *Strain of Violence: Historical Studies of American Violence and Vigilantism*. New York: Oxford University Press, 1975.

Brownmiller, Susan. *Against Our Will: Men, Women, and Rape*. New York: Simon and Schuster, 1975.

Bruce, Philip Alexander. *The Plantation Negro as a Freeman*. New York: Putnam's, 1889.

Burke, Fielding. *Call Home the Heart*. London: Longmans, Green, 1932.

Butterfield, Stephen. *Black Autobiography in America*. Amherst: University of Massachusetts Press, 1974.

Cade, Toni, ed. *The Black Woman: An Anthology*. New York: New American Library, Mentor Books, 1970.

Cantril, Hadley. *The Psychology of Social Movements*. New York: Wiley, 1941.

Carson, Josephine. *Silent Voices: The Southern Negro Woman Today*. New York: Dell, 1969.

Carter, Dan T. *Scottsboro: A Tragedy of the American South*. Baton Rouge: Louisiana State University Press, 1969.

Cash, W. J. *The Mind of the South*. New York: Knopf, 1941.

Catt, C. C., and N. R. Schuler. *Woman Suffrage and Politics*. New York: Scribner's, 1926.

Caughey, John W., ed. *Their Majesties, the Mob*. Chicago: University of Chicago Press, 1960.

Cayton, Horace. *Long Old Road*. 1964. Reprint, Seattle: University of Washington Press, 1970.

Chadbourn, James Harmon. *Lynching and the Law*. Chapel Hill: University of North Carolina Press, 1933.

Chafe, William H. *The American Woman*. New York: Oxford University Press, 1972.

—— *Women and Equality: Changing Patterns in American Culture*. New York: Oxford University Press, 1977.

Clark, Septima. *Echo in My Soul*. New York: Dutton, 1962.

Cleaver, Eldridge. *Soul on Ice*. New York: McGraw-Hill, 1968.

Colllins, Winfield H. *The Truth About Lynching and the Negro in the South, in Which the Author Pleads That the South Be Made Safe for the White Race*. New York: Neale Publishing Co., 1918.

Commission on Interracial Cooperation. *The Mob Still Rides: A Review of the Lynching Record, 1931–1935*. Atlanta: Commission on Interracial Cooperation, n.d.

Cott, Nancy F. *The Bonds of Womanhood: "Woman's Sphere" in New England, 1780–1835*. New Haven and London: Yale University Press, 1977.

Cutler, James E. *Lynch-Law: An Investigation into the History of Lynching in the United States*. New York: Longmans, Green, 1905.

Dabney, Virginius. *Below the Potomac: A Book About the New South*. 1942. Reprint, New York: Kennikat Press, 1969.

—— *Liberalism in the South*. Chapel Hill: University of North Carolina Press, 1932.

Daniel, Pete. *The Shadow of Slavery: Peonage in the South, 1901–1969*. Urbana: University of Illinois Press, 1972.

Daniel, Sadie Iola. *Women Builders*. Washington, D.C.: Associated Publishers, 1931.

Daniels, Jonathan. *A Southerner Discovers the South*. 1938. Reprint, New York: Da Capo Press, 1970.

Dann, Martin E., ed. *The Black Press, 1827–1890: The Quest for National Identity*. New York: Putnam's, 1971.

Davis, Allison, Burleigh B. Gardner, and Mary R. Gardner. *Deep South: A Social Anthropological Study of Caste and Class*. Chicago: University of Chicago Press, 1941.

Davis, Lenwood G. *The Black Woman in American Society: A Selected Annotated Bibliography*. Boston: G. K. Hall, 1975.

Degler, Carl. *The Other South: Southern Dissenters in the Nineteenth Century*. New York: Harper and Row, 1974.

Deutsch, Helene. *The Psychology of Women*. New York: Grune and Stratton, 1944.

Dinnerstein, Leonard. *The Leo Frank Case*. New York: Columbia University Press, 1968.

Dixon, Thomas, Jr. *The Clansman: An Historical Romance of the Ku Klux Klan*. New York: Doubleday, Page, 1905.

—— *The Leopard's Spots: A Romance of the White Man's Burden, 1865–1900*. New York: Doubleday, Page, 1902.

Dollard, John. *Caste and Class in a Southern Town*. 1937. Reprint, Garden City, N.Y.: Doubleday, 1957.

——, et al. *Frustration and Aggression*. New Haven: Yale University Press, 1939.

Douglas, Ann. *The Feminization of American Culture*. New York: Knopf, 1977.

Du Bois, W.E.B. *Darkwater: Voices from Within the Veil*. New York: Harcourt Brace and Howe, 1920.

—— *Dusk of Dawn: An Essay Toward an Autobiography of a Race Concept*. New York: Harcourt, Brace, 1940.

—— "A Mild Suggestion," in *The Seventh Son: The Thought and Writings of W.E.B. Du Bois*. Edited by Julius Lester. New York: Random House, 1971.

Dunn, Mary Noreen. *Women and Home Missions*. Nashville: Cokesbury Press, 1936.

Durkheim, Emile. *The Division of Labor in Society*. 1893. Reprint, New York: Free Press, 1964.

Dykeman, Wilma. *Prophet of Plenty: The First Ninety Years of W. D. Weatherford*. Knoxville: University of Tennessee Press, 1966.

—— and James Stokely. *Seeds of Southern Change: The Life of Will Alexander*. Chicago: University of Chicago Press, 1962.

Earhart, Mary. *Frances Willard: From Prayers to Politics*. Chicago: University of Chicago Press, 1944.

Eaton, Clement. *The Freedom-of-Thought Struggle in the Old South*. New York: Harper and Row, 1964.

Eighmy, John Lee. *Churches in Cultural Captivity: A History of the Social Attitudes of Southern Baptists*. Knoxville: University of Tennessee Press, 1972.

Eleazer, Robert B. *Southern Women and the South's Race Problem*. Atlanta: Commission on Interracial Cooperation, n.d. [1929].

Ellison, Ralph. *Invisible Man*. New York: Signet, 1952.

—— *Shadow and Act*. 1953. Reprint, New York: Signet, 1966.

Embree, Edwin R. *Brown America: The Story of a New Race*. New York: Viking, 1931.

Erikson, Erik H. *Childhood and Society*. New York: Norton, 1963.

—— *Identity and the Life Cycle*. New York: International Universities Press, 1959.

Ferguson, Charles W. *Organizing to Beat the Devil*. Garden City, N.Y.: Doubleday, 1971.

Fiedler, Leslie. *Love and Death in the American Novel*. Rev. ed. New York: Delta, 1966.

Filene, Peter Gabriel. *Him/Her/Self: Sex Roles in Modern America*. New York: Harcourt Brace Jovanovich, 1975.

Flexner, Eleanor. *Century of Struggle: The Woman's Rights Movement in the United States*. Cambridge, Mass.: Belknap Press, Harvard University Press, 1959.

Frazier, E. Franklin. *Black Bourgeoisie*. Glencoe, Ill.: Free Press, 1957.

—— *The Negro Family in the United States*. Rev. and abridged ed. Chicago: University of Chicago Press, 1966.

Frederickson, George M. *The Black Image in the White Mind: The Debate on Afro-American Character and Destiny, 1817–1914*. New York: Harper and Row, 1971.

Friedman, Leon, ed. *Southern Justice*. New York: Meridian, 1967.

Fuller, Paul E. *Laura Clay and the Woman's Rights Movement*. Lexington: University of Kentucky Press, 1975.

Gaston, Paul M. *The New South Creed: A Study in Southern Mythmaking*. New York: Knopf, 1970.

Gavins, Raymond. *The Perils and Prospects of Southern Black Leadership: Gordon Blaine Hancock, 1884–1970*. Durham: Duke University Press, 1977.

Geertz, Clifford. *The Interpretation of Cultures: Selected Essays by Clifford Geertz*. New York: Basic Books, 1973.

Gilmore, Al-Tony. *Bad Nigger! The National Impact of Jack Johnson*. Port Washington, N.Y.: Kennikat Press, 1975.

Ginzburg, Ralph, ed. *100 Years of Lynchings*. New York: Lancer Books, 1962.

Glasgow, Ellen. *The Woman Within*. New York: Harcourt, Brace, 1954.

Goldstein, Naomi. *The Roots of Prejudice Against the Negro in the United States*. Boston: Boston University Press, 1948.

Goodwyn, Lawrence. *Democratic Promise: The Populist Movement in America*. New York: Oxford University Press, 1976.

Gould, Lewis L. *Progressives and Prohibitionists: Texas Democrats in the Wilson Era*. Austin: University of Texas Press, 1973.

Graham, Otis L. *An Encore for Reform: The Old Progressives and the New Deal*. New York: Oxford University Press, 1967.

Grant, Donald L. *The Anti-Lynching Movement, 1883–1932*. San Francisco: R and E Research Associates, 1975.

Graves, John Temple. *The Fighting South*. New York: Putnam's, 1943.

Grimes, Alan P. *The Puritan Ethic and Woman Suffrage*. New York: Oxford University Press, 1967.

Grimshaw, Allen D., ed. *Racial Violence in the United States*. Chicago: Aldine, 1969.

Grubbs, Donald H. *Cry from the Cotton: The Southern Tenant Farmers' Union and the New Deal*. Chapel Hill: University of North Carolina Press, 1971.

Gutman, Herbert G. *The Black Family in Slavery and Freedom, 1750–1925*. New York: Pantheon, 1976.

Hammond, Lily H. *Race and the South: Two Studies, 1914–1922*. New York:

Arno Press, 1972. Originally published in two volumes as *In Black and White: An Interpretation of Southern Life.* New York: Fleming H. Revell, 1914, and *In the Vanguard of a Race.* New York: Council of Women for Home Missions and Missionary Education Movement of the United States and Canada, 1922.

—— *Southern Women and Racial Adjustment.* Lynchburg, Va.: J. P. Bell, 1917.

Haskin, Sara Estelle. *Women and Missions in the Methodist Episcopal Church, South.* Nashville: Publishing House of the Methodist Episcopal Church, South, 1921.

Haynes, George Edmund. *Toward Interracial Cooperation.* New York: Federal Council of Churches, 1926.

Helm, Mary. *From Darkness to Light.* New York: Fleming H. Revell, 1909.

—— *The Upward Path: The Evolution of a Race.* New York: Young People's Missionary Movement of the United States and Canada, 1909.

Hofstadter, Richard, and Michael Wallace, eds. *American Violence: A Documentary History.* New York: Random House, 1971.

Holiday, Billie. *Lady Sings the Blues.* London: Barrie and Jenkins, 1973.

Holt, Rakham. *Mary McLeod Bethune: A Biography.* Garden City, N. Y.: Doubleday, 1964.

Horney, Karen. *Feminine Psychology.* Edited and with an introduction by Harold Kelman. New York: Norton, 1967.

Howell, Mabel Katharine. *Women and the Kingdom.* Nashville: Cokesbury Press, 1928.

Hurston, Zora Neale. *Their Eyes Were Watching God.* Philadelphia: Lippincott, 1937.

Irwin, Will. *Propaganda and the News.* New York: McGraw-Hill, 1936.

Jackson, Kenneth T. *The Ku Klux Klan in the City, 1915–1930.* New York: Oxford University Press, 1967.

Johnson, Charles S. *Growing Up in the Black Belt: Negro Youth in the Rural South.* Washington, D.C.: American Council on Education, 1941.

——, Edwin R. Embree, and Will W. Alexander. *The Collapse of Cotton Tenancy.* Chapel Hill: University of North Carolina Press, 1935.

——, et al. *Into the Main Stream: a Survey of Best Practices in Race Relations in the South.* Chapel Hill: University of North Carolina Press, 1947.

Johnson, James Weldon. *Autobiography of an Ex-Colored Man, Three Negro Classics.* Introduction by John Hope Franklin. New York: Avon, 1965.

Johnston, James Hugo. *Race Relations in Virginia and Miscegenation in the South, 1776–1860.* Amherst, Mass.: University of Massachusetts Press, 1970.

Jones, LeRoi. *Dutchman and the Slave: Two Plays.* New York: Morrow, 1964.

Jordan, Winthrop. *White Over Black: American Attitudes Toward the Negro, 1550–1812.* Baltimore: Penguin, 1969.

Kearney, Belle. *A Slaveholder's Daughter.* New York: Abbey Press, 1900.

Kearns, Doris. *Lyndon Johnson and the American Dream.* New York: Harper and Row, 1976.

Kellogg, Charles Flint. *NAACP: A History of the National Association for the Advancement of Colored People.* Baltimore: Johns Hopkins Press, 1967.

Kerlin, Robert T., ed. *The Voice of the Negro, 1919.* New York Dutton, 1920.

Kester, Howard. *The Lynching of Claude Neal.* New York: National Association for the Advancement of Colored People, November 30, 1934.

—— *Lynching Goes Underground.* Sponsored by Senators Wagner and Arthur Capper, and Congressmen Joseph Gavagan and Hamilton Fish. January 1940.

Kirby, Jack Temple. *Darkness at the Dawning: Race and Reform in the Progressive South.* Philadelphia: Lippincott, 1972.

Kousser, J. Morgan. *The Shaping of Southern Politics: Suffrage Restriction and the Establishment of the One-Party South, 1880–1910.* New Haven: Yale University Press, 1974.

Kraditor, Aileen. *The Ideas of the Woman Suffrage Movement, 1890–1920.* Garden City, N.Y.: Anchor, 1971.

Krueger, Thomas A. *And Promises to Keep: The Southern Conference for Human Welfare, 1938–1948.* Nashville: Vanderbilt University Press, 1967.

Kundsin, Ruth B. *Women & Success: The Anatomy of Achievement.* New York: Morrow, 1974.

Lacy, Dan Mabry. *The White Use of Blacks in America.* New York: Atheneum, 1972.

Ladner, Joyce A. *Tomorrow's Tomorrow: The Black Woman.* Garden City, N.Y.: Doubleday, 1971.

Lash, Joseph P. *Eleanor and Franklin.* New York: Norton, 1971.

Lasswell, Harold D. *Propaganda Technique in the World War.* New York: Knopf, 1927.

—— *Psychopathology and Politics.* Chicago and London: University of Chicago Press, 1930.

Lederer, Wolfgang. *The Fear of Women.* New York: Grune and Stratton, 1968.

Lemons, J. Stanley. *The Woman Citizen: Social Feminism in the 1920's.* Urbana: University of Illinois Press, 1973.

Lerner, Gerda, ed. *Black Women in White America: A Documentary History.* New York: Random House, 1972.

—— *The Grimké Sisters of South Carolina: Rebels Against Slavery.* Boston: Houghton Mifflin, 1967.

Levine, Lawrence W. *Black Culture and Black Consciousness: Afro-American Folk Thought from Slavery to Freedom.* New York: Oxford University Press, 1977.

Lessing, Doris. *The Grass is Singing.* London: Michael Joseph, 1950.

Lewinson, Paul. *Race, Class, and Party: A History of Negro Suffrage and White Politics in the South.* 1932. Reprint, New York: Universal Library, 1965.

Loescher, Frank S. *The Protestant Church and the Negro.* New York: Association Press, 1948.

Loewenberg, Bert James, and Ruth Bogin, eds. *Black Women in Nineteenth-Century American Life: Their Words, Their Thoughts, Their Feelings.* University Park: Pennsylvania State University Press, 1976.

Logan, Rayford W. *The Betrayal of the Negro: From Rutherford B. Hayes to Woodrow Wilson.* New York: Macmillan, 1965. First published as *The Negro in American Life and Thought: The Nadir, 1877–1901,* 1954.

——, ed. *What the Negro Wants*. Chapel Hill: University of North Carolina, 1944.

Lumpkin, Grace. *A Sign for Cain*. New York: Lee Furman, 1935.

Lumpkin, Katharine Du Pre. *The Making of a Southerner*. New York: Knopf, 1947.

—— *The South in Progress*. New York: International Publishers, 1940.

Lundberg, Ferdinand, and Marynia Farnham. *Modern Woman: The Lost Sex*. New York: Harper and Bros., 1947.

McCullers, Carson. *The Heart is a Lonely Hunter*. Boston: Houghton Mifflin, 1940.

McCulloch, James, ed. *Battling for Social Betterment: The Southern Sociological Congress, 1914*. Nashville: Southern Sociological Congress, 1914.

MacDonell, Mrs. R. W. *Belle Harris Bennett: Her Life Work*. Nashville: Board of Missions, Methodist Episcopal Church, South, 1928.

—— *Shifts of Emphasis*. Nashville: Department of Education and Promotion, Woman's Section, Board of Missions, Methodist Episcopal Church, South, 1928.

McLaurin, Melton Alonza. *Paternalism and Protest: Southern Cotton Mill Workers and Organized Labor, 1875–1905*. Westport, Conn.: Greenwood, 1971.

McPherson, James M. *The Abolitionist Legacy: From Reconstruction to the NAACP*. Princeton: Princeton University Press, 1975.

Mars, Florence. *Witness in Philadelphia*. Baton Rouge: Louisiana State University Press, 1977.

Martin, George Madden, Mrs. *Children of the Mist*. New York: Appleton, 1920.

Mason, Lucy Randolph. *Standards for Workers in Southern Industry*. New York: National Consumers' League, 1931.

—— *To Win These Rights: A Personal Story of the CIO in the South*. New York: Harper, 1952.

Mathews, Donald G. *Religion in the Old South*. Chicago and London: University of Chicago Press, 1977.

Mays, Benjamin F. *Born to Rebel: An Autobiography*. New York: Scribner's, 1971.

Meier, August. *Negro Thought in America, 1880–1915*. Ann Arbor: University of Michigan Press, 1968.

Meriwether, Elizabeth Avery. *Recollections of Ninety-Two Years, 1824–1916*. Nashville: Tennessee Historical Commission, 1958.

Miller, Robert Moats. *American Protestantism and Social Issues, 1919–1939*. Chapel Hill: University of North Carolina Press, 1958.

Mims, Edwin. *The Advancing South: Stories of Progress and Reaction*. Garden City, N.Y.: Doubleday, Page, 1926.

Mitchell, Juliet. *Psychoanalysis and Feminism*. New York: Pantheon, 1974.

Morgan, David. *Suffragists and Democrats: The Politics of Woman Suffrage in America*. East Lansing: Michigan State University Press, 1972.

Morrison, Toni. *The Bluest Eye*. New York: Holt, Rinehart and Winston, 1970.

—— *Sula*. New York: Knopf, 1974.

Murray, Pauli. *Proud Shoes: The Story of an American Family.* New York: Harper and Row, 1956.

Myrdal, Gunnar, Richard Sterner, and Arnold Rose. *An American Dilemma: The Negro Problem and Modern Democracy.* 2 vols. New York: Harper and Row, 1942.

National Association for the Advancement of Colored People. *Thirty Years of Lynching in the United States, 1889–1918.* New York: National Association for the Advancement of Colored People, 1919.

Newby, I. A. *Black Carolinians: A History of Blacks in South Carolina from 1895–1968.* Columbia: University of South Carolina Press, 1973.

—— *Jim Crow's Defense: Anti-Negro Thought in America, 1900–1930.* Baton Rouge: Louisiana State University Press, 1965.

Newell, Mrs. W. A. *Handbook for Interracial Committees.* Nashville: Department of Education and Promotion, Woman's Section, Board of Missions, Methodist Episcopal Church, South, n.d.

Odum, Howard W. *Race and Rumors of Race: Challenge to American Crisis.* Chapel Hill: University of North Carolina Press, 1943.

Olcott, Jane, comp. *The Work of Colored Women.* New York: Young Women's Christian Association, 1919.

O'Neill, William L. *Everyone Was Brave: The Rise and Fall of Feminism in America.* Chicago: Quadrangle, 1969.

Ovington, Mary White. *The Walls Came Tumbling Down.* New York: Schocken, 1970.

Page, Dorothy Myra. *Gathering Storm: A Story of the Black Belt.* New York: International Publishers, 1932.

Page, Thomas Nelson. *The Negro: The Southerner's Problem.* New York: Young People's Missionary Movement of the United States and Canada, 1904.

Parker, Gail Thain, ed. *The Oven Birds: American Women on Womanhood, 1820–1920.* Garden City, N.Y.: Doubleday, 1972.

Parris, Guichard, and Lester Brooks. *Blacks in the City: A History of the National Urban League.* Boston: Little, Brown, 1971.

Paulson, Ross Evans. *Women's Suffrage and Prohibition: A Comparative Study of Equality and Social Control.* Glenview, Ill.: Scott, Foresman, 1973.

Peane, C. O. *Mary McLeod Bethune.* New York: Vanguard, 1951.

Peck, Mary Gray. *Carrie Chapman Catt: A Biography.* New York: Wilson, 1944.

Peirce, Neal R. *The Megastates of America: People, Politics and Power in the Ten Great States.* New York: Norton, 1972.

Percy, William Alexander. *Lanterns on the Levee: Recollections of a Planter's Son.* New York: Knopf, 1941.

Pickens, William. *Lynching and Debt Slavery.* New York: American Civil Liberties Union, 1921.

Powdermaker, Hortense. *After Freedom: A Cultural Study in the Deep South.* 1939. Reprint, New York: Atheneum, 1968.

Raper, Arthur F., and Ira De A. Reid. *Sharecroppers All.* Chapel Hill: University of North Carolina Press, 1941.

—— *The Tragedy of Lynching*. 1933. Reprint, New York: Dover, 1970.

Record, Wilson. *Race and Radicalism*. Chapel Hill: University of North Carolina Press, 1951.

Reed, John Shelton. *The Enduring South: Subcultural Persistence in Mass Society*. Lexington, Mass.: D. C. Heath, 1972.

Report of Commission on Woman's Place of Service in the Church. Nashville: Woman's Missionary Council, Methodist Episcopal Church, South, 1930.

Reports of the Methodist Episcopal Church, South, Woman's Missionary Council, 1911–1940. Nashville, Tennessee: Publishing House of the Methodist Episcopal Church, South, 1911–40.

Rogin, Michael Paul. *Fathers and Children: Andrew Jackson and the Subjugation of the American Indian*. New York: Vintage, 1976.

Rose, Arnold. *The Negro in America*. Boston: Beacon Press, 1962.

Rose, Thomas, ed. *Violence in America: A Historical and Contemporary Reader*. New York: Random House, 1969.

Rosenbaum, Jon, and Peter C. Sederberg, eds., *Vigilante Politics*. Philadelphia: University of Pennsylvania Press, 1976.

Rosengarten, Theodore. *All God's Dangers: The Life of Nate Shaw*. New York: Avon, 1974.

Ross, B. Joyce. *J. E. Spingarn and the Rise of the NAACP, 1911–1939*. New York: Atheneum, 1972.

Scarbrough, Clara Sterns. *Land of Good Water: A Williamson County, Texas, History*. Georgetown: Williamson County Sun Publishers, 1973.

Scott, Anne Firor. *The Southern Lady: From Pedestal to Politics, 1830–1930*. Chicago: University of Chicago Press, 1970.

——, and Andrew M. Scott. *One Half the People: The Fight for Woman Suffrage*. Philadelphia: Lippincott, 1975.

Shay, Frank. *Judge Lynch: His First Hundred Years*. New York: Ives Washburn, 1938.

Sims, Mary S. *The YWCA: An Unfolding Purpose*. New York: Woman's Press, 1950.

Skaggs, William H. *The Southern Oligarchy: An Appeal in Behalf of the Silent Masses of Our Country Against the Despotic Rule of the Few*. New York: Devin-Adair, 1924.

Smelser, Neil J. *Theory of Collective Behavior*. New York: Free Press, 1963.

Smith, Lillian. *Killers of the Dream*. 1949. Reprint, Garden City, N.Y.: Doubleday, 1963.

—— *Strange Fruit*. New York: Reynal and Hitchcock, 1944.

Sosna, Morton. *In Search of the Silent South: Southern Liberals and the Race Issue*. New York: Columbia University Press, 1977.

Southeastern Federation of Colored Women's Clubs. *Southern Negro Women and Race Co-operation*. Atlanta: Southeastern Federation of Colored Women's Clubs, 1921.

Southern Commission on the Study of Lynching. *Lynchings and What They Mean: General Findings of the Southern Commission on the Study of Lynching*. Atlanta: Commission on Interracial Cooperation, 1931.

—— *The Mob Murder of S. S. Mincy*. Atlanta: Southern Commission on the Study of Lynching, n.d.

Southern Commission on the Study of Lynchings. *The Plight of Tuscaloosa.* Atlanta: Southern Commission on the Study of Lynching, 1933.

Southern Regional Council. *The Southern Regional Council, 1944–1964.* Atlanta: Southern Regional Council, 1964.

Stanton, Elizabeth Cady. *Eighty Years and More: Reminiscences, 1815–1897.* Edited by Gail Thain Parker. New York: Schocken, 1971.

———, Susan B. Anthony, Matilda Joslyn Gage, and Ida Husted Harper, eds. *History of Woman Suffrage.* 6 vols. Rochester, N.Y.: Charles Mann Printing Co., 1881–1922.

Sternsher, Bernard, ed. *The Negro in Depression and War: Prelude to Revolution, 1930–1945.* Chicago: Quadrangle, 1969.

Stott, William. *Documentary Expression and Thirties America.* New York: Oxford University Press, 1973.

Sullivan, Mary Loretta, and Bertha Blair. *Women in Texas Industries.* Bulletin of the Women's Bureau, no. 26. Washington: U.S. Government Printing Office, 1936.

Talmadge, John E. *Rebecca Latimer Felton: Nine Stormy Decades.* Athens: University of Georgia Press, 1960.

Tannenbaum, Frank. *Darker Phases of the South.* New York: Putnam's, 1924.

Tatum, Noreen Dunn. *A Crown of Service: A Story of Woman's Work in the Methodist Episcopal Church, South, from 1878–1940.* Nashville: Parthenon, 1960.

Taylor, William R. *Cavalier and Yankee: The Old South and American National Character.* Garden City, New York: Anchor, 1963.

Thompson, Ernest Trice. *Presbyterians in the South.* 3 vols. Richmond, Va.: John Knox Press, 1963–1973.

Thorpe, Earl E. *Eros and Freedom in Southern Life and Thought.* Durham: Seeman Printery, 1967.

Tindall, George Brown. *The Emergence of the New South, 1913–1945.* Baton Rouge: Louisiana State University Press, 1967.

——— *South Carolina Negroes, 1877–1900.* 1952. Reprint, Baton Rouge: Louisiana State University Press, 1966.

Toomer, Jean. *Cane.* New York: Harper and Row, 1969.

Torrence, Fred Ridgely. *The Story of John Hope.* New York: Macmillan, 1948.

Trelease, Allen W. *White Terror: The Ku Klux Klan Conspiracy and Southern Reconstruction.* New York: Harper and Row, 1971.

Vance, Rupert B., and Nicholas Demerath, eds. *The Urban South.* Chapel Hill: University of North Carolina Press, 1954.

Van den Berghe, Pierre L. *Race and Racism: A Comparative Perspective.* New York: Wiley, 1967.

Walker, Alice. *In Love and Trouble: Stories of Black Women.* New York: Harcourt Brace Jovanovich, 1974.

Waskow, Arthur I. *From Race Riot to Sit-In, 1919 to the 1960s.* Garden City, N.Y.: Anchor, 1966.

Washington, Mary Helen, ed. *Black-Eyed Susans: Classic Stories By and About Black Women.* Garden City, New York: Anchor, 1975.

Weare, Walter B. *Black Business in the New South: A Social History of the North Carolina Mutual Life Insurance Company*. Urbana: University of Illinois Press, 1973.

Weatherford, W. D. *Lynching: Removing Its Causes*. Nashville: Southern Sociological Congress, 1916.

Webb, Walter Prescott. *The Great Plains*. Boston: Ginn, 1931.

Weiss, Nancy J. *The National Urban League, 1910–1940*. New York: Oxford University Press, 1974.

Wells, Ida B. *Crusade for Justice: The Autobiography of Ida B. Wells*. Edited by Alfreda Duster. Chicago: University of Chicago Press, 1970.

Wells-Barnett, Ida B. *On Lynchings: Southern Horrors; A Red Record; Mob Rule in New Orleans*. New York: Arno Press, 1969. First published in 3 vols., 1892, 1895, and 1900.

White, Walter Francis. *The Fire in the Flint*. New York: A. A. Knopf, 1924.

—— *A Man Called White: The Autobiography of Walter White*. New York: Viking, 1948.

—— *Rope and Faggot: A Biography of Judge Lynch*. New York: Knopf, 1929.

Wiebe, Robert H. *The Search for Order, 1877–1920*. New York: Hill and Wang, 1967.

Williams, Daniel T. *Eight Negro Bibliographies*. New York: Kraus Reprint Co., 1970.

Williams, Roger M. *The Bonds: An American Family*. New York: Atheneum, 1971.

Williamson, Joel. *After Slavery: The Negro in South Carolina During Reconstruction, 1869–1877*. Chapel Hill: University of North Carolina Press, 1965.

Wolters, Raymond. *Negroes and the Great Depression: The Problem of Economic Recovery*. Westport, Conn.: Greenwood Press, 1970.

—— *The New Negro on Campus: Black College Rebellions of the 1920s*. Princeton: Princeton University Press, 1975.

Wood, Forrest G. *Black Scare: The Racist Response to Emancipation and Reconstruction*. 1968. Reprint, Berkeley: University of California Press, 1970.

Woodson, Carter G. *The Mis-education of the Negro*. Washington, D.C.: Associated Publishers, 1933.

Woodward, C. Vann. *American Counterpoint: Slavery and Racism in the North-South Dialogue*. Boston: Little, Brown, 1971.

—— *Origins of the New South, 1877–1913*. Baton Rouge: Louisiana State University Press, 1951.

—— *Tom Watson: Agrarian Rebel*. London: Oxford University Press, 1963.

Woofter, Thomas J., Jr. *The Basis of Racial Adjustment*. Boston: Ginn, 1925.

Work, Monroe, ed. *The Negro Year Book: An Annual Encyclopedia of the Negro, 1912–1956*. Tuskegee: Negro Year Book Publishing Co., 1912–56.

Wright, Richard. *Black Boy: A Record of Childhood and Youth*. 1945. Reprint, New York: Harper and Row, 1966.

—— *Uncle Tom's Children*. New York: Signet, 1947.

Young, Wayland. *Eros Denied: Sex in Western Society.* New York: Grove Press, 1964.

Articles

Abernathy, Mollie C. "Southern Women, Social Reconstruction and the Church in the 1920's." *Louisiana Studies,* 13 (Winter 1974), 289–312.

"Against Lynching: Association of Southern Women for the Prevention of Lynching." *Commonweal,* 17 (April 19, 1933), 675–76.

Alexander, Will W. "The Negro Migration." *The Christian Index* (June 14, 1923), pp. 6–8.

—— "Our Conflicting Racial Policies." *Harper's Magazine,* 190 (January 1945), 172–79.

—— "A Usable Piece of Community Machinery." *Journal of Social Forces,* 1 (1923), 41–42.

"All Honor to the Women of Georgia!" *Christian Century,* 48 (January 28, 1931), 123.

Ames, Jessie Daniel. "Editorial Treatment of Lynching." *Public Opinion Quarterly,* 2 (January 1938), 77–84.

—— "The Mote and the Beam." *World Outlook,* 23 (January 1933), 18, 40.

—— "The New Negro," in *Robert Russa Moton of Hampton and Tuskegee.* Edited by William Hardin Hughes and Frederick D. Patterson. Chapel Hill: University of North Carolina Press, 1956.

—— "The Shame of a Christian People." *World Outlook,* 24 (February 1934), 21, 32.

—— "Southern Women Against Lynching." *Christian Index,* 131 (November 5, 1931), 647.

—— "Southern Women and Lynching." *Crime Survey,* 1 (April 1935), ASWPL Reprint.

—— "Start the Women—They Won't Quit." *World Outlook,* 23 (February 1933), 18, 27.

—— "Whither Leads the Mob?" *Missionary Voice,* 22 (January 1932), 20, 46.

—— "Women and Lawlessness." *Missionary Voice,* 22 (February 1932), 31, 47–48.

Athey, Louis L. "Florence Kelley and the Quest for Negro Equality." *Journal of Negro History,* 56 (October 1971), 249–61.

Baptist History and Heritage, 12 (January 1977). Special issue on "The Role of Women in Baptist History."

Barber, Henry E. "The Association of Southern Women for the Prevention of Lynching, 1930–1942." *Phylon,* 34 (December 1973), 378–89.

de Bardeleben, Mary. "Can We Do Less?" *Missionary Voice*, 10 (March 1920), 92.

Bennett, Belle H. "The President's Message." *Our Homes*, 18 (December 1909), 9.

Blackwelder, Julia Kirk. "Quiet Suffering: Atlanta Women in the 1930s." *Georgia Historical Quarterly*, 61 (Summer 1977), 112–24.

Bond, Horace Mann. "Should the Negro Care Who Wins the War?" *Annals*, 223 (September 1942), 81–84.

—— "What Lies Behind Lynching." *The Nation*, 128 (March 27, 1929), 370–71.

Braden, Anne. "A Second Open Letter to Southern White Women." *Southern Exposure*, 4 (Winter 1977), 50–53.

—— "The Wansley Case: An Open Letter to the White Women of the South." *Southern Patriot* (December 1972), 7.

Breed, Warren. "Comparative Newspaper Handling of the Emmett Till Case." *Journalism Quarterly*, 35 (Summer 1958), 291–98.

Brown, Ina Corinne. "Hearings on the Costigan-Wagner Bill." *World Outlook*, 24 (April 1934), 21, 34.

Brown, Juanita. "Sara Estelle Haskin." *World Outlook*, September 1943, 15–17.

Brown, William O. "Interracial Cooperation: Some of Its Problems." *Opportunity*, 11 (September 1933), 272–73, 285.

Carter, Dan T. "The Anatomy of Fear: The Christmas Day Insurrection Scare of 1865." *Journal of Southern History*, 42 (August 1976), 345–64.

Cayton, Horace R. "Fighting for White Folks?" *The Nation*, 155 (September 26, 1942), 267–70.

Chodorow, Nancy. "Family Structure and Feminine Personality," in *Woman, Culture and Society*. Edited by Michelle Zimbalist Rosaldo and Louise Lamphere. Stanford: Stanford University Press, 1974.

Clayton, Cranston. "College Interracialism in the South." *Opportunity*, 12 (1934), 267–69, 288.

Cole, William E. "The Role of the Commission on Interracial Cooperation in War and Peace." *Social Forces*, 21 (May 1943), 456–63.

Crowe, Charles. "Racial Violence and Social Reform—Origins of the Atlanta Riot of 1906." *Journal of Negro History*, 53 (July 1968), 234–56.

Cunningham, Minnie Fisher. "Too Gallant a Walk." *The Woman's Journal*, 14 (January 1929), 12–13, 46–47.

Dabney, Virginius. "Dixie Rejects Lynching." *The Nation*, 145 (November 27, 1937), 579–80.

—— "Nearer and Nearer the Precipice." *Atlantic Monthly*, 171 (January 1943), 94–100.

—— "Press and Morale." *Saturday Review of Literature*, 25 (July 4, 1942), 5–6, 24–25.

Dalfiume, Richard M. "The 'Forgotten Years' of the Negro Revolution." *Journal of American History*, 55 (June 1968), 90–106.

Davis, Horace B. "A Substitute for Lynching." *The Nation*, 130 (January 1, 1930), 12–14.

Degler, Carl N. "What Ought to Be and What Was: Women's Sexuality in the Nineteenth Century." *American Historical Review*, 79 (December 1974), 1467–1490.

Dew, Lee A. "The Lynching of 'Boll Weevil.'" *Midwest Quarterly*, 12 (Winter 1971), 145–53.

Douglass, Frederick C. "Lynch Law in the South." *North American Review*, 155 (July 1892), 17–24.

DuBois, Ellen. "The Radicalism of the Woman Suffrage Movement: Notes Toward the Reconstruction of Nineteenth-Century Feminism." *Feminist Studies*, 3 (Fall 1975), 63–71.

Du Bois, W. E. B. "Inter-racial Comity." *The Crisis*, 22 (May 1921), 6–7.

—— "The Liberal South." *The Crisis*, 21 (April 1921), 247–48.

—— "The Newer South." *The Crisis*, 31 (February 1926), 163–65.

—— "Votes for Women." *The Crisis*, 8 (August 1914), 179–80.

Duffus, Robert L. "Counter-Mining the Ku Klux Klan." *The World's Work*, 46 (July 1923), 275–84.

Durr, Virginia Foster. "The Emancipation of Pure, White, Southern Womanhood." *New South*, 26 (Winter 1971), 46–54.

—— [Eliza Heard, pseud.] "In the Name of Southern Womanhood." *New South*, 17 (November–December 1962), 16–18.

Eaton, Clement. "Mob Violence in the Old South." *Mississippi Valley Historical Review*, 29 (December 1942), 351–70.

Edwards, George Clifton. "Texas: The Big Southwestern Specimen." *The Nation*, 116 (March 21, 1923), 334–37.

Eleazer, Robert B. "Southern Women Against the Mob." *Southern Workman*, 60 (March 1931), 126–31.

Ethridge, W. S. "Salesmen of Violence." *Outlook and Independent*, 156 (November 19, 1930), 457–59.

—— "Southern Women Attack Lynching." *The Nation*, 131 (December 10, 1930), 647, 650.

Evans, Sara. "Women's Consciousness and the Southern Black Movement." *Southern Exposure*, 4 (Winter 1977), 10–18.

Faragher, Johnny and Christine Stansell. "Women and Their Families on the Overland Trail, 1842–1867." *Feminist Studies*, 2 (1975), 150–66.

Finkle, Lee. "The Conservative Aims of Militant Rhetoric: Black Protest During World War II." *Journal of American History*, 60 (December 1973), 692–713.

"Forcible and Statutory Rape: An Exploration of the Operation and Objectives of the Consent Standard." *Yale Law Journal*, 62 (December 1952), 55–83.

Fox, Greer Litton. "'Nice Girl': Social Control of Women Through a Value Construct." *Signs*, 2 (Summer 1977), 805–17.

Frederickson, Mary. "The Southern Summer School for Women Workers." *Southern Exposure*, 4 (Spring 1977), 70–75.

Fuller, Helen. "The Ring Around the President." *New Republic*, 109 (October 25, 1943), 563–65.

Gavins, Raymond. "Gordon Blaine Hancock: A Black Profile from the New South." *Journal of Negro History*, 59 (July 1974), 207–27.

Gerber, David A. "Lynching and Law and Order: Origin and Passage of the Ohio Anti-Lynching Law of 1896." *Ohio History*, 83 (Winter 1974), 33–50.

Goodwyn, Lawrence C. "Populist Dreams and Negro Rights: East Texas as a Case Study." *American Historical Review*, 76 (December 1971), 1435–56.

Gutman, Herbert G. "Work, Culture, and Society in Industrializing America, 1815–1919." *American Historical Review*, 78 (June 1973), 531–88.

Hackney, Sheldon. "Southern Violence." *American Historical Review*, 74 (February 1969), 906–25.

Hageman, Alice L. "Women and Missions: The Cost of Liberation," in *Sexist Religion and Women in the Church: No More Silence*. Edited by Alice Hageman. New York: Association Press, 1974.

Hammond, L. H. "A Lover of All Races." *Missionary Voice*, 12 (October 1922), 304.

—— "Negro Boys Make Good." *Survey*, 32 (September 12, 1914), 603.

"The Hand on the Cradle." *Our Homes*, 11 (January 1902), 1.

Harris, Julia C. "The Spirit of Revolt in Current Fiction." *Journal of Social Forces*, 3 (March 1925), 427–31.

Haskin, Sara Estelle. "Southern Women and Mob Violence." *Missionary Voice*, 22 (February 1932), 34.

—— "Women of the Left Wing." *World Outlook*, 23 (February 1933), 28–30.

Helm, Lucinda B. "The Negro Problem." *Our Homes*, 6 (September 1897), 3.

Hoffman, Erwin D. "The Genesis of the Modern Movement for Equal Rights in South Carolina, 1930–1939." *Journal of Negro History*, 44 (October 1959), 346–69.

Holmes, William F. "Whitecapping: Agrarian Violence in Mississippi, 1902–1906." *Journal of Southern History*, 35 (May 1969), 165–85.

"Interracial Cooperation, Constructive Measures Recommended by Southern White Women." *Southern Workman*, 50 (January, 1921), 35–37.

Inverarity, James M. "Populism and Lynching in Louisiana, 1889–1896: A Test of Erikson's Theory of the Relationship Between Boundary Crises and Repressive Justice." *American Sociological Review*, 41 (April 1976), 262–80.

Jeffrey, Julie Roy. "Women in the Southern Farmers' Alliance: A Reconsideration of the Role and Status of Women in the Late Nineteenth-Century South." *Feminist Studies*, 3 (Fall 1975), 72–91.

Jenson, Richard. "Family, Career, and Reform: Women Leaders in the Progressive Era," in *The American Family in Social-Historical Perspective*. Edited by Michael Gordon. New York: St. Martin's Press, 1973.

Johnson, Guy B. "Southern Offensive." *Common Ground*, 4 (Summer 1944), 87–93.

Johnson, Kenneth R. "Kate Gordon and the Woman Suffrage Movement in the South." *Journal of Southern History*, 38 (August 1972), 365–92.

Johnson, Oakley C. "Is the Punishment of Rape Equally Administered to

Negroes and Whites in the State of Louisiana?" in *We Charge Genocide*. Edited by William L. Patterson. 1951. Reprint, New York: International Publishers, 1970.

Jones, Lester M. "The Editorial Policy of Negro Newspapers of 1917–18 as Compared with That of 1941–42." *Journal of Negro History*, 29 (January 1944), 24–31.

Lamon, Lester C. "The Black Community in Nashville and the Fisk University Student Strike of 1924–1925." *Journal of Southern History*, 40 (May 1974), 225–44.

Lebsock, Suzanne D. "Radical Reconstruction and the Property Rights of Southern Women." *Journal of Southern History*, 43 (May 1977), 195–216.

Lerner, Gerda. "Early Community Work of Black Club Women." *Journal of Negro History*, 59 (April 1974), 158–67.

—— "Women's Rights and American Feminism." *The American Scholar*, 40 (Spring 1971), 235–48.

Lewis, Diane K. "A Response to Inequality: Black Women, Racism, and Sexism." *Signs*, 3 (Winter 1977), 339–61.

Lomax, John A. "Governor Ferguson and the University of Texas." *Southwest Review*, 28 (1942–1943), 11–29.

"Lynchless South in 1933." *Commonweal*, 17 (November 30, 1932), 116.

McCallum, Jane Y. "Activities of Women in Texas Politics," in *Texas Democracy*, vol. 1. Edited by Frank C. Adams. Austin: Democratic Historical Association, 1937.

—— "Women's Joint Legislative Council," in *The Handbook of Texas*, vol. 1. Edited by Walter P. Webb, 2 vols. Austin: The Texas State Historical Association, 1952.

Martin, George Madden. "American Women and Paternalism." *Atlantic Monthly*, 133 (June 1924), 744–53.

—— "American Women and Public Affairs." *Atlantic Monthly*, 133 (February 1924), 169–71.

—— "The American Woman and Representative Government." *Atlantic Monthly*, 135 (March 1925), 363–71.

Martin, Mrs. George (Madden). "Race Cooperation." *McClure's*, 54 (October 1922), 9–20.

Meier, August, and Elliott Redwick. "Negro Retaliatory Violence in the Twentieth Century." *New Politics*, 5 (Winter 1966), 41–51.

Miller, Robert Moats. "The Attitudes of American Protestantism Toward the Negro, 1919–1939." *Journal of Negro History*, 41 (July 1956), 215–40.

—— "The Protestant Churches and Lynching, 1919–1939." *Journal of Negro History*, 42 (April 1957), 118–31.

Milton, George Fort. "The Impeachment of Judge Lynch." *Virginia Quarterly Review*, 8 (April 1932), 247–56.

"Missouri Leads 1931 Lynching Parade." *Literary Digest*, 108 (January 31, 1931), 17–18.

Mitchell, Norma Taylor. "From Social to Radical Feminism: A Survey of Emerging Diversity in Methodist Women's Organizations, 1869–1974." *Methodist History*, 13 (April 1975), 21–44.

Murray, Pauli. "The Liberation of Black Women," in *Our American Sisters: Women in American Life and Thought.* Edited by Jean E. Friedman and William C. Shade. Rev. ed. Boston: Allyn and Bacon, 1976.

Nordyke, Lewis T. "The Ladies and the Lynchers." *Reader's Digest,* 35 (November 1939), 110–13.

—— "Ladies and Lynchings." *Survey Graphic,* 28 (November 1939), 683–86.

O'Brien, Michael. "C. Vann Woodward and the Burden of Southern Liberalism." *American Historical Review,* 78 (June 1973), 589–604.

Odum, Howard. "Lynchings, Fears, and Folkways." *The Nation,* 133 (December 30, 1931), 719–20.

"Our Outlook." *Our Homes,* 7 (May 1898), 4.

Ovington, Mary White. "Is Mob Violence the Texas Solution of the Race Problem?" *The Independent,* 99 (September 6, 1919), 320.

—— "Revisiting the South." *The Crisis,* 34 (April 1927), 42–43, 60–61.

Ottley, Roi. "A White Folks' War?" *Common Ground,* 2 (Spring 1942), 28–31.

"Paine College and Its Annex." *Our Homes,* 19 (March 1910), 6–9.

Parrott, Lisbeth. "Seven Thousand Women Pledge to Eradicate Mob Violence." *World Outlook,* 23 (August 1933), 23, 31.

Partington, Donald H. "The Incidence of the Death Penalty for Rape in Virginia." *Washington and Lee Law Review,* 22 (1965), 43–75.

Pickens, William. "The Woman Voter Hits the Color Line." *The Nation,* 111 (October 6, 1920), 372–73.

Pipkin, Charles W. "Social Legislation," in *Culture in the South.* Edited by W. T. Couch. Chapel Hill: University of North Carolina Press, 1934.

Potter, David M. "American Women and the National Character." *Stetson University Bulletin,* 62 (Summer 1962), reprinted in *American History and the Social Sciences.* Edited by Edward N. Saveth. New York: Free Press, 1964.

Pruden, Durwood. "A Sociological Study of a Texas Lynching." *Studies in Sociology,* 1 (Dallas: Southern Methodist University, 1936), 3–9.

Redding, J. Saunders. "Southern Defensive—I." *Common Ground,* 4 (Spring 1944), 36–42.

Reed, John Shelton. "An Evaluation of an Anti-Lynching Organization." *Social Problems,* 16 (Fall 1968), 172–82.

—— "Percent Black and Lynching: A Test of Blalock's Theory." *Social Forces,* 50 (March 1972), 356–60.

Robinson, Jo Ann. "Lillian Smith: Reflections on Race and Sex." *Southern Exposure,* 4 (Winter 1977), 43–48.

Ross, B. Joyce. "Mary McLeod Bethune and the National Youth Administration: A Case Study of Power Relationships in the Black Cabinet of Franklin D. Roosevelt." *Journal of Negro History,* 60 (January 1975), 1–28.

Scott, Anne Firor. "After Suffrage: Southern Women in the Twenties." *Journal of Southern History,* 30 (August 1964), 298–318.

Scott, Anne Firor. "The 'New Woman' in the New South." *South Atlantic Quarterly,* 61 (Autumn 1962), 473–83.

—— "Women, Religion, and Social Change in the South, 1830–1930," in *Religion and the Solid South*. Edited by Samuel S. Hill. Nashville: Abingdon Press, 1972.

—— "Women's Perspective on the Patriarchy in the 1850's." *Journal of American History*, 61 (June 1974), 52–64.

Seligmann, Herbert J. "Protecting Southern Womanhood." *The Nation*, 108 (June 14, 1919), 938–39.

Seymour, Ann. "Lawd, Does Yo 'Undahstan'?" in *Representative One-Act Plays by American Authors*. Edited by Margaret Mayorga. Boston: Little, Brown, 1937.

de Silver, Albert. "The Ku Klux Klan—'Soul of Chivalry.' " *The Nation*, 113 (September 14, 1921), 285–86.

Simkins, Francis Butler. "Ben Tillman's View of the Negro." *Journal of Southern History*, 3 (May 1937), 161–74.

Singal, Daniel Joseph. "Ulrich B. Phillips: The Old South as the New." *Journal of American History*, 63 (March 1977), 871–91.

Sitkoff, Harvard. "Racial Militancy and Interracial Violence in the Second World War." *Journal of American History*, 58 (December 1971), 661–81.

Smith, Egbert W. "Origin and Growth of the Organized Women's Work of the Southern Presbyterian Church." *Union Seminary Review*, 40 (October 1928), 23–34.

Smith, Helena H. "Mrs. Tilly's Crusade." *Collier's*, 126 (December 30, 1950), 28–29, 66–67.

Smith, Lillian. "Addressed to White Liberals." *New Republic*, 111 (September 18, 1944), 331–33.

—— "Southern Defensive—II." *Common Ground*, 4 (Spring 1944), 43–45.

Smith-Rosenberg, Carroll. "Beauty, the Beast and the Militant Woman: A Case Study in Sex Roles and Social Stress in Jacksonian America." *American Quarterly*, 23 (October 1971), 562–84.

—— "The Female World of Love and Ritual: Relations Between Women in Nineteenth-Century America." *Signs*, 1 (Autumn 1975), 1–30.

"Southern Women Fight Lynching Evil." *Literary Digest*, 117 (January 27, 1934), 22.

"Southern Women and Lynching." *Journal of Social Forces*, 1 (May 1923), 469–70.

"Southern Women Speak Out." *World Tomorrow*, 13 (December 1930), 487.

Stevens, Thelma. "At the Greater Bethlehem House in Augusta, Georgia." *Missionary Voice*, 22 (April 1930), 30–31.

Strom, Sharon Hartman. "Leadership and Tactics in the American Woman Suffrage Movement: A New Perspective from Massachusetts." *Journal of American History*, 62 (September 1975), 296–315.

Tanner, Nancy. "Matrifocality in Indonesia and Africa and Among Black Americans," in *Woman, Culture and Society*. Edited by Michelle Zimbalist Rosaldo and Louise Lamphere. Stanford: Stanford University Press, 1974.

Taylor, A. Elizabeth. "The Woman Suffrage Movement in Texas." *Journal of Southern History*, 17 (May 1951), 194–215.

Taylor, Graham. "The Southern Social Awakening." *Survey*, 28 (September 14, 1912), 744–45.

"Tennessee Mobilizing for Law and Order." *Survey*, 39 (March 23, 1918), 690–91.

"These Women and Lynching." *Holland's, The Magazine of the South*, 59 (February 1940), 3.

Thomas, Keith. "The Double Standard." *Journal of the History of Ideas*, 20 (April 1959), 195–216.

Tippett, Tom. "Short Cut to a Lynching." *The Crisis*, 43 (January 1936), 8–10, 26.

Tobias, Channing H. "Two Southern Women Pioneers." *World Outlook*, 22 (October 1932), 29.

Townsend, Mrs. F. L. "Why I Am Opposed to Woman's Suffrage." *The Methodist Quarterly Review*, 57 (January 1913), 98–107.

Villard, Oswald Garrison. "The Race Problem." *The Nation*, 99 (December 24, 1914), 738–40.

Wells-Barnett, Ida B. "Our Country's Lynching Record." *Survey*, 29 (February 1, 1913), 573–74.

Welter, Barbara. "The Feminization of American Religion, 1800–1860," in *Clio's Consciousness Raised: New Perspectives on the History of Women*. Edited by Mary Hartman and Lois W. Banner. New York: Harper and Row, 1974.

"What a Deaconess Is and What She Is Not." *Our Homes*, 11 (March 1902), 1.

"The White Woman's Burden." *The Nation*, 112 (February 16, 1921), 257–58.

Wimpy, W. E. "Lynching, An Evil of County Government." *Manufacturers' Record*, 70 (August 24, 1916), 49–50.

—— "Mob Lynching Lynches the Law." *Manufacturers' Record*, 76 (December 25, 1919), 113–14.

"Women and Lynch Law." *Commonweal*, 13 (December 17, 1930), 171–72.

Young, Earl Fiske. "The Relation of Lynching to the Size of Population Areas." *Sociology and Social Research*, 12 (March–April, 1928), 348–53.

Index

Abolitionism, 19–20, 66
Abzug, Bella, 266
Addams, Jane, 57
African American Women in Defense of Ourselves, xx
Afro-American Federation of Colored Women, 320n100
"After the War Program," 62
Alexander, Will W., 62, 65, 66, 87, 126, 171, 252, 271; view of blacks, 73; and organization of women's conference (1920), 90; attitude toward Ames, 124, 257; anti-lynching stand of, 159–60, 161, 163; and Scottsboro case, 199; posts held after CIC, 257
Alford, Bessie C. (Mrs. L. W.), 173, 183, 187, 188, 352n72; lectures for ASWPL, 215–16; and prevention of lynching, 229–30
All God's Dangers (Shaw), 143–44
American Association of University Women (AAUW), Texas Branch, 52; supports social reform, 309n106
American Dilemma, An (Myrdal), 168–69, 331n3
Ames, Frederick Daniel (son), 14, 119, 327n37
Ames, Frederick W., 12
Ames, Jessie Daniel, ix, xx, xxi, xxv; early life, 1–14; place in history of, xxxviii, 272–73; relationship with father, 5, 6, 8–9, 14, 27, 28, 277–78; affective life of, 5, 8, 15–18, 30, 56, 57–58, 118, 123, 262–63, 297n39; education of, 8–9; relationship with men, 9; relationship with sister Lulu, 9, 14, 16–17, 280–86; marriage to Roger Post Ames, 11–14, 277–78; children of, 13, 296n37; feminism of, 13, 26–30, 52–53, 58, 280n123; sexual orientation of, 13, 15, 269n40; effects of early life leadership style, 15–16; and femininity, 16–17, 57, 270n42;

relationship with other women, 17, 286; relationship with mother, 17, 28–29, 283–84; beginning of public role, 19–58; interest in politics, 27, 28; as businesswoman, 28–31; in suffrage movement, 30–35, 38–39; search for personal identity, 31, 301–2n45; president of Georgetown Equal Suffrage League, 31–32; relationship with Minnie Fisher Cummingham, 32–34, 47–48, 116–18; and female "influence," 33, 234, 250; and public speaker, 33–34, 211–15; political activities of, 35, 114–16, 326–27n25; rejection of dependency, 39; and fight for ratification of 19th amendment, 41–42; first president of Texas League of Women Voters, 44–56; and prison reform, 50; move to racial liberalism, 53–55, 107–19; views of women, 57–58, 248–49; work in CIC, 59–128, 256–57; role conflict in, 107; criticized for anti-lynching stand, 112, 150–51, 218; alienation from suffragist allies, 116–18; economic situation of, 119–23; campaign against lynching, 127–28, 217–21, 249–53; on lynching, 136, 140, 142, 169, 207–8, 229–31, 250; on interracial sex, 154, 156, 203–4; uses CIC anti-lynching interest to found women's organization, 161–64, 171; emphases in organization of ASWPL, 178–79, 181; view of social reform, 182; on Scottsboro case, 199–200; on legal justice for blacks, 200–1; *Whither Leads the Mob?*, 201; on women's fear of rape, 203; on double standard, 205–6; on status of Negro, 214; addresses Southern Newspaper Publishers' Association, 219–20; opposes NAACP anti-lynching strategy, 237, 239–53; leadership style of, 248, 251–53; paternalistic attitude of, 250; relationship with blacks, 250–51;

The block print on the cover was created by Hale A. Woodruff, an art instructor at Atlanta University, where he developed an important group of younger African-American artists. In 1938 he was commissioned to do the Amistad Murals for Talladega College. The print appeared in Alain Locke, ed., *The Negro in Art: A Pictorial Record of the Negro Artist and of the Negro Theme in Art* (Washington, D.C.: Associates in Negro Folk Education, 1940, 1957).